T0189918

Communications
in Computer and Information Science   **1513**

More information about this series at https://link.springer.com/bookseries/7899

Weijia Cao · Aydogan Ozcan · Haidong Xie ·
Bei Guan (Eds.)

Computing and Data Science

Third International Conference, CONF-CDS 2021
Virtual Event, August 12–17, 2021
Proceedings

 Springer

Editors
Weijia Cao ⓘ
Chinese Academy of Sciences
Beijing, China

Aydogan Ozcan ⓘ
University of California
Los Angeles, CA, USA

Haidong Xie
China Academy of Space Technology
Beijing, China

Bei Guan
Chinese Academy of Sciences
Beijing, China

ISSN 1865-0929   ISSN 1865-0937 (electronic)
Communications in Computer and Information Science
ISBN 978-981-16-8884-3   ISBN 978-981-16-8885-0 (eBook)
https://doi.org/10.1007/978-981-16-8885-0

This Springer imprint is published by the registered company Springer Nature Singapore Pte Ltd.
The registered company address is: 152 Beach Road, #21-01/04 Gateway East, Singapore 189721, Singapore

Preface

The International Conference on Computing and Data Science (CONF-CDS) is a leading conference on computing technology, machine learning, computer science, and data science hosted by Eliwise Academy. Participants worldwide are welcome to share their findings and inspirations in relevant fields through research papers and speeches and presentations. CONF-CDS hopes to build an international platform for researchers, scholars, and academicians to carry out academic exchange and thus promote cooperation.

This volume contains the papers of the 3rd International Conference on Computing and Data Science (CONF-CDS III) held during August 12–17, 2021. Submissions were reviewed by the editorial team and professional reviewers. Each paper was examined and evaluated for its theme, content, structure, language, and other necessary elements of an academic paper. CONF-CDS III received a total of 85 submissions, and 31 of them were accepted and are published in this volume of conference proceedings. These papers all lie in the field of computing and data science, focusing on topics such as various algorithms, machine learning, and neural networks, amongst others.

In consideration of the COVID-19 pandemic, CONF-CDS III was held online on YouTube. Authors of high-quality papers were invited to deliver presentations of their works. Naira Hovakimyan from the University of Illinois Urbana-Champaign, Alex Siow from the National University of Singapore, Gerhard Klimeck from Purdue University, and Kourosh Khoshelham from the University of Melbourne were invited as keynote speakers and gave brilliant speeches on their latest research and frontier technologies.

We would like to give sincere thanks to all authors who submitted their papers to CONF-CDS III, the editors and reviewers who guaranteed the quality of papers with their expertise, and the committee members who devoted themselves to the success of this conference. We are also grateful to Springer for publishing the conference proceedings. We hope you find it enjoyable and draw inspiration from this volume.

November 2021

Weijia Cao
Aydogan Ozcan
Haidong Xie
Bei Guan

Organization

General Chair

Aydogan Ozcan   University of California, Los Angeles, USA

Technical Program Committee

Weijia Cao (Co-chair)	Chinese Academy of Sciences, China
Haidong Xie (Co-chair)	China Academy of Space Technology, China
Bei Guan (Co-chair)	Chinese Academy of Sciences, China
Xiufeng Liu	Technical University of Denmark, Denmark
Yuhang Liu	Chinese Academy of Sciences, China
Kourosh Khoshelham	University of Melbourne, Australia
Ying Xing	Beijing University of Posts and Telecommunications, China
Shuai Shao	OPPO Research Institute
Chenkai Guo	Nankai University, China
Yulong Fu	China Electric Power Research Institute, China
Zachary Ziegler	Harvard University, USA
Long Bao	Tufts University, USA

Organizing Committee

Hang Lu (Chair)	Chinese Academy of Sciences, China
Alex Siow	National University of Singapore, Singapore
Ce Li	China University of Mining and Technology, China
Brajendra Panda	University of Arkansas, USA
Ke Wang	Beijing University of Posts and Telecommunications, China
Di Wu	China Academy of Information and Communications Technology, China
Ruipeng Gao	Beijing Jiaotong University, China
Guoqing Xiang	Peking University, China
Karen Works	Florida State University, USA
Yanzhao Hou	Beijing University of Posts and Telecommunications, China
Lu Wang	Chinese Academy of Sciences, China
Zhanwei Liu	Cornell University, USA
Gongzhuang Peng	University of Science and Technology Beijing, China
Rahul Kumar Dubey	Robert Bosch GmbH, India
Wenliang Lin	Beijing University of Posts and Telecommunications, China
Yi Guo	University of Southern California, USA
Lei Shu	University of Texas at Austin, USA
Shibiao Wan	University of Pennsylvania, USA
Liqing Wang	China Academy of Aerospace Electronics Technology, China
Xiaoguang Wang	Virginia Polytechnic Institute and State University, USA

Publicity Committee

Xiaolong Li (Chair)	Beijing University of Posts and Telecommunications, China
James Duncan-Brown	University of South Africa, South Africa
Yuqing Zhao	Johns Hopkins University, USA

Contents

Algorithms in Machine Learning and Statistics

Advances in Natural Language Processing

Advances in Deep Learning

Video Denoise Algorithms Research and Analysis

Hongfei Du[✉]

Tianjin University of Commerce, Tianjin 300134, China

Abstract. Noise in video images is inevitable, so it is necessary to study video denoising. After many years of research on video image noise reduction by researchers, many effective video image noise reduction algorithms have been presented. In this paper, we will research and analyze the mainstream video image denoising algorithms on their characteristics, strengths, and weakness including traditional methods and learning-based methods. Necessary comments and analysis have also been presented for these algorithms later, by which the advantages and disadvantages of each algorithm are evaluated. Finally, we carefully produce the probable directions of future video image denoising algorithms for better denoise performance including the combination of traditional and learning-based algorithms for different applications.

Keywords: Video denoise · Video/image characteristics · Traditional methods · Learning-based methods

1 Introduction

Image noise is a kind of interference factor which is affected by the internal circuit and environment of the system and can make the image quality decline. The video noise is similar to the image noise, while which is also affected by the time domain factors, such as the flash noise caused by the sampling frequency among frames. The classical noise includes Pepper noise and Gaussian noise. The amplitude of Pepper noise is constant, but not the noise position is random. While the amplitude of Gaussian noise is random, but every pixel is defected by noise. To reduce the image and video noises, several efficient denoise methods are proposed.

Typical image denoising methods consist of the non-local means (NLM) denoising method [1] and the denoising method based on sparse representation [2]. Non-local filtering is the main characteristic of NLM. Firstly, the model searches similar regions in the whole image based on image blocks. Next, the average value of the similar regions is calculated, and finally, the Gaussian noise of the image is removed. The denoising method based on sparse representation is another classical denoising method. How to describe the energy of the signal as much as possible by the minimum number of coefficients is the main research problem of sparse representation. Firstly, the image is decomposed and reconstructed by Orthogonal Matching Pursuit (OMP) in a discrete cosine dictionary (DCT) dictionary, which can effectively remove the additive noise. Then logarithmic transformation is applied to the reconstructed image to adapt to the sparse representation denoising model.

© Springer Nature Singapore Pte Ltd. 2021
W. Cao et al. (Eds.): CONF-CDS 2021, CCIS 1513, pp. 3–14, 2021.
https://doi.org/10.1007/978-981-16-8885-0_1

As to the video denoise typical methods, which includes the motion characteristics considerations. In [3], an adaptive video denoising framework that integrates robust optical flow into an NLM framework with noise level estimation is presented. In the method, spatial regularization in optical flow is the key to ensure temporal coherence in removing structured noise, which achieves better denoise performance. Pablo et al. has proposed another method with the Kalman filtering of patches for frame-recursive video denoising [4]. The method is a simple frame recursive method that is fast with low memory complexity and achieves competitive results. Although these traditional video denoise methods can achieve acceptable quality, the CNN (Convolutional Neural Network) based methods have been researched in depth recently including the ViDeNN [5] and the FastDVDnet [6] methods, which can outperform the traditional methods.

It can be seen that traditional video denoising methods mainly consider the characteristics of the frame level, which means each frame uses the same denoising model and strength. These methods have not considered that video denoising according to the content difference of different regions in a video image, which means the universal applicability cannot guarantee the best denoising effect of each frame region.

While the CNN based video denoising methods can achieve better denoising results than traditional methods, the denoising performance is limited by video training and test model. Due to the denoising model dependence on the different training and test sets, these methods cannot be self-adaptive always for other video sequences. It is difficult to maintain a stable denoising performance for only one specific CNN based video denoising method in different video scenes.

Therefore, in this paper, we will study the typical video denoising methods in recent years including several traditional and CNN based methods, to deeply analyze the video denoising characteristics and their development trend, and put forward the possible development improvement and future development direction in the future.

This paper is organized as follows: Sect. 2 describes traditional video denoise work, Sect. 3 analyzes the learning-based video denoise methods, and Sect. 4 concludes this paper.

2   Traditional Video Denoise Methods Analysis

In this section, we will analyze the classic methods of video image denoising including spatial, temporal, and spatial-temporal methods with their characteristics, and the deep analysis is given finally.

Firstly, there are many traditional spatial denoising methods, which generally have the characteristics of searching the pixel points or similar areas in the current frame image one or more times, such as the simplest median filter [7] and Gaussian filter [8]. The median filter takes the values of adjacent coefficients around the target pixel to be filtered and sorts them from small to large with the target pixel. Then the median value of the sequence is determined as the filtered data value of the pixel, while the Gaussian filter takes the pixel to be filtered in the Gaussian noise and brings it into the function to obtain the filtering effect. There is also a bilateral filtering method [9] that adds the weight term of pixel value based on Gaussian filtering, that is to say, considering the distance factor as well as the influence of pixel value difference. For typical spatial denoising method characteristics analysis further, here we focus on the analysis of the NLM method as follows.

NLM algorithm determines two windows, which is a similar window and search window. A similar window is selected to compare the similarity of two pixels, while the search window determines the region and range to search for a similar structure. Let v be the noisy image and $\tilde{u}$ be the denoised image. The gray value of the pixel x in $\tilde{u}$ is obtained in the following way,

$$\tilde{u} = \sum_{y \in I} w(x, y) * v(y) \tag{1}$$

The weight w(x, y) represents the similarity between x and y pixels, and its value is determined by the distance between V(x) and V(y), which are rectangular neighborhoods centered on x and y,

$$w(x, y) = \frac{1}{Z(x)} exp(-\frac{\|V(x) - V(y)\|^2}{h^2}) \tag{2}$$

$$\|V(x) - V(y)\|^2 = \frac{1}{d^2} \sum_{\|z\|_\infty \leq ds} \|v(x+z) - v(y+z)\|^2 \tag{3}$$

$$Z(x) = \sum_{y} exp\left(-\frac{V(x) - V(y)^2}{h^2}\right) \tag{4}$$

where Z(x) is the normalization coefficient and h is the smoothing parameter, which controls the attenuation of the Gaussian function. The larger the h is, the smoother the change of Gaussian function is, the higher the denoising level is, the more edge details are preserved, but too many noise points will remain. The specific value of h is based on the noise level in the image. In the image with Gaussian noise after NLM filtering process as shown in Fig. 1 [1], it will get a good result as depicted in Fig. 2 [1].

Fig. 1. Interpretation of NLM process [1]

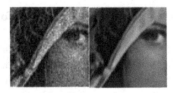

Fig. 2. Comparison of NLM filtering effect [2]

Secondly, corresponding to the spatial domain, we introduce temporal filtering. This method is only used for video denoising, but not for image denoising, due to the filtering is carried out in the time domain. These methods always need to use the most similar content of time-domain reference frame or pixel block for weighted filtering, and then motion estimation (ME) and motion compensation (MC) measures to solve the problem of time-domain noise. For example, the Block Method of 3-Dimension (VBM3D) [10], a method based on 3D fast matching, not only has a high signal-to-noise ratio but also has a very good visual effect. The only disadvantage is the high time complexity. There is also a time-domain filtering method called multi-hypothesis motion compensated filter (MHMCF) [11]. This kind of filter has less input and easier operation. Here we will introduce the MHMCF method in detail as a representative temporal filtering method as follows.

Let s_0 be the current frame, s_μ be the other frames, z_μ be the remaining frames, n_μ be the noise, $\mu = 1, 2, \ldots, N$, Then the noise-contaminated video signal under N assumptions can be represented as Fig. 3. Assuming $\overrightarrow{Y} = [s_0', c_1', c_2', \cdots, c_N']^T$ as the noisy observations, $\overrightarrow{H} = [1, 1, \cdots, 1]^T$ is the (N + 1) × 1 transition matrix, $\overrightarrow{Z} = [0, z_1', z_2', \cdots, z_N']^T$ is residue vector and $\overrightarrow{N} = [n_0, n_1, n_2, \cdots, n_N]^T$ is noise vector, the expression can be expressed as,

$$\overrightarrow{Y} = \overrightarrow{H} s_0 + \overrightarrow{Z} + \overrightarrow{N} \tag{5}$$

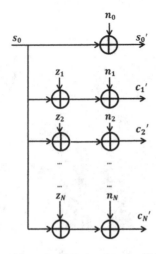

Fig. 3. The noise-contaminated video signal under N frames assumption [11]

Assuming that the average value of z_μ is not equal to 0, there should be a constant d to reduce the estimation error. Let $\widehat{s_0}$ be the estimated value of s_0, $\overrightarrow{B}$ be the filter coefficient, and d be a constant, then the expression is as follows:

$$\widehat{s_0} = \overrightarrow{B}\,\overrightarrow{Y} + d \tag{6}$$

Based on the minimum least squares estimator, we find the values of $\overrightarrow{B}$ and d to minimize the estimation error.

$$\overrightarrow{B} = (\overrightarrow{H}^T(Cov(\overrightarrow{Z}+\overrightarrow{N}))^{-1}\overrightarrow{H})^{-1}\overrightarrow{H}^T(Cov(\overrightarrow{Z}+\overrightarrow{N}))^{-1} \tag{7}$$

$$d = -\overrightarrow{B}\,\overrightarrow{Z} \tag{8}$$

Figure 4 is the filtering result picture of MHMCF method, from the figure (a) to (f) are original picture, unfiltered, filtered by JNT, filtered by 1 HMCF, filtered by 2 HMCF, and filtered by 3 HMCF. Obviously, the more the multi-hypothesis frames, the better the quality can be obtained.

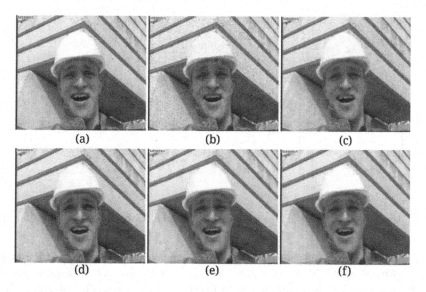

Fig. 4. Comparison of filtering effect of MHMCF [11]

Thirdly, we naturally think of a filtering method that combines temporal and spatial filtering. It combines the characteristics of the two methods. The filtering method mentioned in [3] is such a filtering method. NLM reflects the consideration of the noise reduction process in the spatial domain, and the robust optical flow reflects its time-domain characteristics. This method can be divided into three steps: Approximate K-nearest neighbors (AKNN), optical flow and NLM.

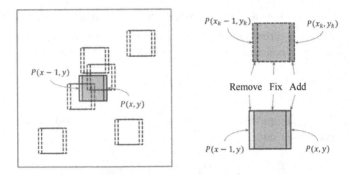

Fig. 5. AKNN searching for similar blocks [3]

In the first step, AKNN method is used to find the first K similar block sets of the most similar point, and the difference values are arranged from small to large as shown in Fig. 5.

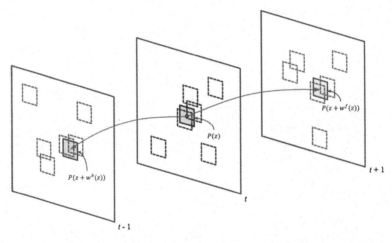

Fig. 6. Using optical flow to find the position of the target block before and after the frame [3]

In the second step, as shown in Fig. 6, the optical flow is used to find the target block positions of AKNN similar block sets in the previous and subsequent frames, which are executed several times to get the first K similar block sets in different frames.

In the last step, NLM weighting is applied to similar blocks by adding Gaussian distribution. The equation is as follows:

$$\hat{i}(z) = \frac{1}{Z}\sum_{i=t-H}^{t+H}\gamma^{|i-l|}\sum_{j=1}^{K}I(Z_{ij})exp\left\{-\frac{D_w\left(P(z),P(z_{ij})\right)}{2\sigma_t^2}\right\} \tag{9}$$

$$Z = \sum_{i=t-H}^{t+H} \gamma^{|i-l|} \sum_{j=1}^{K} exp\left\{-\frac{D_w\left(P(z), P(z_{ij})\right)}{2\sigma_t^2}\right\} \tag{10}$$

$$D_w\left(P(z), P(z_{ij})\right) = \frac{1}{Z'} \sum_{u \in [-s,s] \times [-s,s] \times 0} \left(P(z_1+u) - P(z_2+u)\right)^2 exp\left\{-\frac{\|u\|^2}{2\sigma_t^2}\right\}$$
$$\tag{11}$$

where t is the current frame, H is the time interval, the first H frame is $(t + H)$, and the last H frame is $(t - H)$, K is the most similar first K in AKNN, s is the search radius, $Dw(\cdot, \cdot)$ is a weighted SSD function of spatial offset, and Z' is the normalization factor. As can be seen from Fig. 7, the final filtering result is also very good.

Fig. 7. AKNN filter result picture [3]

The above models are mainly processed from the perspective of signal statistics, but they do not consider the subjective perception characteristics of image content, which means that from the perspective of human eyes, there may be excessive filtering in some regions and insufficient filtering in some regions. A good denoising model not only needs to consider the filter core modeling, filter window size, filter strength calculation and adaptive, but also needs to consider the complexity and so on. For example, the denoising result of the grassland area is not easy to be observed, while the filtering result of the sky area is easy to be found, and so on. This means that, to improve the subjective feeling after denoising, future video denoising may need to model the video content understanding based on the consideration of signal distribution characteristics.

3 Learning Based Video Denoise Methods Analysis

In this section, we will analyze the video denoising methods based on learning methods including CNN, DNN, GNN, NLCNN, and other methods with related deep analysis are given finally.

With the popularity of machine learning in recent years, and to add machine understanding of video content in the process of noise reduction, the denoising methods based on learning methods including CNN have been widely studied and applied recently.

For image denoise, additive white gaussian noise [12] (AWGN) is presented, which is a typical CNN based method. To improve the performance of video denoise, researchers put forward the CBDnet [13], DnCNN [14], etc. Although these kinds of methods can improve the quality of image, they are too complex for video denoise while processing frame by frame as an image. Therefore, for the video denoise, DVDnet [15], FastDVDnet [6] are proposed. Here the CBDnet and FastDVDnet methods are selected as reprehensive methods for image and video denoise with analysis as follows, respectively.

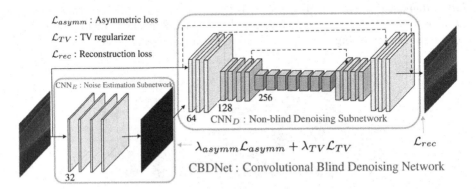

Fig. 8. CBDnet denoising process [13]

Firstly, the CBDnet consists of a noise estimation subnet (CNN_E) and a non blind denoising subnet (CNN_D). CNN_E generates the estimated noise level map $\hat{\sigma}(y) = F_E(y; W_E)$ by noise observation coefficient y, where W_E is the network parameter of CNN_E. Since CNN_E has the same size as the input y and can be estimated by the complete convolution network, its output can be utilized as the noise level mapping. In the next step, CNN_D takes y and $\hat{\sigma}(y)$ as input to get the final denoising result $x = F_D(y, \hat{\sigma}(y); W_D)$, where W_D represents the network parameters of CNN_D. In addition, CNN_E allows the estimated noise level map $\hat{\sigma}(y)$ to be adjusted before CNN_D. The Fig. 8 depicts the process of CBDnet.

In detail, CNN_E is a five layer convolutional network without pooling and batch normalization (BN) operation. Each convolution layer has 32 characteristic channels and the filter size is 3×3. There is a ReLU after each build-up layer. While the CNN_D adopts U-Net architecture, with y and $\hat{\sigma}(y)$ as input, and gives prediction x in noiseless and clean image. Residual mapping $R(y, \hat{\sigma}(y); W_D)$ is learned by residual learning, and then $x = y + R(y, \hat{\sigma}(y); W_D)$ is predicted. The 16 layer U-Net architecture of CNN_E introduces symmetric jump connection, step convolution and transpose convolution to utilize multi-scale information and expand receptive field. All filters are 3×3 in size. Except for the last one, a ReLU is added after each convolution layer.

The asymmetric loss defined below is introduced into the noise estimation subnet and combined with the reconstruction loss to train the complete CBDNet,

$$L_{asymm} = \sum_i \left| \alpha - II_{(\hat{\sigma}(y_i) - \sigma(y_i)) < 0} \right| \cdot (\hat{\sigma}(y_i) - \sigma(y_i))^2 \tag{12}$$

where II_e equals to 1 or 0 when e < 0 and 0, respectively. In addition, a global variation (TV) regularization is introduced to constrain the smoothness of $\hat{\sigma}(y)$,

$$L_{TV} = \|\nabla_h \hat{\sigma}(y)\|_2^2 + \|\nabla_v \hat{\sigma}(y)\|_2^2 \tag{13}$$

where ∇_h and ∇_v represent gradient operators along the horizontal or vertical direction, respectively. The cost of reconstruction is

$$L_{rec} = \|\hat{x} - x\|_2^2 \tag{14}$$

The total loss function is as follows, and Fig. 9 is the noise reduction result of CBDnet.

$$L = L_{rec} + \lambda_{asymm} L_{asymm} + \lambda_{TV} L_{TV} \tag{15}$$

(a) Noisy image   (b) Denoised patches

Fig. 9. Denoising effect of CBDnet [13]

Secondly, the FastDVDnet is a kind of video denoising methods. Its typical process is depicted in Fig. 10. It can be seen from Fig. 10 (a) that the model is a two-stage structure, which takes five consecutive frames and one noise estimation as the input of the network, in which the middle frame is the denoised frame, and then the five frames are divided into three groups as the input of Denoise Block 1, and three Denoise Block 1 as the input of Denoise Block 2. Three of them share parameters, Denoise Block 1 and Denoise Block 2 have the same structure, such as Fig. 10 (b), which is a modified version of U-Net. To solve the problem of alignment difficulties caused by motion, the DVDnet method chooses to use the optical flow estimation method. However, this method is time-consuming. Based on the DVDnet method, the FastDVDnet method uses a U-Net method that has alignment within the range of perception. Therefore, FastDVDnet inherits the advantages of DVDnet, while it also has lower time complexity and faster speed. Figure 11 shows the comparison of the denoise results

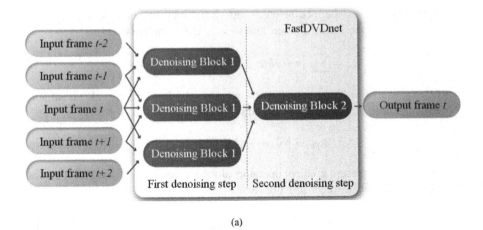

(a)

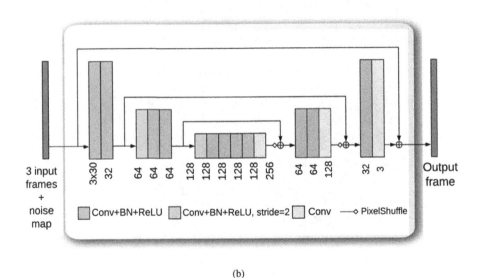

(b)

Fig. 10. Structure diagram of FastDVDnet [6]

between other denoising methods and FastDVDnet, where Fig. 11 (a) is DVDnet, and Fig. 11 (b) is FastDVDnet. It can be seen that the edges of the image after denoising by these two methods are smoother and the details are better preserved.

Finally, it can be seen that, compared with traditional denoise methods, the image and video denoising methods based on CNN do not need to establish the noise model and estimate the noise intensity. It means that these methods can achieve better performance without the mathematic model loss risk. However, these kinds of methods need a lot of training, and the performance of different data sets may have a big gap. For better and practical denoise methods, the learning-based methods can combine with the traditional denoising models to explore their different characteristics. For example, the method NLCNN [16], a non-local processing method based on the introduction of the deep network for non-local processing can achieve better and robust performance. Therefore, in the future, it may be necessary to combine the advantages of traditional methods and learning-based methods to consider the content and noise characteristics when building network models.

(a)   (b)

Fig. 11. Denoising results comparison (a) DVDnet (b) FastDVDnet [6]

4   Conclusions

This paper mainly evaluates and studies different methods of video image noise reduction, including traditional methods and learning-based methods, and predicts the future development direction of video image noise reduction. In the traditional methods, we analyzed the NLM algorithm in the spatial domain, the MHMCF algorithm in the time domain, and the AKNN algorithm combining the spatial and time domains, and found that although most traditional methods have good adaptability, while they lack subjective image characteristics of subjective perception analysis. In learning-based methods, we mainly studied and analyzed various video denoising methods based on CNN, and concluded that this type of method can achieve better performance without the risk of loss of mathematical models, but it also has disadvantages. They require more optimistic adaptability and training for different circumstances. Combining the conclusions of the two types of methods, we believe that it will help to achieve better performance. In the future, we will continue to analyze the video denoise methods more deeply, including noise characteristics, model characteristics, etc., for proposing better denoising methods.

References

1. Buades, A., Coli, B., Morel, J.M.: A non-local algorithm for image denoising. In: Computer Vision and Pattern Recognition 2005, CVPR 2005, vol. 2, pp. 60–65 (2008)
2. Wu, D., Du, X., Wang, K.: An effective approach for underwater sonar image denoising based on sparse representation. In: 2018 IEEE 3rd International Conference on Image, Vision and Computing (ICIVC), pp. 389–393, March 2018
3. Liu, C., Freeman, W.T.: A high-quality video denoising algorithm based on reliable motion estimation. In: Daniilidis, K., Maragos, P., Paragios, N. (eds.) ECCV 2010. LNCS, vol. 6313, pp. 706–719. Springer, Heidelberg (2010). https://doi.org/10.1007/978-3-642-15558-1_51

4. Arias, P., Morel, J.: Kalman filtering of patches for frame-recursive video denoising. In: 2019 IEEE/CVF Conference on Computer Vision and Pattern Recognition Workshops (CVPRW), Long Beach, CA, USA, pp. 1917–1926 (2019). https://doi.org/10.1109/CVPRW.2019.00243

5. Claus, M., Gemert, J.V.: ViDeNN: deep blind video denoising. In: 2019 IEEE/CVF Conference on Computer Vision and Pattern Recognition Workshops (CVPRW), Long Beach, CA, USA, pp. 1843–1852 (2019). https://doi.org/10.1109/CVPRW.2019.00235

6. Tassano, M., Delon, J., Veit, T.: FastDVDnet: towards real-time deep video denoising without flow estimation. In: 2020 IEEE/CVF Conference on Computer Vision and Pattern Recognition (CVPR), Seattle, WA, USA, pp. 1351–1360 (2020). https://doi.org/10.1109/CVPR42600.2020.00143

7. George, G., Oommen, R.M., Shelly, S., Philipose, S.S., Varghese, A.M.: A survey on various median filtering techniques for removal of impulse noise from digital image. In: 2018 Conference on Emerging Devices and Smart Systems (ICEDSS), Tiruchengode, pp. 235–238 (2018). https://doi.org/10.1109/ICEDSS.2018.8544273

8. Jain, A., Gupta, R.: Gaussian filter threshold modulation for filtering flat and texture area of an image. In: 2015 International Conference on Advances in Computer Engineering and Applications, Ghaziabad, pp. 760–763 (2015). https://doi.org/10.1109/ICACEA.2015.7164804

9. Wenxuan, S., Jie, L.I., Minyuan, W.U.: An image denoising method based on multiscale wavelet thresholding and bilateral filtering. Wuhan Univ. J. Nat. Sci. **2**, 148–152 (2010)

10. Dabov, K., Foi, A., Egiazarian, K.: Video denoising by sparse 3D transform-domain collaborative filtering. In: 2007 15th European Signal Processing Conference, Poznan, pp. 145–149 (2007)

11. Guo, L., Au, O.C., Ma, M., et al.: A multihypothesis motion-compensated temporal filter for video denoising. In: IEEE International Conference on Image Processing. IEEE (2006)

12. Naserzadeh, S., Jalali, M.: Channel estimation and symbol detection in AWGN channel for new structure of CDMA signals. In: 2011 Eighth International Conference on Information Technology: New Generations, Las Vegas, NV, pp. 1080–1081 (2011). https://doi.org/10.1109/ITNG.2011.197

13. Guo, S., Yan, Z., Zhang, K., Zuo, W., Zhang, L.: Toward convolutional blind denoising of real photographs. In: 2019 IEEE/CVF Conference on Computer Vision and Pattern Recognition (CVPR), Long Beach, CA, USA, pp. 1712–1722 (2019). https://doi.org/10.1109/CVPR.2019.00181

14. Zhang, K., Zuo, W., Chen, Y., Meng, D., Zhang, L.: Beyond a Gaussian denoiser: residual learning of deep CNN for image denoising. IEEE Trans. Image Process. **26**(7), 3142–3155 (2017). https://doi.org/10.1109/TIP.2017.2662206

15. Tassano, M., Delon, J., Veit, T.: DVDNET: a fast network for deep video denoising. In: 2019 IEEE International Conference on Image Processing (ICIP), Taipei, Taiwan, pp. 1805–1809 (2019). https://doi.org/10.1109/ICIP.2019.8803136

16. Lefkimmiatis, S.: Non-local color image denoising with convolutional neural networks. In: 2017 IEEE Conference on Computer Vision and Pattern Recognition (CVPR), Honolulu, HI, pp. 5882–5891 (2017). https://doi.org/10.1109/CVPR.2017.623

Stock Market Movement Prediction: A Comparative Study Between Machine Learning and Deep Time Series Models

Leheng Sheng[✉]

Southeast University, Nanjing 211189, China
213182080@seu.edu.cn

Abstract. The stock market is one of the most important financial markets. It can not only provide financial support for listed companies, but also enable common shareholders to obtain profits through market transactions. In the literature, time series model, machine learning model and deep learning model are used for stock prediction. Because of the development of artificial intelligence, more and more advanced time series models have been proposed and achieved good results on a series of problems. However, whether these models can work on stock market movement prediction has not been studied. In this paper, based on the stock index data of the United States and China, we try to compare and predict the movement by two machine learning models and four deep learning models for different horizon lengths. Our results show that deep learning models are more prone to over fitting than SVM and XGBoost models, and the result is not as good as traditional machine learning model.

Keywords: Stock market movement prediction · Machine learning · Deep learning · Time series models

1 Introduction

People can make profits through financial transactions, so there are various trading markets around the world, such as stock market, futures trading and foreign exchange trading market. Among these financial markets, the stock market is the most widely accepted. Taking China and the United States as examples, there are Shenzhen Stock Exchange, Shanghai Stock Exchange and other trading markets in China. And the total market value of China's stock market has exceeded 11 trillion US dollars in 2020. Similarly, there are several stock markets in US. As China is one of the most representative developing countries and the United States is a typical developed country, we choose the stock markets of these two countries to study in this paper.

There are two opinions about whether the stock price can be predicted. One is the proponent of the Efficient Market Hypothesis (EMH). This hypothesis holds that if a stock market is highly regulated, transparent and competitive, the stock price trend will reflect all valuable information timely and accurately, such as the current and future value of the company. When EMH is established, there is no way to forecast the stock price of tomorrow by analyzing the past data. Another view is the opposition to the

© Springer Nature Singapore Pte Ltd. 2021
W. Cao et al. (Eds.): CONF-CDS 2021, CCIS 1513, pp. 15–27, 2021.
https://doi.org/10.1007/978-981-16-8885-0_2

EMH. Because of the factors of insider trading and false trading, the stock market in real world is not effective. At the same time, with the rise of mobile Internet, people can collect more and more data as input features. Different input characteristics, including historical price, technical indicators, emotional indicators of stock evaluation text, are used to achieve higher accuracy in predicting the trend.

In this study, we mainly rely on historical price to forecast the market index movement 1 day, 5 day and 10 days later. We also calculate technical indicators as input features. Based on the stock index data of the United States and China, we try to compare the movement prediction of two machine learning models and four deep learning models for different horizon lengths. Our results show that deep learning models are more prone to over fitting than SVM and XGBoost models, and the result is not as good as traditional machine learning model.

This paper is arranged as follows. In Sect. 2, previous studies concerning to this paper are discussed. In Sect. 3, we give the dataset and problem description. In Sect. 4, we give the feature engineering as well as the prediction models. In Sect. 5, we give the implementation details as well as the results. In Sect. 6, we give the conclusion.

2   Related Works

The financial market is a complex system. Traditional econometric models, although highly theoretical and explanatory, often fail to perform as well as novel machine learning models. In recent years, artificial intelligence has been more and more widely used in the financial field and showed outstanding performance.

The knowledge of experts is used for financial prediction in Misuk [1], which is incorporated in a data mining scheme with a focus on model interpretability and prediction metrics.

Wei Chen et al. [2] propose a method for trend forecasting with convolution neural network (CNN) model based on graph convolution feature. And this model achieves an accuracy over 51% on the dataset of China stock market.

Yi et al. [3] propose a new hybrid model based on long short term memory (LSTM) and particle swarm optimization (IPSO). They use adaptive mutation factor in this work as a parameter in model optimization. This technology keep model away from converging to local optimum too early. And the R^2 of this model on Australian stock market exceeds 0.94.

Sezer et al. [4] propose CNN-TA using a two-dimensional CNN based on image processing characteristics. The time series are transformed into two-dimensional images and processed by CNN. The accuracy of their model on test data (Dow-30) is 58%.

Thibaut et al. [5] use the method of deep reinforcement learning (DRL) to build a novel trading model. This algorithmic trading system works efficiently. The Sharpe Ratio of this strategy on Apple stock is 1.484 which is higher than B&H, S&H and TF methods.

Althelaya et al. [6] study how the combination of deep learning technology and multi-resolution analysis improves the prediction accuracy. And their method is evaluated with the S&P500 index.

Yldrm et al. [7] merge two LSTM models together to predict the direction of the EUR and USD currency pair. One LSTM is based on the data of financial factors, while the other is based on technical indicators. Their hybrid model achieves an accuracy of about 73.09% on the prediction of EUR and USD currency pair.

Adesola and Michael [8] use machine learning to predict the trend reverse. They apply this model on data from 20 foreign exchange market and find out this model is widely applicable.

Yilin et al. [9] study how RF, SVR, LSTM, DMLP and CNN advance the mean-variance and omega models. They find out RF + MVF has the best result and SVR based omega model performs best among OF models.

Sarbjit et al. [10] use a soft computing model of discrete wavelet transform, wavelet denoising and autoregressive model to predict the weekly closing price and daily closing price of the BSE100 S&P Sensex index.

Pooja et al. [11] propose a fusion supervision framework SDCF. The framework relies on a novel CTL model. The experiment is based on dataset from several markets and this novel model achieves an average F1 score of 0.62 on 15 Indian stocks. This result is better than 1-D CNN approach.

Gite et al. [12] propose an efficient machine learning technology using LSTM and XAI to forecast the movement of stock market and explain why AI would make this choice. They settle the model on the data of National Stock Exchange and news headlines. They not only give the prediction of stock movement, but also present the explanation that why AI will make this prediction by using XAI.

More related work can be referred to some recent reviews [13, 14].

3 Dataset and Problem Description

3.1 Dataset

The stock indices we use cover both the US and China markets, with the following four indices:

1. SSE Composite: It is a stock market index which contains all stocks trading at the Shanghai Stock Exchange, including A shares and B shares traded in the China market. The currency of this index is CNY.
2. S&P 500: It contains 500 large companies listed in the US market. The company list may change and may not necessarily have the exact number of 500. As one of the most commonly used equity indices, S&P 500 has been widely used in previous studies. The currency of this index is USD.
3. NASDAQ Composite: It is an index containing all stocks listed in a specific US stock market, i.e., the Nasdaq stock market. The currency of this index is USD.
4. NYSE Composite: It is also a stock market index of all stocks listed in a specific US market, i.e., the New York market. The currency of this index is USD.

The original daily data we get from Yahoo Finance include the following fields: the open/high/low/close prices, the adjusted close price, and the trading volume. The adjusted prices reflect the stock's value after considering the corporate actions,

including the stock's dividends, stock splits and new stock offerings. We adjust the
open/high/low prices accordingly, e.g., the adjusted open price = open price * (adjusted close price/close price). In the following parts, we use the adjusted prices unless
specifically noted.

We obtain the daily data for more than ten years, from Jan 1, 2009 to Dec 12, 2020.
We show the market situations of the four indices in Fig. 1, 2, 3 and 4.

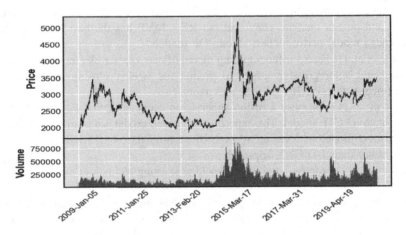

Fig. 1. The market situation of SSE Composite.

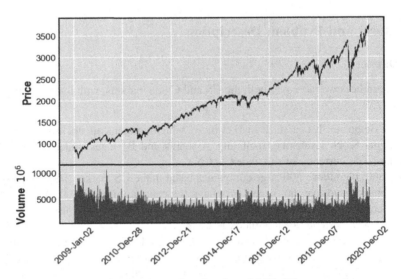

Fig. 2. The market situation of S&P 500.

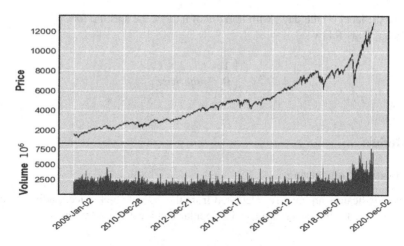

Fig. 3. The market situation of NASDAQ Composite.

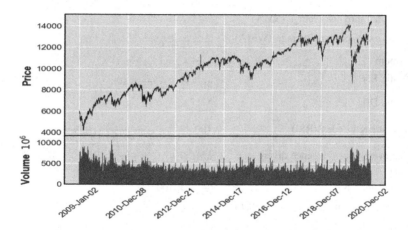

Fig. 4. The market situation of NYSE Composite.

Following a standard machine learning scheme, the raw data is divided into three subsets, namely, training, validation and testing sets. The data from 2009 to 2016 is for training models. The data from 2017 to 2018 is the validation set. The data from 2019 to 2020 is the testing set. The models would be trained on the training set, the hyper parameters would be chosen according to the validation set, and the final performance would be evaluated in the testing set in the following parts.

3.2 Problem

According to the future adjusted close price relative to today's change, we label 0 or 1 distribution to represent the decline and rise. Therefore, we can define a classification problem. We use three different horizons, i.e., 1 day, 5 days and 10 days to label the data. For the label on the day t with horizon of n days, the specific formula to calculate the label y_t is as follows.

$$y_t = \begin{cases} 1, & C_{t+n} > C_t \\ 0, & otherwise \end{cases}$$

4   Models

4.1   Feature Engineering

Technical indicators are mainly calculated from the data of stock price, trading volume or price index. In this paper, we use 10 popular technical indicators as follows.

Table 1. Selected technical indicators.

Name	Formula
Simple n-day moving average (SMA)	$\frac{C_t + C_{t-1} + \ldots + C_{t-n-1}}{n}$
Weighted n-day moving average (WMA)	$\frac{nC_t + (n-1)C_{t-1} + \ldots + C_{t-n-1}}{n + (n-1) + \ldots + 1}$
Momentum	$C_t - C_{t-(n-1)}$
Stochastic K%	$\frac{C_t - LL_{t-(n-1)}}{HH_{t-(n-1)} - LL_{t-(n-1)}} \times 100$
Stochastic D%	$\frac{\sum_{i=0}^{n-1} K_{t-i}}{10} \%$
Relative strength index (RSI)	$100 - \frac{100}{1 + \left(\sum_{i=0}^{n-1} UP_{t-i}/n\right) / \left(\sum_{i=0}^{n-1} DW_{t-i}/n\right)}$
Moving average convergence divergence (MACD)	$MACD(n)_{t-1} + \frac{2}{n+1} \times (DIFF_t - MACD(n)_{t-1})$
Larry William's R%	$\frac{H_n - C_t}{H_n - L_n} \times 100$
Accumulation/distribution (A/D) oscillator	$\frac{H_t - C_{t-1}}{H_t - L_t}$
Commodity channel index (CCI)	$\frac{M_t - SM_t}{0.015 D_t}$

C_t is the closing price of day t, L_t is the low price and L_t is the high price at time t, LL_t and HH_t are lowest low and highest high price in the last t days, respectively. UP_t means upward price change while DW_t is the downward price change at time t.

Some other indicators are calculated as follows:

$$DIFF_t = EMA(12)_t - EMA(26)_t$$

$$M_t = \frac{H_t + L_t + C_t}{3}$$

$$SM_t = \frac{\sum_{i=1}^{n} M_{t-i+1}}{n}$$

$$D_t = \frac{\sum_{i=1}^{n} |M_{t-i+1} - SM_t|}{n}$$

4.2 Machine Learning Models

We adopt two machine learning models which are also often considered in previous studies, namely, Support Vector Machine (SVM) and eXtreme Gradient Boosting (XGBoost) [15].

SVM is a widely used supervised machine learning, which is suitable for the classification problems we are dealing with. A hyperplane with the largest amount of margin is built iteratively by SVM, which aims to separate data of different types. SVM has the advantages of both the elegant mathematical formulation as well as the theoretical performance guarantee.

XGBoost is an ensemble machine learning model that is based on the framework of gradient boosting. The weak learner used as the base estimator is usually the decision tree, which is prone to overfitting. By boosting individual tree models, all the trees are built sequentially with the aim to reduce the errors in previous ones. XGBoost also makes many engineering improvements and algorithmic optimizations than the standard boosting process.

4.3 Deep Learning Models

We adopt four models, namely, Gated Recurrent Units (GRU) [16], Long Short Term Memory (LSTM) [17], Temporal Convolutional Network (TCN) [18], and Time Series Transformer (TST) [19].

GRU and LSTM are both RNN (Recurrent Neural Network) variants, which are designed for time series. RNNs allow previous outputs to be used as inputs, so that the information from previous time steps to be kept. While the idea is simple, RNNs is troubled by the problems of the vanishing gradient problem, which makes training the neural network weights impossible. To solve the problem of vanishing gradient, GRU uses the two gates to control what information to be passed to the output, i.e., update gate and reset gate. LSTM is similar to GRU, by introducing three gates to control how much and which information to retain.

TCN extends the parallel processing ability of convolutions in the image processing field to the temporal area. CNN has been extremely successful in the image processing problems, which are usually two dimensional. By reducing the convolution operation to the one dimensional time series, TCN manages to be applied to the time series problems and has been proven effective in time series classification and prediction, while retaining the parallel processing ability of convolutions.

TST extends the successful structure of Transformer in the NLP (Natural Language Processing) field to the problems of time series. This is the first time that TST is applied to both US and China markets in the literature. Transformer abandons the common structures of RNNs and CNNs. Instead, Transformer is fully based on the attention mechanism. At first, this specific structure is used for NLP and contributes many successful language models. Then the idea is extended to all sequential data, including time series, by taking these data as the languages. This extension has been proven effective unexpectedly, even in the visual field by taking image patches from a big picture and organize them in a sequential manner.

5 Results

5.1 Settings

We used Tsai[1] as the programming platform. Tsai is an open-source deep learning package based on Pytorch[2] & fastai.[3] This framework focuses on most advanced techniques for time series classification, regression and forecasting. Also, we use the package of hyperopt[4] to search for the best hyperparameter.

We use the accuracy and weighted F1 score for evaluation metrics.

Accuracy is the proportion of the correct sample number to the total sample number. However, it is not a good evaluation index when the model is overfitting. It is possible to have the highest accuracy when the model is predicted to be 1 or 0. As the harmonic average of precision and recall, F1 score is widely used as the final evaluation method in many machine learning competitions. Therefore, we also introduce F1 score as the evaluation index. Also, we draw the confusion matrix. Confusion matrix is a visual method for comparing the true and predicted labels. The diagonal elements are the sample numbers that are correctly classified.

5.2 Results

We first collate the results of different models on 1-day, 5-day and 10 day scales. The accuracies and F1 scores of the models we compare are presented in Table 1, 2, 3, and 4 (Table 5).

---

[1] https://timeseriesai.github.io/tsai/.

[2] https://pytorch.org/.

[3] https://docs.fast.ai/.

[4] http://hyperopt.github.io/hyperopt/.

Table 2. The accuracies and F1 scores for SSE Composite.

Model	1-day movement		5-days movement		10-days movement	
	Accuracy	F1 score	Accuracy	F1 score	Accuracy	F1 score
SVM	0.530	**0.530**	0.553	**0.554**	0.579	**0.586**
XGBoost	0.520	0.520	0.538	**0.540**	0.588	**0.586**
GRU	0.524	0.451	0.578	0.423	0.627	0.483
LSTM	0.527	0.390	0.577	0.422	0.627	0.483
TCN	0.534	0.397	0.577	0.423	0.627	0.483
TST	0.507	0.410	0.542	0.469	0.594	0.582

Table 3. The accuracies and F1 scores for S&P 500.

Model	1-day movement		5-days movement		10-days movement	
	Accuracy	F1 score	Accuracy	F1 score	Accuracy	F1 score
SVM	0.477	0.480	0.531	0.521	0.578	0.588
XGBoost	0.519	0.520	0.669	**0.537**	0.685	**0.641**
GRU	0.582	0.428	0.669	**0.537**	0.717	0.607
LSTM	0.582	0.428	0.669	**0.537**	0.727	0.612
TCN	0.582	0.428	0.669	**0.537**	0.727	0.612
TST	0.544	**0.540**	0.451	0.448	0.455	0.464

Table 4. The accuracies and F1 scores for NASDAQ Composite.

Model	1-day movement		5-days movement		10-days movement	
	Accuracy	F1 score	Accuracy	F1 score	Accuracy	F1 score
SVM	0.523	**0.509**	0.521	0.521	0.545	0.560
XGBoost	0.489	0.494	0.642	**0.539**	0.760	0.660
GRU	0.600	0.478	0.665	0.532	0.764	**0.662**
LSTM	0.598	0.448	0.665	0.532	0.764	**0.662**
TCN	0.598	0.448	0.665	0.532	0.746	0.660
TST	0.598	0.448	0.661	0.533	0.764	**0.662**

From Table 1, although the accuracy of deep learning method on some data sets is higher than that of traditional machine learning method, the F1 score is often lower than that of traditional machine learning method. This is because the deep learning model is too complex, in many cases, there is a phenomenon of overfitting, that is, for any data input data on any test set, the output of the deep learning model is 1. In contrast, the over fitting problem of machine learning is not so serious. Specifically, we draw the confusion matrix for each machine learning model. It is clear to see that in most cases, the machine learning model does not only predict 1 or 0 (Figs. 5, 6, 7, 8, 9, 10, 11 and 12).

Table 5. The accuracies and F1 scores for NYSE Composite

Model	1-day movement		5-days movement		10-days movement	
	Accuracy	F1 score	Accuracy	F1 score	Accuracy	F1 score
SVM	0.521	0.521	0.487	0.497	0.521	0.534
XGBoost	0.525	**0.526**	0.537	0.547	0.584	**0.591**
GRU	0.556	0.390	0.650	**0.551**	0.669	0.537
LSTM	0.556	0.397	0.670	0.511	0.669	0.537
TCN	0.556	0.390	0.650	**0.551**	0.669	0.537
TST	0.556	0.390	0.648	0.518	0.669	0.537

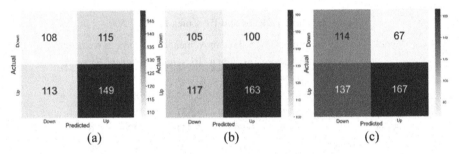

Fig. 5. Confusion matrices of SVM for SSE Composite for 1, 5, and 10 days.

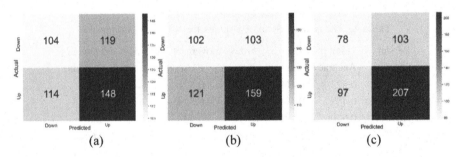

Fig. 6. Confusion matrices of XGBoost for SSE Composite for 1, 5, and 10 days.

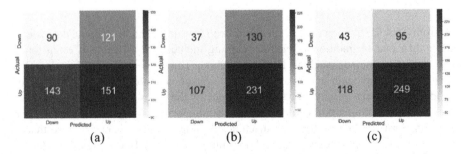

Fig. 7. Confusion matrices of SVM for S&P 500 for 1, 5, and 10 days.

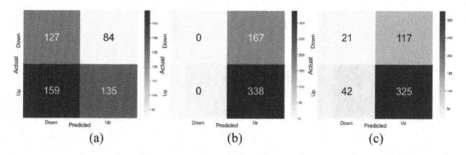

Fig. 8. Confusion matrices of XGBoost for S&P 500 for 1, 5, and 10 days.

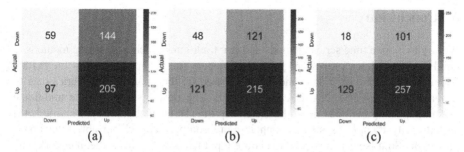

Fig. 9. Confusion matrices of SVM for NASDAQ Composite for 1, 5, and 10 days.

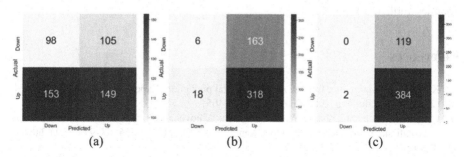

Fig. 10. Confusion matrices of XGBoost for NASDAQ Composite for 1, 5, and 10 days.

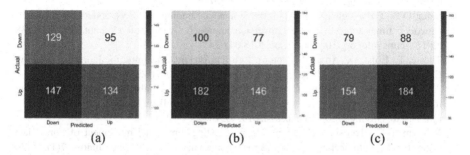

Fig. 11. Confusion matrices of SVM for NYSE Composite for 1, 5, and 10 days.

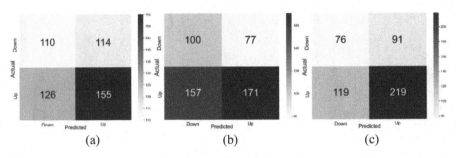

Fig. 12. Confusion matrices of XGBoost for NYSE Composite for 1, 5, and 10 days.

6   Conclusion

We use four deep time series methods and two traditional machine learning methods to build the stock index movement prediction model. The paper also studies the market fluctuation after 1 day, 5 days and 10 days based on the financial time series data of China SSE, S & P500, NASDAQ and NYSE. The results show that the traditional machine learning method tend to beat the deep time series method. Financial market is an extremely complex system, which is more complex and changeable than image prediction. So it is very important to choose input features. At this stage, the work only stays in the analysis of historical data. In future work, we will consider adding more input features, such as sentiment factors and market fundamentals, to improve the accuracy further.

References

1. Kim, M.: A data mining framework for financial prediction. Expert Syst. Appl. **173**, 114651 (2021). https://doi.org/10.1016/j.eswa.2021.114651
2. Chen, W., Jiang, M., Zhang, W.-G., Chen, Z.: A novel graph convolutional feature based convolutional neural network for stock trend prediction. Inf. Sci. **556**, 67–94 (2021). https://doi.org/10.1016/j.ins.2020.12.068
3. Ji, Y., Liew, A.W.-C., Yang, L.: A novel improved particle swarm optimization with long-short term memory hybrid model for stock indices forecast. IEEE Access **9**, 23660–23671 (2021). https://doi.org/10.1109/access.2021.3056713
4. Sezer, O.B., Ozbayoglu, A.M.: Algorithmic financial trading with deep convolutional neural networks: time series to image conversion approach. Appl. Soft Comput. **70**, 525–538 (2018). https://doi.org/10.1016/j.asoc.2018.04.024
5. Théate, T., Ernst, D.: An application of deep reinforcement learning to algorithmic trading. Expert Syst. Appl. **173**, 114632 (2021). https://doi.org/10.1016/j.eswa.2021.114632
6. Althelaya, K.A., Mohammed, S.A., El-Alfy, E.S.M.: Combining deep learning and multiresolution analysis for stock market forecasting. IEEE Access **9**, 13099–13111 (2021). https://doi.org/10.1109/access.2021.3051872
7. Yıldırım, D.C., Toroslu, I.H., Fiore, U.: Forecasting directional movement of Forex data using LSTM with technical and macroeconomic indicators. Financ. Innov. **7**(1), 1–36 (2021). https://doi.org/10.1186/s40854-020-00220-2

8. Adegboye, A., Kampouridis, M.: Machine learning classification and regression models for predicting directional changes trend reversal in FX markets. Expert Syst. Appl. **173**, 114645 (2021). https://doi.org/10.1016/j.eswa.2021.114645

9. Ma, Y., Han, R., Wang, W.: Portfolio optimization with return prediction using deep learning and machine learning. Expert Syst. Appl. **165**, 113973 (2021). https://doi.org/10.1016/j.eswa.2020.113973

10. Singh, S., Parmar, K.S., Kumar, J.: Soft computing model coupled with statistical models to estimate future of stock market. Neural Comput. Appl. **33**(13), 7629–7647 (2021). https://doi.org/10.1007/s00521-020-05506-1

11. Gupta, P., Majumdar, A., Chouzenoux, E., Chierchia, G.: SuperDeConFuse: a supervised deep convolutional transform based fusion framework for financial trading systems. Expert Syst. Appl. **169**, 114206 (2021). https://doi.org/10.1016/j.eswa.2020.114206

12. Shilpa, G., Hrituja, K., Priyam, M., Ketan, K., Shilpi, S., Neerav, P.: Explainable stock prices prediction from financial news articles using sentiment analysis. PeerJ Comput. Sci. **7**, e340 (2021). https://doi.org/10.7717/peerj-cs.340

13. Jiang, W.: Applications of deep learning in stock market prediction: recent progress. arXiv preprint arXiv:2003.01859 (2020)

14. Thakkar, A., Chaudhari, K.: A comprehensive survey on deep neural networks for stock market: the need, challenges, and future directions. Expert Syst. Appl. **177**, 114800 (2021). https://doi.org/10.1016/j.eswa.2021.114800

15. Chen, T., Guestrin, C.: XGBoost: a scalable tree boosting system. In: Proceedings of the 22nd ACM SIGKDD International Conference on Knowledge Discovery and Data Mining, pp. 785–794 (2016)

16. Cho, K., Van Merriënboer, B., Gulcehre, C., et al.: Learning phrase representations using RNN encoder-decoder for statistical machine translation. arXiv preprint arXiv:1406.1078 (2014)

17. Hochreiter, S., Schmidhuber, J.: Long short-term memory. Neural Comput. **9**(8), 1735–1780 (1997)

18. Bai, S., Kolter, J.Z., Koltun, V.: An empirical evaluation of generic convolutional and recurrent networks for sequence modeling. arXiv preprint arXiv:1803.01271 (2018)

19. Zerveas, G., Jayaraman, S., Patel, D., Bhamidipaty, A., Eickhoff, C.: A transformer-based framework for multivariate time series representation learning. arXiv preprint arXiv:2010.02803v2 (2020)

Occluded Face Recognition with Deep Learning

Qin Jiayu[⊠]

School of Information Science and Technology, Fudan University,
Shanghai, China
qinjiayu@fudan.edu.cn

Abstract. Face recognition is an research topic of great importance in both the academia and industry, with a large number of applications based on this technology. Occluded face recognition is even more challenging when the whole face is not available. We find this problem has not been completely solved and is still a hot topic in recent years. Based on a real-world masked face dataset, we conduct a series of experiments with an aim of evaluating five advanced deep learning models and find that DenseNet performs the best with a test accuracy of 0.8012.

Keywords: Recognition of occluded face · Convolutional neural network · Deep learning

1 Introduction

Face Recognition [1] is a biometric technology that can recognize or verify the identity of a subject in an image or video based on facial feature information of a person. A series of related technical assemblies that use an image acquisition tool (such as a camera) to collect an image or video stream containing sufficient human facial features and automatically detect and track faces in the image to recognize and verify the detected faces.

Face recognition using deep learning can be applied to the following scenarios: identity identification/authentication in national security and public safety, specific scenarios include exit and entry administration, photo comparison of suspects, identification of conference representatives, identification of passports, face identification for kindergarten transport, whole database search of missing persons, repeated screening of multiple cards for one person; face image attendance system and other enterprise applications; examinee identification and other areas of education; e-commerce authentication, financial user authentication and other financial security fields.

Research on face recognition began in the 1950s. Researchers in the field of psychology have tried to explain how people recognize faces in terms of cognitive psychology and brain science. Since 1970, there have been researches that are closely related to current face recognition technologies. The research can be split into three stages. Stage one is the cyborg identification stage. In one of the earliest study [2], the researchers transformed the facial image into a grayscale image. Face recognition in this period is manual in nature, and the system can no longer complete the process of

© Springer Nature Singapore Pte Ltd. 2021
W. Cao et al. (Eds.): CONF-CDS 2021, CCIS 1513, pp. 28–35, 2021.
https://doi.org/10.1007/978-981-16-8885-0_3

face recognition without operators. The second stage is the human-computer interaction recognition stage, which is mainly characterized by relatively simple representation methods, such as geometric feature parameters or Euclidean distance, to represent the advanced features of human face. This phase requires the introduction of prior knowledge of the operator.

The third stage is marked by the occurrence of deep learning algorithms. With the introduction of deep learning algorithms, the error rate of face recognition has been greatly reduced. In the 2015 visual AI system recognition project ImageNet competition [3], ResNet [4] achieved an error rate of 3.57% for the first time below that of human vision at 5.19%. With the continuous development of deep learning models and applications [5, 6], the field of recognition has been extended to mobile intelligent terminals such as emotional robots, vehicle-mounted auxiliary systems and so on.

During the covid-19 epidemic, the problem of facial occlusion is particularly acute. Everyone is wearing a mask, which makes the existing face recognition technology almost completely ineffective, causing great difficulties in the areas of authentication that rely on face recognition, such as neighborhood access, railway station security, face payment, suspect hunting and so on. Especially at public security checkpoints such as train stations, a portal based on traditional facial recognition system cannot effectively detect a masked face, and removing the mask increases the risk of virus infection. Since covid-19 virus can spread through contact, password or fingerprint-based unlocking systems are not secure. To address the above problems, existing facial recognition methods, which rely heavily on all facial features, must be improved to reliably authenticate a face even if it is not fully exposed.

In this paper, we firstly review the latest progress of occluded face recognition studies, especially the ones based on deep learning algorithms. Then based on a real-world masked face dataset, we conducted several experiments in order to assess and compare the performance of different deep learning models. We present the findings and the results in this paper.

This article is structured in the following way. Section 2 shows the work related to applying techniques such as deep learning to solve the occlusion face recognition problem. Section 3 presents the dataset and experiments. Conclusions are given in Sect. 4.

2   Related Work

This section reviews the work related to closed face recognition from both academic and industry practice perspectives. While the study of face recognition has gone through a long path, there are still many challenges in this area, e.g., head deflection, light change, registration error, facial occlusion and identity difference [7]. In this paper, our focus is the occluded situation, when the face is partially occluded, e.g., by masks during the covid-19 epidemic.

In the practical application of face recognition, the large number of occluded faces recognition has been among the main problems. Occlusion in images can degrade the performance of full-image based methods. The method in [8] divides the image into modules. Different modules are assigned different weights using weighting functions based on the Fisher modulator index and moduler residuals. Module weights can be used to reduce the influence of low discrimination modules.

Inspired by the neural features of human vision where people use context information under occlusion instead of focusing on the facial parts to recognize faces. In [9], the authors presented an efficient method of extracting features that combines information from both local and the context to perform face recognition. They also proposed a method of Adaptive Fusion that incorporates the proposed structural features, concatenated bead labeling features and Reinforced Centrosymmetric Local Binary Pattern (RCSLBP).

In [10], the authors employ Convolutional Neural Networks to act as feature extraction engines and use dictionaries to linearly encode the extracted depth features. The dictionary consists of a graphical library comprising the depth features from the training set samples and a secondary part consisting of matching vectors obtained from subjects inside and outside the training set, which are linked to the occlusion patterns of the test face samples.

Using single sample per person (SSPP) for face recognition is another important issue in practical facial recognition systems because of its lack of available information in the sample data; in [11], the discriminative multiscale sparse coding (DMSC) method is presented in this paper. In this work, possible occlusion differences are modeled using a vocabulary learned from subsamples. By having one training sample per subject, most types of occlusion differences can be efficiently handled.

A different approach was proposed in [12] to deal with three problems: 1) non-uniform illumination, 2) partially occluded, 3) restricted number of available training data. In this novel approach, illumination normalization, occlusion improvement, as well as the final face recognition are performed on the basis of locating the largest matching area (LMA) in each face point, in contrast to the traditional approach based on a fixed size local area. Reliability is achieved through new feature extraction methods, LMA matching methods for faces, and modeling of inexperienced data.

In [13], there is a proposed framework for robustness called Nuclear Norms for Adapted Occlusion Dictionary Learning (NNAODL). They first introduce a kernel norm based error model to describe the occluded and damaged regions of the search image. Then, they integrate the error images with training instances to create a dictionary that can accurately reconstruct the corrupted and undamaged regions of the query images. In addition, they use a two-dimensional structure to represent and adjust the sampling weights to retain further information about the structure. The above mentioned benefits are combined into one target function and an algorithm for solving the model efficiently is proposed.

Generative Adversarial Networks (GANs) are particularly well suited for reconstructing visually plausible occlusions through face coloring. Inspired by these occlusal obstacles, the authors of [14] offered a variety of identities in coloring to facilitate the recognition of occluded faces. The main idea was to integrate GAN with an up-optimized, pre-prepared CNN discriminator. This CNN recognizer would act as a third player against the generator, identifying diversity within the same class of identity.

Taking inspiration that the human vision system clearly disregards occlusions and focuses only on unoccupied parts of the face, the authors [15] suggested a strategy for learning masks to find and remove corrupted features from recognition. First, they use a novel pairwise differential Simulation Network (PDSN) design that exploits the top-twitch feature differences between occluded and non-occluded face pairs to construct a mask dictionary. Each element in this dictionary captures the similarity between the occluded face region and the damaged element, called the feature discard mask (FDM). For images of faces with random part occluded faces, the authors pooled the corresponding dictionary elements to generate the FDM and multiplied it by the original features to eliminate the damaged traits for recognition.

Other than the above academic studies, many companies also propose their solutions to the occluded face recognition problem. In view of the incomplete facial image information with masks, Huawei proposed to use face recognition network to conduct face recognition on face reconstruction images. Through image reconstruction network, face images with accessories (glasses, masks, hats, etc.) can be reconstructed into face images without accessories [16].

In another work [17], a block face image library is built, specifically in the judgment of the need to identify mask on the face image (such as glasses, masks, etc.). The obstructions are picked up and added to the reference database. Then the face image is identified by the reference image matching search in the library, so as to complete the identification process.

Alibaba also proposes a new approach to improve accuracy [18], through a comprehensive local organs image matching technology to complete recognition, not only can the local organ is the eye image, nose, mouth and ears images, etc., can also be the chin area, face contour, birthmarks or moles images, and so on. According to the similarity evaluation indexes of multiple local organs of the face and the corresponding weights, the overall similarity evaluation indexes can be obtained, so as to obtain more accurate facial recognition results under occlusion.

Recently, some technology groups have achieved some success in face recognition with masks in the news. Sense Time reported a pass rate of 85% when the person exposes 50% of the nose [19]. Hanwang technology facial recognition can also recognize the face while wearing a mask, with an accuracy of 85% [20].

3 Dataset and Experiments

3.1 Dataset

This section we perform our experiments over a real-world masked dataset [21]. This data set finds images from the Internet and filters them manually. According to the description of the original paper, the data set includes 5,000 mask faces and 90,000 Normal faces of 525 people. The total number of people without masks in the data set is 460, while the total number of people with masks is 525. We took the intersection, that is, only 460 people were used. We used 90,468 pictures of 460 people without masks, and a total of 92,413 pictures with masks.

Figures 1 and 2 show examples of images with and without masks, respectively.

Fig. 1. An example of the face picture without a mask.

Fig. 2. An example of face picture with a mask.

In order to make the picture suitable for training, the first step is to preprocess the picture. The first step is to normalize the data. We divide the value of each pixel on each channel by 255, so that its value is between 0 and 1. The second step is to divide the training and validation sets: with 20% of our dataset as a validation set. The third step is to adjust the size of the image: there are different adjustment methods according to different algorithms.

3.2 Experiments

During the experiment, different convolutional neural networks were used for training respectively. We give a short introduction as well as the performance of these networks in this part.

MobileNet [22]. MobileNet is a lightweight and efficient CNN model. First, convolution of different input channels is made by MobileNet with the depthwise convolution, and the above output results are then combined with pointwise convolutions, reducing the computational effort and the number of model parameters significantly. Parameters on ImageNet are not used. Batch size was set to 32. Learning rate was first set to 0.05, then reduced as 0.01 for fine training. On the training set, the accuracy reached 0.8164, but only 0.2883 on the validation set, showing a serious overfitting phenomenon. Then the early stopping mechanism is introduced. If the accuracy of the validation set after 10 epochs was not improved, then the training would be stopped. After introducing the early stopping mechanism, the accuracy on the training set was 0.9609, and on the validation set was 0.3666. Final accuracy on the test set was 0.3696.

ResNet [4]. The ResNet framework allows very fast training of neural networks and the accuracy of the models is greatly improved.The basic concept of ResNet is the insertion of a forward link, i.e., a highway network. The forward structure represents a nonlinear representation for the performance inputs, whereas the highway network allows to keep some part of outputs of the forward network layers.ResNet allows to pass the information of the original inputs to the later layers directly.

During training, a $224 \times 224 \times 3$ input is used. Batch size was set to 8. Learning rate was first set to 0.05, then set to 0.01 for fine training. And an early stopping ping mechanism is used. After 16 rounds of training, the accuracies were 0.9991 on the training set and 0.6011 on the validation set. The accuracy on the final test set was 0.5942.

Inception [23]. A very deep convolutional network that was developed by Google is the InceptionV3 network. Model's input size is 299 × 299 by default and has three channels. The settings are the same with the other networks. The input size is made to 299 × 299. The accuracy on training set is 0.9993 after 13 epochs. And the accuracy of the validation set is 0.7786. Final accuracy of this test set is 0.7734.

Xception [24]. Xception was developed by Google in 2017. Its purpose is similar to that of the MobileNet series, using Inception V3 as the template and replacing the Inception module with Depthwise Conv and Pointwise Conv with residual active. In the training process, an input size of 299 × 299 × 3 was used. After 19 epochs of training, the accuracy was 0.9993 on the training set and 0.6613 on the validation set. Final accuracy of this test set is 0.6644.

DenseNet [25]. A densely connected convolutional network (DenseNet) joins every layer to all previous layers. While a conventional L-layer convolutional neural network has L connections from each layer to the next layer, DenseNet has L(L + 1)/2 connections directly. As to each layer, its input is composed of all feature maps of the previous layers, which itself serves as input for all succeeding layers.DenseNet has seven compelling advantages: it mitigates gradient loss, enhances the propagation of features, stimulates the reuse of features, and reduces dramatically on the number of parameters.There are several versions of DenseNet with different number of layers, and in this study we use is DenseNet201. As the name suggests, DenseNet201 has 201 layers. During the training process, a 224 × 224 × 3 input is used. After 16 rounds of fine-tuning, the average accuracy was 0.9989 on the training set and 0.8043 on the validation set. The final accuracy on the test set was 0.8012.

The results are summarized in Table 1. After comparison, we found that DenseNet201 had the highest accurate rate of 0.8012 on the test set, but this performance was still not satisfactory compared to the case without the mask, which may indicate that wearing a mask is still a big challenge for convolutional neural networks in occluded face recognition scenarios.

Table 1. Performance summary of different models.

Model	Training accuracy	Validation accuracy	Test accuracy
MobileNet	0.9609	0.3666	0.3696
ResNet	0.9991	0.6011	0.5942
InceptionV3	0.9993	0.7786	0.7734
Xception	0.9993	0.6613	0.6644
DenseNet201	0.9989	0.8043	0.8012

4 Conclusion

In this paper, we find that the study for occluded face recognition studies is still very active in the past few years, with a lot of challenges remaining unsolved and the deep learning approach as the mainstream solution. Based on a real-world masked face dataset, we conduct a series of experiments and evaluate different deep learning models and find that the DenseNet201 model performs the best with a test accuracy of 0.8012, which still leaves a great space for improvement in the future research.

References

1. Liu, X.: A brief talk on face recognition technology based on deep learning. Inf. Commun. **06**, 18–20 (2019)
2. Parke, F.I.: Computer generated animation of faces. In: Proceedings of the ACM Annual Conference, vol. 1, pp. 451–457 (1972)
3. Deng, J., Dong, W., Socher, R., et al.: Imagenet: a large-scale hierarchical image database. In: 2009 IEEE Conference on Computer Vision and Pattern Recognition, pp. 248–255. IEEE (2009)
4. He, K., Zhang, X., Ren, S., et al.: Deep residual learning for image recognition. In: Proceedings of the IEEE Conference on Computer Vision and Pattern Recognition, pp. 770–778 (2016)
5. Jiang, W., Zhang, L.: Geospatial data to images: a deep-learning framework for traffic forecasting. Tsinghua Sci. Technol. **24**(1), 52–64 (2018)
6. Jiang, W.: Applications of deep learning in stock market prediction: recent progress. arXiv preprint arXiv:2003.01859 (2020)
7. Sariyanidi, E., Gunes, H., Cavallaro, A.: Automatic analysis of facial affect: a survey of registration, representation, and recognition. IEEE Trans. Pattern Anal. Mach. Intell. **37**(6), 1113–1133 (2014)
8. Zhao, S., Hu, Z.: A modular weighted sparse representation based on fisher discriminant and sparse residual for face recognition with occlusion. Inf. Process. Lett. **115**(9), 677–683 (2015)
9. Zheng, W., Gou, C., Wang, F.Y.: A novel approach inspired by optic nerve characteristics for few-shot occluded face recognition. Neurocomputing **376**, 25–41 (2020)
10. Cen, F., Wang, G.: Dictionary representation of deep features for occlusion-robust face recognition. IEEE Access **7**, 26595–26605 (2019)
11. Yu, Y.F., Dai, D.Q., Ren, C.X., et al.: Discriminative multi-scale sparse coding for single-sample face recognition with occlusion. Pattern Recogn. **66**, 302–312 (2017)
12. McLaughlin, N., Ming, J., Crookes, D.: Largest matching areas for illumination and occlusion robust face recognition. IEEE Trans. Cybern. **47**(3), 796–808 (2016)
13. Du, L., Hu, H.: Nuclear norm based adapted occlusion dictionary learning for face recognition with occlusion and illumination changes. Neurocomputing **340**, 133–144 (2019)
14. Ge, S., Li, C., Zhao, S., et al.: Occluded face recognition in the wild by identity-diversity inpainting. IEEE Trans. Circ. Syst. Video Technol. **30**, 3387–3397 (2020)
15. Song, L., Gong, D., Li, Z., et al.: Occlusion robust face recognition based on mask learning with pairwise differential siamese network. In:Proceedings of the IEEE International Conference on Computer Vision, pp. 773–782 (2019)

16. Jia, X., Li, Y., Zhang, J., Kan, M., Shan, S.: Face recognition method, device and computer-readable medium. CN110399764A, 01 Nov 2019
17. Li, W., Xu, C., Liu, J.: A face recognition method and system. CN105095829A, 25 Nov 2015
18. Jiangnan: A face recognition method and device. CN109145720A, 04 Jan 2019
19. http://ai.cps.com.cn/article/202002/937650.html. Accessed 25 Aug 2020
20. https://baijiahao.baidu.com/s?id=1658872342983093939&wfr=spider&for=pc. Accessed 25 Aug 2020
21. Wang, Z., Wang, G., Huang, B., et al.: Masked face recognition dataset and application. arXiv preprint arXiv:2003.09093 (2020)
22. Howard, A.G., Zhu, M., Chen, B., et al.: Mobilenets: efficient convolutional neural networks for mobile vision applications. arXiv preprint arXiv:1704.04861 (2017)
23. Szegedy, C., Vanhoucke, V., Ioffe, S., et al.: Rethinking the inception architecture for computer vision. In: Proceedings of the IEEE Conference on Computer Vision and Pattern Recognition, pp. 2818–2826 (2016)
24. Chollet, F.: Xception: deep learning with depthwise separable convolutions. In: Proceedings of the IEEE Conference on Computer Vision and Pattern Recognition, pp. 1251–1258 (2017)
25. Huang, G., Liu, Z., Van Der Maaten, L., et al.: Densely connected convolutional networks. In: Proceedings of the IEEE Conference on Computer Vision and Pattern Recognition, pp. 4700–4708 (2017)

Fake News Detection Based on a Bi-directional LSTM with CNN

Yu Ji[✉]

University of California, Santa Cruz, Santa Cruz, CA 95060, USA
yji34@ucsc.edu

Abstract. The misleading information brought by fake news has troubled our society for a long time. Recently, the increasing spreading rate of fake news has more severe consequences than ever in the past. Many types of neural networks have been applied to solve fake news detection and other natural language problems during these years. Nevertheless, due to the limitation of each structure, a hybrid neural network would often achieve a preferable accuracy. In this paper, a novel deep neural network is proposed for the fake news detection problem based on Convolutional Neural Network and Bi-directional Long Short Term Memory network. Sequential information will be captured by using Bi-LSTM and hidden features will be captured at a detailed level using CNN. The model will be tested on large-scale datasets, which demonstrated better performance than conventional neural networks.

Keywords: Machine learning · Deep learning · Convolution network · Bi-LSTM · Natural language processing

1 Introduction

The rapid growth of social media platforms indeed brings information accessibility to their users. Unfortunately, fake news has also been wildly spreading via traditional print and online social media, which obtain economic or political benefits while manipulates its readers. Therefore, fake news detection becomes a practical natural language processing (NLP) problem to prevent people from misleading by false information.

Although detecting fake news is a long-discovered problem in human life, people could only define the trueness of a piece of news with their mind most time during the past centuries. However, the development of machine learning and deep learning algorithm has brought a new perspective into this field. In the past few years, there have been various experiments and approaches in NLP problems based on machine learning and deep learning algorithms. Naïve Bayes was chosen to perform the classification as one of the most traditional machine learning methods. Nonetheless, this experiment has been done by Granik in 2017 has a great start, it still leaves some space for improvement. [1] Then, other machine learning models are also introduced by Ahman. Etc, such as linear SVM, logistic regression, multiplayer perceptron, K nearest neighbors, and random forests. [2] These models have been tested with multiple datasets. Even though the logistic regression model outperformance other methods, all

© Springer Nature Singapore Pte Ltd. 2021
W. Cao et al. (Eds.): CONF-CDS 2021, CCIS 1513, pp. 36–44, 2021.
https://doi.org/10.1007/978-981-16-8885-0_4

of them achieve less accuracy than ensemble techniques, deep learning methods. According to Yang. Etc., TI-CNN model, which extracts explicit and latent features, can identify fake news effectively. [3] However, their model relies on the combined information from both the text and image. There also have been researches on formats of the dataset. Dong, etc. introduces his CNN-based model to solve fake news detection problem seeing as semi-supervised learning. [4] By only providing part of the label, the model spends a large amount of time on calculation. Aldwairi and Alwahedi approach fake news detection in social media networks with various groups of datasets which are distinguished by numbers and other marks. [5] On the other hand, LSTM and other RNN models are tested by Shen and Zhang on the sentence classification task. [6] Later on, many hybrid models are introduced by others in the NLP area. Okoro, etc. achieved great accuracy by combining the human literacy news detection tool and the machine linguistic and network-based approaches. [7] Zhang, etc. have developed their deep diffusive neural network to solve the same problem. [8] In addition, a combination of CNN and RNN approach is proposed by Zhang, etc. called RCNN. [9] Meanwhile, Bahad, etc. also have built their model using Bi-directional LSTM network. [10] Based on that, a more advanced hybrid network is generated from the combination of a CNN with an attention mechanism and a Bi-LSTM network [11].

In this paper, a hybrid neural network is applied to the fake news detection problem. The part of Bi-LSTM will firstly uncover the sequential information in both forward and backward order. The part of CNN will be used to reveal the hidden connections at a detailed level. This proposed hybrid neural network model will solve the fake news detection problem in a more effective way.

The rest of this paper is structured as follows: Sect. 2 is the summary of related works in the field. Section 3 demonstrates the neural network models that have been developed and used for comparison. Section 4 concludes our work.

2 Method

2.1 An Overview of the Proposed BiLSTM-CNN Algorithm

The proposed approach consists of two main parts, which are text preprocessing and deep neural network. The input datasets are two sets of classified news sets, either true or fake. Removing stopwords and punctuations of the dataset is the first step of the preprocessed pipeline. Then embedding dictionary is set up using Word2Vec algorithm. Next is the neural network, shown in Fig. 1. The generated matrix representation of sentences produced by the embedding layer will be sent into a hyper neural network structure. Sequential information will be captured by the first level of structure, Bi-LSTM. And the next level neural network CNN will extract the hidden connection of the words.

2.2 Text Preprocessing

Preprocessing the unstructured data, such as text, is one of the cores of natural language processing. The machine learning models often require the matrix form of the input from both extraction and manipulation of the texts. Specifically, removing punctuation, lowercase conversion, and word embedding are applied in the experiment. In addition, removing the Stopwords is also used to perform data cleaning. Stopwords, such as "the, and, who," often appears in English sentences but with limited information knowledge. The information density will remain the same without them. In this experiment with a Python3 environment, the English Stopwords sublibrary in the Natural Language Toolkit (NLTK) is applied.

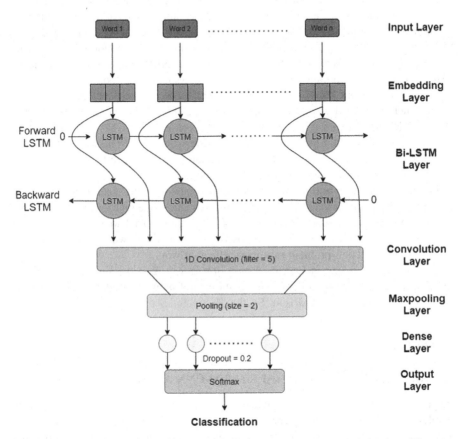

Fig. 1. This is an architecture diagram of the proposed model. The input information will stream through the Bi-LSTM part, which consists of the embedding layer and Bi-LSTM layer. Then the information will be used to adjust the connection in the CNN structure. After all, the last layer will use a SoftMax function to output classification.

2.3   Sequential Information Captured by Bi-LSTM

The Bi-LSTM model used contains a word embedding layer and a two-part LSTM structure. The embedding layer will convert each word to a vector representation according to a pre-learned algorithm. The similar meaning of the words will result in a closer distance in the vector space. Specifically, the continuous skip-gram model (Fig. 2) is chosen from Word2Vec algorithms is used in this experiment. As a reversed structure of the CBOW algorithm, skip-gram is wildly used to solve unsupervised learning problems by finding the most related words for a given word. Under this structure, input is designed to be the target word and output is designed to be the context word.

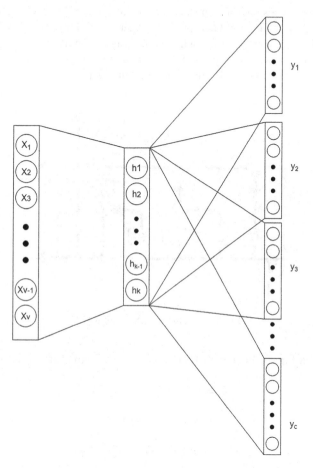

Fig. 2. This is a structural representation of the Skip-Gram Model. The x_i is the input given. The middle layer is the only one hidden layer. There is no activation function side of the hidden layer. The output layer on the right side computes the output y_i from the dot product of the hidden layer h_i and weight matrix.

In the experiment, each piece of news contains a sequence of words $w_1, w_2, ..., w_n$. Based on that, the average log probability will be used to predict context words given the target word within a limited training context with the size c.

$$\frac{1}{I} \sum_{i=1}^{I} \sum_{-c \le j \le c, j \ne 0} \log P(W_{i+j}|W_j) \tag{1}$$

The other part of the model is the Bi-LSTM layer. This layer consists of two LSTM layers, from both forwards and backwards. LSTM can handle long-term dependency because both cell states and hidden states are included in an LSTM structure, where a vanilla RNN only contains a hidden state. The other reason for choosing the LSTM unit instead of RNN is to prevent the gradient vanishing situation. In addition to a single layer, Bi-LSTM is used to represent both sequential information in forward and backward, which are connected to the same output layer.

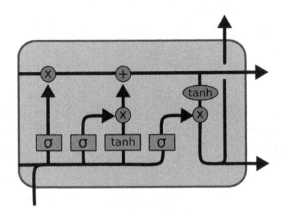

Fig. 3. A Complete LSTM unit [12]

As shown in Fig. 3, the current LSTM unit can be calculated as follows at a time t:

$$f_t = \sigma\left(W_f \cdot [h_{t-1}, x_t] + b_f\right) \tag{2}$$

$$i_t = \sigma\left(W_i \cdot [h_{t-1}, x_t] + b_i\right) \tag{3}$$

$$C_t = tanh(W_C \cdot [h_{t-1}, x_t] + b_C) \tag{4}$$

$$C_t = f_t * C_{t-1} + i_t * C_t \tag{5}$$

$$o_t = \sigma(W_0 \cdot [h_{t-1}, x_t] + b_0) \tag{6}$$

$$h_t = o_t * tanh(C_t) \tag{7}$$

In those equations, σ represents the sigmoid activation function. Weights are updated according to the flowchart from the bottom left to the top right. X_t is the input vector at the time t; W_i, W_f, W_C, W_o represent the weight associated with X_t in different gates; h_{t-1}, h_t represent the hidden state; b_f, b_C, b_o represent the bias offset of each gate. And * is the elementwise multiplication.

The first step, f_t, is used to forget the information sent from the last round. Then, i_t and C_t are combined to determine the information stored in the current cell state. This is also as known as updating the cell state. After C_t, the tanh layer, is used to update the current one, it also has to update the old cell state C_{t-1} to C_t by multiplying f_t and adding the new candidate values. Later, a sigmoid layer and a tanh layer will decide the final output of a LSTM cell. Eventually, a complete Bi-LSTM structure will have its result by calculating the elementwise sum of h_i forward and h_i backward.

2.4   Convolutional Neural Network

After the weights are passed from the Bi-LSTM layers, a traditional convolutional neural network (CNN) is utilized to finish the true or fake news categorization. Each convolutional layer will decrease the window size to generate a new feature representation of the information. And a max-pooling layer will concatenate and capture the hidden representation. A combination of both layer structures is applied to make the final prediction with a SoftMax activation function (Fig. 4).

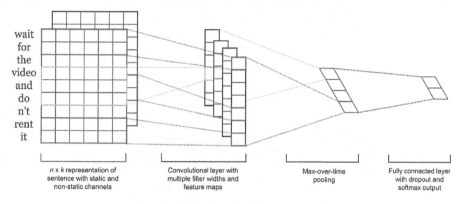

wait
for
the
video
and
do
n't
rent
it

n x k representation of
sentence with static and
non-static channels

Convolutional layer with
multiple filter widths and
feature maps

Max-over-time
pooling

Fully connected layer
with dropout and
softmax output

Fig. 4. A Complete CNN structure [13]

3   Experiment and Result

All codes are written in Python 3.7 using TensorFlow 1.14. All experiments have been performed on a Core processor Intel CPU i7-7800X 3.5 GHz with 32 GB RAM and a 1080Ti graphic card. The dataset is obtained from Fake and real new Dataset at Kaggle.

Dataset: The dataset is from the Kaggle website. [14] As one of the most popular datasets used in the NLP research, this dataset contains the fake and real news from during the American presidential election period in 2016. There are two pre-labeled files, true and fake accordingly, containing more than 20000 pieces of news each. Title, Text, Subject, and Date, a total of four attributes are introduced in each news. The content under the Text attribute is used as the input of the experiment. Also, 0 is given to the FAKE set, and 1 is given to the TRUE set as the label to distinguish two sets.

The experiment has 100 as the batch size, 10 as the epochs, and 0.2 as the validation split rate. The performance accuracy of the models is evaluated according to the prediction accuracy, whether the news is correctly classified as TRUE or FAKE (Figs. 5 and 6) (Table 1).

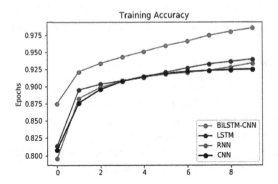

Fig. 5. Training accuracy among all four tested models

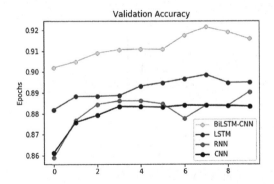

Fig. 6. Validation accuracy among all four tested models

Table 1. Evaluation of the proposed model and some common neural networks (Proposed Model is in bold)

Model	Accuracy	Precision	Recall	F1 Score
CNN	0.883	0.893	0.891	0.892
Vanilla RNN	0.890	0.899	0.903	0.901
LSTM	0.895	0.909	0.908	0.908
BiLSTM-CNN	**0.916**	**0.918**	**0.914**	**0.916**

Four models are tested in the experiment: CNN, RNN, LSTM, BiLSTM-CNN (proposed model). Overall, the new BiLSTM-CNN model solves this and returns a better prediction accuracy, precision, recall, and F1 score than all other models.

4 Conclusion and Future Work

In this paper, fake news is classified by a complex deep learning structure. Firstly, the Word2Vec word embedding layer is to produce the matrix representation of the input news. Then, the deep learning models learn and predict the label of given news. Given an evaluation and a comparison, BiLSTM-CNN outperforms CNN, vanilla RNN, and LSTM. Both advantages of Bi-LSTM and CNN are included in this hyper model. Specifically, the hidden connection between sentences and sequential information from forward and backward are captured. As a result, the proposed model shows its outstanding performance in a task for long-term-text categorical classification.

The dataset used in this paper focuses on the news related to the reports of the American presidential election. Although the designed model and classification receive a preferable accuracy on this dataset, it does not represent it is eligible to solve problems in other fields. Thus, future work will extend the topic and languages in fake news detection problems. If possible, the tone of reporting the news should also be considered as a parameter in the analysis.

References

1. Granik, M., Mesyura, V.: Fake new detection using naïve Bayes classifier. In: 2017 IEEE Ukraine Conference on Electrical and Computer Engineering (UKRCON), pp. 900–903. IEEE, Kyiv, Ukraine (2017)
2. Ahmad, I., Yousaf, M., Yousaf, S., Ahmad, M.O..: Fake news detection using machine learning ensemble methods. Complexity in Deep Neural Networks 1(1), (2020)
3. Yang, Y., Zheng, L., Zhang, J., Cui, Q., Li, Z., Yu, P.S.: TI-CNN: convolutional neural networks for fake news detection. arXiv (2018)
4. Dong, X., Victor, U., Qian, L.: Two-path deep semisupervised learning for timely fake news detection. IEEE Trans. Comput. Soc. Syst. 7(6), 1386–1398 (2020)
5. Aldwairi, M., Alwahedi, A.: Detecting fake news in social media networks. Procedia Comput. Sci. 141, 215–222 (2018)
6. Shen, L., Zhang, J.: Empirical evaluation of RNN architectures on sentence classification task. arXiv (2019)
7. Okoro, E.M., Abara, B.A., Umagba, A.O., Ajonye, A.A. Isa, Z.S.: A hybrid approach to fake news detection on social media. Nigerian Journal of Technology 37(2), 454–462 (2018)
8. Zhang, J., Dong, B, Philip, S.Y.: FAKEDETECTOR: effective fake news detection with deep diffusive neural network. arXiv (2018)
9. Zhang, X., Chen, F., Huang, R.: A combination of RNN and CNN for attention-based relation classification. Procedia Comput. Sci. 131(1), 911–917 (2018)
10. Bahad, P., Saxena, P., Kamal, R.: Fake news detection using bi-directional LSTM recurrent neural network. Procedia Comput. Sci. 165, 74–82 (2019)

11. Xu, T., Du, Y., Fu, C., Xie, C.: Incorporating forward and backward instances in a bi-lstm-cnn model for relation classification. In: 2018 IEEE 4th International Conference on Computer and Communications, pp. 2133–2137. IEEE, Chengdu, China (2018)

12. Colah Homepage. https://colah.github.io/posts/2015-08-Understanding-LSTMs. Accessed 24 Mar 2021

13. WILDML   Homepage.   http://www.wildml.com/2015/12/implementing-a-cnn-for-text-classification-in-tensorflow/. Accessed 24 Mar 2021

14. Kaggle   Homepage.   https://www.kaggle.com/clmentbisaillon/fake-and-real-news-dataset. Accessed 30 Dec 2020

Prediction and Prevention of Metro Station Congestion Based on LSTM Neural Network and AnyLogic

Xuyan Zhao[✉]

Beijing University of Civil Engineering and Architecture, Beijing 100044, China

Abstract. Metro is one of the most important public transportation tools in large cities. Periodic congestion easily occurs in certain areas of metro stations because of the periodic peak of travel demand. Congestion will bring inconvenience to passenger's travel and increase the risk of accidents such as trampling. In this paper, a method based on LSTM neural network and AnyLogic is proposed to predict and prevent the occurrence of congestion in specific areas in metro stations in advance. Firstly, the congestion is predicted by LSTM and historical data, and then a reasonable way to solve the congestion is discovered based on AnyLogic simulations. The proposed method is expected to provide general suggestions for metro station managers. According to the simulation results, the proposed method can effectively alleviate the congestion in metro stations and reduce the probability of high passenger density areas.

Keywords: Simulation · Passenger flow management · Congestion avoidance

1 Introduction

With the rapid development of urban transportation, rail public transportation has gradually become one of the primary travel modes and played a crucial role in daily life. Nowadays, in rush hour or some transfer stations, crowd congestion jams are prevalent in the megalopolis. Scientists try to simulate and analyze the process to alleviate the above problem. Zhu et al. [1] based on the analysis of the traffic flow characteristics of the surrounding areas in 2009, the land use strategies of high-speed railway stations are found. This study improves the utilization rate of station land.

In order to simulate the evacuation and queuing of passengers, Shigeyuki Okazaki et al. [2] simulated the pedestrian movement in buildings and urban spaces by using the pedestrian movement model with evacuation and queuing in 2012, which provided an effective method to manage the passenger flow in public places such as metro stations. However, the generalizability is not tested in both papers. Bohari et al. [3] simulated the passenger moment pattern to reduce the congestion and improve the accessibility of passengers. However, it requires a large number of employees to implement this method, which is challenging to be deployed in different conditions in 2014. In order to provide guidance for the passenger flow, Li et al. [4] quality analyzed the short-term traffic flow prediction method of the dynamic highway traffic model. The simulation results show that the method is effective also feasible, which provides strong support

© Springer Nature Singapore Pte Ltd. 2021
W. Cao et al. (Eds.): CONF-CDS 2021, CCIS 1513, pp. 45–52, 2021.
https://doi.org/10.1007/978-981-16-8885-0_5

for the traffic management department. However, this method has not been studied in traffic information optimization, so there may be some deficiencies in the actual road problems. The paper written by Hualan Wang et al. is based on AnyLogic, which analyzes the ways to improve the operation capacity of Zhongchuan High-speed Railway Station by optimizing passenger flow lines [5]. Although the walking distance of passengers entering the ticket hall has increased after the optimization, the effective separation of the crowd has become clearer. By doing this, the cross interference is reduced and station capacity is increased. However, in some special or novel structure stations, the simulation may not play such a good effect.

Wang and Xu et al. [6] established a model on an island platform. The model is used to simulate the process of passengers getting on and off the bus under different conditions. According to the calculation results, the main factors affecting the average time of getting on and off the bus and their influencing trends are obtained. Jiang and Yan et al. analyzed the train dispatch scheme and carrying capacity of Changsha South Railway Station [7]. By analyzing several aspects like the train headway, the station layout, and the utilization of tracks. In order to give effective suggestions for these limiting factors. But this paper only analyzes a few specific factors; This is not enough for all stations. Tian and Chen et al. analyzed the passenger flow conflict under the different layouts of service facilities [8]. On the basis of AnyLogic, constructive suggestions for alleviating station congestion are put forward. In future research, passengers' micro-behaviors can be included in the selection model to make the research more in-depth and detailed. According to the literature review, there are few scholars to make combined passenger flow prediction and simulation for passenger guidance research. This research proposes a method, which uses the historical traffic data and LSTM neural network to predict the upcoming congestion and uses AnyLogic simulation method to explore the strategy of relieving congestion. Finally, the prediction and simulation are combined to alleviate congestion. The contributions of this study are as follows:

1. Through the prediction model, the time of daily congestion can be analyzed in order to inform the metro station managers in advance and prevent the upcoming congestion.
2. By using simulation, the location and deployment time of the deployment staff are proposed.
3. The data obtained from the model analysis can provide data for the optimization of metro stations in the future.

2   Methodology

Figure 1 shows the control framework of this project design. The passenger flow management of the station is realized through the cooperation between an automation management platform and the managers.

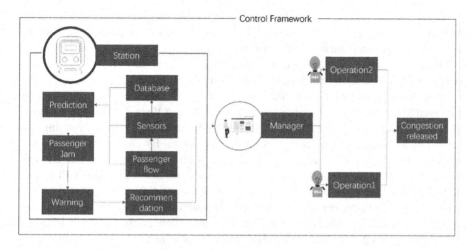

Fig. 1. Demonstration of the control framework

The three functions of the automatic management platform are to predict passenger flow, to provide early warning of congestion, and to provide suggestions for passenger flow guidance when congestion is predicted. The passenger flow prediction function is based on a trained Long Short-Term Memory (LSTM) neural network. The network is trained based on the historical data of card swiping, and a well-trained LSTM network is able to support accurate prediction. The adopted input and target data for training the LSTM is shown in Fig. 2. The input for the first LSTM is the observed predictor feature, but for all future LSTM, the input is the expected deviation term for time and the output value of the previous LSTM. In this figure, the variable names are explained as follows: $D(t(n))$: passenger density in key areas, $\widehat{D(t(n))}$: the prediction of key area's passenger flow density, $CP(t(n))$: the number of passengers who swiped the card into the station within the corresponding time. $TH1(t(n))$: the headway for trains in direction 1. $TH2(t(n))$ the headway for trains in direction 2. The prediction can be obtained by setting up the LSTM network and input $CP(t(1))$, $TH1(t(1))$, $TH2(t(1))$.

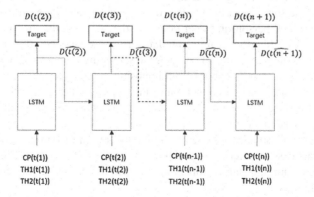

Fig. 2. Adopted LSTM model

The proposed system will send a warning to the station managers when it detects the impending congestion. The early warning part of congestion needs to provide the staff with the predicted areas where congestion will occur and the congestion degree. It is difficult to collect such data in practice. For a specific station, the direction of passengers' travel during peak hours is often periodic. Thus AnyLogic can be used to simulate and explore mitigation strategies in advance. Therefore, the AnyLogic is employed to obtain the demand data through simulation. A three-dimensional model of the corresponding station is established in AnyLogic, and the passengers entering and leaving each station could be controlled in the simulation. By changing the frequency and speed of passengers entering the station, the high-density areas in different scenarios can be obtained. The passenger density in some areas of the station will exceed the safety standard in some scenarios, and the corresponding input parameters and areas where congestion occurs are recorded. The simulated data can be used as the preliminary data for realizing congestion area prediction in the platform with the continuous accumulation of recorded data. The data obtained from the simulation can be compared and adjusted according to the real data collected by the sensors when congestion occurs, in reality, to continuously improve the accuracy of early warning.

The third function is to provide suggestions for preventing congestion. Guiding passenger flow in advance is a way to avoid congestion. In the model, engineers test the guidance modes in different scenarios and carry out verification tests in the AnyLogic model. Each solution is numbered and then stored in the database. The platform first seeks solutions to similar congestion in the database when the intelligent prediction platform predicts that congestion is about to happen, and it gives suggestions to the staff and if similar solutions are found. If it is not found, however, the early warning information will be recorded, and the engineer will conduct a new solution modeling test according to the marked early warning information in the short future.

3 Case Study

The case study uses AnyLogic to verify the efficiency of the proposed system. The created model includes two floors. Each floor has an area of around 512 m^2. The B1 floor mainly simulates a series of processes, such as passengers buying tickets at the station, security check, taking the escalator to the platform, and getting out of the station. During the simulation, the number of passengers entering each metro entrance to the B1 floor is 100 person-times per hour. On the B2 floor, the metro arrives at the station every 120 s. This floor mainly simulates the passengers boarding and alighting the metro, leaving the platform, and entering the station by escalator. During the study, the B1 floor and B2 floor are separate from imposing different conditions of constraints so that the flow of passengers into and out of the station will be congested on different floors. After the congestion has formed, there are two ways to change the congestion and relieved the passenger flow.

Two congestion scenarios are created and alleviated in the simulation. Passengers jam at the entrance, security check, and ticket gate in the first scenario. The solution for this scenario is to arrange staff members in a certain area to guide the passenger flow (as shown in Fig. 3).

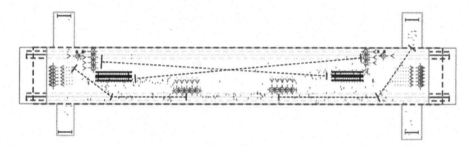

Fig. 3. Solution for the first scenario

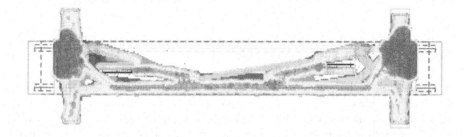

(a). Passenger Density without Guidance

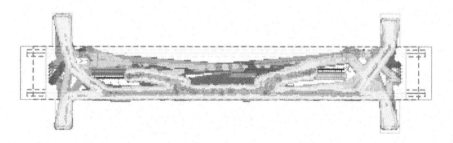

(b). Passenger Density with Guidance

Fig. 4. Passenger density distribution comparison of the first scenario

Figure 4 shows the passenger density distribution comparison between with and without the guidance within the station, and Fig. 5 shows the highest density comparison. As shown in the figure, density decreased significantly and dropped.

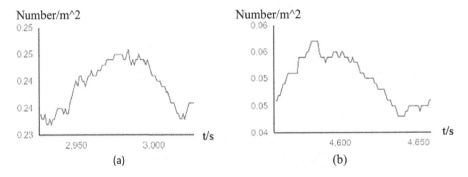

Fig. 5. Highest passenger density comparison of the first scenario.

By comparing with Figs. 4 and 5, the congestion has been significantly reduced. So there is no doubt that this is a very feasible approach.

Congestion occurs at the B2 floor in the second scenario.

Congestion in the second scenario is caused by the headway. When the evening rush hour and other factors arrive, more passengers can be gathered in a short time on the B2 floor. So, at this point, the original headway cannot satisfy the requirement of that passenger flow. Thus, it caused congestion. It also leads to a gradual increase in the number of passengers waiting for the metro on the B2 floor, resulting in the congestion phenomenon, which is more obvious when the metro arrives at the station. When it comes to the solution, the flow can be relieved by shortening the metro's arrival time,

(a). Passenger Density of the Second Scenario without Headway Adjustment

(b). Passenger Density of the Second Scenario with Headway Adjustment

Fig. 6. Passenger density distribution comparison of the second scenario

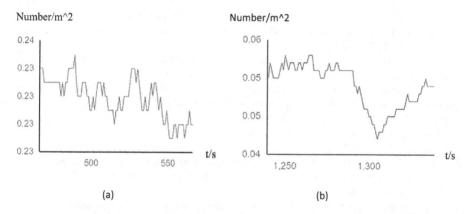

Fig. 7. Highest passenger density comparison of the second scenario

which is collected by a large amount of historical data to ensure that the operation of the metro will not cause unnecessary safety risks by shortening the headway. In the past, the metro arrives at the station every 120 s. But when the headway changes to every 45 min, the congestion has been greatly reduced (Fig 6).

Figure 7(a) shows without change the headway during the rush hour, the peak density of the B1 floor is very congested and even reaches 0.24. Figure 7(b) shows that the population density decreased significantly after shortening the headway and dropped even to 0.04. The test result of the two scenarios proves the proposed system is feasible and is able to reduce the congestion on the different floors effectively.

4   Conclusion

This paper proposes a system that is able to predict the congestion and provide guidance to alleviate it. The prediction is realized by the LSTM neural network, and the AnyLogic is adopted to test different solutions. By analyzing the data and improving the management measures of the metro station, the original congestion has been relieved significantly. Although the case study proves the system could relieve the congestion, there are some limitations. The prediction part is not tested in the case study due to lack of data. Consider the LSTM is well tested in many research areas, it is reasonable to assume the model could provide acceptable prediction accuracy. It is expected to further discover the proposed system and refine the method in the future.

References

1. Zhu, Y., Wang, H., Xue, B.: Land usage and development in high-speed train stations and its traffic impact analysis. In: International Conference on Transportation Engineering, pp. 1152–1157 (2009)
2. Okazaki, S., Matsushita, S.: A study of simulation model for pedestrian movement with evacuation and queuing. J. Architect. Plan. Environ. Eng. (Trans. AIJ) **432** (1993)

3. Bohari, Z.A., Bachok, S., Osman, M.M.: Improving the quality of public transportation system: application of simulation model for passenger movement. Procedia Soc. Behav. Sci. **153**, 542–552 (2014)
4. Li, S.B., et al.: Research on the method of traffic organization and optimization based on dynamic traffic flow model. Discret. Dyn. Nat. Soc. **2017**, 1–9 (2017)
5. Wang, H., et al.: Analysis and optimization of passenger flowlines at Zhongchuan high-speed railway station. Model. Simul. Eng. **2018**(21), 1–8 (2018)
6. Wang, Z., Xu, J.: A simulation analysis of subway passengers' per capita boarding and alighting time's influence rule based on CA. In: American Society of Civil Engineers, ASCE, pp. 6265–6273, July 2019
7. Jiang, Y., et al.: Analysis of the limiting factors of carrying capacity at changsha south railway station. In: American Society of Civil Engineers, ASCE, pp. 981–989, January 2020, https://doi.org/10.1061/9780784482742.113
8. Tan, B., et al.: Research on simulation and optimization of facility layout of urban rail transit station based on anylogic. In: 20th COTA International Conference of Transportation Professionals (2020)

Drought Level Prediction with Deep Learning

Chenhao Liu[(✉)]

University of Electronic Science and Technology of China, Chengdu,
Sichuan, China

Abstract. The forecast of drought levels is important for agricultural development and ecological protection. Some previous approaches include statistical methods, machine learning and so forth. To predict the drought level more accurately, we use the deep learning method, which avoids the addition of professional meteorological auxiliary information as in the previous research, so that the prediction system can automatically predict without the help of professionals. In this study, we have built a number of different deep learning models that combine RNN, CNN and attention mechanism, and use a public meteorological dataset named US Drought & Meteorological Data. At the same time, we compared deep learning with other prediction methods. Our results show that deep learning network of Inception combined with LSTM and attention mechanism achieves the best F1 score of 0.728 and it performs better at distinguishing higher drought levels than other methods. Overall, we conclude that deep learning models have the best performance which exceeds machine learning, but under the current drought grade classification standards, the existing methods cannot distinguish the higher drought grades well.

Keywords: Drought level prediction · Machine learning · Meteorological data

1 Introduction

Drought is a long-term climate phenomenon with lots of reasons and effects. Human civilization has been affected by natural disasters such as drought since ancient times. Although science and technology are gradually developing, drought still causes many inevitable disasters and economic losses of up to 300 billion U.S. dollars to the world every year. The drought mainly affects the following aspects:

- Agriculture: Lack of water will reduce crop yields and even famine.
- Manufacturing: Water is widely used in the industry and drought would increase the difficulty towards using water for manufacturing. Many companies may face suspension of production.
- Hydropower: The amount of hydropower generation has decreased, and power consumption in some areas has been in short supply, and even power outages have brought serious difficulties to people's lives.
- Daily life: Domestic water is in short supply, which will affect drinking water in severe cases, threaten human life and health, may lead to the extinction of precious species, reduce biodiversity, and road exposure may cause problems and affect traffic.

© Springer Nature Singapore Pte Ltd. 2021
W. Cao et al. (Eds.): CONF-CDS 2021, CCIS 1513, pp. 53–65, 2021.
https://doi.org/10.1007/978-981-16-8885-0_6

If we can predict whether a drought will occur in advance through various meteorological indicators, then we can avoid the above problems, and greatly increase people's trust in agriculture and new water-related energy industries, and increase the investment in these industries, finally alleviate the severity of important global issues such as food and resource shortages.

With the development of science and technology, scientists use different mathematical methods to solve the problem of drought prediction. We can simply summarize them into three categories, statistical methods [1–3], machine learning methods [4–6], and deep learning methods including Long Short Term Memory (LSTM) [7–11]. Statistical methods generally standardize meteorological data or make other conversions, input them into mathematical models, cluster or convert the output feature vectors into normal distributions, and then discuss probabilities. This method can quickly obtain classification results based on the data, but since the training needs to adjust the coefficient weight, the experimenter needs a lot of experience, and the accuracy is difficult to improve. Machine learning methods include XGBoost, random forest, etc. They can be well extended to large-scale data, and the process is easier to understand by experimenters, and it is easier to improve the data, but they are difficult to deal with missing data. In this method, overfitting and ignoring the attributes relationship in the data set often appear. Thirdly, deep learning methods such as LSTM have made breakthroughs in time series prediction and classification tasks in various fields [12–15]. However, in the field of drought prediction, most studies only use the neural network of LSTM or only combine LSTM with the above two methods of learning, but despite this, it still achieved results that are no less than other methods.

In this work, we use both advanced machine learning as well as deep learning methods for the problem of drought level prediction, based on a real-world dataset that is publicly available. After a comprehensive comparison, we find that most methods are at the similar level for drought prediction, in which Inception combined with LSTM and attention mechanism has the best performance, achieving an F1 score of 0.728.

2   Problem Description

In this study, we deal with the drought prediction problem based on the meteorological indictors in the history. The dataset we use is US Drought & Meteorological Data, a manually created drought measurement data set, released on Kaggle publicly. The problem is to use meteorological data to predict drought levels, and to promote this technology from the United States to the world. The drought level is divided into six categories, five of which represent different degrees of drought and the last one without drought. However, the cases of no drought are not contained in this dataset and thus omitted in this study. The meteorological indicators are composed of 18 items as shown in Table 1. Each item is a collection of meteorological indicators and drought levels for 90 days before a specific time and place.

Table 1. The list of the meteorological indicators.

Indicator	Description
WS10M_MIN	Minimum wind speed at 10 m (m/s)
QV2M	Specific humidity at 2 m (g/kg)
T2M_RANGE	Temperature range at 2 m (C)
WS10M	Wind speed at 10 m (m/s)
T2M	Temperature at 2 m (C)
WS50M_MIN	Minimum wind speed at 50 m (m/s)
T2M_MAX	Maximum temperature at 2 m (C)
WS50M	Wind speed at 50 m (m/s)
TS	Earth skin temperature (C)
WS50M_RANGE	Wind speed range at 50 m (m/s)
WS50M_MAX	Maximum wind speed at 50 m (m/s)
WS10M_MAX	Maximum wind speed at 10 m (m/s)
WS10M_RANGE	Wind speed range at 10 m (m/s)
PS	Surface pressure (kPa)
T2MDEW	Dew/Frost point at 2 m (C)
T2M_MIN	Minimum temperature at 2 m (C)
T2MWET	Wet bulb temperature at 2 m (C)
PRECTOT	Precipitation (mm day-1)
WS10M_MIN	Minimum wind speed at 10 m (m/s)
QV2M	Specific humidity at 2 m (g/kg)
T2M_RANGE	Temperature range at 2 m (C)
WS10M	Wind speed at 10 m (m/s)
T2M	Temperature at 2 m (C)
WS50M_MIN	Minimum wind speed at 50 m (m/s)
T2M_MAX	Maximum temperature at 2 m (C)
WS50M	Wind speed at 50 m (m/s)
TS	Earth skin temperature (C)
WS50M_RANGE	Wind speed range at 50 m (m/s)
WS50M_MAX	Maximum wind speed at 50 m (m/s)
WS10M_MAX	Maximum Wind Speed at 10 m (m/s)
WS10M_RANGE	Wind speed range at 10 m (m/s)
PS	Surface pressure (kPa)
T2MDEW	Dew/Frost point at 2 m (C)
T2M_MIN	Minimum temperature at 2 m (C)
T2MWET	Wet bulb temperature at 2 m (C)
PRECTOT	Precipitation (mm day-1)

We divide the top 47% of the data as the training set, 10% of the data as the validation set, and the remaining 43% of the data as the test set. The time range for each subset is shown in Table 2. In the training set, test set and validation set, the proportion of each category is basically the same, but it can be found that the data distribution is very uneven, with D0 accounting for more than 50% ratio. As the drought level increases, the proportion of data in each drought category becomes less, e.g., the D4 case only has a data ratio of 3.4–3.8%. We show the data distributions in Fig. 1 for all the three subsets.

Table 2. The time range of data subsets.

Data subset	Year range (inclusive)	Percentage (approximately)
Training set	2000–2009	47%
Validation set	2010–2011	10%
Test set	2012–2020	43%

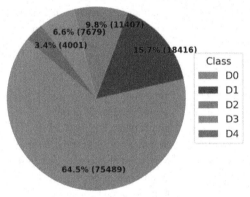

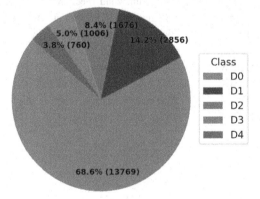

Fig. 1. Class distribution of the training set, validation set, test set.

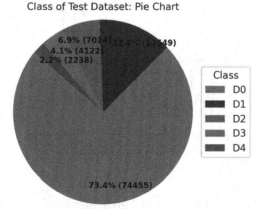

Fig. 1. (*continued*)

3 Methodology

3.1 Model

LSTM and GRU. In this part, we use Long Short-Term Memory (LSTM), which is a special kind of Recurrent Neural Network (RNN) and solves the problems of gradient vanishing and gradient explosion during long sequence training in RNN training. Compared with the ordinary RNN, LSTM can perform better in longer sequences.

As shown in Fig. 2, structurally speaking, LSTM is three inputs $x^{(t)}$, $h^{(t-1)}$, $c^{(t-1)}$, and two outputs. LSTM has three gates, input and output forget gate. The calculation process is as follows:

$$i^{(t)} = \sigma\left(W^{(f)}x^{(t)} + U^{(i)}h^{(t-1)}\right) \tag{1}$$

$$f^{(t)} = \sigma\left(W^{(f)}x^{(t)} + U^{(f)}h^{(t-1)}\right) \tag{2}$$

$$o^{(t)} = \sigma\left(W^{(o)}x^{(t)} + U^{(o)}h^{(t-1)}\right) \tag{3}$$

$$\tilde{c}^{(t)} = \tanh\left(W^{(c)}x^{(t)} + U^{(o)}h^{(t-1)}\right) \tag{4}$$

$$c^{(t)} = f^{(t)} \circ c^{(t-1)} + i^{(t)} \circ e^{(t)} \tag{5}$$

$$h^{(t)} = o^{(t)} \circ \tan\left(c^{(t)}\right) \tag{6}$$

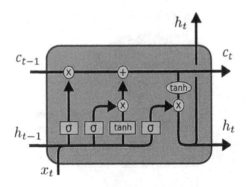

**LSTM
(Long–Short Term Memory)**

Fig. 2. The LSTM structure.

Gated Recurrent Units (GRU) is another variant of RNN. GRU has two inputs $x^{(t)}$, $h^{(t-1)}$, one output $h^{(t)}$, and the output is state. The calculation process is as follows:

$$z^{(t)} = \sigma\left(W^{(z)}\right) \cdot \left[h^{(t-1)}, x^{(t)}\right] \tag{7}$$

$$r^{(t)} = \sigma\left(W^{(r)}\right) \cdot \left[h^{(t-1)}, x^{(t)}\right] \tag{8}$$

$$\tilde{h}^{(t)} = \tanh\left(W \cdot \left[r^{(t-1)} * h^{(t-1)}, x^{(t)}\right]\right) \tag{9}$$

$$h^{(t)} = \left(1 - z^{(t)}\right) * h^{(t-1)} + z^{(t)} * \tilde{h}(t) \tag{10}$$

GRU has two gates, i.e., reset and update, as shown in Fig. 3. GRU has less parameters compared to LSTM, and training speed is faster. In contrast, less data is required. If there is enough data, the effect of LSTM may be better than GRU.

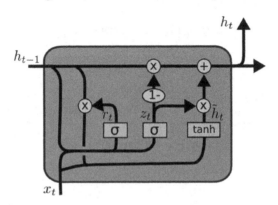

Fig. 3. The GRU structure.

Transformer. Transformer [16] is solely based on the attention mechanism. The attention mechanism is the new frontier of artificial intelligence research. It is used to capture the receptive field in an image or video. It is also used in Natural Language Processing (NLP) to locate key tokens or features. Without using any component similar to CNN or RNN, the entire Transformer framework is based on attention. Precisely speaking, only self-attention and feed forward neural network are used in Transformer. In this study, Transformer Encoder is used instead of LSTM to process and encode the time series. Though the final result was not as good as LSTM with a slight gap, it was still competitive.

Attention Layer. Different from the normal classifier approach, in order to achieve better results, we use the attention layer [17] connected behind the RNN to replace the fully connected layer. The principle of RNN with attention is shown in the Fig. 4. Compared with the method of connecting linear layer after LSTM used in traditional time series prediction, adding attention layer after LSTM establishes the corresponding relationship between input features and output. Simply speaking, the neural network constantly updates the features of a specific input and a specific position, reducing the feature to a certain extent, so as to achieve better results.

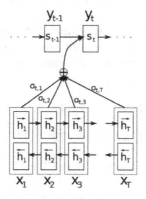

Fig. 4. RNN with attention.

Convolutional Neural Network. CNN is usually used in the field of computer vision. In this study, we also tried to process the data with CNN first and then input the processed data into the RNN network. This is because CNN can make model more sensitive to partial information. We adopted ResNet and Inception as our CNN network.

Machine Learning Models. As we mentioned before, the mainstream drought prediction method is still machine learning, so we also applied the machine learning method to this data set. In this study, we mainly use the machine learning methods of XGBoost and random forest, which have been proven effective in many previous studies [18].

3.2 Other Techniques

Data Augmentation. During the experiment, we found that the skewness of the drought data distribution seriously affected the model's prediction performance. In order to reduce the impact of data imbalance, we used the data augmentation method to balance the training set. We use SMOTE and over sample methods to add a relatively small number of categories to achieve the purpose of data enhancement.

Parametric Search. In the experiments, we used the parameter search method to adjust the parameters of various models, including learning rate, optimizer, learning period and RNN layer number. We used the hyperopt package. It can set each hyperparameter range accordingly, and apply all combinations to the model to achieve the purpose of parameter search.

4 Experiment

4.1 Settings

All the models are implemented with Python 3.7, using scikit-learn and PyTorch packages.

We mainly use F1 score as evaluation metrics. Precision and recall are defined by the ratio of true positive samples. F1 score simultaneously considers precision and recall, so that both reach the highest at the same time. We give their definitions as follows:

$$Recall = TP/(TP + FN) \tag{11}$$

$$Recall = TP/(TP + FN) \tag{12}$$

$$F1 = 2/(1/Precision + 1/Recall) = 2^*(Recall^*Precision)/(Precision + Recall) \tag{13}$$

In which TP, FN, FP and TN are defined in Table 3. We also use the different versions of accuracy as our evaluation metrics, which calculates the weighted ratio of correctly classified samples.

Table 3. The definitions of TP, FN, FP and TN.

Label	Prediction	
	1	0
1	True Positive (TP)	False Negative (FN)
0	False Positive (FP)	True Negative (TN)

4.2   Results

During the experiment, we found that Inception with LSTM has the best performance in deep learning and machine learning, respectively. When using parameter search to adjust the parameters, we searched for the number of RNN layers, the number of cycles, and the learning rate. The search space for the number of RNN layers is defined as 2, 3, 4. For the number of cycles, the search space is defined as 10, 30, 100. The search space for learning rate is defined as 0.001, 0.0001, 0.00001. We found that the model generally performed the best when the learning rate was 0.0001 for 10 epochs in a large number of parameter searches. And we also found that overfitting occurs after the sixth epoch of training. The val_loss in the validation set cannot continue to decrease. Therefore, we set the epoch number of subsequent experiments to 10 and save the best model on val_loss. Similarly, when we use the hyperopt package, we find that the RNN has the best performance when the number of layers is 2.

We show the final experimental results in Table 4. The Inception model connecting LSTM with attention has the best result, and the performance of machine learning is not bad when compared with more complex deep learning models. We also compare the confusion matrix for different models in Figs. 5, 6, 7, 8 and 9. In Fig. 8, XGBoost predicts more than 90% of the data as D0, especially in category D4 and D5, it cannot make correct predictions. Therefore, the reason for the high F1 score of machine learning is that the data is unbalanced and 64% of the cases correspond to category D0, while the scores of deep learning methods on macro avg and weighted avg are much better than machine learning. It is mentioned in the methodology that we have used data augmentation, but the results are not ideal. From the E graph and Table 4, it is not difficult to find that the recall of D5 and D4, F1 is still very low, compared with no data augmentation, there is no improvement, and the overall F1 value has dropped.

Table 4. Results of different models.

Model	F1 score	Accuracy	Macro avg	Weighted_avg
LSTM+attention (10 epochs)	0.724023	0.72	0.27	0.69
LSTM+attention (100 epochs)	0.667568	0.67	0.27	0.67
BiLSTM+attention	0.720605	0.72	0.28	**0.70**
TranformerEncoder+attention	0.723574	0.72	0.27	0.69
Incetion+LSTM+attention	**0.727686**	**0.73**	0.28	0.69
GRU+attention	0.726553	**0.73**	**0.30**	**0.70**
XGBoost	0.722816	0.72	0.23	0.67
Random Forest	0.724846	0.72	0.17	0.63
Inception+LSTM+attention (Data Augmentation)	0.587871	0.59	0.29	0.64

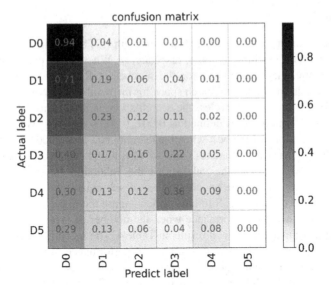

Fig. 5. Confusion matrix. LSTM + attention

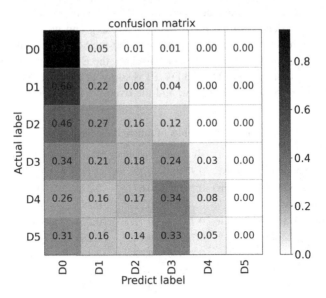

Fig. 6. Confusion matrix. Inception + LSM + attention

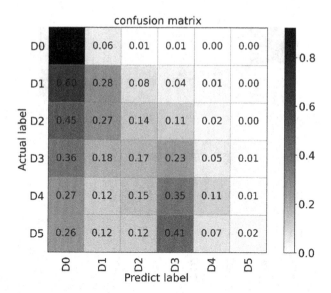

Fig. 7. Confusion matrix. GRU + attention

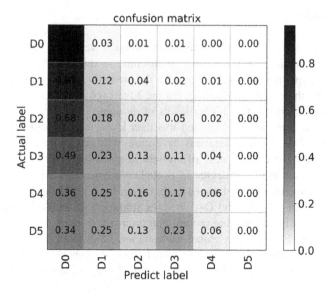

Fig. 8. Confusion matrix. XGBoost.

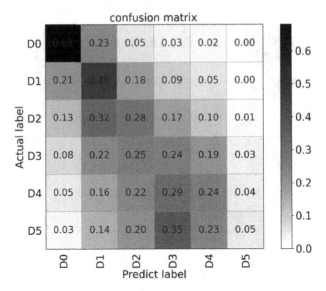

Fig. 9. Confusion matrix. Inception + LSTM + attention (Data Augmentation)

5   Conclusion

In summary, before the start of the experiment, although we expect that the deep model can far surpass previous methods such as machine learning in the field of drought prediction, the experimental results show that the predictive ability of RNN with CNN is slightly better than machine learning, but the advantage of deep learning is that it is more capable of distinguishing higher levels of drought.

Based on our previous research and this data level, it is not difficult to find that although most of the existing data sets have quite rich and comprehensive meteorological index data, the classification of drought levels is more subjective and lacks a quantitative assessment of the degree of drought. Judgment criteria such as the concentration of inorganic salts, estimated output, etc., have made the model difficult to distinguish between D2, D3, and D4. Previous studies have found that adding expert analysis data to the model training process can improve the predictive ability of model to a certain extent. In the future, global warming and other factors will cause droughts to appear more frequently, so researchers can get more data about droughts. We believe that after the completion of the data set, the ability of deep learning to predict droughts will be improved.

References

1. Hao, Z., Hao, F., Singh, V.P., et al.: A theoretical drought classification method for the multivariate drought index based on distribution properties of standardized drought indices. Adv. Water Resour. **92**, 240–247 (2016)

2. Ali, Z., Hussain, I., Faisal, M., et al.: An ensemble procedure for pattern recognition of regional drought. Int. J. Climatol. **40**(1), 94–114 (2020)
3. Zhou, K., Li, J., Zhang, T., et al.: The use of combined soil moisture data to characterize agricultural drought conditions and the relationship among different drought types in China. Agric. Water Manage. **243**, 106479 (2021)
4. Gou, R., Zhao, J.: Eco-environmental quality monitoring in Beijing, China, using an RSEI-based approach combined with random forest algorithms. IEEE Access **8**, 196657–196666 (2020)
5. Dikshit, A., Pradhan, B., Alamri, A.M.: Short-term spatio-temporal drought forecasting using random forests model at New South Wales, Australia. Appl. Sci. **10**(12), 4254 (2020)
6. Dikshit, A., Pradhan, B., Alamri, A.M.: Temporal hydrological drought index forecasting for New South Wales, Australia using machine learning approaches. Atmosphere **11**(6), 585 (2020)
7. Dikshit, A., Pradhan, B., Huete, A.: An improved SPEI drought forecasting approach using the long short-term memory neural network. J. Environ. Manage. **283**, 111979 (2021)
8. Rahmati, O., Panahi, M., Kalantari, Z., et al.: Capability and robustness of novel hybridized models used for drought hazard modeling in southeast Queensland, Australia. Sci. Total Environ. **718**, 134656 (2020)
9. Zhu, S., Xu, Z., Luo, X., et al.: Internal and external coupling of Gaussian mixture model and deep recurrent network for probabilistic drought forecasting. Int. J. Environ. Sci. Technol. **18**, 1–16 (2020)
10. Dikshit, A., Pradhan, B., Alamri, A.M.: Long lead time drought forecasting using lagged climate variables and a stacked long short-term memory model. Sci. Total Environ. **755**, 142638 (2021)
11. Wu, X., Zhou, J., Yu, H., et al.: The Development of a hybrid wavelet-ARIMA-LSTM model for precipitation amounts and drought analysis. Atmosphere **12**(1), 74 (2021)
12. Jiang, W., Zhang, L.: Geospatial data to images: a deep-learning framework for traffic forecasting. Tsinghua Sci. Technol. **24**(1), 52–64 (2018)
13. Jiang, W.: Applications of deep learning in stock market prediction: recent progress. arXiv preprint arXiv:2003.01859 (2020)
14. Jiang, W., Luo, J.: Graph neural network for traffic forecasting: a survey. arXiv preprint arXiv:2101.11174 (2021)
15. Jiang, W.: Time series classification: nearest neighbor versus deep learning models. SN Appl. Sci. **2**(4), 1–17 (2020)
16. Vaswani, A., Shazeer, N., Parmar, N., et al.: Attention is all you need. In: Proceedings of the 31st International Conference on Neural Information Processing Systems, pp. 6000–6010 (2017)
17. Luong, M.T., Pham, H., Manning, C.D.: Effective approaches to attention-based neural machine translation. arXiv preprint arXiv:1508.04025 (2015)
18. Chen, T., Guestrin, C.: Xgboost: a scalable tree boosting system. In: Proceedings of the 22nd ACM SIGKDD International Conference on Knowledge Discovery and Data Mining, pp. 785–794 (2016)

Comparing Different CNN Training Strategies in Low-Level CT Image-Processing Tasks

Alexander Huang[✉]

Beckman High School, Irvine, CA, USA

Abstract. Image artifact removal in computed tomography (CT) allows clinicians to make more accurate diagnoses. One method of artifact removal is iterative reconstruction. However, reconstructing large amounts of CT data using this method is tedious, which is why researchers have proposed using filtered back-projection paired with neural networks. The purpose of this paper is to compare the performances of various forms of training data for convolutional neural networks in three low level CT image processing tasks: sinogram completion, Poisson noise removal, and focal spot deblurring. Specifically, modified U-nets are trained with either CT sinogram data or reconstruction data for each of the tasks. Then, the predicted results of each model are compared in terms of image quality and viability in a clinical setting. The predictions show strong evidence of increased image quality when training models with reconstruction data, thus the reconstruction strategy possesses a clear edge in practicality over the sinogram strategy.

Keywords: Computed tomography · X-ray · Sinogram completion · Poisson noise removal · Focal spot deconvolution · Convolutional neural networks

1 Introduction

Computed Tomography is a commonly used medical imaging modality due to its advantages over other conventional imaging methods. These advantages include rapid image acquisition, larger amounts of data, and clear, detailed images of internal structures [1]. While CT possesses many advantages over other imaging modalities, a prominent issue that CT medical professionals struggle to deal with are image artifacts, which refer to misrepresentations of the scanned objects. Deep learning techniques such as convolutional neural networks (CNN) have been seeing increased attention in medical imaging [2–5]. Most of these applications have been focusing on using CNN for classification tasks such as pathology identification [6] and tumor segmentation [7]. However, the application of CNNs in low-level medical imaging tasks is an under-studied area. When using CNN for CT, there are two main strategies used for model training due to the fact that CT images have two domains. These two strategies differ because one uses sinogram data3 for training and the other uses reconstruction data. A sinogram is the direct output of the CT detector, which consists of all the X-ray projections taken from different angles (See Fig. 1). The reconstruction is the result after a reconstruction algorithm [8] has been applied on the sinogram, and this three-

© Springer Nature Singapore Pte Ltd. 2021
W. Cao et al. (Eds.): CONF-CDS 2021, CCIS 1513, pp. 66–77, 2021.
https://doi.org/10.1007/978-981-16-8885-0_7

dimensional image is what allows professionals to analyze the internal structure of objects or patients.

A benchmark of the performance of these two strategies is missing, and the purpose of this study is to compare these strategies through three different CT imaging tasks. The tasks consist of sinogram completion (See second column of Fig. 9), Poisson noise removal (See second column of Fig. 11), and focal spot deblurring (See second column of Fig. 13). These are all common CT artifacts, which lower the image quality and make analysis more difficult. The cause of these artifacts is due to the nature of CT scans requiring the use of X-ray beams. Since X-ray is a form of radiation, exposure to it also increases the likelihood of developing cancer. Therefore, doctors must find a careful balance when selecting the radiation dose. While a high dose produces a high-quality image, it also increases the patient's chance of developing cancer. On the other hand, having a lower dose reduces the risk for cancer, but it also introduces the aforementioned image artifacts, lowering the image quality and making diagnosis harder. Sinogram completion and Poisson noise artifacts are introduced from lower dose images, while focal spot deblurring comes from the X-ray source itself.

The first task, sinogram completion, stems from a scanning method named sparse-sampling, where the CT scanner produces X-ray beams at fewer angles than a full sample. For example, a sparse sample's sinogram could include 180 angles around the patient's body while a full sample includes 360. A full sample sinogram produces a higher quality image than the sparse sampled one, but a sparse sample scan reduces the patient's radiation exposure by a large margin. Another way to reduce radiation dose is to lower the scanner's tube current (mA), causing it to emit a lower amount of X-ray photons in each projection, which produces Poisson noise throughout the image. The final task isn't controlled by the radiation dose; it is due to the size of the X-ray source. An image with no blur requires the source to be infinitely small, which isn't possible in the real world. Even then, extremely small sources will not be able to handle large amounts of X-ray output due to overheating. Therefore, normal X-ray sources will produce images with a reasonable amount of blur, and thus, the need for deblurring arises. Success of this work will help others understand the benefits and downsides of the two strategies (Fig. 1).

Fig. 1. Example of a sinogram and its reconstruction

2   Materials and Methods

2.1   Dataset

Experimentation involved the use of sinogram data obtained from the FIPS Open X-Ray Tomographic Datasets. Four sinograms were used, and they were created from four different objects: a walnut, carved cheese, a lotus, and a cross phantom. The walnut data was a 1200 × 2296 sinogram, signifying that it consisted of projections taken from 1200 angles. The rest of the data had a significantly lower amount of projections, with the lotus sinogram having dimensions of 366 × 2240, and the carved cheese and cross phantom being 360 × 2240 (Fig. 2).

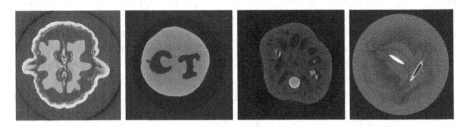

Fig. 2. FIPS Data reconstructions

2.2   Network Architecture

The model used to conduct this study is a modified U-Net [9], which was initially used for segmentation in biomedical images [10, 11]. The original structure used 2 × 2 max pooling to down sample the input data. One of the modifications involved replacing the max pooling layer with a convolutional layer with a stride of 2. This allows the down sampling process to be learn-able, which improves the overall ability of the network. The second modification was an addition of a residual block in the last layer. This allows the network to learn how to approximate the difference between the input and target and also accounts for the vanishing gradient issue common in networks with many layers. Both of these modifications improve the approximation ability of the model, making it a better fit for regression tasks as opposed to its original segmentation purpose. The architecture of the modified model is shown in Fig. 6. In order to generate input images to train the models for the sinogram domain, image artifacts were simulated over the original sinogram, and the ground truth sinogram was used as the desired output. For the reconstruction domain, the Poisson noise and focal spot deblurring tasks used the reconstruction of the estimated sinogram from the sinogram domain model as input and the ground truth sinogram's reconstruction as output. The sinogram completion model used the sparse sinogram's reconstruction as input and the ground truth sinogram's reconstruction as output, and an explanation of this difference is in the Focal Spot Deconvolution section. Training and testing data was split by using the walnut, carved cheese, and lotus as the training set, while the cross phantom was used as the test set. Since using the entire image data for training would be too computationally expensive and only net four sets of data for training, the model utilizes patch-based training, each patch being a 64 × 64 portion of the entire image. This results in train and test sets consisting of 66,848 and 12,672 patches, respectively. The final predicted result would then be all the patches pieced back together after going through the model. During training, an Adam optimizer with learning rate 0.001 was used, along with a callback that reduced the learning rate by half if no improvement was seen over three epochs. A mean squared loss function calculated the average of how far off each predicted pixel was from the ground truth, its equation given by (Fig. 3): scikit-image

$$MSE = \frac{1}{N} \sum_{i=1}^{n} \left(Y - Y_{pred} \right)^2 \tag{1}$$

Afterwards, the model was trained for 100 epochs, and the model was able to learn very quickly, as shown by the learning curve (taken from the sinogram completion model that was trained in the sinogram domain) in Fig. 7.

2.3   Image Artifact Simulation

Sinogram Completion. To generate the input images for this task, a python for loop with a step of 10 was used over the original sinogram, and the input image only contained values at these slices, with the rest of the image having a zero-pixel value. This method successfully reduced the sinogram to only 10% of the original amount of slices (Fig. 4).

Fig. 3. Example of a sparse sampled sinogram's reconstruction

Fig. 4. Example of a reconstruction with Poisson noise artifacts

Poisson Noise Removal. In order to add noise to the original images, a python function modeled after [12] was used. The function takes 3 parameters that determine the amount of noise, along with a fourth parameter which is the original low-noise sinogram. The function then returns an array that represents a high-noise version of the original sinogram (Fig. 5).

Focal Spot Deconvolution. The method introduced in [13] was used for the focal spot deconvolution. The simulation of focal spot deconvolution is very straightforward with the help of the gaussian function from the scikit-image library. The [14] function takes a parameter named σ, which is the standard deviation of the gaussian kernel, to determine the amount of blur that will be applied to the image. The higher the σ the blurrier the image. We used σ = 2 for the input image simulation. Finally, the function returns the desired blurry image that simulates the focal spot blur artifact (Fig. 6).

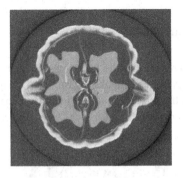

Fig. 5. Example of a reconstruction with the focal spot blurring issue

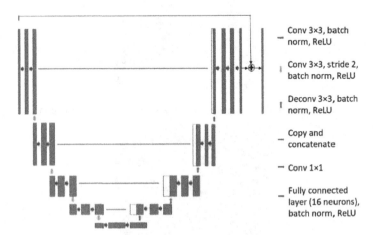

Fig. 6. Architecture of the U-Net used in this study. 64 × 64 patches were used as input and output images during training

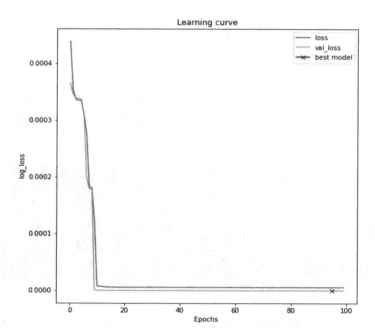

Fig. 7. Graph of the model's loss over 100 epochs

3 Results

3.1 Sinogram Completion

Looking at the walnut data (Fig. 8), both predicted reconstructions perform well in removing the streak artifacts prevalent throughout the sparse reconstruction. However, looking at the zoomed in portions, the quality at the center of the walnut for the sinogram domain reconstruction has decreased substantially when compared to the ground truth. The reconstruction domain result, on the other hand, is very close to the ground truth, quality wise, and it outperforms the sinogram domain for the walnut data. Without looking closely, it is hard to find noticeable differences between the recon-struction domain image and the ground truth, but when magnifying the center of the walnut, it is clear that the model smooths over intricate details, which could prove troublesome when applied on complex structures like the heart. The remaining data (Fig. 9) followed a similar trend, the predicted reconstructions successfully removed the streak artifacts (with one exception), but the centers of the sinogram domain images are heavily warped, making details and edges of the image difficult to see, which render the images useless for diagnosis in a clinical setting. After inspection, the recon-struction domain achieves better performance than the sinogram domain, maintaining higher quality images that are close to the ground truth. However, it still isn't the same as a full sinogram due to the bright spots introduced in the cheese and lotus data, and the small streak artifacts still present in the cross phantom data. These issues are small

72   A. Huang

compared to the warping in the sinogram domain and the streak artifacts covering the image in the sparse reconstructions. We can conclude that training in the reconstruction domain works best for the sinogram completion task.

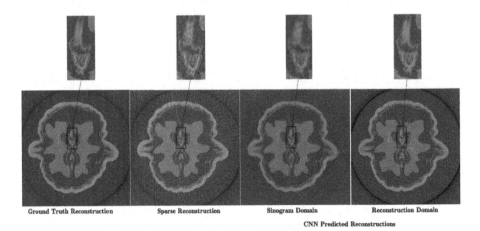

Fig. 8. Walnut data results with magnification for the sinogram completion task

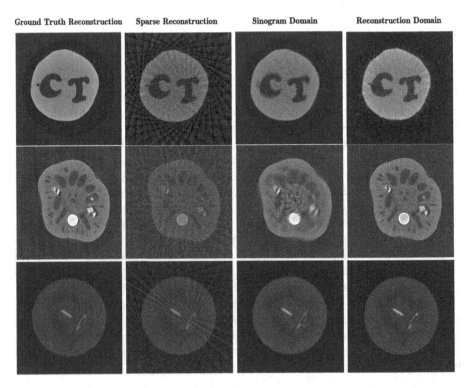

Fig. 9. Results for the remaining data

3.2 Poisson Noise Removal

At first, it is difficult to tell the difference between the four cross phantom images (See Fig. 10), but magnifying a portion of the image helps us easily differentiate and compare the results. The noisy reconstruction is covered with tiny black spots that make up Poisson noise, and the noise gives the image a static texture. Although the noise level isn't extremely high in this experiment, the results can still tell us which strategy works better for denoising. Both models perform very similarly in removing the actual noise artifacts from the image, but the sinogram domain's result changes the quality of the image, making it blurrier than the reconstruction domain and noisy reconstructions. Because of this, the reconstruction domain strategy outperforms the sinogram domain strategy for the cross phantom data, due to a closer image quality to the ground truth.

Some of the remaining results (Fig. 11) differ from that of the cross phantom. For the walnut data, the two predicted reconstructions appear to be virtually the same, meaning in some instances, the two strategies achieve the same performance. This could be due to the fact that the walnut data makes up a large amount of the training data set, and this shows that the reconstruction domain strategy for denoising works better in cases with less data provided. A similar trend to the cross phantom data is seen in the rest of the images, with the sinogram domain result tending to be a blurrier and lower quality image than the reconstruction domain, but overall, both training strategies successfully remove most of the noise from the image. Again, the reconstruction domain has a better performance than the sinogram domain overall, though in some instances, the two strategies have similar results.

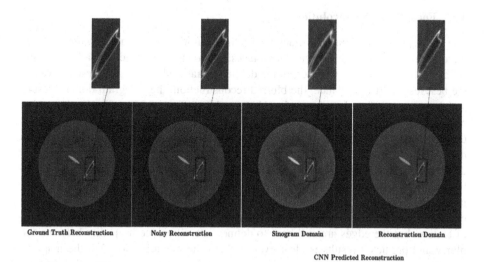

Ground Truth Reconstruction   Noisy Reconstruction   Sinogram Domain   Reconstruction Domain

CNN Predicted Reconstruction

Fig. 10. Cross Phantom results with magnification for the Poisson noise removal task

Ground Truth Reconstruction   Noisy Reconstruction   Sinogram Domain   Reconstruction Domain

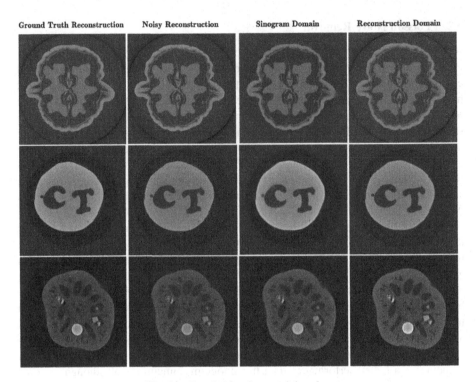

Fig. 11. Results for the remaining data

3.3   Focal Spot Deconvolution

The focal spot deconvolution artifact proved to be harder for the models to remove than the other two tasks. In the previous two tasks, the models removed virtually all of the streak artifacts or noise, however, in the deblurring task, blur was still present, even in the best result. At first glance, the blurred reconstruction, the sinogram domain result, and the reconstruction domain result all have a clear difference in quality for the carved cheese (See Fig. 12). The image with nothing done to it is the lowest in quality, while the sinogram domain image is in the middle, and the reconstruction domain image is the highest in quality. Upon magnification of the hole to the left of the "C", the difference is even more pronounced. The circle's edges are very hard to define in the blurred reconstruction, and its shape has been slightly altered. The texture of the cheese itself has changed as well, looking smooth instead of textured like the original. The circle shape is easier to see in the predicted results, and the background isn't as devoid of texture, but the edges are still hard to define. The difference in quality between the blurry and predicted results is clear even without the magnification, but the magnification helps clarify that the predicted results do a lot better at approximating texture, and it makes the difference in quality between the two predicted results clearer.

As for the rest of the results (Fig. 13), the two strategies have little difference in performance for the walnut and lotus data. Both strategies achieve better image clarity than the blurred image, meaning that for these two cases, it doesn't matter which type of training is performed. The cross-phantom's results are the same case as the carved cheese, where the sinogram domain was blurrier than the reconstruction domain.

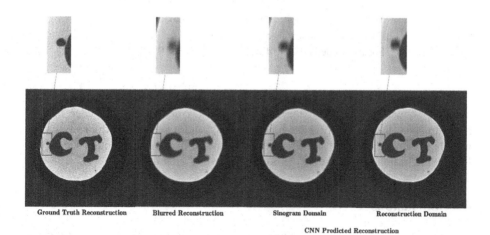

Ground Truth Reconstruction   Blurred Reconstruction   Sinogram Domain   Reconstruction Domain

CNN Predicted Reconstruction

Fig. 12. Carved Cheese results with magnification for the Focal Spot Deconvolution Task

Ground Truth Reconstruction   Blurred Reconstruction   Sinogram Domain   Reconstruction Domain

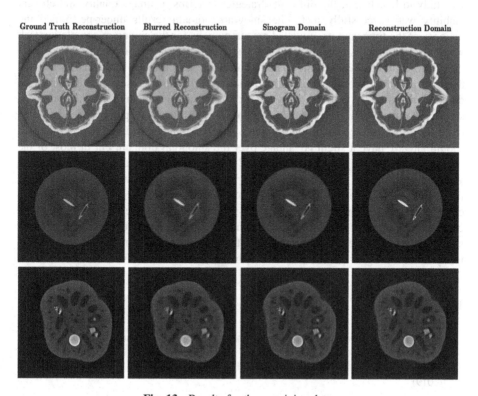

Fig. 13. Results for the remaining data

Table 1. PSNR values calculated between walnut results and original walnut reconstruction

	CNN training method		
	None	Sinogram	Reconstruction
Sinogram completion	38.30	35.36	43.52
Poisson noise removal	38.10	35.65	47.30
Focal spot deblurring	47.33	35.23	35.19

The PSNR values of predicted results, when compared to the original, for all three tasks are shown in Table 1 for the walnut data. They demonstrate the edge that the reconstruction domain has over the other methods, and it verifies the difficulty for the models to remove the blur artifact. The lotus, cheese, and cross phantom values followed similar trends, and they were omitted to avoid redundancy.

4   Conclusions

In this work, the performance of different CNN training strategies in medical CT was compared through three common low level image-processing tasks, and the target of the study to benchmark the different strategies in terms of image quality and clinical viability was successfully met. The sinogram domain results under-performed the majority of the time, and its predicted reconstructions for the sinogram completion task were not even used as training input for the reconstruction domain due to the fact that the results achieved by using the sparse reconstruction as training input were better. On the contrary, the reconstruction domain never performed worse than the sinogram domain, making it the better strategy to pick when training a model for CT. However, a surprising outcome was that the two strategies had the same performance in some cases. Because the reconstruction domain's input has already been through a model, it should already have a slight advantage over the sinogram domain, but in most of the walnut results and the lotus results for focal spot deconvolution, the two strategies had virtually no difference in performance. This interesting result shows that in a few cases, the extra step included in the reconstruction domain wasn't necessary, and the less computationally expensive strategy, he sinogram domain, achieved the same results. In conclusion, this paper successfully bench-marked and compared the two main training strategies, and as a result discovered that the reconstruction domain strategy consistently achieves higher performances than the sinogram domain, with few exceptions.

References

1. Bushberg, J.T., Boone, J.M.: The essential physics of medical imaging. Lippincott Williams and Wilkins (2011)
2. Maier, J., et al.: Focal spot deconvolution using convolutional neural networks, vol. 03, p. 25 (2019)

3. Lee, H., Lee, J., Kim, H., Cho, B., Cho, S.: Deep-neural-network-based sinogram synthesis for sparse-view ct image reconstruction. IEEE Trans. Radiation Plasma Med. Sci. **3**(2), 109–119 (2019)
4. Lin, W.A., et al: Dudonet: Dual domain network for ct metal artifact reduction (2019)
5. Zhao, Z., Sun, Y., Cong, P.: Sparse-view ct reconstruction via generative adversarial networks. In: 2018 IEEE Nuclear Science Symposium and Medical Imaging Conference Proceedings (NSS/MIC), pp. 1–5 (2018)
6. Bar, Y., Diamant, I., Wolf, L., Greenspan, H.: Deep learning with non-medical training used for chest pathology identification. In: Medical Imaging 2015: Computer-Aided Diagnosis. International Society for Optics and Photonics, vol. 9414, p. 94140V (2015)
7. Iqbal, S., Ghani, M.U., Saba, T., Rehman, A.: Brain tumor segmentation inmulti-spectral mri using convolutional neural networks (cnn). Microscopy Res. Tech. **81**(4), 419–427 (2018)
8. Lucas, L., et al.: State of the art: iterative ct reconstruction techniques. Radiology, **276**(2), 339–357 (2015) PMID: 26203706
9. Ronneberger, O., Fischer, P., Brox, T.: U-net: convolutional networks for biomedical image segmentation (2015)
10. Hartmann, A., et al.: Bayesian u-net for segmenting glaciers in sar imagery, (2021)
11. Bandyopadhyay, H., Dasgupta, T., Das, N., Nasipuri, M.: A gated and bifurcated stacked u-net module for document image dewarping (2020)
12. Zeng, D., et al.: A simple low-dose x-ray ct simulation from high-dose scan. IEEE Trans. Nucl. Sci. **62**(5), 2226–2233 (2015)
13. Sawall, S., Backs, J., Kachelrieß, M., Kuntz, J.: Focal spot deconvolution using convolutional neural networks. In: Medical Imaging 2019: Physics of Medical Imaging International Society for Optics and Photonics, vol. 10948, p. 109480Q (2019)
14. van der Walt, S.J., et al.: Scikit-image: image processing in python. PeerJ, **2**, e453 (2014)

Sound-Based Respiratory Disease Recognition with Machine Learning

Xiaoran Xu[✉]

Electrical and Computer Engineering Department,
New York Institute of Technology, Newyork, USA
xxu23@nyit.edu

Abstract. Due to the effects of respiratory diseases, a large number of people die every year. Last year, the new coronavirus COVID-19 swept the world even more, causing the huge loss of personnel and economic decline around the world. To fight against this huge epidemic, relying on hospitals only to detect the such large number of people is obviously inefficient. Therefore, this paper proposes to relieve the pressure of medical workers through sound detection, in a framework of combing the Mel Frequency Cepstral Coefficient (MFCC) and Convolutional Neural Networks (CNN). To compare different voice types and disease types, we selected three open data sets, namely, ICBHI, Coswara and Verify. Then we compared CNN with the Multi-layer Perceptron, Random Forest and XGBoost models. Finally, it is concluded that CNN has the highest accuracy rate on the three data sets.

Keywords: COVID-19 · Respiratory disease · Mel Frequency Cepstral Coefficient · Convolutional Neural Network

1 Introduction

Respiratory diseases are one of the largest causes of death in the world. Currently, approximately 3.8 million people die from respiratory diseases every year [1]. Multiple research data indicate that due to smoking and declining air quality, the incidence of respiratory diseases is increasing. The World Health Organization (WHO) predicts that the number of deaths from respiratory diseases will reach 10 million in 2025 [1]. Among them, common diseases such as acute and chronic nasopharyngitis, influenza, tonsillitis, tracheitis and chronic bronchitis account for 80% of the entire respiratory diseases.

Especially in 2020, with the outbreak of the COVID-19, more than 4 million people were infected and more than 72,000 deaths were reported in the week before December 27, 2020 [1]. Clinically, patients with the COVID-19 and other respiratory diseases have similar symptoms, such as difficult breathing and coughing. The transmission mode of COVID-19 is mainly aerosol and contact transmission, and there are many asymptomatic infections, so the transmission capacity is very strong. Ordinary people are very susceptible to infection without paying attention, and it is not easy to find out that they are sick. At present, the main detection method is based on diagnostic testing, based on a sample of mucus from the nose or throat, or a sample of saliva. If the testing is positive, further examination in the hospital is needed. In this process, the risk of

W. Cao et al. (Eds.): CONF-CDS 2021, CCIS 1513, pp. 78–90, 2021.
https://doi.org/10.1007/978-981-16-8885-0_8

infection has actually increased than staying inside. People need to go to a professional place for nucleic acid testing. If there are symptoms, they need to be isolated. After arriving at the hospital, a series of inspections such as X-ray [2] and CT-scan [3] can be further conducted. In addition to the high cost of detection, the radiation itself can also cause certain harm to the human body. There are news reports [4] that some hospitals have forgotten to disinfect the X-ray rooms used by COVID-19 patients and caused other patients to contract COVID-19.

Therefore, we hope that we can accurately diagnose COVID-19 patients before going to the hospital for further diagnosis. We can distinguish between healthy and unhealthy people through the difference in their breathing sounds, which show the abnormalities if infected. In this article, we intend to use audio signals to determine respiratory diseases, through breathing, coughing, and normal pronunciation collected by smartphones or computer microphones. Since all personal electronic devices can be used, the patients do not need to go to a medical facility for sound pattern collection, and it is very convenient for patients with the COVID-19, normal people and patients with suspected COVID-19 to complete the data collection process independently at home. If collected in a quiet place at home, it also helps to reduce noise interference and improve data quality.

Similar ideas have also appeared in previous studies, such as data collected by video recordings on the Internet [5], and data collected by crowdsourced personal smartphones [6, 7], or well-designed apps [5, 8, 9]. Previous research has also explored the use of machine learning models, such as random forest [6], SVM [5, 8], MLP [10], as well as the deep learning models, such as CNN [9, 11, 12], which has been proven effective in a series of problems [13–15]. There are also some studies verifying the feasibility of voice judgment for COVID-19 [9, 16]. And research on the classification of vocalization types [17]. Based on the trained models, free or commercial applications have been developed for individual users [18].

However, there are still some shortcomings in the previous studies, for example, the amount of data is not very large, the result accuracy is not high enough, the amount of change considered is relatively small, and there is no comparison with other models, or it fails to take into account the new challenges posed by the COVID-19 epidemic.

In this work, we propose a framework that combines the Mel Frequency Cepstral Coefficient (MFCC) and Convolutional Neural Networks (CNN) and demonstrate that it is superior to other methods. Specifically, MFCC is used as the first step to extract features in the frequency domain, followed by CNN as the classification model. We compare the CNN model with the multi-layer perceptron, random forest, XGBoost [19] models in three datasets, namely, the ICBHI data set [20], Coswara [6], and Virufy data set [11]. These three datasets provide different types of breathing sounds, e.g., Coswara collects nine types of sound, namely, heavy breathing, shallow breathing, heavy cough, shallow cough, fast counting, normal number and sustained vowel phonation (three kinds; /ey/ as in made, /i/ as in beet, /u:/ as in cool). Our classification target also changes with the datasets. For the ICBHI data set, the CNN model distinguishes among different diseases. While for the Coswara and COVID shared data, the CNN model makes a binary classification. By using these diverse datasets, our work takes into account normal pneumonia and COVID-19 pneumonia simultaneously. After a comprehensive evaluation, we show that MFCC-CNN framework is superior to other solutions in all three datasets.

The main contributions of our method are summarized as follows:

1. We consider normal respiratory diseases and COVID-19 pneumonia simultaneously, by analyzing the breathing, cough, and voice of individual users.
2. We compare multiple models, such as the fully connected network, random forest and XGBoost model with the MFCC-CNN framework, with three evaluation metrics, namely, accuracy, ROC curve, and confusion matrix. The evaluation on three diverse datasets show that that MFCC-CNN framework is superior to other solutions.

The following arrangements of this article are as follows. Section 2 gives a systematic summary of related work. Section 3 introduces the source as well as the description of the data set used in this paper. Section 4 presents a detailed description of methods and experimental descriptions. Section 5 summarizes the conclusion and findings as well as the future research directions.

2 Related Work

In this section, we give a detailed discussion about the relevant studies, especially their datasets and models.

In the literature, there are some open dataset for the sound classification problem. In the three public data set ESC-10, ESC-50, and UrbanSound8K, CNN is proven effective in Bales et al. [21], with an accuracy of 89.60%. However, this work fails to compare the CNN model with other models. Later, there are datasets specified for the respiratory sound classification problem, e.g., ICBHI, which has 6895 respiratory cycles and 126 subjects. Monaco et al. [10] compare different models, e.g., random forest, MLP, SVM and DNN, in the ICBHI dataset, and find that the accuracy of MLP is the best, with a value of 85%. Rocha et al. [20] creates a database including 920 recordings acquired from 126 participants and two sets of annotations. This database is released to the public. It is useful to the research community by bringing the attention in respiratory sound classification problem.

With the emerging COVID-19 in 2020, researchers are trying to collect different types of sound files to combat with this virus. Voice information of 19 speakers extracted from YouTube TV videos are used in Ritwik et al. [5]. Sharma et al. [6] collect 6,507 clean and 1,117 noisy sound data sets by using mobile phones and laptops. Three datasets are used in Dunne et al. [11], namely, Google's audio set, Coswara project, and 17 samples of cough sounds infected with COVID-19. Based on the mobile app, the COVID-19 symptoms of 2,618,862 participants are collected in Menni et al. [7]. In Brown et al. [8], 4,352 unique users are involved through web applications and 2,261 unique users are involved from Android applications, including 4,352 and 5,634 samples respectively. This is the first public crowdsourcing method to collect audio data to judge the COVID-19 epidemic. In Imran et al. [9], 1,838 cough sound and 3,597 environmental sound of no cough are used.

Based on these datasets, different types of models are tried and compared, including the machine learning and deep learning models. In Schuller et al. [16], it mainly discusses the possibility of using machine learning analysis to diagnose symptoms through sound. SVM is used in Ritwik et al. [5], with an accuracy rate of 88.6% and a F-score of 0.927. However, this performance is not convincing because the dataset they use is too small. SVM is also the best in Brown et al. [8], when compared with LR, and Gradient Boosting Decision Tree. Random forest is used in Sharma et al. [6], with an accuracy rate of 66.74%. This accuracy is not high enough and there are no distinction different health conditions. SVM and CNN are compared in Dunne et al. [11], in which CNN is better with an accuracy rate of 97.5%. However, their problem is also the small data size. CNN is also proven effective in Imran et al. [9]. Logistic regression is used to analyze 805,753 individuals with symptoms that have not been tested for SARS-CoV-2 in Menni et al. [7] and achieves an accuracy about 95%.

While different models may present diverse performances on different datasets, we need to consider the feasibility of applying these models in a real-world system. Faezipour et al. [18] provides some theoretical support for the use of mobile phones to diagnose the COVID-19 symptom. This type of self-examination will be an early step before the doctor orders further examinations such as lung CT and X-rays. However, their work lacks of the specific data support.

3 Dataset Description

In this study, we use three open datasets from the literature.

3.1 ICBHI Data Set [20]

This dataset contains sound examples recorded by the exploration group of the Respiratory Research and Rehabilitation Laboratory of the School of Health Sciences, University of Aveiro. The hints of pneumonia, COPD and asthma were gathered successively with an advanced stethoscope. In different examinations, bronchiolitis, bronchiectasis, and cystic fibrosis, the sounds were gathered at the same time utilizing either seven stethoscopes with a receiver in the fundamental cylinder or seven air coupled electret amplifiers situated in cases made of teflon. Respiratory sounds were gained utilizing the Computerized Lung Auscultation—Sound System. Tests were recorded in Aveiro, Portugal, at ESSUA and Hospital Infante D. Pedro, in Porto, Portugal, at Hospital Santa Maria and Lusíadas, and at the Faculty of Health Sciences, University of Southampton, England.

This information base incorporates 920 accounts procured from 126 members and two arrangements of explanations. Sounds were recorded from the windpipe and six chest areas: left and right foremost, back, and horizontal. Sounds were gathered in clinical and non-clinical (home) settings. The obtaining of respiratory sounds was performed on members, everything being equal. Members included patients with lower respiratory plot diseases, upper respiratory parcel contaminations, pneumonia, COPD, asthma, bronchiolitis, bronchiectasis, and cystic fibrosis.

3.2   Coswara [6]

The Coswara dataset zeroed in on connecting with the human populace across the globe. For this reason, they made a site application giving a straightforward and intuitive UI. A client could open the application in an internet browser (PC or cell phone), give metadata, and continue to recording the sound examples utilizing the gadget receiver.

The size of dataset has 6,507 clean and 1,117 noisy audio files corresponding to respiratory sound samples from 941 participants. For sound information, Coswara centers around nine unique classifications, specifically, breathing (two sorts; shallow and profound), hack (two sorts; shallow and weighty), supported vowel phonation (three sorts;/ey/as in made,/I/as in beet,/u:/as in cool), and one to twenty digits checking (two sorts; typical and quick moving). Later, we would use these different categories of sound data and compare their performance for symptom classification.

3.3   Virufy Dataset [5]

The Virufy dataset is exact in light of the fact that it was gathered at a clinic under management by doctors adhering to Standard Operating Procedures and educated patient assent. This information is preprocessed and named with COVID-19 status (procured from PCR testing), alongside tolerant socioeconomics (age, sex, clinical history). A sum of 749 sound documents which contains 2 sorts of information are thought about, COVID-19 or not.

4   Experiments

4.1   MFCC

For speech recognition and speaker recognition, the most commonly used feature is Mel-scale Frequency Cepstral Coefficients (MFCC), which is shown in Fig. 1.

The pre-accentuation measure is the initial phase, wherein the discourse signal experiences a high-pass channel. The reason for pre-accentuation is to help the high recurrence part and straighten the recurrence range of the sign.

After pre-accentuation, we need to isolate the sign into brief timeframe outlines. The recurrence in the sign that changes with time isn't reasonable for Fourier change of the whole sign. To stay away from the present circumstance, we can securely expect that the recurrence in the sign is steady in a brief timeframe. Along these lines, by performing Fourier change in this brief timeframe outline, we can get a decent guess of the recurrence profile of the sign by associating neighboring casings.

In the wake of partitioning the sign into outlines, we apply a window work, (for example, a Hamming window) to each casing. There are a few motivations to apply a window capacity to the window outline, particularly to balance the endless information expected by the FFT and diminish range spillage.

Since the change of the sign in the time area is typically hard to introduce the attributes of the sign. It is typically changed over to the energy conveyance in the recurrence space for perception. Diverse energy disseminations can speak to the

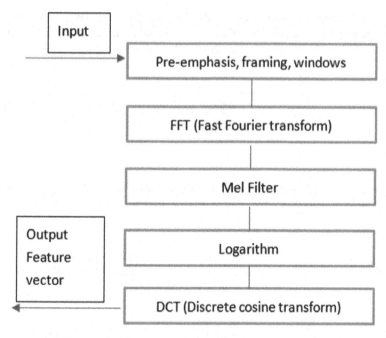

Fig. 1. The process of MFCC.

qualities of various voices. In this way, in the wake of increasing the Hamming window, each edge should go through a quick Fourier change to get the energy circulation on the recurrence range. Quick Fourier change is performed on each casing signal after casing division and windowing to acquire the recurrence range of each casing. At that point we take the modulus square of the recurrence range of the discourse sign to get the force range of the discourse signal.

The three-sided bandpass channel has two primary purposes, e.g., to smooth the recurrence range, wipe out the impact of sounds, and feature the formant of the first voice. Also, the quantity of counts can be decreased. At that point we figure the logarithmic energy yield by each channel bank. Incidentally, the channel bank coefficients determined in the past advance are profoundly connected, which might be hazardous in some AI calculations. Subsequently, we can apply Discrete Cosine Transform (DCT) to decorrelate the channel bank coefficients and produce a compacted portrayal of the channel bank.

4.2 CNN

Based on the extracted MFCC features, we propose to use a convolutional neural network model for further classification. The structure of the CNN model is shown in Fig. 2. It has a sequential structure, consisting of four Conv2D convolutional layers and the filter size is set as 2×2. The first layer uses the input shape of (40, 862, 1), where 40 is the number of MFCC features, 862 is the number of frames. A small Dropout value of 20% is used after the convolutional layers. Each convolutional layer is followed by the max pooling layer and the final convolutional layer is followed by a global average pooling layer. The final part is three dense layers, and the last layer has the same number of neurons equal to the number of sound classes.

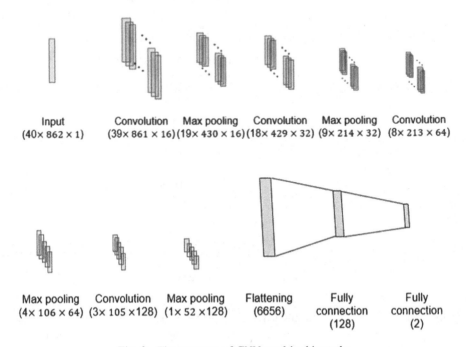

Input
(40× 862 × 1)

Convolution
(39× 861 × 16)

Max pooling
(19× 430 × 16)

Convolution
(18× 429 × 32)

Max pooling
(9× 214 × 32)

Convolution
(8× 213 × 64)

Max pooling
(4× 106 × 64)

Convolution
(3× 105 ×128)

Max pooling
(1× 52 ×128)

Flattening
(6656)

Fully
connection
(128)

Fully
connection
(2)

Fig. 2. The structure of CNN used in this study.

The essential unit of the convolutional layer block followed by the greatest pooling layer behind the convolutional layer. The convolutional layer is utilized to distinguish spatial examples in picture, for example, lines and item parts, and the ensuing most extreme pooling layer is utilized to diminish the convolutional layer's affectability to area. The convolutional layer block is made out of two essential units over and over. In the convolution layer block, every convolution portion has similar size as the channels. The quantity of yield channels of the first convolutional layer is 16, and the quantity of yield channels of the second convolutional layer is expanded to 32. This is on the grounds that the info tallness and width of the second convolutional layer are more modest than those of the first convolutional layer. In this way, expanding the yield channel makes the boundary sizes of the two convolutional layers comparative. The window state of the two max pooling layers of the convolutional layer block is 2 × 2, and the step is 2. Since the pooling window has a similar shape as the step, the zone covered by each sliding of the pooling window on the information doesn't cover one another.

At the point when the yield of the convolutional layer block is passed into the completely associated layer block, the completely associated layer square will smooth each example in the small-scale cluster. All in all, the info state of the completely associated layer will get two-dimensional, where the first measurement is the examples in quite a while clump, the subsequent measurement is the vector portrayal after each example is leveled, and the vector length is the channel, stature and width the result of. The completely associated layer block contains 3 completely associated layers.

5   Conclusion

The accuracy is mainly used as the evaluation metric. Also, we show the confusion matrix and ROC curve. We compared CNN with MLP, Random Forest and XGBoost model as the benchmark method. The Random Forest and XGBoost already have very strong robustness in machine learning. They have been tested in many experiments and previous studies and proven to be very strong ensemble learning models, which are better than many other machines learning model. MLP is also a deep learning model, but we find that it is not as effective as the CNN model in this study. The results are shown in the form of accuracy in Table 1.

It can be seen from Table 1 that CNN performs better than MLP, Random forest and XGBoost models in Verify and ICBHI dataset, and there is no overfitting during training. Although the accuracy of CNN in Coswara is slightly inferior to other models, and the others are seriously overfitted during the training process (Fig. 4). The performance of the Coswara dataset is different in sounds (Fig. 5). Shallow breathing, shallow cough, fast counting, and vowel a perform better than other types of sound (Fig. 6). The vowels e and o have the worst performance (Fig. 7). The following figures show the best-performing confusion matrix and part of the ROC curve (Fig. 8).

Table 1.   The accuracy of different models on each dataset

	CNN	MLP	Random Forest	XGBoost
Coswara (Breathing deep)	0.728	0.714	0.801	0.801
Coswara (Breathing shallow)	0.734	0.752	0.794	0.804
Coswara (cough-heavy)	0.718	0.774	0.798	0.805
Coswara (cough-shallow)	0.739	0.739	0.801	0.794
Cowara (counting fast)	0.725	0.756	0.805	0.801
Cowara (counting normal)	0.721	0.735	0.808	0.808
Coswara (vowel a)	0.746	0.732	0.791	0.794
Coswara (vowel e)	0.686	0.739	0.798	0.774
Coswara (vowel o)	0.661	0.675	0.790	0.790
Verify	0.993	0.987	0.980	0.987
ICBHI	0.891	0.886	0.870	0.891

In conclusion, we find that the CNN model is better than the Multi-layer Perceptron, Random Forest and XGBoost models, after a comprehensive comparison on these open datasets and is more promising of being used in practice to fight against the respiratory diseases, especially the recent COVID-19 (Fig. 3).

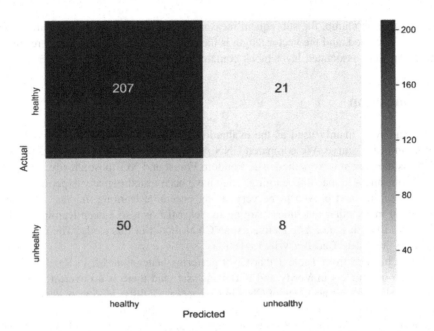

Fig. 3. The confusion matrix of CNN on Coswara (breathing shallow) data.

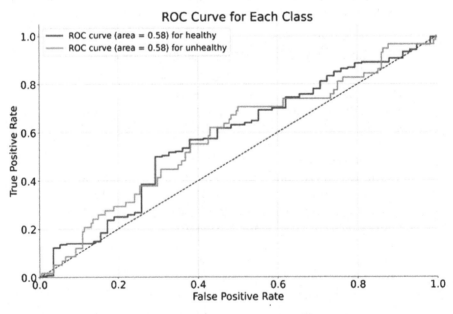

Fig. 4. The ROC curve of CNN on Coswara (breathing shallow) data.

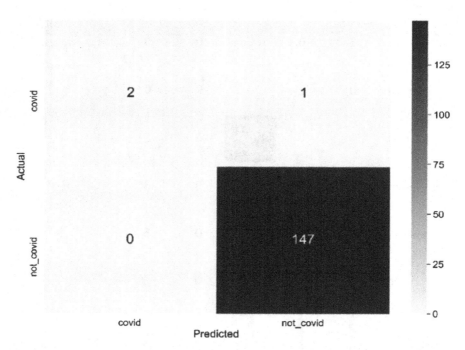

Fig. 5. The confusion matrix of CNN on Verify data.

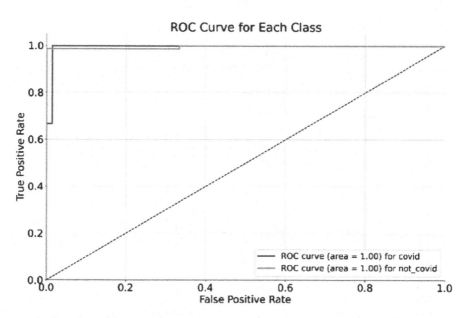

Fig. 6. The ROC curve of CNN on Verify data.

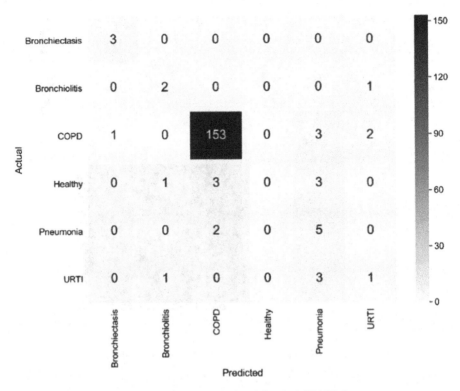

Fig. 7. The confusion matrix of CNN on ICBHI data.

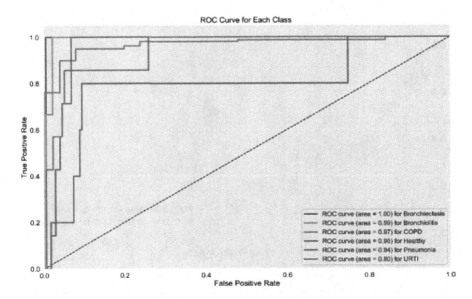

Fig. 8. The ROC curve of CNN on ICBHI data.

References

1. World Health Organization. World health statistics 2020: monitoring health for the SDGs sustainable development goals. World Health Organization (2020)
2. Hira, S., Bai, A., Hira, S.: An automatic approach based on CNN architecture to detect Covid-19 disease from chest X-ray images. Appl. Intell. **51**(5), 2864–2889 (2020). https://doi.org/10.1007/s10489-020-02010-w
3. Ardakani, A.A., et al.: Application of deep learning technique to manage COVID-19 in routine clinical practice using CT images: results of 10 convolutional neural networks. Comput. Biol. Med. 103795 (2020)
4. DXY.cn. Determined to be infected by the shared CT room! Qingdao has had a new crown hospital feeling incident before. (in Chinese). https://k.sina.cn/article_2212518065_83e058b101900v7cw.html. Accessed 3 Jan 2020
5. Ritwik, K.V.S., Kalluri, S.B., Vijayasenan, D.: COVID-19 patient detection from telephone quality speech data (2020). arXiv preprint arXiv:2011.04299
6. Sharma, N., et al.: Coswara–a database of breathing, cough, and voice sounds for COVID-19 diagnosis (2020). arXiv preprint arXiv:2005.10548
7. Menni, C., et al.: Real-time tracking of self-reported symptoms to predict potential COVID-19. Nat. Med., 1–4 (2020)
8. Brown, C., et al.: Exploring automatic diagnosis of COVID-19 from crowdsourced respiratory sound data (2020). arXiv preprint arXiv:2006.05919
9. Imran, A., et al.: AI4COVID-19: AI enabled preliminary diagnosis for COVID-19 from cough samples via an app (2020). arXiv preprint arXiv:2004.01275
10. Monaco, A., et al.: Multi-time-scale features for accurate respiratory sound classification. Appl. Sci. **10**(23), 8606 (2020)
11. Dunne, R., Morris, T., Harper, S.: High accuracy classification of COVID-19 coughs using Mel-frequency cepstral coefficients and a Convolutional Neural Network with a use case for smart home devices (2020)
12. Hershey, S., et al.: CNN architectures for large-scale audio classification. In: 2017 IEEE international conference on acoustics, speech and signal processing (icassp). IEEE (2017)
13. Jiang, W., Zhang, L.: Geospatial data to images: a deep-learning framework for traffic forecasting. Tsinghua Sci. Technol. **24**(1), 52–64 (2018)
14. He, K., Zhang, X., Ren, S., et al.: Deep residual learning for image recognition. In: Proceedings of the IEEE conference on computer vision and pattern recognition, pp. 770–778 (2016)
15. Jiang, W.: Applications of deep learning in stock market prediction: recent progress (2020). arXiv preprint arXiv:2003.01859
16. Schuller, B.W., et al.: Covid-19 and computer audition: an overview on what speech and sound analysis could contribute in the SARS-CoV-2 Corona crisis (2020). arXiv preprint arXiv:2003.11117
17. Wang, Y., et al.: Abnormal respiratory patterns classifier may contribute to large-scale screening of people infected with COVID-19 in an accurate and unobtrusive manner (2020). arXiv preprint arXiv:2002.05534
18. Faezipour, M., Abuzneid, A.: Smartphone-based self-testing of COVID-19 using breathing sounds. Telemedicine e-Health (2020)
19. Chen, T., Guestrin, C.: Xgboost: a scalable tree boosting system. In: Proceedings of the 22nd ACM Sigkdd International Conference on Knowledge Discovery and Data Mining, pp. 785–794 (2016)

20. Rocha, B.M., et al.: An open access database for the evaluation of respiratory sound classification algorithms. Physiol. Measur. **40**(3), 035001 (2019)
21. Bales, C., et al.: Can machine learning be used to recognize and diagnose coughs? (2020). arXiv preprint arXiv:2004.01495

Stock Prediction with Adaptive-Factors Temporal Convolutional Attention-Based Network

Rui Qi$^{(\boxtimes)}$ and Weimin Pan

Beijing University of Post and Telecommunications, 10 Xitucheng Road, Haidian, Beijing, China
qirui@bupt.edu.cn

Abstract. The stock prediction has been a hot and challenging research theme for a long time. With the rise of deep learning, the application of deep learning methods to financial time series forecasting has attracted much attention. This paper models the stock prediction problem by combining both technical factors and financial factors in market. We innovatively use Temporal Convolutional Attention-based Network (TCAN) for stock factor feature extraction. What's more, we proposed Factor Attention (FA) to weight the importance of different input factors adaptively, so that we can eliminate factor noise and focus on the main factors. Finally, it is verified in Chinese stock market. Experimental results show that our method effectively improves the accuracy of stock return prediction, up to 59.95%. At the same time, the cumulative yield curve is significantly better than HS-300 index when using our model to select stocks and adjust portfolio. Compared with other stock prediction models, our model also has the certain advantage in multiple investment indicators.

Keywords: Deep learning · Stock prediction · Time series forecast · Stock selection

1 Introduction

Stock prediction is a classic research issue in the field of computing finance. With the rise of deep learning, it has been extensively studied again in recent years. More and more deep learning methods are applied into stock prediction [1, 2]. Studying stock prediction has great application value in our real life, which can enhance the interpretability of stock return. A key point of stock prediction is the feature extraction of financial time series data. In view of the powerful feature extraction capability of convolutional neural network, the two branch model [3] took the input data as images and used 2-d CNN to extract the feature for each factor separately. However, the disadvantage is that general 2-d CNN ignores the time series characteristic of input data. So it can not effectively retain its temporal structure characteristic.

In order to solve the disadvantage of the two branch model, this paper uses the Temporal Convolutional Attention-based Network (TCAN) [4] for feature extraction. The combined features of factors at different moments will be fully mined, so as to

© Springer Nature Singapore Pte Ltd. 2021
W. Cao et al. (Eds.): CONF-CDS 2021, CCIS 1513, pp. 91–104, 2021.
https://doi.org/10.1007/978-981-16-8885-0_9

make better use of its time series characteristic. **Temporal Convolutional Network** (TCN) [5] is a variant of CNN, which combines the aspect of RNN and CNN's architecture. On the basis of TCN, TCAN adds a temporal attention block between every two convolution modules, which gives different weights to historical moments' features extracted by the previous layer. As a result, it can better integrate the characteristics of different moments. Relevant researches [4] show that TCAN's performance on many tasks surpasses traditional time series prediction models such as LSTM [6] and GRU [7]

Another key point in stock prediction is the selection of candidate factors. This paper proposes an attention mechanism to solve it, named as Factors Attention. There are many factors that can be used for stock prediction, but not all of these factors are always strongly related to stock return at every moment. That is to say, there may be some redundant or failure factors. The existence of those factors is likely to interfere with stock prediction. For example, both factor x and factor y are related to stock returns, but at different moments, the contribution value of x and y to the stock return is different, or they are redundant factors at some moment. Therefore, it is very necessary to explicitly assign importance weights to different factors. In order to increase the attention to high-quality factors and reduce the weight of redundant factors, we propose the factor attention. It can play a role in factor screening.

Our newly proposed model in this paper is named as **A**daptive-**F**actors **T**emporal **C**onvolutional **A**ttention-based **N**etwork (AF-TCAN). The experimental results show that for the prediction of stock return classification in this paper, the accuracy of AF-TCAN can achieve the best result, which is higher than linear model, LSTM and two-branch CNN model. In the backtesting experiment, the cumulative return rate of stock adjustment using AF-TCAN can outperform HS-300 and other stock prediction models.

The remainder of the paper is organized as follows. Section 2 presents a brief review of the related work. Section 3 details our prediction model proposed in this paper. Section 4 presents the factors, data preprocessing and experimental results. Section 5 gives the summary and prospect of the work.

2   Related Work

In the financial field, the relevant attribute which can explain the stock return by the cross-section analysis is called the "factor". The most classic model that uses factors to explain the stock return is the Fama-French three-factor model [8]. In 1992, Fama and French studied the factors that determine the difference in the return of different stocks in the U.S. stock market. They found that the excess return of the stock market can be explained by the exposure of three factors, which are market portfolio, market capitalization and price book-value ratio respectively. In 1995, Carhart improved the three-factor model by adding a momentum factor on the basis of the original three factors. And the Carhart four-factor model [9] was proposed, which made up for the lack of interpretation of the market trend effect by the three-factor model. In 2013, Fama and French found that the profit factor and investment factor also have an impact on the return of stock assets. These two additional factors were added to the Fama-French three-factor model, and the Fama-French five-factor model [10] was proposed. In addition, a lot of other factors have been found one after another. According to the statistics [11], more than 300 factors have been discovered just until 2012. Therefore, the factors that investors should consider are increasing rapidly. But due to the curse of dimensional, it is difficult to simultaneously examine all factors at the same time. As well, some factors may become invalid over time. In terms of models, cross-section analysis methods mostly use linear regression model because it is easy to handle statistics and robust in financial. However, the relation between the factors and stock's return is very complicated [12]. Linear model can not fully explain the relation between factors and stock return. Its prediction accuracy is limited.

Since nonlinear behaviors were found in financial time series data, nonlinear models such as KNN, SVM and DNN have been applied to stock prediction. In 2013, Jianxue Chen [13] studied how to use SVM to learn the relationship between technical factors and stock prices. The results showed that SVM could bring certain improvement in financial time series forecasting performance. Entering the era of deep learning, in 2015, Kai Chen [14] only used the LSTM to predict stock returns on the Chinese stock market, dividing stocks into 7 categories according to the return interval. But its accuracy rate was only 27.2%, because his method was only limited for stock prices. Other important features such as technical indicators and financial indicators that have a greater guiding significance for the stock market were not considered. In 2016, Cavalcante [15] proposed a review of the application of a variety of machine learning methods in the financial field, most of which are forecasts based on time series analysis such as representative RNN, LSTM, SVM and ensemble learning models. In 2018, Masaya and Nakagawa [16] used a multi-layer perceptron neural network and combined with multiple factors, to conduct a research on Japanese stock market. It was proved that the use of deep learning to nonlinear combination of factors can improve the accuracy of stock return prediction than simply linear combination of various factors and other machine learning models. This also pointed out the general direction of using deep learning to predict stock returns for other researchers. In the same year, Gao Tingwei [17] ultilized LSTM with technical factors to make stock return prediction. Specially, PCA was innovatively used to remove factor noise by reducing dimensionality. This method comprehensively considered technical factors that affect the stock price. It also considered the removal of redundant factor's noise. However, it did not consider the impact of financial indicators. Feng Fuli [18] used the attention-based LSTM to model the time series sequence. And it used the adversarial approach for model training. The result showed that the attention mechanism and adversarial training approach could effectively improve the stock prediction performance. However, it was also a prediction only based on price data, without considering other factors. In 2021, the two-branch CNN model [3] comprehensively took account of both technical and financial factors for stock prediction. However, it used CNN to extract the feature of each factor separately and discarded the time series feature of sequence data. Also, it treated all input factors equally, without fully considering the relative importance between them.

The model proposed in this paper comprehensively considers both technical factors and financial factors. As well, it weights the importance of each factor to remove noise. What's more, it ultilizes advanced temporal convolutional attention-based network for feature extraction. In some way, it solved the existed problems in the above.

3   Methods

3.1   Factor Attention

In fact, not all factors are strongly related to stock returns at every time. There may be some redundant and irrelevant factors as time goes by. However, the trend of stocks is only affected by the most relevant factors. Irrelevant factors will bring noise to the forecasting task. Besides, as time goes by, the importance of some factor is also changing. Therefore, it is particularly important to pay more attention to the important factors. Inspired by the work in [19], we designed a factor screening method based on attention mechanism, name as Factor Attention (FA). With FA, we can effectively solve the problem by assigning different weights to different factors at different moments.

FA is used to adaptively extract the relevant factors at each moment, which plays a role in factor screening in some way. It can highlight the importance of strong correlation factors in the current market environment and eliminate the noise of weak correlation factors. Accordingly, all factors will be used more rationally. The process is shown in Fig. 1.

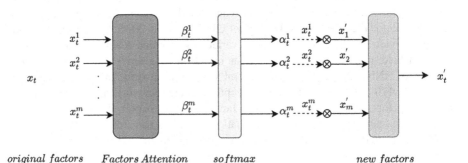

original factors   Factors Attention   softmax   new factors

Fig. 1. Factor attention

Given the input sequence of factor k, $x^k = \left(x_1^k, x_2^k, x_3^k, x_4^k, \ldots, x_n^k\right)$,

$$\beta^k = \tanh\left(w_a x^k + b_a\right) \tag{1}$$

where $w_a \in \mathbb{R}^{n*n}, b_a \in \mathbb{R}^n$. w_a and b_a are the parameters that need to be learned. Now we get the score vector of x^k distributed in n time steps, $\beta^k = \left(\beta_1^k, \beta_2^k, \beta_3^k, \ldots, \beta_n^k\right) \in \mathbb{R}^n$.

$$\alpha_t^k = \frac{exp^{\beta_t^k}}{\sum_{i=1}^{m} exp^{\beta_t^i}} \tag{2}$$

Then we obtain α_t^k by β_t through the *softmax* function, which is the attention weight of the k-th factor at time t. The factor weight is multiplied by the corresponding factor, and finally the weighted factor sequence $x^{'k}$ is obtained.

$$x^{k} = \left(\alpha_t^1 x_t^1, \alpha_t^2 x_t^2, \alpha_t^3 x_t^3, \alpha_t^4 x_t^4, \ldots, \alpha_t^m x_t^m \right) \tag{3}$$

As shown in Fig. 1, the original input sequence at time t is $x_t = \left(x_t^1, x_t^2, x_t^3, x_t^4, \ldots, x_t^m \right)$. Through the above mentioned factors attention, we can obtain the weighted factor sequence $x_t' = \left(\alpha_t^1 x_t^1, \alpha_t^2 x_t^2, \alpha_t^3 x_t^3, \alpha_t^4 x_t^4, \ldots, \alpha_t^m x_t^m \right)$. Then, for the input at each moment, a certain attention weight is assigned to each influencing factor. The importance of different factors at each moment is measured, so that the model can focus on the important driving factors. Rather than treating all factors equally, it is more reasonable and efficient.

3.2 Temporal Convolutional Attention-Based Network

Temporal Convolutional Attention-based Network (TCAN) is an extension of Temporal Convolutional Network (TCN). The evaluation of TCN shows that its convolutional architecture has better performance than recurrent networks on various tasks [5]. As well, it has longer effective memory. TCN uses causal dilated convolution as the standard convolutional layer. Every two such convolutional layers and identity mapping are encapsulated as a residual module. Stacked by such modules, the complete fully convolutional deep network is built with convolution layer in the last few layers. Compared with TCN, TCAN introduces attention mechanism between convolutional layers, which can effectively integrate the features of historical and current moments. In general, TCAN is composed of causal dilated convolution, residual connection and temporal attention.

Causal Dilated Convolution. Causal convolution [20] can only perform operations on the input at the past moments, which is similar to masking the ordinary convolution operation by half. For the causal convolution in TCAN, it performs convolution operations on the previous layer's elements earlier to obtain the current layer's output at current moment. So it avoids information leakage from the future to the past. But it requires a large number of layers or a larger convolution kernel to widen the receptive field. A larger receptive field is necessary for the construction of long-term memory. If we do not expect to expand the receptive field through increasing the amount of calculation, we need to use the dilated convolution [20]. It can expand the receptive field by skipping part of the input, so that the convolution kernel can be applied to an area larger than its own length. Besides, the dilated convolution can avoid gradient disappearance, complex training and poor fitting effect problem caused by the increase of the convolutional layers' number.

Residual Connection. The residual connection is based on the nonlinear transformation. Specially, it introduces a short connection which applies the input directly to the output of the nonlinear layer [21]. It extracts important information from the shallow layer and migrates to the deep layer, thereby enhancing the feature expression of the shallow information. In this way, through multiple stacked residual modules in TCAN, the low-level feature of factors can be utilized. Note that the traditional three-factor model and four-factor model only use first-order features, which show the importance of shallow factor features in stock return prediction.

Temporal Attention. The essence of temporal attention is inspired by self-attention in transformer [22], but it is different from the conventional attention mechanism in terms of internal causality. The general self-attention mechanism uses information of all moments, including the past and future. But for time series data, we can only deal with past information. Its input at time t is a function of the previous layer's output $x[1:t]$, thus ensuring that information will not leak from the future to the past.

3.3   Fusion Model

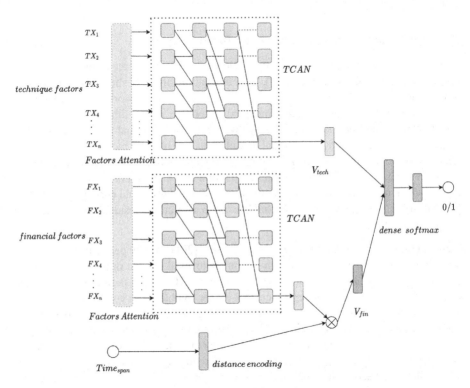

Fig. 2. Fusion model overview

As shown in Fig. 2, the fusion model combines **Factors Attention** (FA) and **Temporal Convolutional Attention-based Network** (TCAN), which is name as **Adaptive-Factors Temporal Convolutional Attention-based Network** (AF-TCAN). It has two channels: the technical factor channel and the financial factor channel, which deals with technical factors and financial factors respectively. At last, the two channels are merged and predict the final stock return rate jointly through the fully connected layer.

The input of the technical channel is $TX_i \in \mathbb{R}^{29}$, which represents the 29 technical factors of historical trading day i, where $i \in [1, 90]$. Then its deep representation embedding will be extracted by FA and TCAN. The input of the financial channel is

$FX_i \in \mathbb{R}^{10}$, which represents the 10 financial factors of historical financial report i, where $i \in [1, 4]$. As well, $Time_{span}$ needs to be sent to the financial channel, which represents the time interval between the latest financial report's release date and prediction date. It's used to deal with the difference of granularity between financial factors and technical factors. Similar with the position embedding in BERT [23], the $Time_{span}$ of financial factors obtains its distance embedding d through the distance encoding layer. The embedding d indicates the effectiveness of factors, which simulates that the delay of time will weaken the value of the information capacity. Then, it is applied to the financial embedding extracted by FA and TCAN to obtain the final financial factor embedding.

Considering the timeliness of stock return prediction in real life, people often refer to the factor value at the latest moment. In practice, the stock trend is indeed most affected by recent moments. As a result, the paper uses the output h_t at the last moment of TCAN as the feature embedding V of that factor category. The feature embeddings of two channels are V_{tech} and V_{fin} respectively. Next, they are concatenated and deep high-level feature extraction is performed through the fully connected layer. At last, the prediction result is obtained through the nonlinear *softmax* layer.

4   Experiments

4.1   Model Sample

This paper uses a total of 29 technical factors and 10 financial factors [18], as shown in Tables 1 and 2. They cover as much as possible all factors that have an impact on stock return in practice. Technical factors are mainly divided into seven categories: valuation factor, risk factor, overbought-oversold factor, volume factor, volume-price factor, energy-type factor and trend-type factor. Financial factors are mainly divided into four categories: share factor, profitability factor, capital structure factor and cash flow factor.

Table 1. 29 technical factors

Category	No.	Factor description
Valuation	1	PE
	2	PB
	3	PCF
Risk	4	20-day return variance
	5	20-day peak of stock earnings
	6	20-day positive return variance
	7	20-day loss variance
	8	20-day income-loss variance ratio

(continued)

Table 1. (*continued*)

Category	No.	Factor description
Overbought-oversold	9	Price momentum of last 5 days
	10	Price momentum of last 10 days
	11	Maximum daily return in the past month
	12	LN
	13	(Current price/average price of last month) - 1
	14	Price momentum difference
	15	Sustainable skewness in the past 20 days
Volume	16	5-day average turnover rate
	17	10-day average turnover rate
	18	Moving average of 6-day transaction amount
	19	Moving average of 20-day transaction amount
	20	Standard deviation of 6-day transaction amount
	21	Standard deviation of 20-day transaction amount
Quantity-price	22	Money flow
	23	WVAD 6-day average
Energy	24	AR
	25	BR
	26	CR
Trend	27	Arron-Up
	28	Arron-Down
	29	Arron-Osc

Table 2. 10 financial factors

Category	No.	Factor description
Share	1	Earnings per share
	2	Undistributed profit per share
	3	Net assets per share
	4	Capital reserve per share
	5	Basic earnings per share
Profitability	6	Return on net assets
Capital structure	7	Current assets ratio
	8	Gearing ratio
Cash flow	9	Net profit margin
	10	Net cash flow per share

Feature. The sample's feature X is composed of two major types of factors: technical factors and financial factors. We select 29 technical factors of the latest 90 historical trading days to act as the technical part $X_{tech} \in \mathbb{R}^{90*29}$ of the sample, listed in Table 1 for details. There are 4 financial reports every year for each stock. We selected 10 representative financial factors of the latest 4 periods of financial reports to act as the financial part $X_{fin} \in \mathbb{R}^{4*10}$, listed in Table 2 for details. The time interval T_{span} between the latest the financial factors' release time and the current time is also calculated to simulate the effectiveness of financial factors. At last, the complete feature of the sample is $X = (X_{tech}, X_{fin}, T_{span})$.

Label. The sample's label y is obtained according to the rank place of the log cumulative return $\log_{return}$ of all stocks in the next 30 trading days. We sort all stocks according to their log cumulative return from high to low. The top 30% stocks are marked as positive labels, and the bottom 30% stocks are marked as negative labels.

$$y = \begin{cases} 1, & \text{if } \log_{return} \text{ in top } 30\% \\ 0, & \text{if } \log_{return} \text{ in bottom } 30\% \end{cases}$$

By rolling at the time interval of 30 trading days, the samples' feature and label are generated in the above way. The process is shown in Fig. 3.

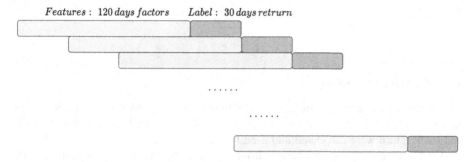

Fig. 3. How to make samples

4.2 Data Preprocessing

Remove Extreme Value. Note the sequence of factor i is f_i, the median of the sequence f_i is M_i , and M'_i is the median of the sequence $|f_i - M_i|$.

$$f_i = \begin{cases} M_i + 5 * M'_i, & \text{if } f_i > M_i + 5 * M'_i \\ M_i - 5 * M'_i, & \text{if } f_i < M_i - 5 * M'_i \end{cases}$$

Fill Missing Value. The missing value is reset to the average value of stocks in the same Shenwan industry. For the value $f_{i,k}$ of stock k and factor i, assuming that there are N stocks in the same industry and the factor value of individual stock j in the same industry is $f_{i,j}$.

$$f_{i,k} = \begin{cases} f_{i,k}, & \text{if } f_{i,k} \neq None \\ \frac{\sum f_{i,j}}{N}, & \text{if } f_{i,k} = None \end{cases}$$

Industry-Market Value Neutralization. The process performs linear regression of the exposure sequence f_i on the industry dummy variable V^i and the market value M^i after taking the logarithm. Then take the residual ε obtained from the regression as the new factor exposure sequence $\tilde{f}_i$.

$$f_i = \log(M^i) + wV^i + \varepsilon$$

$$\tilde{f}_i = \varepsilon$$

Suppose there are n industries in total, and stock i belongs to industry k, then its industry dummy variable $V^i = (V_1^i, V_2^i, \ldots, V_n^i)$, where $V_j^i = \begin{cases} 1, & if\ j = k \\ 0, & if\ j \neq k \end{cases}$.

Standardization. The factor sequence is subtracted from its mean value μ, and then divided by its standard deviation σ, to obtain a new factor exposure sequence that approximates the normal distribution of $N(0, 1)$.

$$f_i = \frac{f_i - \mu}{\sigma}$$

4.3   Experimental Setting

The experiment was on the stock data of Chinese market, which was obtained from Juchao Information. According to the original data, technical factor, financial factor and stock return were calculated and used to generate samples of the stock prediction model. The time range of the dataset is from 2010 to 2019, in which the data from 2010 to 2018 is selected as the training dataset, and the data from 2018 to 2019 is used as the test dataset.

As for the backtesting experiment, its timeline is from 2018.6 to 2019.4. Every 30 trading days, we take a reposition for the portfolio. On relocation date, we select 8 stocks to buy in as our new portfolio and empty the old portfolio.

4.4   Results

Baselines. For comparison, the baselines chosen are LSTM, linear model and two-branch CNN model. The evaluation metrics are divided into two categories: model accuracy and backtesting risk indicators. Risk indicators include cumulative return, alpha, information ratio and max drawdown.

Model Accuracy Comparison. As shown in Table 3, the stock return prediction accuracy of our newly proposed model reaches 59.95%, which is significantly better than two-branch CNN model, LSTM and linear model. AF-TCAN is more effective in stock returns prediction.

Table 3. Accuracy

Method	Accuracy
Linear model	56.58%
LSTM	56.75%
Two-branch CNN	58.42%
AF-TCAN	**59.95%**

Backtesting Performance Comparison. According to the experimental setup, we carried out the backtesting experiment. We used the prediction results of the above four prediction models separately to select stocks and adjust the asset portfolio. The cumulative return rate was calculated during the period. As shown in Figs. 4, 5 and 6, from July 2018 to May 2019, the cumulative yield curve of AF-TCAN is generally better than other three models and HS-300. Specially, AF-TCAN performed better than the two branch CNN model at every moment throughout the backtesting period. Besides, except that the performance in the early period was more unstable than LSTM and linear model, our model's performance achieved overtake in the subsequent backtesting interval. And finally, the cumulative return of newly proposed AF-TCAN in the entire period is much higher than the other three models. At the same time, as shown in Table 4, our model also has certain advantages in other risk indicators. As a result, it has better investment effect, which risk is controlled when the income increases.

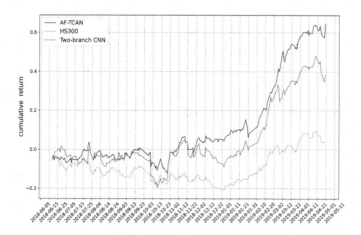

Fig. 4. The cumulative yield curve of AF-TCAN and two-branch CNN

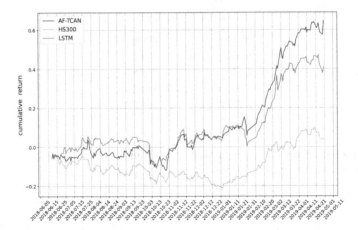

Fig. 5. The cumulative yield curve of AF-TCAN and LSTM

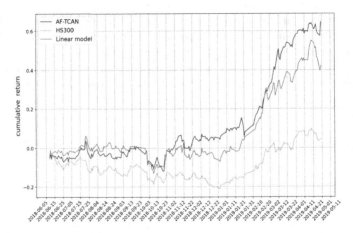

Fig. 6. The cumulative yield curve of AF-TCAN and linear model

Table 4. Backtesting risk indicators

Method	Cumulative return	Alpha	Information ratio	Max drawdown
Linear model	42.13%	44.61%	12.06%	230.93%
LSTM	41.02%	43.38%	13.60%	340.66%
Two-branch CNN	38.46%	40.22%	10.46%	**210.59%**
AF-TCAN	**64.61%**	**71.10%**	**21.14%**	269.74%

5   Conclusions

The study shows that our newly designed stock prediction model AF-TCAN has achieved remarkable results. Its accuracy on the evaluation set in this paper is significantly higher than two-branch CNN, LSTM and linear model, which indicates that our proposed model can more effectively predict the cumulative return of stocks in the future. In the backtesting experiment, the return of stock selection based on our model's prediction result was also better than other models. As a result, it confirmed the rationality and effectiveness of AF-TCAN proposed in this paper.

In the future, we will try to add news text data and explore the feasibility of news factors in stock prediction through modeling between news events and stock return. By integrating news-event model with the current model in this paper, we can use all these three types of factors at the same time. A key point of that plan is the authenticity and effectiveness of news used. There must be a reliable source of financial news in Chinese market. As well, we need to further clean the data to improve the factor's quality. In addition, exploring a more reasonable model structure is also a feasible optimization direction.

References

1. Abe, M., Nakagawa, K.: Deep learning for multi-factor models in regional and global stock markets. In: Sakamoto, M., Okazaki, N., Mineshima, K., Satoh, K. (eds.) JSAI-isAI 2019. LNCS (LNAI), vol. 12331, pp. 87–102. Springer, Cham (2020). https://doi.org/10.1007/978-3-030-58790-1_6
2. Nelson, D.M.Q., Pereira, A.C.M., de Oliveira, R.A.: Stock market's price movement prediction with LSTM neural networks. In: 2017 International joint conference on neural networks (IJCNN). IEEE (2017)
3. Jia, C., Pan, W.: Two branch risk factors model for stock prediction. ISEEIE (2021)
4. Hao, H., et al.: Temporal convolutional attention-based network for sequence modeling. arXiv preprint arXiv:2002.12530 (2020)
5. Bai, S., Zico Kolter, J., Koltun, V.: An empirical evaluation of generic convolutional and recurrent networks for sequence modeling. arXiv preprint arXiv:1803.01271 (2018)
6. Hochreiter, S., Schmidhuber, J.: Long short-term memory. Neural Comput. 9(8), 1735–1780 (1997)
7. Chung, J., et al.: Empirical evaluation of gated recurrent neural networks on sequence modeling. arXiv preprint arXiv:1412.3555 (2014)
8. Fama, E.F., French, K.R.: Common risk factors in the returns on stocks and bonds. J. Financ. Econ. 33(1), 3–56 (1993)
9. Carhart, M.M.: On persistence in mutual fund performance. J. Financ. 52(1), 57–82 (1997)
10. Fama, E.F., French, K.R.: A five-factor asset pricing model. J. Financ. Econ. 116(1), 1–22 (2015)
11. Harvey, C.R., Liu, Y., Zhu, H.: and the cross-section of expected returns. Rev. Finan. Stud. 29(1), 5–68 (2016)
12. Levin, A.U.: Stock selection via nonlinear multi-factor models. In: Proceedings of the 8th International Conference on Neural Information Processing Systems (1995)

13. Chen, J.: SVM application of financial time series forecasting using empirical technical indicators. In: 2010 International Conference on Information, Networking and Automation (ICINA), vol. 1. IEEE (2010)
14. Chen, K., Zhou, Y., Dai, F.: A LSTM-based method for stock returns prediction: a case study of China stock market. In: 2015 IEEE International Conference on Big Data (Big Data). IEEE (2015)
15. Cavalcante, R.C., et al.: Computational intelligence and financial markets: a survey and future directions. Expert Syst. Appl. **55**, 194–211 (2016)
16. Abe, M., Nakayama, H.: Deep learning for forecasting stock returns in the cross-section. In: Pacific-Asia Conference on Knowledge Discovery and Data Mining. Springer, Cham (2018)
17. Gao, T., Chai, Y.: Improving stock closing price prediction using recurrent neural network and technical indicators. Neural Comput. **30**(10), 2833–2854 (2018)
18. Feng, F., et al.: Enhancing stock movement prediction with adversarial training. arXiv preprint arXiv:1810.09936 (2018)
19. Qin, Y., et al.: A dual-stage attention-based recurrent neural network for time series prediction. arXiv preprint arXiv:1704.02971 (2017)
20. van den Aaron, O., et al.: WaveNet: a generative model for raw audio. arXiv preprint arXiv:1609.03499 (2016)
21. He, K., et al.: Deep residual learning for image recognition. In: Proceedings of the IEEE Conference on Computer Vision and Pattern Recognition (2016)
22. Ashish, V., et al.: Attention is all you need. arXiv preprint arXiv:1706.03762 (2017)
23. Devlin, J., et al.: BERT: pre-training of deep bidirectional transformers for language understanding. arXiv preprint arXiv:1810.04805 (2018)

Car First or Pedestrian First? Motion Prediction and Planning in Human-Robot Interactions

Xu Lian[✉]

Shenzhen Middle School, Shenzhen, China
lancelian8086@yeah.net

Abstract. As the demand for autonomous agents such as intelligent vehicles and robots' increases, effective and safe human-machine interaction must be ensured. Therefore, machines should be able to anticipate the motions of humans and solve appropriate schemes to achieve their goals. To accomplish this, a sequence of future positions must be generated according to some historical positions extracted from videos by the predictive neuron network, and the planning algorithm has to find and execute the best scheme in a limited window. In the paper, we propose to use a long-short-term-memory (LSTM) network for prediction and an A* algorithm to solve the planning problem. With these methods, we successfully combined these two parts and conducted simulations where autonomous cars have to reach targets efficiently while avoiding pedestrians in a safe manner. Besides, we compared our predictive models with other models on the UCY data-set. We also conducted experiments to compare the resulting paths with our prediction and those with naive and simple linear prediction. The result showed that our system can effectively generate safe and efficient future paths for autonomous vehicles.

Keywords: Human-robot interaction · Pedestrian trajectory · Motion planning · Long-short-term-memory network · A* search

1 Introduction

Nowadays, research about human-robot interaction is perpetually under the spotlight because of the emergence of complex artificial intelligence (AI). Researchers from all over the world have developed uncountable innovative inventions based on AI. For example, speaktoit assistants, such as Siri and Cortana, facilitate immediate information communication to the end-user; another instance is the introduction of intelligent robotics in industrial and manufacturing applications that improve efficiency and eliminate hazards. Autonomous driving belongs in this promising emergent domain studied by many researchers. Currently, autonomous vehicles remain plagued by limitations in performance, in particular, motion prediction, a necessary module to enable prophetic decision making. If we can develop a precise and effective prediction model, many new techniques will process significantly. For instance, autonomous vehicles need to get to the given destinations as soon as possible while avoiding potential hazards such as collisions with pedestrians and other vehicles. Without

© Springer Nature Singapore Pte Ltd. 2021
W. Cao et al. (Eds.): CONF-CDS 2021, CCIS 1513, pp. 105–129, 2021.
https://doi.org/10.1007/978-981-16-8885-0_10

predictions of the pedestrians' positions, the vehicle cannot decide how to behave next. Similarly, other service robots for household and industrial applications also need to be designed with the reduction of risk to people within its operational scope. Such prediction models are in severe demand in every situation where robots have to navigate themselves to goals in a human-occupied environment. By now, many studies have been conducted by researchers to address these problems, and while many models have been designed, this remains a significant challenge for researchers in autonomous guidance.

Beyond prediction models, motion planning is another crucial module for robots to make decisions. After predicting the positions of different kinds of obstacles, the vehicle has to decide on its acceleration and direction, which will further determine the motor power and the future positions of the vehicle. In this way, the car and pedestrians can interact actively and safely in the same environment.

In our study, we designed a long-short-term-memory (LSTM) [1] model for prediction, and we formulated the planning problem as a MDP [2] planning problem and designed an A* search algorithm for it. In addition, we connected these two models together and created a complete model to simulate a common situation where the car is asked to get the goal on a map with meandering pedestrians. To underscore the significance of the prediction, we compare the prediction results of our trained prediction model and a simple linear prediction which assumes the pedestrian will maintain the same velocity. In addition, we extended our comparisons to other existing models to find the advantages and drawbacks of our model on the public data set UCY [3]. (Fig. 1)

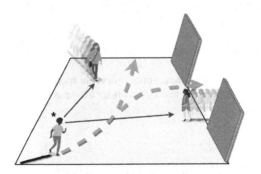

Fig. 1. Pedestrians trajectory prediction

2   Related Work

2.1   Prediction [4]

The software configurations of an intelligent vehicle can be generally summarized as three core components: perception, planning and control [5]. The perception module captures information presented in the environment such as positions, times, states, predictions, and sends it to other module in the system. The planning module employs the information gathered by perception to generate a full plan of actions toward the goals. Such a plan is passed to the controller module to be conducted, which translates the plan into commands for the devices on the vehicle while employing different methods to reduce the error. Therefore, the vehicle is incapable of operation in absence of any of these three elements.

Traditional Models. Before the wide adoption of deep learning in this field, the researchers' general conception was to formulate this question based on physics or sociology and calculate the future positions of the pedestrians with some specific rules that were derived by them. For instance, an easy model is to assume that pedestrians will keep their current velocities or accelerations during the following time steps [6]. It becomes immediately apparent that these linear models are too simple to perceive complex interactions among pedestrians. Comparatively, recent models were developed with the ability to take such interactions into account. The vanguard of these approaches, the social-force model which was conducted by helbing, uses concepts from sociology to construct a system able to formulate the behaviors of human beings [7]. It models the interaction between humans by two virtual forces: an attractive force and a repulsive force. They bring such two forces into the prediction of future trajectories. This model has been proven to be effective and competitive in a number of scenarios and datasets [3, 8]. Based on this idea, some impressive and elaborate modifications have been proposed by other researchers [9, 10]. Moreover, by further observing into this task, researchers extracted more key information that affected pedestrians' trajectories from videos and took these factors into consideration in the model, and a variety of innovative formulations have been constructed by them. For instance, tay used a gussian process [11] to solve such a problem; antonini proposed a discrete choice model for prediction [12]; rodriguez came up with a way to analyze crowded scenes from videos; other models derived by lisotto [13] can perceive both interaction among pedestrians and between pedestrians and other crucial objects or scene scale; some other researches [14–16] analyzed people's behaviors via finding out the goal of pedestrians; some other combined pedestrians with similar behavior into clusters and analyzed them as a group [17, 18]. Though such formulated models are quick to train and run, the formulas invented by researchers lack flexibility since there are so many factors that can affect pedestrians' decisions, so the prediction will be terrible if the actual situation has not been formulated by the models. As a result, the neuron networks with abundant weights might have better performance.

Deep Learning Method. On the other hand, rather than using derived formulation to solve the problem, the mainstream has turned to teaching computers to generate a data-based comprehension of the pedestrian trajectory. However, the conventional fully connected neuron network might not be appropriate for spatial-temporal signals because they cannot establish a sense of order and remember the information extracted from previous time steps. Therefore, the recurrent neuron network (RNN) models were proposed to handle this problem. It shows its superiority, but improvement is necessary. So the variants of RNN, long short term memory (LSTM) [4] and gated recurrent units (GRU) [19], were invented as a response and proved their great performance. These modified RNN have been widely adopted in natural language processing (NLP) [20], speech recognition [21], trend forecasts, and machine translation [22]. As they did before, in this challenging field, LSTM and GRU have inspired many new solutions with noble success. For instance, the sequence to sequence structure of LSTM has attained a relatively lower loss than many models [23]; the social LSTM [24], DAG-Net [25] and the social wagdat [26] model successfully set up connections among pedestrians to give the network chances to learn the relationship among agents; the ss-LSTM model [27] integrates the information from the scene and from the social reactions into the network; yagi [28] makes a prediction using first-person video data in order to take the ego-motions which can implicitly show intention of the people into consideration; shi, xiaodan's model [29] is also impressive because it accesses a way to deal with extremely crowded scenarios. These models all show different advantages when dealing with the public datasets [3, 8]. However, even though there are so many attempts to use deep learning in this task, sometimes the simplest constant velocity model can still outperform these complicated models [6], and it is much easier to train. Therefore, in the pedestrian's trajectory prediction problems, there are many different and competitive candidates and not a single "gold" approach exists that can handle all situations.

2.2 Planning [5]

The research of the motion planning module of robots is very popular with a long history. To meet the requirement for navigation in flexible real-life scenarios, the planning module is indispensable for both robots and automated vehicles because they both need to navigate in the flexible real-life scenes and complete their assigned tasks. The basic meaning of motion planning is to make decisions by the information that perception has captured, such as the positions of roads, other cars and pedestrians (what we study in this research). According to this framework, researchers have come up with a large amount of ideas and algorithms during the last few decades. These researches can be categorized into several groups; some of them are so classical models to the degree that a few examples were invented before the advent of computers, while some other algorithms are creative and impressive. Some groups of solutions are introduced below:

Graph Search Planning. The general idea of this branch is to find a series of future states in the state space for the vehicle by searches or other algorithms. When the robot executes along these planned states, it will get optimal reward. A classic example of this kind of algorithm is shown in Fig. 2, what the graph search algorithm does is to generate a search tree that consists of nodes of states based on such a graph; then the nodes in the trees are checked and evaluated until the goal, or final nodes, are met. The pioneer of these algorithms is the dijkstra algorithm [30–32], it can find a single-source shortest path. Inspired by this fundamental algorithm, many other algorithms emerged. DFS (Depth first search) [33] and BFS (Breadth first search) [34] are two simple instances. Then UCS (Uniform cost search) [35], which does BFS according to a cost function in order to reduce the nodes that need to be expanded and is able to make sure that the result is optimal, is implemented. The differences between UCS and BFS are shown in Fig. 3 and Fig. 4. The blue dots are the nodes in the search graph, and the red dots are the goal states. Moreover, extended from Dijkstra algorithm, A* [36] was invented. This search scheme is quicker than other existing methods because of the adoption of heuristics: this algorithm uses the sum of the past costs and the estimation of the distance to the goal as a criterion to find and evaluate the optimal path. Therefore, designing the cost function and heuristics is the most important and challenging task to perform such an algorithm. Across a long term of researching, differently designed variants of A* such as the anytime D* [37], the dynamic A* [36], the Theta* [38], and the field D* [39] were employed in automated robots and vehicles. However, though the graph search algorithms can find the best path with limited information, they also have obvious drawbacks: they plan the path in discrete nodes instead of a smooth track. In addition, they are also time-consuming when dealing with intricate situations because they need to expand and enumerate many nodes in the searching tree, while computational time is extremely crucial in automated driving that has to take reaction to the changes in the environment and replan a new path in a moment. In our work, we design a cost function and heuristics for the vehicle-pedestrian scene.

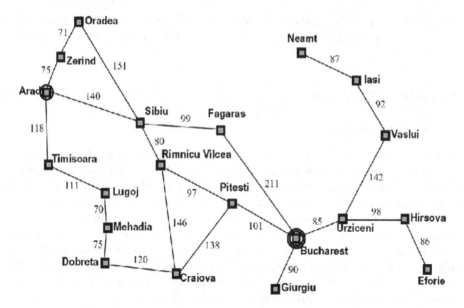

Fig. 2. Traveling in Romania—a classical example of Graph Search

Interpolating Curve Planning. The two approaches discussed above are generally recognized as global planners that can only generate approximate and discrete paths. To complete the solution, interpolating curve planning is applied. Interpolating means to insert data into the rough data given by global planners and output a smooth and continuous trajectory. The Computer-aided Geometric Design (CAGD) [40] is a fundamental technique in the application of this task. Researchers use different curves like clothoid curve [41, 42] and polynomial curve [43, 44] to fit the points and make the path smoother.

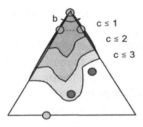

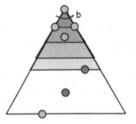

Fig. 3. The UCS search   Fig. 4. The BFS search

Interpolating Curve Planning. The two approaches discussed above are generally recognized as global planners that can only generate approximate and discrete paths. To complete the solution, interpolating curve planning is applied. Interpolating means to insert data into the rough data given by global planners and output a smooth and continuous trajectory. The Computer-aided Geometric Design (CAGD) [40] is a fundamental technique in the application of this task. Researchers use different curves like clothoid curve [41, 42] and polynomial curve [43, 44] to fit the points and make the path smoother.

3 Problem Statement

3.1 Overall Procedure

As Fig. 5 shows, to address the task of navigating, a robot has to be able to complete this looping procedure. At first, the camera that is deployed at the front of the robot captures information from the environment in the form of video. Then, through a Convolutional Neuron Network (CNN) [45], the robot perceives features of the environment such as the historical positions of pedestrians and other objects. This information is sent to the prediction model to predict future positions which are crucial to the planning algorithm. After the planning module has solved an optimal path for the robot, the controller is called to generate a sequence of power commands to the motors to move the robot by only one node of the path, and the rest of the path is abandoned. This is the principle of Model Predictive Control (MPC). This trick is conducted to ensure the planned path depends on true features since the features in the environment undergo constant change and more recent paths can generate more accurate predictions. Finally, when the robot has achieved the next state, factors in the environment, including pedestrians' positions and the robot itself, will change, so a recapture of the information is necessary. As this loop is running, the robot will gradually approach its goal until it achieves it. Our system is represented with the green block in Fig. 5, and it can convert the extracted positions of pedestrians into a proper path for the vehicle given the goal and other stable barriers in the environment.

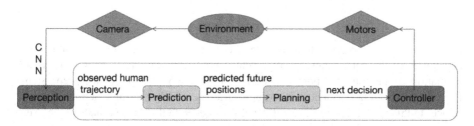

Fig. 5. The overall procedure of the system

3.2 Prediction

In the prediction module, a sequence of the historical positions is translated and read by a computer, and another sequence of predicted future positions returns. Therefore, what our prediction model does can be summarized with the following formula:

$$(\widehat{x},\widehat{y})_{t+1},(\widehat{x},\widehat{y})_{t+1}\cdots(\widehat{x},\widehat{y})_{t+T}=f\big((x,y)_{t-H+1},(x,y)_{t-H+2},\cdots(x,y)_t\big) \qquad (1)$$

Where the f (x) stands for the whole function of prediction; $(x,y)_t$ represents the predicted value of the x and y position at the time t; T is the time horizon the models will predict and H is the length of the historical sequence that is put into the network. Therefore, the prediction problem is a sequence-to-sequence prediction with input and output features of size 2 (x and y position).

3.3 Planning

We expect our robot to do the things shown in Fig. 6: to generate a sequence of actions that result in a path to the goal among different kinds of barriers. The orange dots are the prediction of pedestrians, while the orange lines represent the true paths. The blue line is the planned path of the vehicle, and the blue dots are the actual positions at each time step.

In the planning algorithm, since the next decision only depends on the current state of the agent and the predicted information, this problem can be considered as a Markov Decision Process (MDP) [5]. Thus, the state space and action space have to be defined. In this specific question, the state is actually the attributes of the robot in a certain situation, and our definition is that every state is a vector of size 5: t (current time step), x (x position), y (y position), v (the current velocity of the agent), d (the direction that the robot faces, measured in radians). As shown in the equation:

$$S = (t, x, y, v, d) \qquad (2)$$

On the other hand, the action space is the range of choices available to the robot given the current state to transform to the next state. By simplifying the robot as a point and considering about real scene when we drive, we know that the choice of path at a specific state is actually the choice of acceleration and turning angle. By taking these actions, the robot can reach any state in the state space. So, the action space is defined as follows.

$$a_s = (a, \theta) \tag{3}$$

Moreover, via the prediction module, the robot has received the predicted future trajectories of the pedestrians, we represent it with $(Xp, Yp)_{t+1:t+T}$, which means the estimation of pedestrians' positions during the following T (predicted step) steps. Therefore, we can design a cost function to evaluate whether a single action is a good choice. In this way, the algorithm will be able to generate the planned path step by step because we can update the current state with the chosen action without interference from the previous decisions, and the entire process can be represented by this formula.

$$(a_{t:t+T}, \delta_{t:t+T}) = argmin\left(C\left(S_t, S_{goal}, \widehat{(X_p, Y_p)}_{t+1:t+T}\right)\right) \tag{4}$$

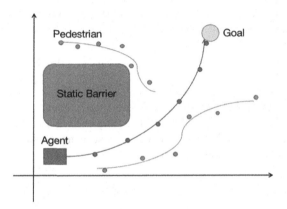

Fig. 6. The situation of our planning program

Where $a_{t:t+T}$ and $\delta_{t:t+T}$ is the planned accelerations and diversions (the action) of the agent in the following T time steps. T is the steps we want to plan (equal to our predicted output); C() is the cost function and St stands for the state of the agent at the time t (current time).

This formula means that the sequence of accelerations and diversions from the source toward the goal in a certain time period is determined by minimizing a cost function that judges and weighs different factors including the risk of colliding with pedestrians. More details regarding the design of the cost functions and the planning algorithm are given in the following sections.

4   Method

4.1   Heuristic and Cost Functions

The heuristic is just a simple estimation of how much work the agent need to do to achieve the goal. However, we should bear in mind a critical rule when designing a heuristic: the heuristics must be admissible and consistent if we want to guarantee the optimality of the path. Admissible and consistent: $\forall \left(H_i - H_j\right) \leq C_{ij}$.

Where H means the heuristic of node i and Cj represents the actual cost form node i to node j. As a result, the heuristic will never overestimate the actual distance and the A-score will never decrease along the expanded nodes. In this specific question, our heuristic is defining as:

$$H = \begin{cases} \infty(0 \times \text{ffff}) & (S \in ICS) \\ \\ W_H \times \left((x - x_{goal})^2 + (y - y_{goal})^2 \right) & (S \notin ICS) \end{cases} \tag{5}$$

Where W_H means a constant weight. We used the square of Euclidean Distance (the straight line distance) to the goal to estimate the cost because this measurement never overestimates the distance, so our algorithm can be optimal. Moreover, we also adopt a trick on H value to reduce the nodes that need to be expanded. We used a concept called Inevitable Collision State(ICS) [46, 47] the state that no matter what the vehicle decides to do, collision, or at least extremely close contact, is inevitable according to the current prediction. Therefore, if the current state is in ICS, we can feel free to set its H-value to a value that is close to infinity because will definitely not choose this path. This can prevent the search from further expanding unnecessary nodes.

Besides H value, G value is also crucial to finding the best path. Since it is the measurement of the total cost from origin to current states, we summarized several costs that the agent will face below and design our G function based on these rules:

- The speed of the vehicle should not be too much bigger than the speed limitation, because over-speeding is always illegal and can be a potential safety threat.
- The vehicles should accelerate or decelerate as minimally as possible, frequent changes of velocity will make passengers uncomfortable.
- Too frequent turnings are also unfriendly to passengers and may giddy them; in addition, more turnings can make the demand of the accuracy of the controller and the motors stricter.
- The vehicles should maintain distance from pedestrians as close contact is a potential risk for collision and the prediction model cannot be relied upon completely.
- In any situation, saving time while reducing potential hazards is the preferred outcome, so the planned path should be as short as possible to a time scale.

We designed G value as the sum of several functions which represent these costs with their weights. Concrete formulas are listed below accordingly (all W is the weight):

$$C_{vlim} = \begin{cases} 0 & v \leq v_{lim} \\ W_{vlim} \times (v - v_{lim})^2 & v > v_{lim} \end{cases} \tag{6}$$

Where v_{lim} stands for the speed limitation. This equation is easy to understand, if the car does not overspeed, the cost should be zero, and the car does have excessive velocity, the cost will increase at a square rate.

$$C_{acc} = W_{quareacc} \times a^2 \tag{7}$$

Where a is the acceleration that need to be executed to the state that is being evaluate.

$$C_{turn} = W_{turn} \times \theta^2 \tag{8}$$

Where 6 stands for the turning angle that need to be conducted to the next state.

$$C_{coll} = \sum_{i=1}^{i \le p} W_{coll} \times e^{-k*\left((x-x_i)^2 + (y-y_i)^2\right)} \tag{9}$$

Where k is another parameter that can make the curve less steep, and p is the number of pedestrians that the agent is able to detect; x_i and y_i are the predicted positions of pedestrians i at current time step. We use exponential function to describe this cost because this function increases at a high rate as x is close to zero, which can match our situation that extremely close distance is absolutely Forbidden.

$$C_{time} = W_{time} \times (\Delta t)^m \tag{10}$$

Where Δt is the time difference between the current state and the initial state. m is also a parameter and m This function increases rapidly at the beginning and then becomes gentle. This is because we want the agent to feel the urgency of the time at the beginning of the search, or it will choose to remain still as time lost is otherwise irrelevant to its decision-making.

By this definition and a time-consuming adjustment of weight, we have built a metric which helps our algorithm to search effectively. (Fig. 7)

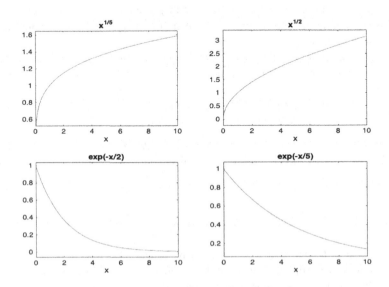

Fig. 7. The graphs of some example functions

4.2   Transitional Function

The algorithm requires a function to update the attributes of the current state after deciding the acceleration and diversion. In our situation, t, v, and d is easy to derive:

$$t_{i+1} = t_i + dt \tag{11}$$

$$v_{i+1} = v_i + a \tag{12}$$

$$d_{i+1} = d_i + \theta \tag{13}$$

Where d_t is the time of a time step, and we define a and θ as using the unit time steps. In addition, to make our model simpler and reduce the computational time, we assumed the car to be a mass point in our search, and the time that the car needs to turn its steering angle is ignored. Since then, the position of the next state after choosing the action has also become uncomplicated:

$$x_{t+1} = x_t + v_i * dt + \left(\frac{1}{2} a dt^2 * \cos(d + \theta) \right) \tag{14}$$

$$y_{t+1} = y_t + v_i * dt + \left(\frac{1}{2} a dt^2 * \sin(d + \theta) \right) \tag{15}$$

In this way, the transition between states is available.

4.3   Search Procedure

In our algorithm, we used Priority Queue [48] to store the fringe nodes and easily select the nodes with the lowest A-score. In addition, we also applied a dictionary to store the parents of the nodes and at the same time serve as a close list that store expanded nodes which should not be expanded again. The procedure of our A* algorithm is shown below, and it is also shown in Fig. 8.

Step 1: Put the origin into the Priority Queue with its A-score as priority.

Step 2: Take the state with the least priority out of the queue.

Step 3: If this node is already being expanded, skip and start from step 2.

Step 4: If the chosen state is a goal state or there is no prediction for the algorithm to continue (have search designed steps), save this node as skip to step 7.

Step 5: For every choice that the agent can take, generate the resulting state and its A-score, push all of them into the priority queue.

Step 6: Set the current state as the parent of all the generated states, return to step 2.

Step 7: Use the saved node to find back to the origin and get a path. update the origin to the first state of the path. If the origin is the goal, then our algorithm is done, but if not, we should re-predict pedestrians' trajectory, clear the queue and parent dictionary, and return to step 1.

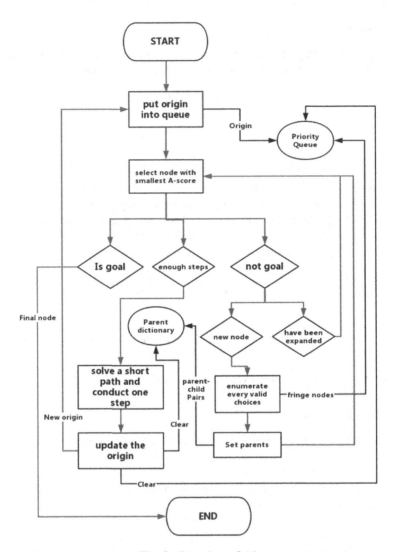

Fig. 8. Procedure of A*

Dataset. We use datasets that originate from two sources. First, we collected some videos of people's footage by drones. After that, we adopted CNN (convoluted neuron network) [45] to translate the videos into historical sequences of positional information. This dataset has a time step of 0.1 s. Moreover, we also utilized the data that has been published by the university of cyprus [3]. This dataset includes many sequences of pedestrians' trajectory, which is represented by positions. There is also a feature called the gaze direction, standing for the direction that pedestrians look. However, in order to maintain the same number of features with the previous dataset, we have abandoned this feature.

Training Configurations. In our training, we modified our hyper parameters for a long time in order to optimize the performance of our models. At last, we found a set of balanced hyper parameters which is listed below:

- Learing rate: 0.01
- Batch size: 25
- Train test validation data ratio: 7: 2: 1
- Epoch: 100
- Activation function: ReLU
- Loss function: MAE (Mean Square Error)
- Optimizer: Adam

With these hyper parameters, our models are able to achieve a relatively good performance and at the same time keep the computational time acceptable.

Prediction Performance. We trained and tested our model with the dataset collected by ourselves. We pre-processed the data and inputted it to our models. The visualizations of the prediction are shown below. The red lines are the historical path; the blue ones are the ground truth. Different colors of scatters represent the prediction by models. Yellow is the simple constant velocity model's, purple stands for our multistep prediction, while green means our feedback model (autoregressive model). These selected graphs are the typical cases that can represent the performance of our models.

In cases (1) and (2), all predictions from all models are precise to an acceptable standard. This is because the behaviors of the pedestrians in these cases are simple: they almost walk along a straight line. Therefore, the constant velocity model can also have acceptable performance (Figs. 9, 10, 11 and 12).

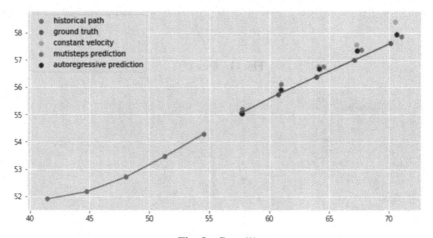

Fig. 9. Case (1)

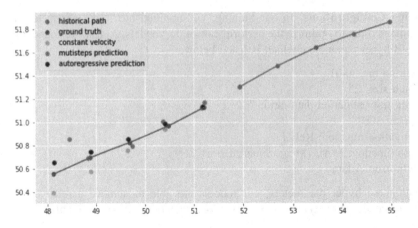

Fig. 10. Case (2)

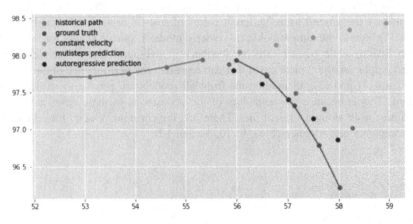

Fig. 11. Case (3)

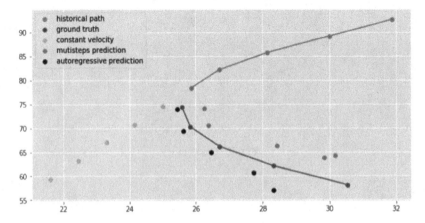

Fig. 12. Case (4)

However, case (3) and (4) show that the superiority of our prediction models is apparent. These two pedestrians suddenly turn right or turn back, and not unsurprisingly, the simple models have no ability to capture their tendencies to turn. However, both of our two models achieve that and generate an approximate prediction.

The judgment on the change of directions from the pedestrians is a far more crucial part than predicting the exact positions of them in autonomous driving since the car always deals with questions like whether the pedestrians will pass the intended path of the car instead of how far they will go. In addition, as pedestrians' speeds are significantly lower than those of cars, the value of error does not matter a lot when we try to decide which model we should use in our search model. As shown in cases (5), (6), (7) and (8), though the pedestrians occasionally behave in unexpected ways, our single-step model prediction successfully predicted the future direction while the other two methods get lost. Moreover, in case (9), the single-step model is also more accurate than the multi-steps model; this superiority indeed exists in the majority of our data-set. As a result, we decided to use the single-step model in our planning (Figs. 13, 14, 15, 16 and 17).

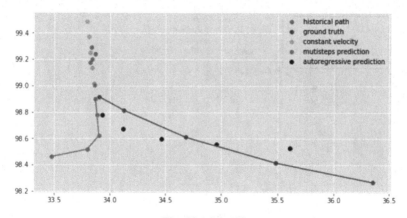

Fig. 13. Case (5)

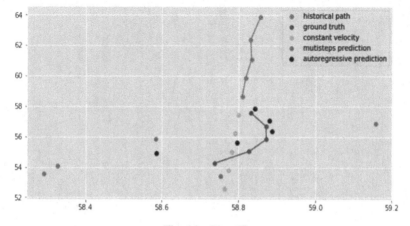

Fig. 14. Case (6)

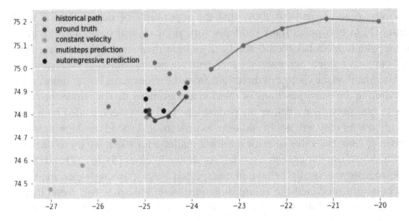

Fig. 15. Case (7)

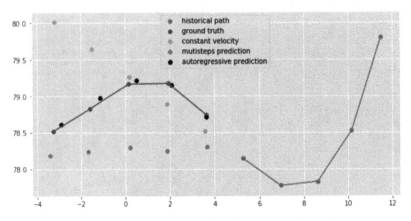

Fig. 16. Case (8)

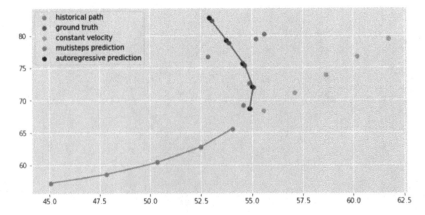

Fig. 17. Case (9)

However, our model still has many limitations. In cases (10) and (11), the pedestrians' behaviors are erratic. The first one takes a sharp turn and accelerates quickly; the second one waits and abruptly turns around. As a result, all of our attempts failed to comprehend such behaviors. This revealed one of our models' limitations that we can only predict a person's path with only his or her historical paths. Hence, it is impossible for our models to successfully take the reactions that he or she has because of other people or objects into account (Figs. 18 and 19).

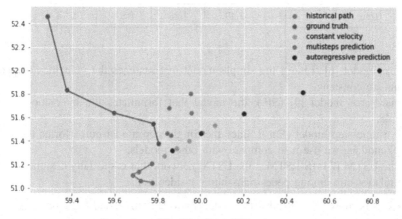

Fig. 18. Case (10)

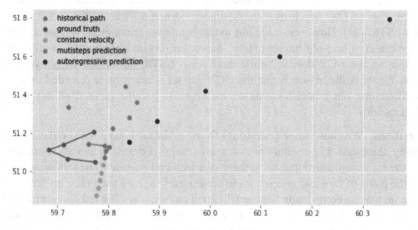

Fig. 19. Case (11)

Comparison Among Our Prediction Models and Other Models. In addition to testing the performance of our prediction model, we also evaluated the MAE (mean absolute error) and compared it to other models that list below.

Table 1. Data comparison among models

error (m) \ models data	Line.	SF.	Sin.	S-LSTM
Zara_1[3]	0.47	0.4	0.26	0.22
Zara_2[3]	0.45	0.4	0.25	0.25
UCY[3]	0.57	0.48	0.46	0.27
Total	1.49	1.28	0.97	0.74

- Linear model [6] (Line.): the simple model that assumes the velocities of pedestrians are constant.
- Social-Force model [9] (SF.): the model that formulates the interaction among people.
- Our Single-step model (Sin.): Since the Single-step model outperforms the multi-steps models, we use it to compare with other models.
- Social-LSTM [24] (S-LSTM.): the LSTM network that is specially designed to take the relationship among pedestrians into consideration.

The loss is shown in the following table. (Zara_1, Zara_2, and UCY datasets are all form University of Cyprus, as mentioned in the dataset subsection) (Table 1).

Unsurprisingly, the Linear model has the greatest error generation among these models; the Social-Force model is better, but it is still too inaccurate to be put into practice. Our LSTM, which uses the traditional structure, was a little worse than the Social-LSTM [24]. However, since our model has fewer parameters, it is an advantage that we can complete our training faster. Moreover, our model resulted in undesirable outcomes on the UCY data set while the Social- LSTM performed far above expectations. We think the reason is that the UCY dataset is much more crowded than other data. Therefore, our model loses its competitiveness because of its disability to learn the interactions.

Simulations. We chose some pedestrians from our data set and ran a simulation of our planning algorithm. In our situation, we used several pedestrians and static barriers to block the car as it planned its path to the goal which had been set. The following figures show the paths of cars and pedestrians in some cases, and we used the same color map in order to make a comparison between different paths easier. The red dot represents the goal, and the block in the red rectangle represents the static barrier. The 3D plot also displays the paths of pedestrians and the car, and the z-axis is time (higher means longer from the initial time).

On track (1), the car has to the pedestrians because of the existence of the static barrier. After turning, it accelerates toward the goal. As shown in Fig. 21, the speed of the car goes up without deceleration. In addition, in Fig. 22, the distances between the car and the pedestrians never become smaller than our predefined safety threshold (lower than 3 m) to cause the risk of collisions. As a result, though the path looks reckless, the car actually prioritized safety above time (Figs. 20 and 23).

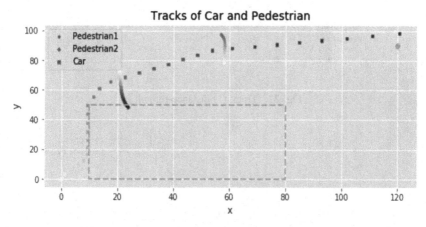

Fig. 20. Track (1)

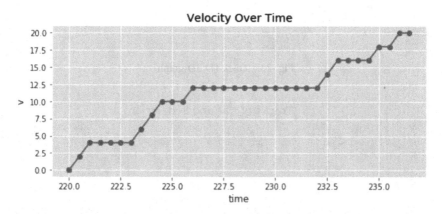

Fig. 21. Track (1) v-t graph

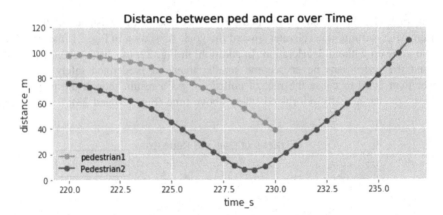

Fig. 22. Track (1) distance-t graph

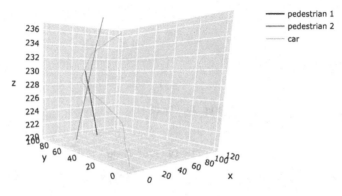

Fig. 23. Track (1) 3D graph

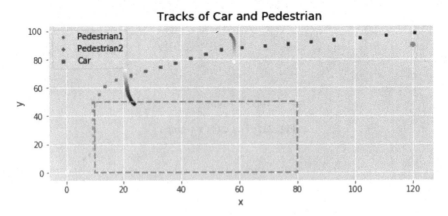

Fig. 24. Track (2)

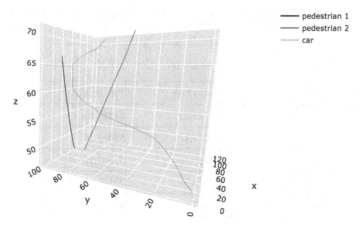

Fig. 25. Track (2) 3D graph

On the other hand, on track (2), as shown in Fig. 24, instead of driving straight to the goal, it chooses to stop and wait for the pedestrians in front of it to clear out. This decision reflects that the car had perceived the risk of collision. Therefore, our algorithm has the ability to answer the simple but crucial question—of who should go first, the car or the pedestrians? (Fig. 25).

Finally, to compare the algorithm's performance when different predictions are used to generate a path, we designed a metric function to evaluate how appropriate the paths are. This function consists of measurements of the paths from different dimensions, including the total distance the car travels, the risk of collisions between pedestrians and the car at every time step, etc. These functions are all added up with their weights. The expression of the metric is shown below:

$$M = W_{time}*t + W_{dist}*s + W_{acc}*\sum a_i^2 + W_{turn}*\sum d_i^2 + W_{coll}*\sum \sigma_i$$

Where different W stand for different weights and are different from those used for planning, t is the total time cost, s is the total distance. a_i and di are the accelerations and the turning angle at time $step_i$. a is the function to evaluate the risk of collision, defined by the following expression:

It is actually almost the same as the C_{coll} in the A* search. The only difference is that x_i and y_i stand for the true positions of pedestrians instead of predicted ones. Therefore, the metric can evaluate the true risk of the path (Table 2)

Apparently, the path generated by the LSTM prediction outperforms the others because in all of the cases tested, the cost metric of the paths with LSTM prediction is lower than those with simple prediction algorithms. Therefore, we can draw the conclusion that a more accurate prediction can indeed assist the planning algorithm in generating a better path.

Table 2. The metrics of planned paths with simple linear prediction and our LSTM prediction in some cases

metric prediction number	simple prediction	LSTM prediction
case1	234312.45	206205.87
case2	99528.83	81584.68
case3	56049.12	54463.79
case4	46537.16	43987.16
case5	74056.99	73593.43
Total	510484.55	459834.93

5   Conclusions

When an autonomous car meets a pedestrian at a crossing, should the car go first or the pedestrian? This problem has to be solved to approach our self-driving dream. Focusing on this problem, we use two LSTM models and A* to designed two modules that are indispensable to autonomous driving and robotic navigation: prediction and planning. Although these two parts have received significant coverage previously, by research, we effectively built a connection between these two sections on our algorithms. These experiments show that computers can generate optimal paths with positive outcomes. It also illustrates that these algorithms have a promising future. Admittedly, our methods are relatively easier than those recent researches have proposed. We did not take the interactions among pedestrians into account like what the mainstream of researches tries to do; we did not use the interpolation curve to make our path smooth rather than discrete. Nevertheless, we have proven that using a better scheme for prediction in motion planning matters a lot by combining and applying previous researchers' intelligence.

References

1. Hochreiter, S., Schmidhuber, J.: Long short-term memory. Neural Comput. **9**(8), 1735–1780 (1997)
2. Koenig, S., Simmons, R., et al.: Xavier: a robot navigation architecture based on partially observable markov decision process models. Artificial Intelligence Based Mobile Robotics: Case Studies of Successful Robot Systems, no. partially, pp. 91–122 (1998)
3. Lerner, A., Chrysanthou, Y., Lischinski, D.: Crowds by example, in Computer graphics forum, vol. 26, pp. 655–664, Wiley Online Library (2007)
4. Rudenko, A., Palmieri, L., Herman, M., Kitani, K.M., Gavrila, D.M., Arras, K.O.: Human motion trajectory prediction: a survey. Int. J. Robot. Res. **39**(8), 895–935 (2020)
5. González, D., Pérez, J., Milanés, V., Nashashibi, F.: A review of motion planning techniques for automated vehicles. IEEE Trans. Intell. Transp. Syst. **17**(4), 1135–1145 (2015)

6. Schöller, C., Aravantinos, V., Lay, F., Knoll, A.: What the constant velocity model can teach us about pedestrian motion prediction. IEEE Robot. Automation Letters **5**(2), 1696–1703 (2020)
7. Helbing, D., Molnar, P.: Social force model for pedestrian dynamics. Phys. Rev. E **51**(5), 4282 (1995)
8. Pellegrini, S., Ess, A., Schindler, K., Van Gool, L.: You'll never walk alone: modeling social behavior for multi-target tracking. In: 2009 IEEE 12th International Conference on Computer Vision, pp. 261–268, IEEE (2009)
9. Yamaguchi, K., Berg, A.C., Ortiz, L.E., Berg, T.L.: Who are you with and where are you going? In: CVPR 2011, pp. 1345–1352, IEEE (2011)
10. Pellegrini, S., Ess, A., Van Gool, L.: Improving data association by joint modeling of pedestrian trajectories and groupings. In: Daniilidis, K., Maragos, P., Paragios, N. (eds.) Computer Vision–ECCV 2010. ECCV 2010. Lecture Notes in Computer Science, vol. 6311. Springer, Heidelberg (2010). https://doi.org/10.1007/978-3-642-15549-9_33
11. Tay, M.K.C., Laugier, C.: Modelling smooth paths using gaussian processes. In: Laugier, C., Siegwart, R. (eds.) Field and Service Robotics. Springer Tracts in Advanced Robotics, vol. 42. Springer, Heidelberg (2008). https://doi.org/10.1007/978-3-540-75404-6_36
12. Antonini, G., Bierlaire, M., Weber, M.: Discrete choice models of pedestrian walking behavior. Transp. Res. Part B: Methodol. **40**(8), 667–687 (2006)
13. Lisotto, M., Coscia, P., Ballan, L.: Social and scene-aware trajectory prediction in crowded spaces. In: Proceedings of the IEEE International Conference on Computer Vision Workshops, p. 0 (2019)
14. Gong, H., Sim, J., Likhachev, M., Shi, J.: Multi-hypothesis motion planning for visual object tracking. In: 2011 International Conference on Computer Vision, pp. 619–626, IEEE (2011)
15. Huang, C., Wu, B., Nevatia, R.: Robust object tracking by hierarchical association of detection responses. In: Forsyth, D., Torr, P., Zisserman, A. (eds.) Computer Vision – ECCV 2008. ECCV 2008. Lecture Notes in Computer Science, vol. 5303. Springer, Heidelberg (2008). https://doi.org/10.1007/978-3-540-88688-4_58
16. Kretzschmar, H., Kuderer, M., Burgard, W.: Learning to predict trajectories of cooperatively navigating agents. In: 2014 IEEE International Conference on Robotics and Automation (ICRA), pp. 4015–4020 (2014)
17. Chandra, R., et al.: Forecasting trajectory and behavior of road-agents using spectral clustering in graphlstms. IEEE Robot. Automation Lett. **5**(3), 4882–4890 (2020)
18. Leal-Taixé, L., Pons-Moll, G., Rosenhahn, B.: Everybody needs somebody: modeling social and grouping behavior on a linear programming multiple people tracker. In: 2011 IEEE International Conference on Computer Vision Workshops (ICCV workshops), pp. 120–127, IEEE (2011)
19. Chung, J., Gulcehre, C., Cho, K., Bengio, Y.: Empirical evaluation of gated recurrent neural networks on sequence modeling (2014). arXiv preprint arXiv:1412.3555
20. Manning, C., Schutze, H.: Foundations of statistical natural language processing. MIT Press (1999)
21. Graves, A., Mohamed, A.-R., Hinton, G.: Speech recognition with deep recurrent neural networks. In: 2013 IEEE International Conference on Acoustics, Speech and Signal Processing, pp. 6645–6649, IEEE (2013)
22. Koehn, P.: Statistical machine translation. Cambridge University Press (2009)
23. Park, S.H., Kim, B., Kang, C.M., Chung, C.C., Choi, J.W.: Sequence-to-sequence prediction of vehicle trajectory via lstm encoder-decoder architecture. In: 2018 IEEE Intelligent Vehicles Symposium (IV), pp. 1672–1678, IEEE (2018)

24. Alahi, A., Goel, K., Ramanathan, V., Robicquet, A., Fei-Fei, L., Savarese, S.: Social lstm: human trajectory prediction in crowded spaces. In: Proceedings of the IEEE conference oncomputer vision and pattern recognition, pp. 961–971 (2016)

25. Monti, A., Bertugli, A., Calderara, S., Cucchiara, R.: Dagnet: double attentive graph neural network for trajectory forecasting (2020). arXiv preprint arXiv:2005.12661

26. Li, J., Ma, H., Zhang, Z., Tomizuka, M.: Social-wagdat: interaction-aware trajectory prediction via wasserstein graph double-attention network (2020). arXiv preprint arXiv: 2002.06241

27. Xue, H., Huynh, D.Q., Reynolds, M., Ss-lstm: a hierarchical lstm model for pedestrian trajectory prediction. In: 2018 IEEE Winter Conference on Applications of Computer Vision (WACV), pp. 1186–1194. IEEE (2018)

28. Yagi, T., Mangalam, K., Yonetani, R., Sato, Y.: Future person localization in first-person videos. In: Proceedings of the IEEE Conference on Computer Vision and Pattern Recognition, pp. 7593–7602 (2018)

29. Shi, X., Shao, X., Guo, Z., Wu, G., Zhang, H., Shibasaki, R.: Pedestrian trajectory prediction in extremely crowded scenarios. Sensors **19**(5), 1223 (2019)

30. LaValle, S.M.: Planning algorithms. Cambridge University Press (2006)

31. Hwang, J.Y., Kim, J.S., Lim, S.S., Park, K.H.: A fast path planning by path graph optimization. IEEE Trans. Syst. Man Cybern. Part A: Syst. Humans **33**(1), 121–129 (2003)

32. Li, Q., Zeng, Z., Yang, B., Zhang, T.: Hierarchical route planning based on taxi gps-trajectories. In: 2009 17th International Conference on Geoinformatics, pp. 1–5, IEEE (2009)

33. Tarjan, R.: Depth-first search and linear graph algorithms. SIAM J. Comput. **1**(2), 146–160 (1972)

34. Beamer, S., Asanovic, K., Patterson, D.: Directionoptimizing breadth-first search. In: SC'12: Proceedings of the International Conference on High Performance Computing, Networking, Storage and Analysis, pp. 1–10, IEEE (2012)

35. Felner, A.: Position paper: Dijkstra's algorithm vs. uniform cost search or a case against Dijkstra's algorithm (2011)

36. Stentz, A.: Optimal and efficient path planning for partially known environments. In: Hebert, M.H., Thorpe, C., Stentz, A. (eds.) Intelligent Unmanned Ground Vehicles. The Springer International Series in Engineering and Computer Science (Robotics: Vision, Manipulation and Sensors), vol. 388. Springer, MA (1997). https://doi.org/10.1007/978-1-4615-6325-9_11

37. Likhachev, M., Ferguson, D., Gordon, G., Stentz, A., Thrun, S.: Anytime search in dynamic graphs. Artif. Intell. **172**(14), 1613–1643 (2008)

38. Nash, A., Daniel, K., Koenig, S., Felner, A.: Theta^*: Anyangle path planning on grids. AAAI **7**, 1177–1183 (2007)

39. Ferguson, D., Stentz, A.: Using interpolation to improve path planning: the field d* algorithm. J. Field Robot. **23**(2), 79–101 (2006)

40. Farin, G.: Curves and surfaces for computer-aided geometric design: a practical guide. Elsevier (2014)

41. Brezak, M., Petrovic, I.: Real-time approximation of clothoids with bounded error for path planning applications. IEEE Trans. Rob. **30**(2), 507–515 (2013)

42. Fraichard, T., Scheuer, A.: From reeds and shepp's to continuous-curvature paths. IEEE Trans. Rob. **20**(6), 1025–1035 (2004)

43. Lee, J.-W., Litkouhi, B.: A unified framework of the automated lane centering/changing control for motion smoothness adaptation. In: 2012 15th International IEEE Conference on Intelligent Transportation Systems, pp. 282–287, IEEE (2012)

44. Petrov, P., Nashashibi, F.: Modeling and nonlinear adaptive control for autonomous vehicle overtaking. IEEE Trans. Intell. Transp. Syst. **15**(4), 1643–1656 (2014)

45. Lawrence, S., Giles, C.L., Tsoi, A.C., Back, A.D.: Face recognition: a convolutional neural-network approach. IEEE Trans. Neural Netw. **8**(1), 98–113 (1997)

46. Fraichard, T., Asama, H.: Inevitable collision states - a step towards safer robots? Adv. Robot. **18**(10), 1001–1024 (2004)

47. Martinez-Gomez, L., Fraichard, T.: An efficient and generic 2d inevitable collision state-checker. In: 2008 IEEE/RSJ International Conference on Intelligent Robots and Systems, pp. 234–241 (2008)

48. Slater, G.S.C., Birney, E.: Automated generation of heuristics for biological sequence comparison. BMC Bioinf. **6**(1), 31 (2005)

Application of Graphical Convolutional Networks to the Safety Assessment of Container Ship Voyages

Yinyin Peng[1($\boxtimes$)], Bin Tan[2], and Xiaoyong Bai[1]

[1] CSSC Marine Technology Co., LTD., Beijing, China
silversilverag@sina.com
[2] Systems Engineering Research Institute, Beijing, China

Abstract. As an important vehicle for maritime transport, container ship accidents may lead to heavy casualties and economic losses. Therefore, the voyage safety of container ships, especially in adverse weather conditions, has always been a particular concern of the water transport industry. With the development of big data technology and artificial intelligence, a number of solutions to complex safety assessment problems have gradually emerged. In this paper, the main influencing factors of container ship voyage safety are analysed in terms of both the marine environment and ship characteristics, and two evaluation indicators are proposed, which construct a safety assessment system for container ship voyage. Based on the previous research, this research innovatively adopts graph convolutional neural networks to design an assessment model for the voyage safety assessment of container ships. A set of historical data is applied to verify the validity of the model. Meanwhile, this method is compared with linear regression model and deep neural networks, which are two popular models for data regression.

Keywords: Container ship · Safety assessment · GCN

1 Introduction

With social progress and economic development, the shipping industry has become one of the most important industries in the world, supporting the trade between countries. Among them, the maritime container transport industry undertakes most of the cargo transportation, which has become the artery of global economic development.

The container ship originated in Britain, with a long, thin shape and a single deck. Cargo is assembled into units so that they can be loaded, unloaded and handled by large machinery or vehicles, thus achieving an efficient and effective transport. This approach greatly accelerates the terminal turnaround while reduces the operation expenses and transport costs. The following Fig. 1 gives an example of container ship loading diagram.

With the rapid development of the maritime transport industry, nowadays the container transport has spread to all the maritime countries in the world. At the same time, the safety of container ships gains more and more concerns. Due to the large windward area, in bad weather, the container ship is susceptible to the influence of

© Springer Nature Singapore Pte Ltd. 2021
W. Cao et al. (Eds.): CONF-CDS 2021, CCIS 1513, pp. 130–140, 2021.
https://doi.org/10.1007/978-981-16-8885-0_11

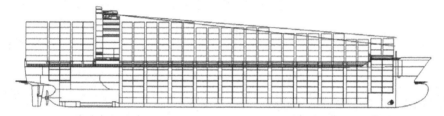

Fig. 1. The 3500 TEU container ship loading diagram for example

wind and waves, which may lead to the lashing loose of the container, or even fall into the sea. In severe cases, it may also cause ships to capsize, resulting in significant casualties and economic losses. Therefore, it is necessary to carry out a voyage safety assessment of container ships.

The United Kingdom is the first country to conduct ship safety assessment and put forward some practical measures and suggestions at the earliest [1]. NJUMO proposed an accident tree assessment method and applied it to ship maintenance [2]. AYHAN, et al. applied the fuzzy data analysis method to risk assessment of cargo ships [3]. Ren, Huilong et al. proposed more detailed solutions to some important problems in safety assessment by using data envelopment methods [4]. Wang Jin-hao et al. selected 400 fishing boat accident cases and divided them into multiple levels to use BP neural network algorithm to provide early warning of the risk level of fishing boat navigation safety, and the results are basically consistent with the actual accident status of fishing boats [5]. In recent years, improved BP neural networks, linear regression models and deep neural networks have also been used to perform safety assessment calculations with good results. These studies have played a positive role in promoting the ship safety evaluation.

2 Assessment Index System

2.1 Factors Affecting the Voyage Safety

When evaluating the safety of a voyage, the first step is to identify the influencing factors. It will be used as input to the calculation model and will influence the accuracy of the evaluation results. It is not possible to be exhaustive, but the main risk factors need to be found and made the focus. Therefore, this paper makes a necessary screening of the factors affecting ship safety.

In the container ship voyage safety assessment index system constructed in this paper, the influencing factors mainly include marine environment and ship characteristics (see Fig. 2) [6, 7].

In the process of sailing, ships are always accompanied by wind, waves and tidal waves, which are greatly affected by external natural conditions such as climate and sea conditions [8]. The environmental conditions of ship navigation mainly include sea meteorological environment conditions, sea geographical environment conditions, sea traffic environment conditions and sea information environment conditions [9]. This

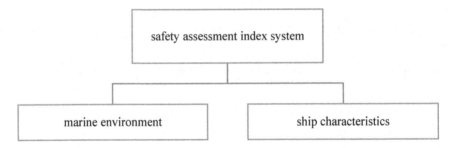

Fig. 2. The composition of safety assessment index system

paper studies the influence of wind, wave and visibility on the voyage safety of container ships. The strong winds acting on container ships can cause the ship to swing violently, and even capsize [10]. The waves will lead to a lot of resistance to the ship in motion, which will not only slow down the sailing speed, but also produce a series of heave shakes [11, 12]. In the case of strong winds and waves, it will result in hull tilt, deck water, hull structure damage and so on [13]. The following Fig. 3 gives an overview of the environmental influencing factors.

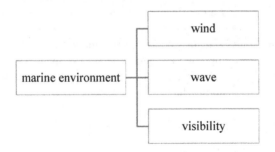

Fig. 3. The composition of environmental influencing factors

Ship characteristics which are closely related to the voyage safety mainly include the volume, tonnage, age, strength, unsinkability and sailing speed [14]. The influence of wind on ship safety is positively correlated with the ship volume above the water surface. The larger the tonnage, the greater the stability of the hull and the higher the risk of collision. With the increase of ship age, the failure rate increases sharply when the ship enters the period of loss and failure. At the same time, hull strength, unsinkability, speed and other factors also greatly affect the voyage safety. The following Fig. 4 gives a summary of all influencing factors.

In addition, operation errors by personnel are also an important factor in voyage safety. But due to the highly random nature, they are not included in this study.

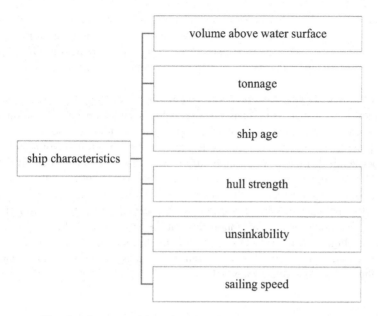

Fig. 4. The composition of environmental influencing factors

2.2 Evaluation Index of Voyage Safety

In order to make a more accurate assessment, two indicators, damage risk and collision risk, are selected in this paper to evaluate the voyage safety of container ships. Damage risk refers to the risk of hull structural damage, equipment electrical failure or even hull capsizing caused by swaying with wind and waves without any collision. Collision risk refers to the risk of the ship running on rocks or colliding with other vessels. The following Table 1 gives a summary of the indicators.

Table 1. Evaluation index

Index	Implication
Damage risk	Hull structural damage, equipment electrical failure, or hull capsizing
Collision risk	Ship running on rocks or colliding with other vessels

3 Method

Neural networks are part of the field of artificial intelligence, which can automatically learn features from large-scale data and generalize the results to unknown data of the same type [15].

Nowadays the most popular neural network is deep convolutional neural networks (CNNs) [16]. Graph convolutional networks (GCNs) are natural extension of convolutional neural network in graph field [17]. There are two main types of graph convolutional neural networks, one based on the spatial domain, the other based on the frequency domain. A GCN can learn the feature information and structure information of nodes end-to-end at the same time, which is the best choice for graph learning task at present. In the tasks such as node classification and edge prediction, GCNs greatly improve the accuracy of the results, which are far better than other methods in public data sets.

GCNs are widely applicable to nodes and graphs of any topology. At present, they have achieved great success in many research fields, such as: image recognition, image segmentation, natural language processing, speech recognition and so on [18].

The process of a GCN algorithm is described as follows. In Convolution Layer 1, every node sends its transformed feature information to its neighbor nodes. At the same time, it also aggregates the feature information of its neighbors for self-update. Then the information is processed by functions such as ReLU to increase the expressive power of the model. After that, the information is passed to the Convolution Layer 2 and ReLU functions for next operation. Repeat the process until the desired depth is reached (see Fig. 5). Similar to GNN, graph convolutional networks also have a local output function, which is used to transform node states (including hidden states and node features) into task-related labels [19].

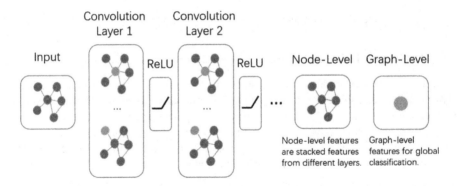

Fig. 5. The process of a GCN algorithm

Based on the above, in this paper, a graph convolutional neural network algorithm is used to evaluate navigation safety.

The adjacency matrix, denoted as A, generated by measuring the Euclidean distances across all the samples. Specifically,

$$a_{ij} = \begin{cases} 1 & if \left\| x_i - x_j \right\|_2 < T \\ 0 & otherwise \end{cases} \tag{1}$$

where $a_{ij} \in A$, x_i and x_j denote the i-th and the j-th sample in the dataset, respectively, and T is the threshold, which was set as 0.95 in this paper.

Once A is given, we create the corresponding graph Laplacian matrix L as follow:

$$L = D - A \tag{2}$$

where D is a diagonal matrix representing the degrees of A, i.e., $D_{i,i} = \sum_j A_{i,j}$ [20, 21]. For the purpose of improving the graph generalization quality [22], we define the symmetric normalized Laplacian matrix (L_{sym}) as:

$$L_{sym} = D^{-\frac{1}{2}}LD^{-\frac{1}{2}} = I - D^{-\frac{1}{2}}AD^{-\frac{1}{2}} \tag{3}$$

where I is the identify matrix.

f and g are defined as two functions. Then convolution of f and g can be expressed as

$$f(t) \star g(t) \triangleq \int_{-\infty}^{\infty} f(t)\, g(t - \tau)\, d\tau \tag{4}$$

where τ represents shifting distance and $\star$ represents convolution operator.

Based on the following theorems and lemma:

Theorem 1. The Fourier transform of the convolution of two functions f and g is equal to the product of their corresponding Fourier transforms.

$$F[f(t)\star g(t)] = F[f(t)] \cdot F[g(t)] \tag{5}$$

Theorem 2. The inverse Fourier transform ($\mathcal{F}^{-1}$) of the convolution of two functions f and g is equal to 2π the product of their corresponding inverse Fourier transforms.

$$\mathcal{F}^{-1}[f(t)\star g(t)] = 2\pi\mathcal{F}^{-1}[f(t)] \cdot \mathcal{F}^{-1}[g(t)] \tag{6}$$

Lemma 2. The basis functions of $\mathcal{F}$ can be equivalently represented by a set of eigenvectors of L.

Then, L can be decomposed as follows [23]:

$$L = U\Lambda U^{-1} = U\Lambda U^{T} \tag{7}$$

where $U = (u_1, u_2 \cdots u_n)$ represents the eigenvectors of L, which is the basis of $\mathcal{F}$. Therefore, the graph convolution can be written as:

$$\mathcal{G}[f\star g_\theta] \approx \sum_{k=0}^{K} \theta'_k T_k(\tilde{L})f \tag{8}$$

where $T_k(\bullet)$ is the Chebyshev polynomials of the variable $\bullet$, and θ'_k represents the Chebyshev coefficients.

By define $K = 1$ and limiting $\lambda_{\max}$ of L to 2 [17], the graph convolution can be transformed to

$$\mathcal{G}[f \star g_\theta] \approx \theta\left(I + D^{-\frac{1}{2}}AD^{-\frac{1}{2}}\right)f \tag{9}$$

According to the above formula, we can derivate the GCNs rule as follow:

$$H^{(\ell+1)} = h\left(\tilde{D}^{-\frac{1}{2}}\tilde{A}\tilde{D}^{-\frac{1}{2}}H^{(\ell)}W^{(\ell)} + b^{(\ell)}\right) \tag{10}$$

where $\tilde{A} = A + I$ is defined as the renormalization terms of A, and $D_{i,i} = \sum_j A_{i,j}$ represents the renormalization terms of D, to enhance network training stability. Besides, $H^{(\ell)}$ is the ℓth layer output and h($\cdot$) denotes the activation function in regard to the weights to-be-learned $\{W^{(\ell)}\}_{\ell=1}^{p}$ and the biases $\{b^{(\ell)}\}_{\ell=1}^{p}$ of the layers ($\ell = 1, 2, \cdots, p$) [24, 25].

4   Instance Verification

4.1   Data and Algorithm

In this paper, 213 groups of data are used as the experiment samples, from Clarkson Ship Database, Marine Accident Report, Accident Database and Other Resources.

50% of the 213 samples were randomly selected as the training data and the reminders were used as test data. All the data were l2-normalized via the feature dimension. The following Table 2 provides some examples.

Table 2. Partial sample data

Category	Factors	S1	S2	S3	S4	S5	S6	S7
Factors	Wind	3	4	5	6	7	9	10
	Wave	1	1	2	3	4	6	7
	Visibility	4	6	2	4	3	6	4
	Volume above water surface	0.5	0.7	0.7	0.7	0.7	0.5	0.5
	Tonnage	0.65	0.85	0.85	0.85	0.85	0.6	0.65
	Ship age	0.75	0.6	0.6	0.6	0.6	0.7	0.7
	Hull strength	0.7	0.8	0.8	0.8	0.8	0.7	0.7
	Unsinkability	0.5	0.6	0.6	0.6	0.6	0.55	0.55
	Sailing speed	0.6	0.8	0.7	0.7	0.7	0.6	0.6
Assessment	Damage risk	0.09	0.07	0.16	0.27	0.36	0.71	0.86
	Collision risk	0.2	0.11	0.63	0.36	0.58	0.64	0.86

We designed the GCN model with three embedding layers. The dimension of the input layer is 9, the same as the data dimension. The dimensions of the hidden layers are set the same as the input dimension, and the number of the output node is 2, which is used to predict the damage risk and collision risk, respectively.

4.2   Experimental Results

After completing the GCN training and testing, an ideal experiment result is presented.

The ground truth and the GCN model output of damage risk are compared in the form of graphs (see Fig. 6).

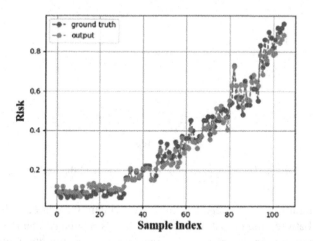

Fig. 6. The visualization of the ground truth and GCN model output for damage risk

The ground truth and the GCN model output of collision risk are compared in the form of graphs (see Fig. 7).

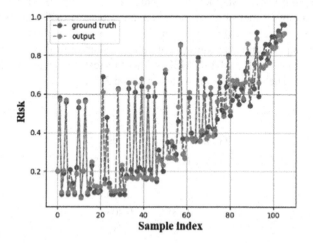

Fig. 7. The visualization of the ground truth and GCN model output for collision risk

The changing trend of the train loss and the test loss is shown in the Fig. 8.

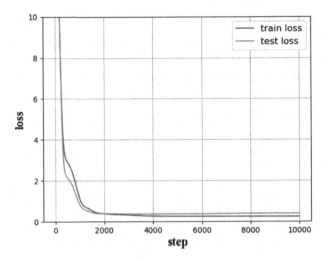

Fig. 8. The visualization of the train loss and the test loss

From the figure, it can be seen that in the experiment the degree of fitting is high, and the error between the output and the truth data is relatively small. Therefore, the GCN model proposed in this paper can be applied to evaluating the voyage safety of the container ship.

4.3 Comparison

This method has been compared with two popular models for data regression. The one is linear regression (LR). Another one is deep neural network (DNN), where the number of layers and dimensions of the layers are the same as the GCN model.

The mean square error (MSE) was applied as the loss function. The model was trained by 104 steps within the training data using Adam optimizer.

Finally, the mean value of the MSE of all the test data was employed as the evaluation metric. The results are presented in Table 3, which shows the advantages of GCN model.

Table 3. Comparison results

Methods	Train MSE	Test MSE
GCN	0.270	0.355
LR	0.650	0.579
DNN	0.235	0.403

5   Conclusion

In order to assess container ship voyage safety, this paper makes an analysis of the evaluation index and the influencing factors, which mainly include marine environment and ship characteristics. On that basis it proposes the assessment index system of container ship voyage safety. And then a graph convolutional network algorithm is put forward for assessment. To verify the validity of the model, a set of historical data is applied for the experiment. At the same time, the data is also applied to a linear regression model and a deep neural network for comparison. After training and testing, the result shows that the GCN model proposed in this paper presents good suitability for the voyage safety assessment, which has a lower MSE compared with the LR model and the DNN.

References

1. Fang, Q., Wang, J., Datubo, A.: FSA and its applications to the safety of ships. Navigation of China, (1), 1–5 (2004)
2. Njumo, D.A.: Fault Tree Analysis (FTA)-Formal Safety Assessment (FSA) in ship repair industry a made easy approach. Int. J. Maritime Eng. **55**(1), 23–32 (2013)
3. Ayhan, M., Hakan, A., Murat, Y., et al.: A FSA based fuzzy DEMATEL approach for risk assessment of cargo ships at coasts and open seas of Turkey. Saf. Sci. **79**, 1–10 (2015)
4. Jiao, J., Ren, H., Sun, S.: Assessment of surface ship-environment adaptability in seaways: a fuzzy comprehensive evaluation method. Int. Naval Arch. Ocean Eng. **8**(4), 344–359 (2016)
5. Wang, J., Li, X., Sun, Y., et al.: Application of BP neural network in fishing vessel navigation safety warning. Fishery Modern. **43**(01), 47–51 (2016)
6. Toffoli, A., Lefèvre, J.M., Bitner-Gregersen, E., et al.: Towards the identification of warning criteria: analysis of a ship accident database. Appl. Ocean Res. **27**(6), 281–291 (2015)
7. Bell, R., Kirtman, B.: Seasonal forecasting of winds, waves and currents in the North Pacific. J. Oper. Oceanogr. **11**, 11–26 (2018)
8. Cardone, V.J., Callahan, B.T., Chen, H., et al.: Global distribution and risk to shipping of very extreme sea states (VESS). Int. J. Climatol. **35**(1), 69–84 (2015)
9. Zhang, H., Shao, Z., Zeng, J.: Ship navigation safety risk assessment based on genetic algorithm and BP neural network. Sci. Res. Rev. **13**, 117 (2020)
10. Gyakum, J.R.: On the evolution of the QE II storm. I: synoptic aspects. Mon Weather Rev. **111**(6), 1137–1155 (1983)
11. France, W.N., Levadou, M., Treakle, T.W., et al.: An investigation of head-sea parametric rolling and its influence on container lashing systems. Mar. Technol. **40**(1), 1–19 (2003)
12. Quilfen, Y., Yurovskaya, M., Chapron, B., et al.: Storm waves focusing and steepening in the Agulhas current: sat- ellite observations and modeling. Remote Sens. Environ. **216**, 561–571 (2018)
13. Wu,H.: Analysis of factors affecting ship navigation safety. China Water Transport **5** (2006)
14. Luo, S., Ma, N., Hirakawa, Y.: Evaluation of resistance increase and speed loss of a ship in wind and waves. J. Ocean Eng. Sci. **1**(3), 212–218 (2016)
15. Klicpera, J., Bojchevski, A.,Günnemann, S.: Predict then propagate: graph neural networks met personalized PageRank. Proc. Int. Conf. Learn. Rep. New Orleans (2019)

16. Chen, Y., Jiang, H., Li, C., Jia, C., Ghamisi, P.: Deep feature extraction and classification of hyperspectral images based on convolutional neural networks, IEEE Trans. Geosci. Remote Sens., **54**(10), 6232–6251 (2016)

17. Kipf, T.N., Welling, M.: Semi-supervised classification with graph convolutional networks, arXiv:1609.02907. http://arxiv.org/abs/1609.02907 (2016)

18. Ying, R., He, R., Chen, K., et al.: Graph convolutional neural networks for web-scale recommender systems. In: Proceedings of the 24th ACM SIGKDD International Conference on Knowledge Discovery and Data Mining, pp. 974–983 (2018)

19. Scarseli, F., Gori, M., Tsoi, A.C., et al.: The graph neural network model. IEEE Trans. Neural Networks **20**(1), 61–80 (2009)

20. Henaf, M.,Bruna, J.,LeCun, Y.: Dep convolutional networks on graph-structured data. arXiv preprint arXiv:1506.05163 (2015)

21. Hong, D., Yokoya, N., Ge, N., Chanussot, J., Zhu, X.X.: Learnable manifold alignment (LeMA): a semi-supervised cross-modality learning framework for land cover and land use classification, ISPRS J. Photogram. Remote Sens., **147**, 193–205 (2019)

22. Xu, B., Shen, H., Cao, Q., et al.: Graph convolutional networks using heat kernel for semi-supervised learning. Proc. 28th Int. Joint Conf. Artif. Intell. (2019)

23. Xu, B., Shen, H., Cao, Q., et al.: Graph wavelet neural network. Proc. Int. Conf. Learn. Represent. New Orleans (2019)

24. Michalski, R.S.: A theory and methodology of inductive learning, Mach. Learn., vol. 110, pp. 83–134 (1983)

25. Zeng, H., Zhou, H., Srivastava, A., Kannan, R., Prasanna, V.: Graph SAINT: graph sampling based inductive learning method, arXiv:1907.04931. http://arxiv.org/abs/1907.04931 (2019)

Evaluation of Quantization Techniques for Deep Neural Networks

Zhiyuan Li[(✉)]

Australian National University, Canberra, ACT 0200, Australia
u6918167@anu.edu.au

Abstract. Over the last few years, different quantization techniques were proposed for Deep Neural Networks (DNNs). This paper makes an overview of some popular and efficient methods. The main purpose of quantization is to help DNNs' deployment on embedded system, and we divide techniques into two categories: Post-training Quantization and Quantization-aware training. In addition, we also compare the results of different methods on two representative networks in DNNs: Resnet and Mobilenet, and analyse some ablation study. Further more, the remaining questions and future direction are summarized to boost the development of quantization method.

Keywords: Quantization · Model compression · Software acceleration

1 Introduction

Deep learning has developed rapidly in the past decade with many applications in complicated challenges, such as speech natural language processing, automatic driving, robotics, cyber-physical systems, etc. However, the large-scale model brings strict requirement of computation intensity and memory accesses which may become a bottleneck for embedded system. This problem rises significant attention in recent years. Some researchers devote many efforts on efficient neural network architecture [1–3] to alleviate the hardware burden, while others try to solve the problem from the software perspective such as pruning [4,5] or quantization [6,7] techniques, etc.

Recently, deep neural network quantization techniques raise much interest with requirements of DNNs deployment on embedded systems. Quantization techniques [8] was proposed when convolution neural networks first appeared. In this decade, with the introduction of new ideas and algorithms, quantization techniques have developed rapidly.

With the development of DNN quantization technique, it empowers more extensive applications with many practical advantages, for example: (1)More suitable for embedded systems; (2)Higher energy efficiency; (3)Fewer memory accesses; (4)Faster computing speed. The above items are beneficial to efficient inference on embedded system. Usually, using 4–8 bit precision can achieve 2-8X speedup and about 20–50% energy saving [9,10]. However, there are many

© Springer Nature Singapore Pte Ltd. 2021
W. Cao et al. (Eds.): CONF-CDS 2021, CCIS 1513, pp. 141–157, 2021.
https://doi.org/10.1007/978-981-16-8885-0_12

pending problems in terms of quantization affecting accuracy and efficiency. For example, neural networks quantization would cause accuracy decrease because of information loss. It is difficult to keep a balance between accuracy and compression rate. Another serious problem comes from retraining. As the quantization process will generate integer which may cause gradient explosion in backward propagation. How to avoid it and getting retrained model is another problem worth thinking about.

According to the above, quantization can bring many benefits but also some problems. It is worthy to summarize and compare recent quantization methods, to guide software or hardware developers to flexibly serve their needs. The rest of paper is organized as follows: Sect. 2 introduces and classifies some mainstream DNNs quantization techniques. Section 3 compares and discusses the results of the mentioned quantization techniques. Conclusion and future work are elaborated in Sect. 4.

2   Model Optimization Techniques

A DNN model that runs efficiently on cloud GPU servers may not maintain the same speed on embedded devices. This might be caused by the significant computation intensity or memory access bandwidth. Therefore, quantization techniques are raised to reduce the storage burden and accelerate the inference. There are many different ways to quantize the DNNs. The schemes are mainly distinguished by the requirement by retraining. Quantization directly enforced on the pre-trained DNN models is called the Post-training Quantization (PTQ). Otherwise, it is called the Quantization-aware training (QAT).

For PTQ, it implements the quantification process on the pre-trained model without introducing retraining. Its advantages reside in its faster deployment and less restrictions compared with QAT.

QAT, as the name suggests, requires to retrain the network during the quantization process which can help the network parameters adapt to the information loss caused by the quantization. Compared to PTQ, it usually maintains relatively higher accuracy but introduces more limitations. In this section, we will elaborate the pros and cons of the two methods and present a thorough study on state-of-the-art work in the literature.

2.1   Post-training Quantization

PTQ is designed to find the best transition manner to shorten the accuracy loss between the vanilla float-point 32(FP32) parameters and lower precision fixed-point parameters(i.e. INT8, INT4, or even INT2). The transition can be described by the following equations:

$$r = S(q - Z)$$
$$q = round(\frac{r}{S} + Z)$$

(1)

where r is the FP32 value used in the vanilla model. q is the corresponding fixed-point value after quantization. S is the scale factor. Z represents the zero point. The purpose of PTQ is to find the best expression to describe the relationship between r and q without the correction from retraining.

The main factor hindering the development of PTQ technique is accuracy loss. According to Eq. (1), the round function will cause information loss in transition which cannot be corrected by retraining process. In this way, exploring PTQ has become a research on finding better mathematical algorithm to describe the conversion process. From this perspective, scientists have explored different ideas to reduce information loss.

Layer-wise Quantization. The most direct method realizing quantization is to do analytical clipping from layer-wise view. For example, Banner et al. [11] propose analytical clipping for integer quantization(ACIQ). The normal clipping function $clip(x, a)$ is defined as follows:

$$clip(x, a) = \begin{cases} x, & if |x| \leq a, \\ sign(x) \cdot a, & if |x| > a, \end{cases} \tag{2}$$

where a is the range number as the clipped tensor is set in the range $[-a, a]$. x is the parameter in tensor. Assuming the range $[-a, a]$ projected into a 2^M integer range where M represents the bit-width of fixed-point number, the quantization step δ between two adjacent values can be computed as following formula:

$$\delta = \frac{2a}{2^M} \tag{3}$$

According to the above equation, the authors assume parameters in tensor fits the Gaussian distribution as shown in Fig. 1. The midpoint $q_i = -a + (2i+1) \cdot \frac{\delta}{2}$ is chosen to represent all the values falling in range $[-a + i \cdot \delta, -a + (i+1) \cdot \delta]$ for every index $i \in [0, 2^M - 1]$. From the distribution image, the expected mean-square-error between original parameter X and its quantized value $Q(X)$ can be written as follows:

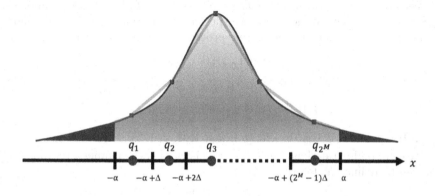

Fig. 1. Uniform quantization from Banner et al. [11]

$$E[(X - Q(X))^2] = \int_{-\infty}^{-a} f(x) \cdot (x + a)^2 dx + \sum_{i=0}^{2^M - 1} \int_{-a+i\delta}^{-a+(i+1)\delta} f(x) \cdot (x - q_i)^2 dx$$

$$+ \int_{a}^{\infty} f(x) \cdot (x - a)^2 dx$$

(4)

The equation can be simplified through quantization noise and clipping noise as the following equation:

$$E[(X - Q(X))^2] \approx 2 \cdot b^2 \cdot e^{-\frac{a}{b}} + \frac{a^2}{3 \cdot 2^{2M}}$$

(5)

where b is from the clipping noise for the case of $Laplace(0, b)$. The optimal clipping value a can be found by calculating derivative equals zero:

$$\frac{\partial E[(X - Q(X))^2]}{\partial a} = \frac{2a}{3 \cdot 2^{2M}} - 2be^{-\frac{a}{b}} = 0$$

(6)

Solve the above derivative equation with different M, the optimal value a^* is shown as follows:

$$a^* = 2.83b, \quad if M = 2$$
$$a^* = 3.89b, \quad if M = 3$$
$$a^* = 5.03b, \quad if M = 4$$

(7)

Kingma et al. [12] explore a local reparameterization technique which can be used for quantization. Banner et al. [13] prove quantized tensor can keep as much information as possible if angle of quantized tensor is close to original one. Migacz [14] uses the KL divergence algorithm to search the best clipping threshold for quantization.

Channel-wise Quantization. Nagel et al. [15] choose channel-wise perspective to realize data-free quantization achieving close-original model performance. The authors compile the range of per channel parameters, for example the first depthwise(DW) convolution layer in MobileNetV2 (see Fig. 2).

Assuming two layers in DNN are given as: $h = f(W^{(1)}x + b^{(1)})$ and $y = f(W^{(2)}h + b^{(2)})$. The authors propose the scaling diagonal matrix S to balance the range of each channel. The scaling process is shown as following equations:

$$y = f(W^{(2)}f(W^{(1)}x + b^{(1)}) + b^{(2)})$$
$$= f(W^{(2)}S\hat{f}(S^{-1}W^{(1)}x + S^{-1}b^{(1)}) + b^{(2)})$$
$$= f(\hat{W}^{(2)}\hat{f}(\hat{W}^{(1)}x + \hat{b}^{(1)}) + b(2))$$

(8)

where $\hat{W}^{(1)} = S^{-1}W^{(1)}; \hat{b}^{(1)} = S^{-1}b^{(1)};$ and $\hat{W}^{(2)} = W^{(2)}S$. The scaling channel theory can be illustrated as Fig. 3. The precision of each channel after quantization can be defined as follows:

$$p_i^{(1)} = \frac{r_i^{(1)}}{R^{(1)}}$$

(9)

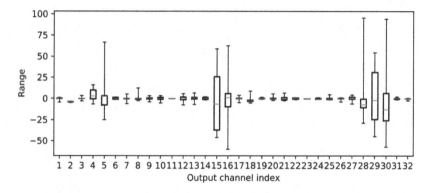

Fig. 2. Per-channel weight ranges of first DW layer in MobileNetV2 from Nagel et al. [15]. The image shows big difference between channel weight ranges which results information loss in quantization process.

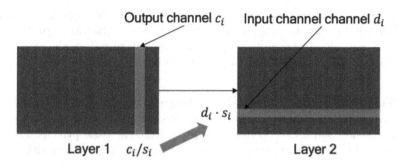

Fig. 3. Rescaling channel process by diagonal matrix S from Nagel et al. [15]

where $r_i^{(1)}$ is the quantization range of channel i in $\hat{W}^{(1)}$, $R^{(1)}$ is the total range of $\hat{W}^{(1)}$. The authors consider the convolution result of two layers instead of finding better algorithm on each layer. Through this way, the optimal question can be converted to find S which can maximize the total precision: $\max_S \sum_i p_i^{(1)} p_i^{(2)}$. where $p_i^{(1)}$ represents the precision of channel i in $\hat{W}^{(1)}$, $p_i^{(2)}$ represents the precision of channel i in $\hat{W}^{(2)}$. The S_i can be solved by given $argmax r_i^{(1)} r_i^{(2)}$ as following formula:

$$S_i = \frac{1}{r_i^{(1)}} \sqrt{r_i^{(1)} r_i^{(2)}} \tag{10}$$

The optimal result of Eq. (10) is $r_i^{(1)} = r_i^{(2)}$. It means channel ranges between two layers must be as close as possible. After cross-layer equalization, the range of per channel parameters of first DW convolution layer in MobileNetV2 is compiled as Fig. 4.

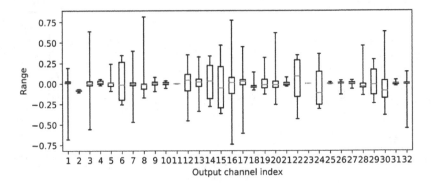

Fig. 4. Per-channel weight ranges of first DW layer in MobileNetV2 after cross-layer equalization from Nagel et al. [15]

Zhao et al. [16] consider the quantization from the view of outlier channel splitting (OCS) with halving channel values to solve the range problem. Lu et al. [17] use a joint convolutional residual network to reduce the overhead of Quantized channel state information (CSI) feedback.

Loss Function Based Quantization. Some experts try to solve accuracy loss question from more basic direction. They consider the loss degradation caused by quantization and try to optimize the result from the basic principle. Li et al. [18] raise dubbed BRECQ technique which pushes the limits of bitwidth in PTQ to INT2.

According to Nagel's idea [19], the effect of quantization on weights is equal to a special case pf weight disturbance. By using Taylor series expansions, the loss degradation caused by quantization can be expressed as follows:

$$E[L(W + \delta W)] - E[L(W)] \approx \delta W^T \bar{g}^{(W)} + \frac{1}{2}\delta W^T \bar{H}^{(W)} \delta W \qquad (11)$$

where $\bar{g}^{(W)} = E[\nabla_W L]$is the gradients; $\bar{H}^{(W)}$ is the hessian matrix; and δW is the weight disturbance. However, full Hessian requires large memory space for calculation to get the optimized result. It needs a special way to calculate it. The authors make two assumptions: Layers are mutual independent; The second order derivatives of activations is the constant diagonal matrix. In this way, Hessian matrix can be computed as following equation:

$$\frac{\partial^2 L}{\partial \theta_i \partial \theta_j} = \sum_{k=1}^{m} \frac{\partial L}{\partial Z_k^{(n)}} \cdot \frac{\partial^2 Z_k^{(n)}}{\partial \theta_i \partial \theta_j} + \sum_{k,l=1}^{m} \frac{\partial Z_k^{(n)}}{\partial \theta_i} \cdot \frac{\partial^2 L}{\partial Z_k^{(n)} \partial Z_l^{(n)}} \cdot \frac{\partial Z_l^{(n)}}{\partial \theta_j} \qquad (12)$$

where $z^{(n)} = f(\theta)$ is the neural network output. $\theta = vec[w^{(1),T}, W^{(2),T}, \cdots]$ is the weight. $L = L(f(\theta))$ is the loss function. As the pretrained model can be regarded as a local minimum, Hessian matrix is assumed as positive-semidefinite and can be converted into Gauss-Newton(GN) matrix:

$$H^{(\theta)} \approx G^{(\theta)} = J_{Z^{(n)}}(\theta)^T H^{Z^{(n)}} J_{Z^{(n)}}(\theta) \tag{13}$$

where $J_{Z^{(n)}}(\theta)$ represents Jacobian matrix form of the output in regard to the network parameters. In this way, quantization effect can be calculated as the product of disturbance. It can be computed through the change in network output $\delta Z^{(n)}$ by the first-order Taylor approximation as follows:

$$\delta Z^{(n)} = \hat{Z}^{(n)} - Z(n) \approx J_{Z^{(n)}}(\theta)\delta\theta \tag{14}$$

According to Eq. (14), it indicates a well-trained teacher model can be well quantized if the initialized student model has the minimized discrepancy. This idea can be realized through the reconstruction of network final output $Z^{(n)}$.

Ghamari et al. [20] consider the L_2 norm of the weight perturbation and add it into the final loss function. Nagel et al. [19] propose AdaRound algorithm which adapts to the training data and task loss.

Comprehensive Method Quantization Several authors do not just consider one method to reduce accuracy loss in quantization process. They just combine several techniques together to solve the problem. Banner et al. [21] combine three new techniques for post-training quantization and achieve very good result.

- Analytical Clipping for Integer Quantization(ACIQ): The authors propose a new way to restrict the range of activation. By analyzing the distribution of tensor through minimizing the mean-square-error measure, they can achieve optimal clipping value to do quantization. More details can be found in previous Layer-wise Quantization part.
- Per-channel bit allocation: The authors develop a bit allocation policy to help determine the optimal bit-width for each channel. The goal of per-channel bit allocation is to minimize the overall mean-square-error.
  The authors suppose the range $[-a_i, a_i]$ of channel i can be quantized by M_i bit precision. By considering Lagrangian equation with a quota of B quantization bins, the optimal question can be defined as following form:

$$\mathcal{L}(M_0, \cdots, M_n, \lambda) = \sum_i (2 \cdot b^2 \cdot e^{-\frac{a_i}{b}} + \frac{a_i^2}{3 \cdot 2^{2M_i}}) + \lambda(\sum_i 2^{M_i} - B) \tag{15}$$

Through simplification and computation, the M_i bit precision for channel i can be expressed as follows:

$$M_i = round(log_2(\frac{a_i^{\frac{2}{3}}}{\sum_i a_i^{\frac{2}{3}}} \cdot B)) \tag{16}$$

where a_i is the threshold of range for channel i. B is a quota of quantization intervals to all different channels.

- Bias-correction: The authors propose a simple way to eliminate the effect of an inherent bias in the mean and variance of weight in quantization process. Denoting the original weights of channel c as W_c and the quantized weights as W_c^q. The expectation and coefficient of error between them can be expressed as follows:

$$\mu_c = E(W_c) - E(W_c^q)$$
$$\xi_c = \frac{||W_c - E(W_c)||_2}{||W_c^q - E(W_c^q)||_2} \tag{17}$$

The compensation of W_c^q to eliminate the bias from W_c for each channel as following form:

$$w \leftarrow \xi_c(w + \mu_c), \quad \forall w \in W_c^q \tag{18}$$

where w is weight in W_c^q, $\xi_c(w + \mu_c)$ is the compensation.

Zhou et al. [22] combine weight partition and group-wise quantization to solve accuracy loss problem. Hubara et al. [23] group AdaQuant, Integer Programming, and Batch-norm tuning together to realize efficient quantization process.

2.2 Quantization-Aware Training

The quantization-aware training idea comes from the binary neural network [24,25] a few years ago. However, due to the integer weights and activation, it causes gradient explosion in the backward propagation. The breakthrough appears with idea of fake quantization in 2017. Jacob et al. [6] propose fake quantization to solve the problem of gradient explosion in retraining process. The author uses a quantization scheme to quantize most weights and activations into 8-bit integer. This method only applies integer arithmetic operations to quantized values. The basic operation is to map integers q to real numbers r as follows:

$$r = S(q - Z) \tag{19}$$

where q is quantized 8-bit integer; S is scale factor; and Z is the zero point. The quantization scheme is only implemented in the forward pass of retraining. The floating-point arithmetic operation allows forward pass to simulate quantized inference. After quantizing weights, they implement convolution with input. Activations are also quantized during inference at points. The range of activations depends on network input. It collects data during training and apply exponential moving averages to make parameters smoothing. For the back-propagation, it uses regular method where the floating point stores all weights and biases which can be used by a small number.

QAT, as the name suggests, is to retrain the network during quantization process. In this way, neural network parameters can adapt to the information loss caused by quantization. Exploring QAT becomes using different algorithm approaching loss function and developing corresponding method to reduce accuracy loss.

Value-aware Quantization. Park et al. [26] ropose a method named value-aware quantization(V-Quant) to realize 4-bit weights and activations. It deals with the problem that most of data concentrated in narrow areas reducing precision while other parameters concentrated in large areas with high precision.

Because quantization causes quality degradation in the training result, the novel technique named quantized activation back-propagation is proposed to prevent accuracy loss of training results. The authors define the weight update during backward propagation as following equation:

$$\Delta w_{ji} = \eta \delta_j y_i \qquad (20)$$

where Δw_{ji} is the weight update from neuron i to neuron j, and η is the learning rate, δ_j is local gradient of neuron j, and y_i is the activation of neuron i. According to Eq. (20), he quantization of activation will cause the perturbation of y_i. To reduce disturbance, the local gradient δ_j can be defined as follows:

$$\delta_j = \varphi'(v_j) \cdot (\Sigma_k \delta_k w_{kj}) \qquad (21)$$

where $\varphi'()$ is the derivate of activation function, v_j is the input of neuron j, and w_{kj} is the weight between neuron j and neuron k. According to Eq. (21), if ReLU activation function is used, $\varphi'(v_j) = 1$, the local gradient becomes independent from sum of activations.

In the paper, another innovation is to provide bit mask information, such as 1-bit memory cost for a neuron, to ReLU to obtain the neuron which back-propagates the error with quantization-induced zero. This is because back-propagate errors from quantization and ReLU activation function are required to achieve same back propagation as the full precision.

Tailor et al. [9] also focus on analysis of values from Graph neural networks(GNNs) and proposed method named Degree-Quant for GNNs quantization. Song et al. [27] raise a regularized learning method based target values determined for quantization aware training.

Loss-aware Quantization. The loss-aware weight quantization is proposed by Lu et al. [28]. The authors apply proximal Newton algorithm to solve the loss caused by quantization. In ternary weight network (TWN), weight is denoted as $w_l = a_l b_l$ where $a_l > 0$ and $b_l \in \{-1, 0, 1\}$. Given loss function l, the second order expansion of the object can be written by using proximal Newton method as follows:

$$\min_{\hat{w}^t} \nabla l(\hat{w}^t - \hat{w}^{t-1}) + \frac{1}{2}(\hat{w}^t - \hat{w}^{t-1})^T D^{t-1}(\hat{w}^t - \hat{w}^{t-1})$$
$$s.t. \quad \hat{w}^t = a_l^t b_l^t, a_l^t > 0, b_l^t \in Q^{n_1}, l = 1, \cdots, L \qquad (22)$$

where $D = diag([diag(D_1)^T, \cdots, diag(D_L)^T]^T)$, D^{t-1} is the estimate of the Hessian of l at $\hat{w}^{t-1}$, Q is the desired quantized value set. If $d_l^{t-1} \equiv diag(D_l^{t-1})$, the object can be written as:

$$\min_{\hat{w}^t} \frac{1}{2} \sum_{l=1}^{L} ||\hat{w}_l^t - w_l^t||^2_{D_l^{t-1}} \qquad (23)$$

where $w_l^t \equiv \hat{w}_l^{t-1} - \nabla l(\hat{w}_l^{t-1}) \oslash d_l^{t-1}$, $\oslash$ is element-wise division.

Therefore, each proximal Newton iteration could minimize the object and it consists of two steps:(1) Get w_l^t according to the gradient descent along $\nabla l(\hat{w}_l^{t-1})$; (2)Quantize w_l^t to $\hat{w}_l^t$ by using above equation. When $d_l(t-1)$ is large, which means the curvature is high. The loss is sensitive to the weight and terrorization error can be more penalized and vice versa.

Mishchenko et al. [29] develop a dynamic quantization from the perspective of cross-entropy loss. Cai et al. [30] combine the latency and training loss to improve accuracy during quantization-aware training.

Hessian-aware Quantization. Dong et al. [31] propose Hessian Aware Quantization (HAWQ) to solve the problem related to different precision for different layers. Mixed precision quantization is used to improve network model size and inference speed, which maintain relatively high precision compared with uniform quantization. However, it has difficulties in determining layers with different precisions and block-wise fine-tuning order. The authors raise a novel second-order quantization method is proposed to solve these problems.

After completing training, neural network has m blocks and each of them are consists of parameters and activations with floating point numbers. The quantization restricts such floating numbers to finite values, which can be described as follows:

$$Q(z) = q_j, \quad z \in (t_j, t_{j+1}] \tag{24}$$

where $(t_j, t_{j+1}]$ is real numbers, $j = 0, \cdots, 2^k - 1$, k is quantization bits, and z is either activation or weight. This function allows all values to map to q_j. Because uniform quantization function cannot promise all layers have the same floating point values distribution and quantization sensitivity, different quantization scheme and second-order information are used for various layers. To explore second-order information, the Hessian matrix can be calculated for each block where eigenvalues of the Hessian matrix can be used to measure sensitivity.

The authors calculate the eigenvalues of Hessian matrix of each block. They evaluate the multiplication of the Hessian matrix and a random vector. The equation is shown as below:

$$\frac{\partial(g_i^T v)}{\partial W_i} = \frac{\partial g_i^T}{\partial W_i} v + g_i^T \frac{\partial v}{\partial W_i} = H_i v \tag{25}$$

where H_i is the Hessian matrix of loss function L with W_i, g_i is the gradient of loss function L with i^{th} block parameters W_i, for a random vector $v = H_i v / ||H_i v||$.

Suppose the Hessian matrix is a block diagonal matrix, with top eigenvalue λ as $H_i \approx \lambda_{i=1}^m$. The below equation is used to sort blocks.

$$S_i = \frac{\lambda_i}{n_i} \tag{26}$$

According to the sorted descending results for S_i, layers with small number of parameters and large eigenvalues are quantized to higher bits, and vice versa. To recover performance affected by low precision quantization, Quantization-aware re-training of the neural network is required. The proposed method is to perform multi-stage fine-tuning. Different blocks are sorted by using below equation:

$$\Omega_i = \lambda_i ||Q(W_i) - W_i||_2^2 \tag{27}$$

where λ_i is Hessian eigenvalue, and $||Q(W_i) - W_i||_2^2$ is the L_2 norm of difference between quantized weight $Q(W_i)$ and W_i

Dong et al. [32] also improve a new algorithm(HAWQ-V2) from Hessian aware view to deal with three shortcomes: (1) a measure of sensitivity; (2) a requirement of manual selection; (3) short of mixed-precision activation quantization.

3 Comparison and Discussion

In order to compare the effects of different quantization method on neural networks, we choose two representative networks in DNNs: Resnet and Mobilenet for the results of quantization techniques on large and small models.

3.1 Large Model-Resnet

Resnet is proposed by He et al. [33] which uses residual learning to deal with degradation problem. Most authors will choose Resnet as a large model of DNNs to test quantization effect. The Table 1 compares the different quantization results on Resnet.

The Table 1 shows QAT techniques achieve better performance than PTQ on Large Models. The state-of-the-art QAT can realize 2-bit and 4-bit quantization for weight and activation perspectively. Lu et al. [28] propose loss-aware quantization which apply proximal Newton algorithm to solve the information loss problem caused by quantization. Dong et al. [32] introduce HAWQ-V2 method to deal with Hessian trace which helps compute sensitivity of bit precision. Both two teams think about the impact of quantization on the models from bottom logic, and find ways to improve techniques. These methods considering from the bottom solve the problem of information loss in the quantification process better than other methods.

3.2 Small Model-Resnet

Mobilenet is a lightweight neural network focused on mobile device raised by Howard et al. [2,34,35]. Mobilenet is another popular neural network chosen for testing quantization techniques (see Table 2)

The Table 2 illustrates the same quantization technique achieve worse performance on small model. Compared with large models, small models have worse robustness for quantization technique. Due to the fewer number of parameters in small networks, they are more sensitive to parameters changing.

Table 1. Different quantizatin techniques on Resnet

Authors	Weight/Activation	Model	Rate
Banner et al. [11]	4-bit/8-bit	Resnet-18	65.8%
	4-bit/8-bit	Resnet-50	71.45%
	4-bit/8-bit	Resnet-101	69.53%
Migacz [14]	8-bit/8-bit	Resnet-50	73.10%
	8-bit/8-bit	Resnet-101	74.40%
Nagel et al. [15]	8-bit/8-bit	Resnet-18	69.70%
	6-bit/6-bit	Resnet-18	66.30%
Zhao et al. [16]	5-bit/5-bit	Resnet-50	71.00%
	4-bit/4-bit	Resnet-50	66.20%
Li et al. [18]	4-bit/4-bit	Resnet-18	69.60%
	4-bit/4-bit	Resnet-50	75.05%
Nagel et al. [19]	4-bit/8-bit	Resnet-18	68.55%
	4-bit/8-bit	Resnet-50	75.01%
Ghamari et al. [20]	4-bit/4-bit	Resnet-50	70.10%
Zhou et al. [22]	5-bit/5-bit	Resnet-18	68.27%
	5-bit/5-bit	Resnet-50	74.81%
Hubara et al. [23]	4-bit/4-bit	Resnet-18	69.4%
	4-bit/4-bit	Resnet-50	71.7%
	4-bit/4-bit	Resnet-101	75.5%
Jacob et al. [6]	8-bit/8-bit	Resnet-50	74.9%
	8-bit/8-bit	Resnet-101	76.60%
Park et al. [26]	32-bit/4-bit	Resnet-50	75.88%
	32-bit/3-bit	Resnet-50	75.92%
	32-bit/2-bit	Resnet-50	75.64%
Lu et al. [28]	**2-bit/4-bit**	**Resnet-50**	**75.48%**
Dong et al. [31]	8-bit/8-bit	Resnet-18	69.34%
	3-bit(mixed)/8-bit	Resnet-18	68.02%
Dong et al. [32]	**2-bit(mixed)/4-bit(mixed)**	**Resnet-50**	**75.76%**

Table 2. Different quantizatin techniques on Mobilenet

Authors	Weight/Activation	Model	Rate
Nagel et al. [15]	8-bit/8-bit	MobilenetV2	71.20%
	8-bit/8-bit	MobilenetV1	70.50%
Li et al. [18]	4-bit/4-bit	MobilenetV2	66.57%
	2-bit/4-bit	MobilenetV2	53.34%
Nagel et al. [19]	**4-bit/8-bit**	**MobilenetV1**	**69.26%**
Ghamari et al. [20]	**4-bit/4-bit**	**MobilenetV1**	**68.20%**
Hubara et al. [23]	8-bit/8-bit	MobilenetV2	71.60%
Park et al. [26]	32-bit/8-bit	MobilenetV2	70.29%
	32-bit/3-bit	MobilenetV2	70.12%
Cai et al. [30]	8-bit/8-bit	MobilenetV2	67.40%

3.3   Ablation Study

Some authors also do ablation experiments on quantization techniques. Banner et al. [21] test four quantization methods combination: (1) ACIQ; (2) Bias-correction; (3) Per-channel bit allocation for weights; (4) Per-channel bit allocation for activations. The combined test results are shown in Fig. 5.

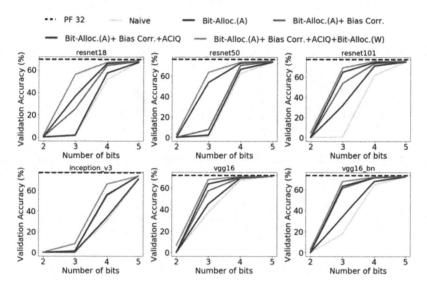

Fig. 5. An ablation test of different techniques on neural networks from Banner et al. [21]

According to Fig. 5, it seems every method contributes to the quantization process. Meanwhile, the validation accuracy has an obvious improvement between 3-bit and 4-bit. Banner's quantization method is more suitable on 4-bit precision.

Hubara et al. [23] do an ablation study on AdaQuant for ResNet50 over ImageNet to optimize the weights, biases, and other parameters combination compared with AdaRound coming from Nagel et al. [19].

The Fig. 6 shows AdaQuant method achieves better performance than AdaRound as it can quantilize paramters of each layer separately. Compared with AdaRound, AdaQuant relieves the restriction of weight changes from ±1 to the real need value because the authors argue that optimizing quantization parameters as well as weight values jointly can achieve better performance.

Tailor et al. [9] compare source of degradation at INT4. In the paper, the authors do a test on accuracy loss for single elements conversion from INT8 to INT4 (see Fig. 7).

The Post-Aggregation and Post-Bias are two most significant element causing performance degradation from 8-bit to 4-bit precision without DQ. Most element have modest effect on accuracy loss compared with INT8 model. In this way, DQ is very important when low bit-precision is required.

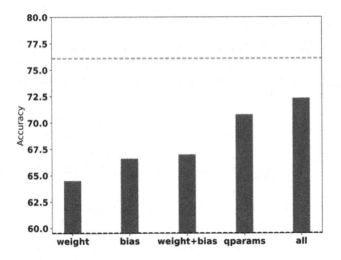

Fig. 6. An ablation study of quantization parameters combination [23]

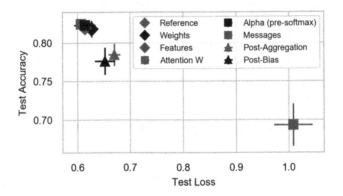

Fig. 7. An ablation study of single elements conversion from INT8 to INT4 [9]

4   Conclusion

In this paper, we have made an illustration on the review of development of quantization techniques. Quantization methods are divided into two main categories: Post-training quantization(PTQ) based on no-retraining and Quantization-aware training(QAT) based on retraining. All these methods push the limit of quantization into smaller bit-width weight and activation for faster inference.

However, there are still left many questions to explore in quantization field. To obtain a high accuracy, it is better to use larger bit-width weight and activation, but it also means lower model compression rate. How to keep a good balance between accuracy and compression rate is still a problem to explore. In another way, people need to explore better algorithm to realize low bit-width quantization with less information loss.

Another problem happens on the gap between PTQ and QAT. With some new technology used on PTQ, the difference between performance of PTQ and QAT becomes very small. However, compared with PTQ, QAT has many restrictions like training data set, time consumption and memory requirement. Since the performance between PTQ and QAT become small, whether QAT is still good choice?

To obtain better performance, it is also possible to combine quantization techniques with some hardware acceleration methods. Quantization is regard as a software model compression technique. If hardware acceleration methods can be added into experiments, it will be much easier to achieve higher compression rate and faster speed.

References

1. Iandola, F.N., Han, S., Moskewicz, M.W., Ashraf, K., Dally, W.J., Keutzer, K.: SqueezeNet: AlexNet-level accuracy with 50x fewer parameters and< 0.5 MB model size (2016). arXiv preprint arXiv:1602.07360
2. Howard, A.G., et al.: Mobilenets: efficient convolutional neural networks for mobile vision applications (2017). arXiv preprint arXiv:1704.04861
3. Zhang, X., Zhou, X., Lin, M., Sun, J.: Shufflenet: an extremely efficient convolutional neural network for mobile devices. In: Proceedings of the IEEE Conference on Computer Vision and Pattern Recognition, pp. 6848–6856 (2018)
4. Li, H., Kadav, A., Durdanovic, I., Samet, H., Graf, H.P.: Pruning filters for efficient convnets (2016). arXiv preprint arXiv:1608.08710
5. Molchanov, P., Tyree, S., Karras, T., Aila, T., Kautz, J.: Pruning convolutional neural networks for resource efficient inference (2016). arXiv:1611.06440
6. Jacob, B., et al.: Quantization and training of neural networks for efficient integer-arithmetic-only inference. In: Proceedings of the IEEE Conference on Computer Vision and Pattern Recognition, pp. 2704–2713 (2018)
7. Yin, P., Zhang, S., Qi, Y., Xin, J.: Quantization and training of low bit-width convolutional neural networks for object detection (2016). arXiv:1612.06052
8. Gray, R.M., Neuhoff, D.L.: IEEE Trans. Inf. Theory. Quantization **44**(6), 2325–2383 (1998)
9. Tailor, S.A., Fernandez-Marques, J., Lane, N.D.: Degree-quant: quantization-aware training for graph neural networks (2020). arXiv preprint arXiv:2008.05000
10. Nayak, P., Zhang, D., Chai, S.: Bit efficient quantization for deep neural networks (2019). arXiv preprint arXiv:1910.04877
11. Banner, R., Nahshan, Y., Hoffer, E., Soudry, D.: ACIQ: Analytical clipping for integer quantization of neural networks (2018)
12. Kingma, D.P., Salimans, T., Welling, M.: Variational dropout and the local reparameterization trick. Adv. Neural Inf. Process. Syst. **28**, 2575–2583 (2015)
13. Banner, R., Hubara, I., Hoffer, E., Soudry, D.: Scalable methods for 8-bit training of neural networks (2018). arXiv preprint arXiv:1805.11046
14. Migacz, S.: 8-bit inference with tensorrt. GPU Technol. Conf. **2**(4), 5 (2017)
15. Nagel, M., Baalen, M.V., Blankevoort, T., Welling, M.: Data-free quantization through weight equalization and bias correction. In: Proceedings of the IEEE/CVF International Conference on Computer Vision, pp. 1325–1334 (2019)

16. Zhao, R., Hu, Y., Dotzel, J., De Sa, C., Zhang, Z.: Improving neural network quantization without retraining using outlier channel splitting. In: International Conference on Machine Learning, pp. 7543–7552. PMLR (2019)
17. Lu, C., Xu, W., Jin, S., Wang, K.: Bit-level optimized neural network for multi-antenna channel quantization. IEEE Wireless Commun. Lett. **9**(1), 87–90 (2019)
18. Li, Y., et al.: BRECQ: Pushing the limit of post-training quantization by block reconstruction (2021). arXiv preprint arXiv:2102.05426
19. Nagel, M., Amjad, R.A., Van Baalen, M., Louizos, C., Blankevoort, T.: November. Up or down? adaptive rounding for post-training quantization. In: International Conference on Machine Learning, pp. 7197–7206. PMLR (2020)
20. Ghamari, S., et al.: Quantization-guided training for compact TinyML models (2021). arXiv preprint arXiv:2103.06231
21. Banner, R., Nahshan, Y., Hoffer, E., Soudry, D.: Post-training 4-bit quantization of convolution networks for rapid-deployment (2018). arXiv preprint arXiv:1810.05723
22. Zhou, A., Yao, A., Guo, Y., Xu, L., Chen, Y.: Incremental network quantization: towards lossless CNNs with low-precision weights (2017). arXiv preprint arXiv:1702.03044
23. Hubara, I., Nahshan, Y., Hanani, Y., Banner, R., Soudry, D.: Improving post training neural quantization: layer-wise calibration and integer programming (2020). arXiv preprint arXiv:2006.10518
24. Courbariaux, M., Bengio, Y., David, J.P.: Binaryconnect: training deep neural networks with binary weights during propagations. In: Advances in Neural Information Processing Systems, pp. 3123–3131 (2015)
25. Han, S., Mao, H., Dally, W.J.: Deep compression: compressing deep neural networks with pruning, trained quantization and Huffman coding (2015). arXiv preprint arXiv:1510.00149
26. Park, E., Yoo, S., Vajda, P.: Value-aware quantization for training and inference of neural networks. In: Proceedings of the European Conference on Computer Vision (ECCV), pp. 580–595 (2018)
27. Song, C., Liu, B., Wen, W., Li, H., Chen, Y.: A quantization-aware regularized learning method in multilevel memristor-based neuromorphic computing system. In: 2017 IEEE 6th Non-Volatile Memory Systems and Applications Symposium (NVMSA), pp. 1–6. IEEE (2017)
28. Hou, L., Kwok, J.T.: Loss-aware weight quantization of deep networks (2018). arXiv preprint arXiv:1802.08635
29. Mishchenko, Y., et al.: Low-bit quantization and quantization-aware training for small-footprint keyword spotting. In: 2019 18th IEEE International Conference on Machine Learning And Applications (ICMLA), pp. 706–711. IEEE (2019)
30. Cai, H., Wang, T., Wu, Z., Wang, K., Lin, J., Han, S.: On-device image classification with proxyless neural architecture search and quantization-aware fine-tuning. In: Proceedings of the IEEE/CVF International Conference on Computer Vision Workshops, pp. 0–0 (2019)
31. Dong, Z., Yao, Z., Gholami, A., Mahoney, M.W., Keutzer, K.: HAWQ: Hessian aware quantization of neural networks with mixed-precision. In: Proceedings of the IEEE/CVF International Conference on Computer Vision, pp. 293–302 (2019)
32. Dong, Z., et al.: HAWQ-v2: Hessian aware trace-weighted quantization of neural networks (2019). arXiv preprint arXiv:1911.03852
33. He, K., Zhang, X., Ren, S., Sun, J.: Deep residual learning for image recognition. In: Proceedings of the IEEE Conference on Computer Vision and Pattern Recognition, pp. 770–778 (2016)

34. Sandler, M., Howard, A., Zhu, M., Zhmoginov, A., Chen, L.C.: Mobilenetv 2: inverted residuals and linear bottlenecks. In: Proceedings of the IEEE Conference on Computer Vision and Pattern Recognition, pp. 4510–4520 (2018)
35. Howard, A., et al.: Searching for mobilenetv3. In: Proceedings of the IEEE/CVF International Conference on Computer Vision, pp. 1314–1324 (2019)

Multi-channel Relation Modeling for Session-Based Recommendation with Self-supervised Learning

Wei Wei[✉]

South China University of Technology, Guangzhou, China

Abstract. Recommender system plays an important role in industrial application, because it can handle the problem of information overload and provide users with content they are interested in. And session recommendation can help anonymous users without auxiliary information or historical interactions. However, previous methods only model a single data relationship. Ignoring the possible existence of chronological relationship, graph structured relationship and mutual relationship among session recommendation items may leads insufficient information mining and then reduces the effect of recommendation task. To handle this problem, we propose Multi-channel Relation Modeling Net, using three classical modules to fully mine information in the data. After that, we design multi-relation factorized pooling module to integrate multi-relation embedding. To get more informative embedding, we then use self-supervised learning to maximizing mutual information between relationships. Our method fully leverages the possible complex structure in the data, which has a certain practical significance in the specific application.

Keywords: Feature fusion · Graph neural network · Session-based recommendation · Self-supervised learning · Transformer

1 Introduction

Recommender system has made some progress in academic research and industrial application [1, 2]. NCF [3] uses neural network to model the double tower model of collaborative filtering, NGCF [4] introduces GCN to recommend and achieves excellent recommendation results. But general recommendation usually requires long-term user-item interaction data and auxiliary information. But in real recommendation scenarios, users are often anonymous and have no historical interaction [5–7].

To deal with these problems, session recommendation has been widely studied. In essence, session is a sequence of items. Hence the work like GRU4Rec [8], NARM [6] naturally introduce RNN. In recent years, GNN is widely used in the field of recommendation and SR-GNN [5], GCE-GNN [7] are works used GNN and got great result for session recommendation. SASRec [9], BERT4Rec [10] and TiSASRec [11] which use self-attention, having great effects in sequence recommendation. However, these models only focus on a single kind of data structure. Session recommendation data are not like the sequence in the strict sense of Natural Language Processing (NLP).

© Springer Nature Singapore Pte Ltd. 2021
W. Cao et al. (Eds.): CONF-CDS 2021, CCIS 1513, pp. 158–170, 2021.
https://doi.org/10.1007/978-981-16-8885-0_13

Chronological information, structured information, or mutual information between the two items in session may all exist in the data as Fig. 1. Only modeling a single relationship data may lose important information and this will affect the result of recommendation.

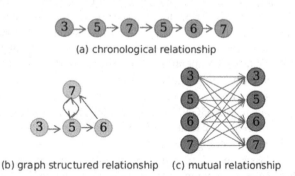

(a) chronological relationship

(b) graph structured relationship   (c) mutual relationship

Fig. 1. Three types of relationships in a session

In order to avoid the omit of information, we propose a model to model the above three relationships to ensure that valid information in the session data can be fully mined. In order to get the embedding of these three relationships, we use RNN, GNN, and Transformer [12] as feature extractor to fully mine the different relations between items. However, the recommendation task only needs a set of embedding. Therefore, we use Multi-model Factorized Billinear Pooling (MFB) [13] to fuse embedding and reasonably aggregate the three type of information.

It is worth noting that the three type of embedding represent the same set of session and item. In addition to exploring their respective differences, we should also pay attention to the common information. To this end, we regard three different embedding as different views, and introduce self-supervised learning by InfoNCE loss [14] to maximize mutual information among views. Finally, after fully mining the differences between data relations and the internal nature of the common, we will get more informative embedding for session recommendation task.

This paper is organized as follows: Sect. 2 describes the main modules, which mainly includes chronological relation modeling, structured relation modeling, mutual relation modeling, feature fusion and self-supervised learning. Section 3 analyzes the functions and advantages of the above main modules. Section 4 introduces the related work of session recommendation and feature fusion. Finally, in Sect. 5, we summarize the work of this paper and put forward the deficiency that need to be improved in the future.

2 Related Work

Session recommendation has applied many classical models in the process of research and development. RNN model is naturally for sequence modeling; Transformer model is excellent in NLP; GNN model is widely studied recently. Part of the work only uses one of them, and part of the work uses two of them in combination. Our work takes advantage of all them, and MFB module is used for the fusion of embedding.

GRU4Rec [8] is the first task to apply GRU to session recommendation. Before that, Markov decision process is the preferred technique to modeling item sequence [15–17]. NARM [6] uses the attention mechanism in GRU and it can capture the relationship between each item in the session and the user's intention [6].

SR-GNN [5] is the first work to introduce graph neural network into session recommendation, and it uses GGNN [18] to model graph structure. Compared with previous work, GCE-GNN [7] focuses on global graph and it uses local graph and global graph to learn embedding of session.

There is no classic model of using Transformer in session recommendation. However, in the sequence recommendation task which is similar to session recommendation, SASRec [9] and BERT4Rec [10] have become classic methods. SASRec is the first self-attention based sequential model. BERT4Rec [10] is a deep bidirectional sequential model and it uses cloze task to randomly mask the items in the sequence to learn the context information. There are other models of innovation based on self-attention, TiSASRec [11] uses the time stamp in the data to add the specific time interval information in the self-attention mechanism, so as to distinguish the relationship between items in the sequence.

The methods above use a single module learning embedding. Some recent methods are more complex in structure and try more combinations. GC-SAN [19] is a graph contextualized self-attention network and it models directed graph from session, and then uses graph neural network to learn item embedding, which contained local contextual information of sequences [19]. Next, it used the self-attention mechanism to learn the global dependence of distant position [19]. TailNet [20] uses GRU and self-attention at the same time. FGNN [21] uses designed GAT and GRU to learn the embedding of item and session respectively.

The simplest feature fusion method is concatenation and element-wise addition. But they are not enough to represent the complex relationship. To solve this problem, MCB [22] MCB uses the vector product of two representations to produce higher dimensional representations for quadratic expansion, and its performance is better than ordinary simple methods. However, MCB needs to maintain high dimension to ensure robust performance, so the limitation of GPU memory may limit its applicability. In order to overcome the problem that MCB occupies too much GPU memory, MLB [23] proposes that it uses Hadamard product and maps features to a lower rank common space. Because MLB can produce deep low rank embedding, it can achieve similar embedding as MCB. Moreover, it only uses fewer parameters. However, the experimental results show that MLB may converge too slowly.

3 Method

In this section, we introduce the proposed model of which is illustrated in Fig. 2. It is composed of three key components: 1) Shared Embedding layer is to mapping index to embedding. 2) Multi-relation learning module applies three modules to model chronological relation, structured relation and mutual relation separately and outputs respective embedding. Then, MFB is used to aggregate embedding. 3) Multi task training module sends embedding of model output to recommendation task and self supervision task respectively to calculating the predictive loss and maximizing mutual information.

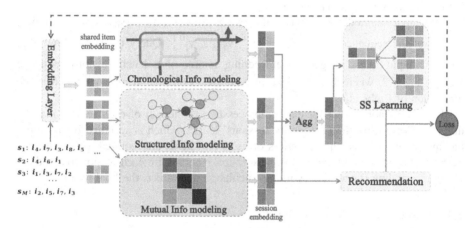

Fig. 2. The structure of model: The model consists of three parts: 1) Shared Embedding layer: Mainly changes the item of the input session into embedding. 2) Multi-relation learning module: Inputing the output of Embedding layer and get three type of the session embedding. 3) Multi-task training module: Joint self-supervised learning and recommendation task training. And then gradient descent, back propagation and update parameters.

3.1 Problem Setting

In session-based recommendation, giving $S = \{s_1, s_2, ..., s_M\}$ to represent the set of sessions in a data set and $\upsilon = \{v_1, v_2, ..., v_N\}$ to represent items in a platform. Each session is a sequence of item $S_i = \left\{ v_1^{(i)}, v_2^{(i)}, ..., v_t^{(i)} \right\}$ in successive order, where v is the selected item in the session S, and t is the length of S.

For a given session S, the task of session-based recommendation is to predict the next item $v_{t+1}^{(i)}$ that the anonymous user will be interested in.

3.2   Shared Embedding Layer

We use one-hot to encode the input of item ID. Then, using a linear fully connected layer without bias to turning a vector into a low dimensional embedding. For the item of the input i-th session $\left\{v_1^{(i)}, v_2^{(i)}, ..., v_t^{(i)}\right\}$, we obtain the embedding of node v_j by the following calculation:

$$e_{v_j} = v_j W_E \tag{1}$$

where $e_{v_j} \in \mathbb{R}^{1 \times d}$ and d is the dimension that the embedding need to transform to. v_j is the one-hot encode of item node. $W_E \in \mathbb{R}^{I \times d}$ is the parameter of linear transformation, I is the total amount of remapped items.

The input of model is a batch of sessions $S = \{s_1, s_2, ..., s_B\}$, each session is consist of the sequence of item $S_i = \left\{v_1^{(i)}, v_2^{(i)}, ..., v_l^{(i)}\right\}$. Query the embedding table with the input index to get the embedding matrix of a batch sessions sequence $E_{input} \in \mathbb{R}^{B \times L \times d}$, where B is the size of batch, L is the length of sequence, d is the dimension of Embedding.

It is worth noting that for data preprocessing, the length of each session may be different. We use padding 0 to unify sessions' length, which is specified by the super parameter. In addition, the subscripts of users and items are required to start from 1 because of padding 0. Moreover, we need to make a mask for each session to avoid the part with padding 0 participates in the calculation and affects the final result.

3.3   Chronological Relation Modeling

The chronological information modeling module uses the common GRU [24] to learn the embedding. Ordinary RNN has the problem of gradient disappearance and gradient explosion. Hidasi et al. [8] suggest that LSTM is not better than GRU in session recommendation task.

The input is the embedding of item in sessions $E_{input} \in \mathbb{R}^{B \times L \times d}$, then we get the output of last RNN cell $E_{GRU} \in \mathbb{R}^{L \times d}$, which is the embedding of a session.

GRU uses gating mechanism to control "input" and "memory" information, and makes prediction at the current time step. The hidden state of the GRU is a linear interpolation between the previous hidden state [1] and the candidate hidden state $\hat{h}_t$

$$h_t = (1 - Z_t)h_{t-1} + Z_t\hat{h}_{t-1} \tag{2}$$

where the update gate is given by:

$$z_t = \sigma(W_z e_t + U_z e_{t-1}) \tag{3}$$

while the candidate hidden layer is obtained by the following calculation:

$$\hat{h}_t = tanh(We_t + U(r_t \odot e_{t-1})) \tag{4}$$

The reset gate is used to calculate the candidate hidden layer is computed as:

$$r_t = \sigma(W_r e_t + U_r e_{t-1}) \tag{5}$$

where $e_t \in \mathbb{R}^{1 \times d}$ is the input of the cell at t time, and e_t is the embedding of the tth item. The final embedding of a single session is recorded as $e_{GRU} \in \mathbb{R}^{1 \times d}$, and the embedding matrix of a batch session is $E_{GRU} \in \mathbb{R}^{B \times d}$.

3.4   Structured Relation Modeling

Weighted Message Passing. Because the importance of neighbors is different, we use attention mechanism to learn weights between nodes. The weights are calculated by element-wise multiplication of two nodes' embedding, then multiplied by the dimension transformation matrix, and finally obtained after the activation function:

$$w_{ij} = PReLU\left(a_{r_{ij}}^T \left(e_{v_i} \odot e_{v_j}\right)\right) \tag{6}$$

where w_{ij} is the importance of node v_j to v_i, and we choose PReLU as activation function.

There are four types of edges in session graph. To take advantage of the information contained in edges, we maintain four kinds of weight vectors. Session graph is very small, and too many GNN layers will cause the oversmoothing [25] problem. Therefore, our session only transmits the information of first-order neighbors. For each node, the weights of all neighbors should be normalized:

$$\alpha_{ij} = \frac{exp\left(PReLU\left(a_{r_{ij}}^T \left(e_{v_i} \odot e_{v_j}\right)\right)\right)}{\sum_{v_k \in N_{v_i}^s} exp\left(PReLU\left(a_{r_{ik}}^T \left(e_{v_i} \odot e_{v_k}\right)\right)\right)} \tag{7}$$

where k is the kth neighbor of an item.

Item Embedding Learning. After getting embedding of session nodes. We obtain the learned item embedding by weighted sum:

$$e_{v_i}^s = \sum_{v_j \in N_{v_j}^s} \alpha_{ij} e_j \tag{8}$$

Session Embedding Learning. The embedding of a session is calculated by the embedding of all nodes in the session. Here, we use attention weight to sum up them. To better predict the users' next clicks, we will pay more attention to the embedding of the last node in a session when learning session embedding:

$$\alpha_i = q^T \sigma(W_1 e_n + W_2 e_i + b) \tag{9}$$

$$e_{GNN} = \sum_{i=1}^{n} \alpha_i V_i \tag{10}$$

where parameters $q \in \mathbb{R}^{1 \times d}$ and $W_1, W_2 \in \mathbb{R}^{d \times d}$ are linear transformation matrices. Finally, the embedding matrix for a batch of session is $E_{GNN} \in \mathbb{R}^{B \times d}$.

3.5 Mutual Relation Modeling

The Scaled Dot-product Attention. The scaled dot-product attention [26] is defined as:

$$Att(Q, K, V) = softmax\left(\frac{QK^T}{\sqrt{d}}\right) V \tag{11}$$

where Q represents the queries, K represents the keys and V represents the values. Intuitively, Att() first calculates the weight between all items. Then, each item is updated by weight sum all embedding. The scale factor $\sqrt{d}$ is to prevent the value from being too large due to inner product.

Self-Attention with Linear Complexity. We use three modules to learn embedding at the same time. Self-attention is low rank [27], in order to reduce the time and space consumption, we introduce linear self-attention [27] which projects the orthogonal dimension $L \times d$ to $S \times d$ first.

The self-attention operation takes $E_{input} \in \mathbb{R}^{B \times L \times d}$ as input, converts it to three matrices through the linear projections, and then feeds them into an attention layer:

$$E_{self-att} = Att\left(E_{input} W^Q, M E_{input} W^K, N E_{input} W^V\right) \tag{12}$$

where the projection matrices $W^Q, W^K, W^V \in \mathbb{R}^{d \times d}$, $M, N \in \mathbb{R}^{L \times S}$.

Point-Wise Feed-Forward Network. Self attention is essentially a linear model. In order to introduce nonlinear factors, we add two layers of fully connected layer after self attention to $E_{self-attetion}$:

$$E_{self-att} = ReLU\left(E_{self-att} W^{(1)} + b^{(1)}\right) W^{(2)} + b^{(2)} \tag{13}$$

where $W^{(1)}, W^{(2)} \in \mathbb{R}^{d \times d}$ matrices and $b^{(1)}, b^{(2)} \in \mathbb{R}^d$.

3.6 Multi-relation Factorized Pooling

We design Multi-relation Factorized Pooling (MFP) module to assembling multi-view embedding:

$$E_{1,2} = SumPooling\left(U_i^T E_1^\circ V_i^T E_2, k\right) \tag{14}$$

where $E_{1,2} \in \mathbb{R}^{d \times 1}$; $U = [U_1, .., U_d] \in \mathbb{R}^{m \times kd}$; $V = [V_1, .., V_d] \in \mathbb{R}^{n \times kd}$ respectively with simple reshape operations; d is the dimension of embedding. The function SumPooling(x, k) means using a one-dimensional non-overlapped window with the size k to perform sum pooling over x.

We combine $E_{GRU} \in \mathbb{R}^{B \times d}$, $E_{GNN} \in \mathbb{R}^{B \times d}$, $E_{self-attention}$ in pairs send into MFB and then implement sum pooling to get the output of the model $E_{output} \in \mathbb{R}^{B \times d}$.

3.7 Self-supervised Learning

Multi-relation learning module fully mined the information of different structural relationships in the data and obtained three type of features. Besides, we should also pay attention the common information. To this end, we adopt InfoNCE [14] loss, using the way of contrastive learning to maximize mutual information. The self-supervised training paradigm can also alleviates the problem of session data sparsity problem. In summary, self-supervised task can be used as an auxiliary task to improve the performance of the main recommendation task.

Self-supervised Signal. MRMS outputs three kinds of session embedding. These embedding essentially represent different views and they correspond to the same set of indexes. If two embedding represent the same index, they are positive sample pairs. The three type of embedding can do the same task in pair.

Contrastive Learning. Given three embedding matrices $E_{GRU} \in \mathbb{R}^{B \times d}$, $E_{GNN} \in \mathbb{R}^{B \times d}$, $E_{self-attention} \in \mathbb{R}^{B \times d}$. Combine them in pairs as different view pairs. For example, for each e_{GRU} in E_{GRU}, there are one corresponding e_{GNN}, $e_{self-attention}$ in E_{GNN} and $E_{self-attention}$ separately. By contraries, for each e_{GRU} in E_{GRU} there are $B - 1$ negative examples in E_{GNN} and $E_{self-attention}$, where B is batch size.

The loss function based on contrastive learning framework maximizes the mutual information of two views is computed as follow:

$$L_{SSL} = -log \frac{exp\left(sim\left(e_i, e_j\right)/\tau\right)}{\sum_{\tilde{e}_j \in E \backslash E_p} exp\left(sim\left(e_i, \tilde{e}_j\right)/\tau\right)} \tag{15}$$

where e_i, e_j have the same index and $e_i, \tilde{e}_j$ are different; τ denotes a temperature parameter for smoothing the result; sim is a similarity function, used to calculate the similarity of two embedding, which can be inner product or cosine similarity. Here we use inner product. $E \backslash E_p$ represents the set that removes positive examples.

3.8 Prediction Score and Loss Function

For recommended tasks, we use the embedding of the model output to calculate the prediction score $\hat{Z}_i$ for each candidate item in set. The classifier calculates the scores in the following way:

$$\hat{Z}_i = e_{output}^T e_{item_i} \tag{16}$$

then the softmax function is apply on the scores:

$$\hat{y} = softmax(\hat{y}) \tag{17}$$

We use cross-entropy as loss function:

$$L_{Rec}(\hat{y}) = -\sum_{i=1}^{m} y_i log(\hat{y}_i + (1 - y_i)log(1 - \hat{y}_i)) \tag{18}$$

where y denotes the one-hot encoding vector of the ground-truth item. Finally, BPR losses and SSL losses are combined by ratio to form the ultimate loss function, and the ratio is determined by the super-parameter:

$$L = \beta L_{Rec} + (1 - \beta)L_{SSL} \tag{19}$$

4 Analysis

In this section, we analyzed the advantages and functions of each important module mentioned above to show the reason for using them. Meanwhile, it is also important to choose the appropriate feature fusion mechanism to generate embedding for the final recommendation task.

4.1 Chronological Relation Module

The most classic model in the field of recommendation is matrix factorization [1]. It decomposes the interaction matrix of user item into the vectors of user and item, and then the inner product is used to fill the interaction matrix. However, due to the lack of user index and other user information, the ordinary matrix factorization is difficult to be applied to session based recommendation.

There are some similarities between session based recommendation task and NLP task. It is reasonable to introduce RNN model into session based recommendation. In the work of session recommendation using recurrent neural network, the first item of user interaction is taken as the initial input of RNN, and then gating and embedding are learned based on the input.

Specifically, we use GRU instead of ordinary RNN or LSTM. Because there is gradient disappearance or gradient explosion in ordinary RNN, and GRU4Rec [8] shows that LSTM is not better than GRU in session recommendation task. GRU has two gating functions: reset gate and update gate. Among them, update gate is the combination of input gate and forget gate. Meanwhile, it also combines cell state with hidden state. GRU has one less gate than LSTM, so it has less matrix multiplication.

4.2   Structured Relation Module

Some session work will learn the relationship between pairs of items serially and successively. They use recurrent neural network or memory network, like GRU4Rec [8] and NARM [6] and memory networks like STAMP [28].

However, these models are just learning about the single line, sequential relationships and may not be sufficient to capture the contexts information. In a session, users may be interested in multiple items, and there may be noisy data due to the randomness of user behavior, and thus the method of sequence model may not be enough to capture the information and relationship in session data correctly and comprehensively, which leads to the lack of complex order and migration in modeling, and then learn the defective embedding.

In order to extend the richness of node transfer and get more meaningful representation for session recommendation, we introduce directed graph from session data. Based on the session graph, GNN can capture more complex transfer relationships between items, modeling the high-order connectivity [4] and earning complex structural information, which is hard to learn from the ordinary work of the same task, like self-attention-based and RNN-based methods.

4.3   Mutual Relation Module

For session sequence modeling, most of the existing methods only focus on the sequence of items, and ignore the possible relationship between items in a session.

In NLP, transformer has achieved great success in machine translation and other tasks. Different from the ideas of recurrence and revolution, transformer uses the structure of encoder decoder to learn the global relationship. Among them, self attention mechanism is widely used in sequence data and has achieved good results, like machine translation [26], sentient analysis [29], sequence recommendation [9] and other tasks [19].

The main reason that transformer can achieve the effect is the self attention module, which can calculate the weights of all objects, and update the representation of each object by adding the weights. Compared with RNN, self attention has stronger ability to capture long-term dependencies, and can be calculated in parallel. Self attention mechanism can constrain the distance between any two positions in a sequence, which is conducive to the learning of session embedding.

4.4   Multi-relation Factorized Pooling

Through the design of the previous module, we fully model different structural information. And the three embedding are indeed the same session. If the embedding of different structural information can not be integrated reasonably and effectively, the next step of the model will be affected. Therefore, a key problem is how to effectively integrate the relevant information for the final recommendation task (Fig. 3).

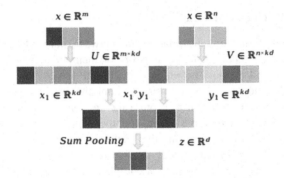

Fig. 3. 1) Mapping embedding to higher dimensions 2) Element wise multiplication in high dimensional space 3) The results of the previous step are divided into three parts: sum pooling

The embedding of multi-relation belongs to different views, and there is a gap between them, simple feature fusion operation like concatenation and element-wise addition are not enough to represent the complex relationship between different views.

For better fusion of different view embedding, we use MFB method. Inspired by the matrix decomposition method, MFB uses a mapping to transform the feature to low rank. The offset is included in the mapping.

Through the above analysis, the feature fusion module can effectively integrate the embedding of different views.

5   Summary

In this work, we found that the relationship modeling of session items is insufficient and propose a self-supervised multi-relation modeling net for session-based recommendation task which including modeling module of three relationships and MFP module to integrate multi-relation. Moreover, to deal with sparsity problem of session data and learn the commonness of different views, we add the self-supervised learning as auxiliary task. After that, we analyze the advantages of modeling multiple relationships and the necessity of using feature fusion module. The current work is only to combine the classical methods for multi-relation modeling. In the future, we will design more specific modules that meet the task scenario and have lower complexity.

References

1. Weimer, M., Karatzoglou, A., Le, Q.V., Smola, A.: Maximum margin matrix factorization for collaborative ranking. Adv. Neural Inf. Process. Syst. (2007)
2. Hamilton, W.L., Ying, R., Leskovec, J.: Inductive representation learning on large graphs. Adv. Neural Inf. Process. Syst. **2017**, 1025–1035 (2017)
3. He, X., Liao, L., Zhang, H., Nie, L., Hu, X., Chua, T.S.: Neural collaborative filtering. In: 26th International World Wide Web Conference, WWW 2017, pp. 173–182 (2017)

4. Wang, X., He, X., Wang, M., Feng, F., Chua, T.S. Neural graph collaborative filtering. In: Proceedings of the 42nd International ACM SIGIR Conference on Research and Development in Information Retrieval (SIGIR 2019), pp. 165–174 (2019)
5. Wu, S., Tang, Y., Zhu, Y., Wang, L., Xie, X., Tan, T.: Session-based recommendation with graph neural networks. In: AAAI, pp. 346–353 (2019)
6. Li, J., Ren, P., Chen, Z., Ren, Z., Lian, T., Ma, J.: Neural attentive session-based recommendation. pp. 1419–1428 (2017). https://arxiv.org/abs/1711.04725
7. Wang, Z., Wei, W., Cong, G., Li, X.L., Mao, X.L., Qiu, M.: Global context enhanced graph neural networks for session-based recommendation. In: Proceedings of the 43rd International ACM SIGIR Conference on Research and Development in Information Retrieval (SIGIR 2020), pp. 169–178 (2020)
8. Hidasi, B., Karatzoglou, A., Baltrunas, L., Tikk, D.: Session-based recommendations with recurrent neural networks. In: Proceedings of the 4th International Conference on Learning Representations (2016)
9. Kang, W.C., McAuley, J.: Self-attentive sequential recommendation. In: Proceedings of the IEEE International Conference on Data Mining, ICDM, November 2018, pp. 197–206 (2018)
10. Sun, F., Liu, J., Wu, J., Pei, C., Lin, X., Ou, W., Jiang, P.: Bert4rec: sequential recommendation with bidirectional encoder representations from transformer. In: Proceedings of the International Conference on Information and Knowledge Management, pp. 1441–1450 (2019)
11. Li, J., Wang, Y., McAuley, J.: Time interval aware self-attention for sequential recommendation. In: Proceedings of the 13th International Conference on Web Search and Data Mining (WSDM 2020), pp. 322–330 (2020)
12. Vaswani, A., et al.: Attention is all you need. Adv. Neural Inf. Process. Syst. **2017**, 5999–6009 (2017)
13. Yu, Z., Yu, J., Fan, J., Tao, D.: Multi-modal Factorized Bilinear Pooling with Co-attention Learning for Visual Question Answering Key Laboratory of Complex Systems Modeling and Simulation, ICCV (2017)
14. Oord, A.V.D., Li, Y., Vinyals, O.: Representation learning with contrastive predictive coding (2018). https://arxiv.org/abs/1807.03748
15. Shani, G., Heckerman, D., Brafman, R.I.: An MDP-based recommender system. J. Mach. Learn. Res. **6**, 1265–1295 (2005)
16. Rendle, S., Freudenthaler, C., Schmidt-Thieme, L.: Factorizing personalized markov chains for next-basket recommendation. In: Proceedings of the 19th International Conference on World Wide Web, pp. 811–820 (2010)
17. Zimdars, A., Chickering, D.M., Meek, C.: Using temporal data for making recommendations (2013). https://arxiv.org/abs/1301.2320
18. Li, Y., Tarlow, D., Brockschmidt, M., Zemel, R.S.: Gated graph sequence neural networks. In: ICLR (2015)
19. Xu, C., et al.: Graph contextualized self-attention network for session-based recommendation. In: IJCAI International Joint Conference on Artificial Intelligence, August 2019, pp. 3940–3946 (2019)
20. Liu, S., Zheng, Y.: Long-tail session-based recommendation. In: Proceedings of the 14th ACM Conference on Recommender Systems (RecSys 2020), pp. 509–514 (2020)
21. Qiu, R., Huang, Z., Li, J., Yin, H.: Rethinking the item order in session-based recommendation with graph neural networks, pp. 579–588 (2019). https://arxiv.org/abs/1911.11942

22. Fukui, A., Park, D.H., Yang, D., Rohrbach, A., Darrell, T., Rohrbach, M.: Multimodal compact bilinear pooling for visual question answering and visual grounding (2016). https://arxiv.org/abs/1606.01847

23. Kim, J.-H., On, K.W., Kim, J., Ha, J.-W., Zhang, B.-T.: Hadamard product for low-rank bilinear pooling (2016). https://arxiv.org/abs/1610.04325

24. Cho, K., van Merrienboer, B., Bahdanau, D., Bengio, Y.: On the properties of neural machine translation: encoder-decoder approaches (2014). https://arxiv.org/abs/1409.1259

25. Klicpera, J., Bojchevski, A., Günnemann, S.: Predict then propagate: graph neural networks meet personalized pagerank. In: ICLR (2019)

26. Vaswani, A., et al.: Attention is all you need. In: NIPS (2017)

27. Wang, S., Li, B.Z., Khabsa, M., Fang, H., Ma, H.: Linformer: self-attention with linear complexity, p. 2048 (2019)

28. Liu, Q., Zeng, Y., Mokhosi, R., Zhang, H.: STAMP: short-term attention/memory priority model for session-based recommendation. In: SIGKDD, pp. 1831–1839 (2018)

29. Lin, Z., et al.: A structured self-attentive sentence embedding. In: ICLR (2017)

Polyp Segmentation Using Fully Convolutional Neural Network with Dropout and CBAM

Yuan Zhong[✉]

Boston University, Boston, MA 02215, USA

Abstract. Colonoscopy is crucial for intestinal polyp detection. If left unnoticed, polyp can gradually become cancer. With the development of endoscopy technology and algorithm-based methods, deep learning models for image segmentation is introduced into the field of colonoscopy to make colonoscopy easier for both physicians and patients. To get better performance, researchers keep on trying new methods and adding new optimization techniques to the existing models. In this paper, we introduced fully convolutional neural network, a classical image segmentation model, and optimized the model with two optimization techniques: convoluted block attention module and dropout. We conducted and evaluated experiments with performance metrics and concluded that convoluted block attention module and dropout have positive influence on the model, and our optimized model has advantage over some state-of-art models.

Keywords: Convolutional block attention module · Dropout · Fully convolutional neural network

1 Introduction

Colorectal cancer is one of the most fatal and commonly occurring type of cancer [1]. In its early stage, polyps form in the inside of colon. If left unnoticed or untreated, the polyp can gradually develop into cancer, and spread to other organs. A common procedure of preventing colon cancer is to remove polyps in its early stage with surgery. In the meantime, ways of aiding physicians of correctly and efficiently identifying colon polyps have been researched to substitute the laborious manual screening. Unlike conventional approaches, such as using chromo-magnifying coloring agent to highlight polyps [2], which are still inefficient, recent research focus on utilizing machine learning models to automatize the process, and the state-of-art methods focus on building deep learning models for real-time screening. For the sake of finding inspirations on colonial polyp detection, this paper utilized fully convolutional neural network as backbone, combined with proven effective methods of improving network's efficiency and accuracy, and optimized the network with experiments. Algorithm performance is also analyzed and compared between models, and the model effective ness, compared with conventional models, is also increased.

The reminder of this paper is organized as follows. In Sect. 2, related works are surveyed in chronological order. In Sect. 3, our model, along with backbone model and optimization techniques, is explained in detail. In Sect. 4, data sets, research questions

© Springer Nature Singapore Pte Ltd. 2021
W. Cao et al. (Eds.): CONF-CDS 2021, CCIS 1513, pp. 171–181, 2021.
https://doi.org/10.1007/978-981-16-8885-0_14

and results table are presented and discussed. And finally, in Sect. 5, we concluded our paper and presented future works.

2 Related Work

The evolution of modern flexible electronic endoscope's screening methods can be summarized in to three main stages. In 1983, medical diagnostic device manufacturer Welch Allyn successfully manufactured the first electronic endoscope. Two decades later, machine learning algorithms were introduced to increase efficiency. With the flourish of deep learning methods and advance in computing power, recent research focuses on applying deep learning models to screening. In the following subsections, we will review the history of endoscopy in chronologically.

2.1 Conventional Methods

The earliest attempt of endoscope development can be traced to Philipp Bozzini, who introduced Lichtleiter as a tool for examining human body [3]. From 1805 to 1932, rigid tubes, combined with light source such as candle and reflecting lenses system, were utilized as tool of endoscopy. The development of semiflexible tube in late 1930s allows physicians to take photo for patient's polyps. In 1957, first fiber optic endoscope was invented by Basil H and Larry C, allows flexible screening of intestine and generating high quality image [4]. In the process of polyp detection, hands on experience and deep-specialized knowledge of the specialist are the key to success. However, the increased number of patients and limited medical care personal required faster methods of screening, and to achieve lower miss rate of polyps a more accurate way of screening was needed.

2.2 Machine Learning Methods

To improve the efficiency and accuracy of colonoscopy, methods aided with algorithms were introduced. The machine learning methods relied heavily on hand crafted features such as texture, color, shape of the polyp. The model is limited by its design: other potential features which can improve the accuracy and efficiency are ruled out as noise, and because of the lack of training data, the model's robustness is not guaranteed. Ellipse fitting techniques, proposed in [5], relied on the shape, edge, and color of the polyp for segmentation task, can only detect small polyps with clear elliptical feature in a small data set of 27 polyp images. [6] proposed a support vector machine with KBF kernel, also relied on texture, color and position-based features. The limitation of the machine learning methods, including complicated mathematical calculation, laborious feature selecting process and limited computational power forced researchers to search for new methods.

2.3 Deep Learning Methods

With the resent boom in algorithm and big data, deep learning was introduced and wildly implemented in polyp detection. [7] first proposed fully convolutional network as a model developed from CNN and was capable of doing efficient and accurate image segmentation task. [8] combined a three dimensional offline and online module with fully convolutional network to generate online probability map and offline probability map and aggregate result. [9] proposed a fully convoluted neural network with extra region refinement stage. Upon receive results from fully convolutional network, the refinement stage utilized texton-based patch representation with a random forest classifier to further refine the prediction.

In the meantime, first proposed in [10], a novel U shape network with heavy emphasis on the use of data augmentation attracted much research attention. [11] adopted the U-net network and added extra pre and post processing layers for data augmentation and pixel-wise prediction. In [12] the U-net architecture was linked to an encoder, which has dilated convolutional layers to learn high level features, and a decoder, which includes post-processing layers to increase prediction accuracy. Similar to the encoder-decoder structure of [12, 13] presented an encoder-decoder network based on VGG16, down sampling and up sampling the features to generate a heatmap for prediction. Other than focusing on overall structure of models, researchers have been searching for methods of optimizing as well. [14] purposed a novel Convolutional Block Attentional Module (CBAM) that combined spatial and channel attention layers to greatly boost performance. [15] purposed a strategy to randomly deactivate neurons to mitigate overfitting. How to combine such layers into model is still to be studied. Resent study of models, such as stated in [16], fitted with optimization above produced promising result with high efficiency.

3 Methodology

In this paper, we took fully convolutional neural network (FCN) as backbone and applied optimization techniques. In the following section our model is explained in detail. Figure 1 is our optimized model which combined CBAM and dropout modules with FCN. The FCN was based on a pretrained VGG-16 model, and its deconvolutional layers were fitted with CBAM and dropout.

Our model takes the original FCN as the base model and combines it with CBAM and dropout. The model takes picture with dimension h*w and color channels d as input and pass the data to 7 convolutional layers with corresponding pooling and activation components. After the convolutional layers, two deconvolutional layers, combining with skip connection layers for up-sampling, refines the feature and send it to the first CBAM. The CBAM is consisted with channel attention module and spatial attention module. Our model adapted two Convolutional Block Attention Modules, one located after skip connection layer, and the other located at last before softmax layer. After the first CBAM module, three deconvolution layers are attached. Two dropout layers are attached to the first and second deconvolution layers for experiment purpose.

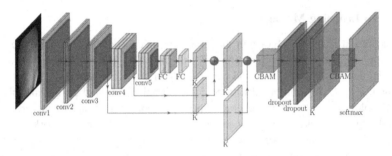

Fig. 1. Model structure

3.1 Convolutional Block Attention Module

The CBAM takes intermediate feature map as input, refines the feature in both channel-wise and spatial-wise attentions, and outputs a feature map with same dimensions of input. The channel attention module uses max polling and average polling across channels with the shared network, then aggregates the feature elementwise, producing a channel attention feature map. The spatial attention feature map is generated by multiplying channel attention feature map with input feature map and pass the refined feature map to next layer. Figure 2 presents the strature of CBAM. The CBAM module's light weightiness and generalness makes it possible to adopt it to many forward feeding convolutional networks without heavy penalty in both computing time and space.

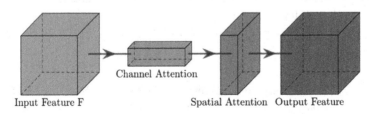

Fig. 2. Convolutional block attention module

3.2 Dropout

Dropout is a simple but efficient way of preventing overfitting. Dropout layer randomly choose a fixed percent of units and temporarily drop them from the network, like in Fig. 3. The network will train in a thinned way, and during test and prediction phase, dropped units will be present in the form of expected output. Thus, the dropout technique reduces over fitting by restricting the network size, while the network remains capable of capturing the influences of dropped unit with expected value.

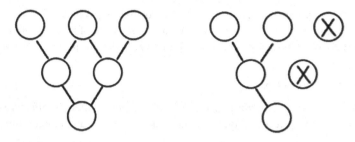

Fig. 3. Dropout. Regular connected neuron (left) VS Dropped out neuron (right)

4 Experiment and Design

The following experiments are performed with pytorch 1.81, torchvision 0.9.1 on a windows 10 machine with AMD 5800x CPU and Nvidia 2080 Ti GPU. Since the experiment focus on segmentizing polyp from background, the binominal cross entropy loss function was chosen along with Adam optimizer.

4.1 Data Set

The chosen data set is CVC-ClinicDB, a publicly available data set for polyp segmentation training [17]. The data set is consisted of 612 images from colonoscopy videos. In the data set, both original image of colonoscopy and ground truth were provided in png and tiff format, and the data set was used in challenges of deep learning network training. Data augmentation techniques were implemented on the data set, including noise addition, flipping, rotating and adjusting luminance. Random test train split was also implemented on the data set, with 90% training data and 10% test data.

4.2 Evaluation Metrics

Accuracy is one of the standardized measures used in binary classification [18], and is adopted as the main metric of tunning:

$$Accuracy(ACC) = \frac{Number\ of\ correct\ predictions}{Total\ number\ of\ predictions} = \frac{TP\_TN}{TP + TN + FP + FN} \quad (1)$$

Where TP = True Positive, TN = True Negative, FP = False Positive, FN = False Negative.

Mean Intersection over Union (MIoU) is the other widely used measure in the field of image segmentation [18]. By computing the intersection over union of ground truth and predicted segmentation, MIoU is a more reliable measure of showing how predicted result fits the ground truth.

$$MIoU = \frac{1}{k+1} \sum_{i=0}^{k} \frac{p_{ii}}{\sum_{j=0}^{k} p_{ij} + \sum_{j=0}^{k} p_{ji} - p_{ii}} \quad (2)$$

Where p_{ii} = Correct Prediction, p_{ji} = False Positive, p_{ij} = False Negative.

Average training time per epoch is chosen as the measure of training efficiency. The measure is calculated by taking the average of time spent during training phase.

4.3   Research Questions

To evaluate our model's performance and optimization strategy's effectiveness, we purposed the following research question and made inference on our experiment result.

Do Dropout and CBAM Affect the Performance of the FCN Model? Answering research question 1, experiments were performed on proposed models and their performance were compared with the original FCN model. Combining dropout and CBAM with the original FCN model, our models experimented are FCN with drop out, FCN with CBAM, FCN with two CBAMs, FCN with dropout and CBAM, FCN with dropout and two CBAMs. The following Table 1 summarizes the experiment results and Fig. 4 presents an example of the prediction results of the methods experimented in comparison.

Table 1. Result of each model's accuracy, mean intersection and union, and average training time per epoch.

Models	ACC	mIoU	Time consumption
FCN	0.992184	0.939245	**03:50**
FCN + Dropout	0.986315	0.956179	03:55
FCN + CBAM	0.995794	0.960328	03:57
FCN + 2 CBAM	0.996159	0.970588	04:03
FCN + CBAM + Dropout	0.996263	0.955472	04:02
FCN + 2 CBAM + Dropout	**0.996758**	**0.978472**	04:09

Overall, our methods of optimization improve accuracy of the model. But with only dropout layer present in the baseline model, the model accuracy decreases by 1%. The model structure of FCN which included batch norm layers could account for this abnormality. Although dropout layers were placed after batch norm layers, as [19] suggested, the performance of the model is still not ideal. In the models with CBAM only, we observed 0.3% of accuracy increase by adding one CBAM into the baseline model, and 0.4% with two CBAMs. What's interesting is that model with both dropout and CBAM raised accuracy 0.4% from base line, even higher than the model with only CBAM. This fact implies that CBAM is a tool that could mitigate the variance shift effect from batch norm and dropout, and could produce a model with higher accuracy overall.

As for mIoU, we achieved 4.2% of performance increase with optimized model (FCN + dropout + CBAM2) compared with the baseline, and the mIoU increases with model complexity in general. Although model with only dropout decreased accuracy, the mIoU of it increased for 1%. Contrary to the expectation that dropout and one CBAM combined would increase mIoU for at least 4%, the model only showed 2%

increase in mIoU. We further evaluated model with dropout and two CBAMs and observed a 4.2 increase in the measure of mIoU.

The optimized model surely achieved the best accuracy and mIoU, with the cost of more time consumed when training. The baseline FCN model spends three minutes and fifty seconds per epoch, while the optimized model used nineteen seconds more. On average, dropout layers in our model takes 5 s to compute, and CBAM takes around 7 s. Hence, there is a tradeoff between model performance and time spent which needs to be taken into consideration.

The optimized model also stays robust against corner cases. In Fig. 4, we present predictions of all our models against a special case. The original picture contains a large polyp, which occupied more than half of the pixels. The picture is special since most polyp is small and round shaped, and this one is large and elongated. From all the predictions of models, the optimized model captures the large polyp with highest accuracy and mIoU. From our point of view, our optimized model most successfully portrayed the general shape of the ground truth and displayed great improvement from the baseline FCN.

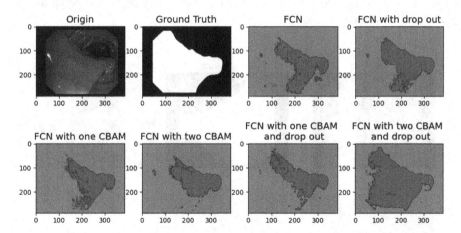

Fig. 4. Prediction **Comparation:** between models experimented: FCN with two CBAMs and dropout outperforms all other models.

While performing experiments on FCN models and optimization techniques, we selected two widely used segmentation models as comparison. SegNet, which upsampling and pooling layers like FCN, has no fully connected layers and produces a heat map like prediction with decode-encode structure. UNet, on the other hand, is another widely researched model in the field of polyp detection with decode-encode structure.

Does the Optimized FCN Model (FCN with Two CBAMs and Dropout) Outperform Other Commonly Used Models in Polyp Recognition? Table 2 summarizes the experiment result. Comparing to SegNet, our optimized FCN model has 1% of increase in accuracy and more than 5% increase in mIoU. Comparing to UNet, our model achieved roughly the same level of accuracy and 1.5% more mIoU. In the measure of time consumption per epoch, our model is 4 s slower than UNet, much faster than SegNet. The result above shows that our optimized FCN model has the best performance with decent time consumption. The predictions in Figs. 5 and 6 show that the optimized FCN model less likely to overfit.

Table 2. Comparison of performance between our optimized model, SegNet and UNet

Models	ACC	mIoU	Time consumption
FCN + 2 CBAM + Dropout	**0.996758**	**0.978472**	04:09
SegNet	0.988424	0.935997	10:40
UNet	0.993185	0.963468	**04:05**

In Fig. 5, our optimized model protrayed the large polyp with highest accuracy and mIoU. The prediction covers most of the ground truth and outlined the shape of the polyp as close as SegNet. UNet, however, does not clearly depict the polyp and its predicted area shatters around.

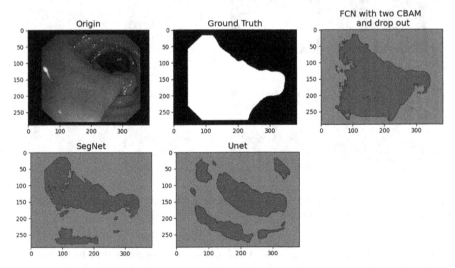

Fig. 5. Predictions **Comparation:** optimized FCN model outperforms competitors segmenting large abnormal polyp.

In Fig. 6, we are presenting predictions against a small, regular polyp. Compare to our optimized model's prediction, both SegNet's and UNet's predictions are influenced by surrounding area's color and brightness, and thus making false predictions scattering around.

Both drop out and CBAM model has observable influence on the FCN model, and different ways of arrangement and number of layers also affect the result. Models with

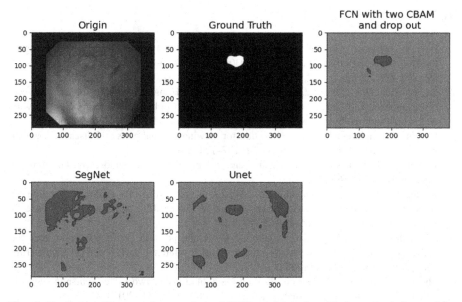

Fig. 6. Prediction **Comparation:** optimized FCN model is less likely to be influenced by brightness and color.

CBAM outperform original model in both metrics. Dropout, in contrast, has negative effect on the accuracy, but if combined with CBAM will have positive influence on the model. Since extra layers were added, it takes longer time per epoch during training phase. The results clearly show that drop out and CBAM are useful techniques for FCN to increase accuracy and mIoU.

5   Conclusion and Future Work

Looking back on the history of colonoscopy and endoscope, it is stunning that a once long and laborious task can be simplified to the extent today. In this paper, we combined FCN, a conventional neural network with deconvolutional layers, with newer optimization techniques for automated polyp segmentation using the data set CVC-ClinicDB from the polyp segmentation challenge. Convolutional block attention module and dropout both proved to be positively influential on the overall performance of the model. In the meantime, the experimental result shows that our model outperforms both SegNet and UNet in accuracy and mIoU, while stays robust against corner cases and shows less sign of overfit. Our future work will be focusing on further optimizing our model with instance distillation methods for faster training and better segmentation performance.

References

1. Bray, F., Jemal, A., Grey, N., Ferlay, J., Forman, D.: Global cancer transitions according to the Human Development Index (2008–2030): a population-based study. Lancet Oncol. **13**(8), 790–801 (2012)
2. Su, L., Pan, H.Z., Weng, J.B., Xu, Y.H., Chen, F., Hong, M.Y.: Relationship between histopathology and surface microstructure of colorectal polyps under chromo-magnifying endoscope with methylene blue. World Chin. J. Digestol. **11**(8), 1227–1229 (2003)
3. Bozzini, P.: Light conductor, an invention for viewing internal parts and diseases, together with illustrations. J. Prac. Med. Surg. **24**, 107–124 (1806)
4. Edmonson, J.M.: History of the instruments for gastrointestinal endoscopy. Gastrointest. Endosc. **37**, S27–S56 (1991)
5. Hwang, S., Oh, J., Tavanapong, W., Wong, J., de Groen, P.C.: Polyp detection in colonoscopy video using elliptical shape feature. In: 2007 IEEE International Conference on Image Processing, pp. II–465–II–468 (2007)
6. Alexandre, L.A., Nobre, N., Casteleiro, J.: Color and position versus texture features for endoscopic polyp detection. In: 2008 International Conference on BioMedical Engineering and Informatics, pp. 38–42 (2008)
7. Shelhamer, E., Long, J., Darrell, T.: Fully convolutional networks for semantic segmentation. IEEE Trans. Pattern Anal. Mach. Intell. **39**(4), 640–651 (2017)
8. Yu, L., Chen, H., Dou, Q., Qin, J., Heng, P.A.: Integrating online and offline three-dimensional deep learning for automated polyp detection in colonoscopy videos. IEEE J. Biomed. Health Inform. **21**(1), 65–75 (2017)
9. Zhang, L., Dolwani, S., Ye, X.: Automated polyp segmentation in colonoscopy frames using fully convolutional neural network and textons. In: Valdés Hernández, M., González-Castro, V. (eds.) MIUA 2017. CCIS, vol. 723, pp. 707–717. Springer, Cham (2017). https://doi.org/10.1007/978-3-319-60964-5_62
10. Ronneberger, O., Fischer, P., Brox, T.: U-Net: convolutional networks for biomedical image segmentation. In: Navab, N., Hornegger, J., Wells, W.M., Frangi, A.F. (eds.) MICCAI 2015. LNCS, vol. 9351, pp. 234–241. Springer, Cham (2015). https://doi.org/10.1007/978-3-319-24574-4_28
11. Tashk, A., Herp, J., Nadimi, E.: Fully automatic polyp detection based on a novel U-Net architecture and morphological post-process. In: 2019 International Conference on Control, Artificial Intelligence, Robotics & Optimization (ICCAIRO), Majorca Island, Spain, pp. 37–41 (2019)
12. Sun, X., Zhang, P., Wang, D., Cao, Y., Liu, B.: Colorectal polyp segmentation by U-Net with dilation convolution. In: 2019 18th IEEE International Conference on Machine Learning and Applications (ICMLA), pp. 851–858 (2019)
13. Badrinarayanan, V., Kendall, A., Cipolla, R.: SegNet: a deep convolutional encoder-decoder architecture for image segmentation. IEEE Trans. Pattern Anal. Mach. Intell. **39**(12), 2481–2495 (2017)
14. Woo, S., Park, J., Lee, J.-Y., Kweon, I.S.: CBAM: convolutional block attention module. In: Ferrari, V., Hebert, M., Sminchisescu, C., Weiss, Y. (eds.) ECCV 2018. LNCS, vol. 11211, pp. 3–19. Springer, Cham (2018). https://doi.org/10.1007/978-3-030-01234-2_1
15. Srivastava, N., Hinton, G., Krizhevsky, A., Sutskever, I., Salakhutdinov, R.: Dropout: a simple way to prevent neural networks from overfitting. J. Mach. Learn. Res. **15**(1), 1929–1958 (2014)
16. Sitaula, C., Hossain, M.B.: Attention-based vgg-16 model for covid-19 chest x-ray image classification. Appl. Intell. **51**(5), 2850–2863 (2020)

17. Jha, D., Smedsrud, P.H., Johansen, D., Lange, T.D., Riegler, M.: A comprehensive study on colorectal polyp segmentation with resunet++, conditional random field and test-time augmentation. IEEE J. Biomed. Health Inf. **25**(6), 2029–2040 (2021)
18. Liang, F.: Evaluating Image Segmentation Models - Towards Data Science. Medium. https://towardsdatascience.com/evaluating-image-segmentation-models-1e9bb89a001b. Accessed 26 July 2021
19. Li, X., Chen, S., Hu, X., Yang, J.: Understanding the disharmony between dropout and batch normalization by variance shift (2018)

Algorithms in Machine Learning
and Statistics

Evaluation of the Effectiveness of COVID-19 Prevention and Control Based on Modified SEIR Model

Menggen Chen and Moshu Xu[✉]

School of Statistics, Beijing Normal University, No. 19 Xinjiekouwai Street, Beijing, People's Republic of China
201911011143@mail.bnu.edu.cn

Abstract. In this paper, the SEIR model is modified. According to the characteristics of COVID-19, a new room of people under quarantine is added, and the incubation period infection rate is introduced. We define the disease-free equilibrium and prove the stability of the equilibrium. Local stability is proved by examining Characteristic polynomial, and global stability is proved by constructing Lyapunov Function. In addition, the effect of the epidemic prevention measures are evaluated by numerical simulation. The research shows that the post exposure infection rate and quarantine rate are the most crucial parameters of this disease.

Keywords: Novel coronavirus · SEIR · Stability analysis · Numerical simulation

1 Background

Many countries in the world today are facing a common global threat-Novel coronavirus. The new outbreak has been named COVID-19 and identified as a pandemic by the World Health Organization.

Many researches [1–4] have shown the considerable role of mathematical models in analyzing the factors that may influence the spread of the disease. Based on these articles, we modified the traditional SEIR model. According to the characteristics of COVID-19, the incubation period infection rate is introduced. And in accordance with the actual means of prevention and control, a new room of quarantined people is added. Firstly, the disease-free equilibrium point of the model is found. Then we analyze its local stability and global stability by examining its characteristic polynomial and using Lyapunov Function.

The COVID-19 imposes great restrictions on the lives, movements, travel (local, national and international) and social relations of billions of people. Local and national governments in almost every country have taken unprecedented measures to control the COVID-19. However, the effect of these measures is mostly unclear. So in this article we try to display it by visualization means.

In the aspect of modeling and stability analysis, some researchers [5, 6] studied the stability of a SEIR model with infectivity under intervention strategy. It is shown that

© Springer Nature Singapore Pte Ltd. 2021
W. Cao et al. (Eds.): CONF-CDS 2021, CCIS 1513, pp. 185–192, 2021.
https://doi.org/10.1007/978-981-16-8885-0_15

the basic reproductive number R_0 plays a crucial role in determining whether the disease is extinct or persistent. Paper [7] and paper [8] studied improved SEIR model. They used the general criteria for the stability of periodic orbits of two dimensional nonlinear autonomous systems and the competitive system theory of differential equations. The stability of the equilibrium point is proved. Paper [9, 10] used Lyapunov Function to analyze the global stability of their systems.

In the aspect of prevention and control effect evaluation, paper [11, 12] used updated mathematical models to simulate different social situations, such as school reopening, social isolation, the use of masks in public places, and evaluated the impact of different strategies on population levels. Paper [13] estimated the effect of physical distancing measures on the progression of the COVID-19 epidemic, finding that physical distancing measures were most effective if the staggered return to work was at the beginning of April. Paper [14] shows that intensive contact tracing followed by quarantine can reduce the control reproduction number and transmission risk.

2   Model

2.1   Modified SEIR Model

Population is divided into five chambers, Susceptible (S), Exposed (E), Infectious with symptoms (I), Recovered (R) and Quarantined (Q).

According to the idea of epidemic dynamics chamber modeling, the following Eq. (1) can be obtained. COVID-19 is characterized by a long incubation period, and the patients that are exposed to the disease and in their incubation period have the same infectivity as the patients who are infectious with symptoms, so on the basis of the SEIR model, the first equation in the Equation Group is modified. Quarantine is a very common way of dealing with this epidemic. People who are quarantined are cut off from other people, so the fourth equation is added. People of room I have a chance to either be quarantined or recover, and people of room Q have another chance to recover.

$$\begin{cases} \frac{dS(t)}{dt} = -\beta S(t)(I(t)+E(t)) \\ \frac{dE(t)}{dt} = \beta S(t)(I(t)+E(t)) - \sigma E(t) \\ \frac{dI(t)}{dt} = \sigma E(t) - (\gamma+\delta)I(t) \\ \frac{dQ(t)}{dt} = \delta I(t) - \varepsilon Q(t) \\ \frac{dR(t)}{dt} = \gamma I(t) + \varepsilon Q(t) \end{cases} \qquad (1)$$

According to the epidemic data that published by the National Health Commission and relevant paper [15], all parameters are summarized in Table 1.

Table 1. Parameter estimates for formula (1)

Parameter	Definitions	Estimated value
$S(t)$	The proportion of susceptible people in the population	$S(0) = 1$
$E(t)$	The proportion exposed people	$E(0) = 0$
$I(t)$	The proportion of people infected with the disease	$I(0) = 0.01$
$R(t)$	The proportion of recovered people	$R(0) = 0$
$Q(t)$	The proportion of the population that is quarantined	$Q(0) = 0$
β	The infection probability of the exposed people and the infected people	0.6
σ	The probability of exposed people becoming infectious	0.125
δ	The probability of an infected person being quarantined	0.128
γ	The probability of being recovered	0.007
ε	The proportion of those quarantined who become recovered	0.014

2.2 The Basic Reproduction Number and Equilibrium Point of the Model

The basic reproduction number is an important index to describe the incidence of infectious diseases. It refers to the expectation of the number of new infections caused by an infected person entering a completely disease-free and susceptible population during the time it's infectious. If an infected person infects on average less than one person during his or her infection period, the disease cannot spread among the population and eventually tends to die out. On the contrary, if the average number of people infected exceeds one, the disease will continue to spread.

Theorem 1. The basic reproductive number of the model is:

$$H_0 = \beta \frac{\gamma + \delta + \sigma}{\sigma(\gamma + \delta)} \tag{2}$$

$1/\sigma$ is the average time of quarantine time. β/σ represents the number of people that a person in room E can infect. $1/(\gamma + \delta)$ is the average time of the symptoms. $\beta/(\gamma + \delta)$ represents the number of people that a person in room I can infect.

When $H_0 \leq 1$ the model has a unique disease-free equilibrium point $P(1, 0, 0, 0, 0)$.

2.3 Stability Analysis of Equilibrium Point

Theorem 2. For Model (1), the disease-free equilibrium is locally asymptotically stable when $H_0 \leq 1$. Since the stability of R is consistent with the stability of the equations, we only need to consider the stability of the first four dimensions.

The Jacobian Matrix of the system at the disease-free equilibrium point $P(1, 0, 0, 0, 0)$ is:

$$J = \begin{pmatrix} 0 & -\beta & -\beta & 0 \\ 0 & \beta - \sigma & \beta & 0 \\ 0 & \sigma & -(\gamma + \delta) & 0 \\ 0 & 0 & \delta & -\varepsilon \end{pmatrix}$$

The corresponding characteristic polynomial is

$$|\lambda E - J| = \begin{vmatrix} \lambda & \beta & \beta & 0 \\ 0 & \lambda - \beta + \sigma & -\beta & 0 \\ 0 & -\sigma & \lambda + \gamma + \delta & 0 \\ 0 & 0 & -\delta & \lambda + \varepsilon \end{vmatrix}$$

The characteristic equation is:

$$\lambda(\lambda + \varepsilon)\left[-\lambda^2 + (\gamma + \delta + \sigma - \beta)\lambda + \sigma\gamma + \sigma\delta - \beta\gamma - \beta\delta - \beta\sigma\right] = 0$$

If all the characteristic value of J has negative real parts, then the disease-free equilibrium point P of model (1) is locally asymptotically stable. When $|\lambda E - J| = 0$, there are two roots: $\lambda 1 = 0$ and $\lambda 2 = -\varepsilon$. In order to make the solution of this equation have negative real parts, and according to Routh-Hurwitz criterion, we need $a_1 > 0$ and

$\begin{vmatrix} a_1 & 0 \\ 1 & a_2 \end{vmatrix} > 0$, $a_1 = \gamma + \delta + \sigma - \beta$, $a_2 = \sigma\gamma + \sigma\delta - \beta\gamma - \beta\delta - \beta\sigma$, We can get

$\beta \frac{\gamma + \delta + \sigma}{\sigma(\gamma + \delta)} = H_0 < 1$, which satisfied the condition. Local asymptotic stability is proved.

Theorem 3. For Model (1), the disease-free equilibrium is globally asymptotically stable when $H_0 \leq 1$.

Construct Lyapunov function

$$V = (\gamma + \delta)E + \beta I$$
$$V' = (\gamma + \delta)[\beta S(E + I) - \sigma E] + \beta[\sigma E - (\gamma + \delta)I]$$
$$= [(\gamma + \delta)\beta S - (\gamma + \delta)\sigma + \beta\sigma]E + [(\gamma + \delta)\beta S - \beta(\gamma + \delta)]I$$
$$\leq [(\gamma + \delta)\beta S - (\gamma + \delta)\sigma + \beta\sigma]E$$
$$\leq [(\gamma + \delta)\beta - (\gamma + \delta)\sigma + \beta\sigma]E$$

When $R_0 < 1$, $V' < 0$, if and only if $E = 0$, equation is satisfied at the disease-free equilibrium $P(1, 0, 0, 0, 0)$. The second method of Lyapunov is satisfied, so the disease-free equilibrium is globally asymptotically stable.

3 Numerical Simulation

3.1 Impact of Post Exposure Infection Rate

We change the infection rate after exposure and simulate the change in the number of infected people (Fig. 1). Under normal circumstances, the proportion of infected people will reach the peak in 22 days, accounting for about 0.347. When the infection rate was 0.5 times and 0.3 times, the peak and peak time of the proportion of the current infected population had significant changes. When the infection rate is 0.5 times, the peak value is about 0.77 times of the normal infection rate peak value, and the time lag of the peak value is about 20 days; when the infection rate is 0.3 times, the peak value is about 0.49 times of the normal contact rate peak value, and the time lag of the peak value is about 46 days. This shows that reducing the transmission rate after contact can significantly control the development of the epidemic. Therefore, mask wearing and vaccination could effectively prevent the transmission of COVID-19 by reducing the transmission rate after contact.

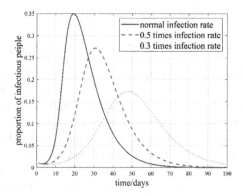

Fig. 1. Effect of changing infection rate

3.2   Impact of Quarantine Rate

We change the quarantine rate and simulate the change in the number of infected people (Fig. 2). Under normal circumstances, the proportion of infected people will reach the peak in 22 days, accounting for about 0.347. When the infection rate is 2 times and 10 times, the peak value of the proportion of the current infected population has a significant change, but the peak time has no significant change. When the quarantine rate is 2 times, the peak value is about 0.63 times of the normal quarantine rate peak value; when the quarantine rate is 10 times, the peak value is about 0.14 times of the normal quarantine rate peak value. This shows that increasing the proportion of quarantine can quickly control the development of the epidemic from the root. Therefore, quarantine of the infected and the susceptible could effectively prevent the spread of COVID-19.

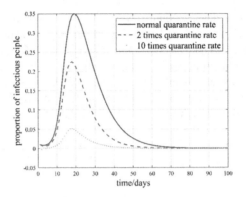

Fig. 2. Effect of changing quarantine rate

3.3   Impact of Recovery Rate on the Development of Epidemic Situation

We change the number of recovery rate and simulate the change in the number of infected people (Fig. 3) and quarantined people (Fig. 4). Under normal circumstances, the proportion of quarantined people will reach the peak in 42 days, accounting for about 0.625. When the recovery rate was 5 times and 10 times, the peak value of the proportion of quarantined people changed significantly. When the recovery rate is 5 times, the peak value is about 0.43 times of the normal rate; when the quarantine rate is 10 times, the peak value is about 0.23 times of the normal rate. When changing the recovery rate, the peak proportion of infected people did not change significantly, because there are two ways for infected people to transform into other people: recovery or quarantine. However, the recovery rate of COVID-19 is very small compared with the quarantine rate, so the recovery rate is not the main reason for the decrease of the proportion of infected people. The only way for the quarantined people to transform into other people is recovery, so changing the recovery rate significantly changes the peak proportion of the quarantined people. The combination of Figs. 2 and 3 shows that the main reason for the effective suppression of COVID-19 is not the increase in recovery rate but the increase in the quarantine rate.

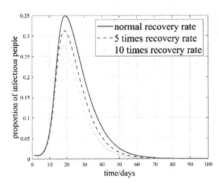

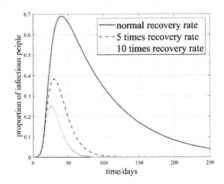

Fig. 3. Effect of changing recovery rate of infected people

Fig. 4. Effect of changing recovery rate of quarantined people

4   Conclusion

Based on the epidemic model, this paper considered the transmission characteristics of the new coronavirus and the practical preventive measures. We build a SEIR model with incubation period infection rate, add quarantined people and analyze the development of epidemic situation and preventive measures. Among them, the incubation period infection rate and quarantine rate are the most critical parameters. Reducing the incubation period infection rate and increasing the quarantine rate could significantly reduce the number of infected people at the peak of the epidemic. Measures such as wearing masks, hospital isolation helps to control the epidemic in this way. However, factors such as age and secondary morbidity, which may have an impact on the development of the epidemic, are also neglected in this model. Therefore, these factors should be taken into account in further researches.

Acknowledgement. This study is supported by Project of Beijing Social Science Fund (18YJB006).

References

1. Altaf Khan, M., Atangana, A.: Modeling the dynamics of novel coronavirus (2019-nCov) with fractional derivative. Alexandria Eng. J. **59**(4), 2379–2389 (2020). https://doi.org/10.1016/j.aej.2020.02.033
2. Li, M.Y., Graef, J.R., Wang, L., Karsai, J.: Global dynamics of a SEIR model with varying total population size. Math. Biosci. (1999)
3. Gatto, M., Bertuzzo, E., Mari, L., et al.: Spread and dynamics of the COVID-19 epidemic in Italy: effects of emergency containment measures. Proc. Natl. Acad. Sci. **117**(19), 202004978 (2020)
4. Wang, H., et al.: Phase-adjusted estimation of the number of Coronavirus Disease 2019 cases in Wuhan, China. Cell Discov. (2020). https://doi.org/10.1038/s41421-020-0148-0
5. Zhou, M., Zhang, T.: Global analysis of an SEIR epidemic model with infectious force under intervention strategies. J. Appl. Math. Phys. **7**, 1706–1717 (2019). https://doi.org/10.4236/jamp.2019.78117
6. Chowell, G., Hengartner, N.W., Castillo-Chavez, C., et al.: The basic reproductive number of Ebola and the effects of public health measures: the cases of Congo and Uganda. J. Theor. Biol. (2012)
7. Li, M.Y., Muldowney, J.S.: Global stability for the SEIR model in epidemiology. Math Biosci. **125**(2), 155–164 (1995). https://doi.org/10.1016/0025-5564(95)92756-5
8. Ansumali, S., Kaushal, S., Kumar, A., Prakash, M.K., Vidyasagar, M.: Modelling a pandemic with asymptomatic patients, impact of lockdown and herd immunity, with applications to SARS-CoV-2. Annu. Rev. Contr. **50**, 432–447 (2020). https://doi.org/10.1016/j.arcontrol.2020.10.003
9. Magal, P., McCluskey, C.C., Webb, G.F.: Lyapunov functional and global asymptotic stability for an infection-age model. Appl. Anal. **89**(7), 1109–1140 (2010)
10. Huang, G., Takeuchi, Y., Ma, W., et al.: Global stability for delay SIR and SEIR epidemic models with nonlinear incidence rate. Bull. Math. Biol. **72**(5), 1192 (2010)

11. Panovska-Griffiths, J., et al.: Determining the optimal strategy for reopening schools, the impact of test and trace interventions, and the risk of occurrence of a second COVID-19 epidemic wave in the UK: a modelling study. Lancet Child Adolesc Health. **4**(11), 817–827 (2020). https://doi.org/10.1016/S2352-4642(20)30250-9

12. Ngonghala, C.N., et al.: Mathematical assessment of the impact of non-pharmaceutical interventions on curtailing the 2019 novel Coronavirus. Math. Biosci. **325**, 108364 (2020). https://doi.org/10.1016/j.mbs.2020.108364

13. Prem, K., et al.: The effect of control strategies to reduce social mixing on outcomes of the COVID-19 epidemic in Wuhan, China: a modelling study. The Lancet Public Health **5**(5), E261–E270 (2020)

14. Tang, B., et al.: Estimation of the transmission risk of the 2019-nCoV and its implication for public health interventions. J. Clin. Med. **9**(2), 462 (2020)

15. Zu, J., Li, M.-L., Li, Z.-F., Shen, M.-W., Xiao, Y.-N., Ji, F.-P.: Transmission patterns of COVID-19 in the Mainland of China and the efficacy of different control strategies: a data- and model-driven study. Infect. Dis. Povert. (2020). https://doi.org/10.1186/s40249-020-00709-z

Finite Difference Method
for Convection-Diffusion Equation

Chenrui Li[(✉)]

Capital Normal University, Beijing 100048, China

Abstract. The convection-diffusion equation is a problem in the field of fluid mechanics. In addition to proving its validity, obvious phenomena of convection and diffusion are also observed. This paper did three numerical experiment using finite difference method (FDM) for trialing feasibility of FDM to solve 1, 2 and 3-dim convection-diffusion equation. We compared this equation's numerical solution with its explicit solution and observed convection and diffusion. In conclusion, we demonstrate the effectiveness of FDM.

Keywords: Finite difference method · Convection-diffusion equation · Convection · Diffusion

1   Introduction

The convection diffusion equation

$$\frac{\partial u}{\partial t} + \nabla \cdot \mathbf{v}u = \nabla \cdot (\mu \nabla u) + f(\mathbf{x}, t) \tag{1}$$

describes quantities in situations where there is both diffusion and convection or advection. It is important to get the solution of the equation with physics situation. Equation (1) is very important in computational fluid dynamics to model the transport phenomena. The coefficients $\mathbf{v}$ and D are convection velocity and diffusion coefficient, $\nabla \cdot \mathbf{v}u$ picture the convention and $\nabla \cdot (\mu \nabla u)$ picture the diffusion. 1 and 2-dimension cases have the analytical solutions. But, in general, it is difficult to obtain the explicit solutions in high space dimensions, which cause trouble in predicting the distribution of matter or energy. Then we have to try to obtain a numerical solution which balances computational speed and accuracy.

This paper deals with solving the convection diffusion equation with 1, 2 or 3 dimensions using the finite difference method.

2   Literature Review

Finite difference method, finite element method and finite volume method are common methods in engineering application. Finite difference method (FDM) is the classical way to calculate the numerical solution of PDE and ODE.

© Springer Nature Singapore Pte Ltd. 2021
W. Cao et al. (Eds.): CONF-CDS 2021, CCIS 1513, pp. 193–203, 2021.
https://doi.org/10.1007/978-981-16-8885-0_16

Cheng Aijie, Zhao Weidong [1] given a economical difference scheme for convection-diffusion equation with Dirichlet's condition.

$$\frac{\partial u}{\partial t} - \nabla \cdot (a(x,y)\nabla u) + \vec{b}(x,y) \cdot \nabla u = f(x,y,t), (x,y) \in \Omega, t \in (0,T] \tag{2}$$

$$u(x,y,0) = u^0(x,y), \quad (x,y) \in \Omega. \tag{3}$$

$$u(x,y,t) = 0, \quad (x,y) \in \partial\Omega \tag{4}$$

$\Omega = (0,1) \times (0,1)$, $\vec{b} = (b_1(x,y), b_2(x,y))$, $a \in C^3(\overline{\Omega})$, $b_1 \in C^0(\overline{\Omega})$, $b_2 \in C^0(\overline{\Omega})$, $f \in C^0((0,T] \times \overline{\Omega})$ and $a(x,y)$ has positive low boundary. By discretizing the equation along characteristics, they have improved the computational efficiency without sacrificing accuracy. When it is a convection-dominated problem, the method of characteristics is faster than CDS. Even some cases will converge on the method of characteristic but CDS when diffusion coefficient is small.

Muhammad Saqib, Shahid Hasnain, Daoud Suleiman Mashat [2] extend Crank-Nicholson and ADI scheme to non-linear two dimension convection-diffusion equation.

$$u_t + uu_x + uu_y - \frac{1}{R}\left(u_{xx} + u_{yy}\right) = 0 \tag{5}$$

To compare with other numerical method, the computational solution is more approach the exact solution.

Murli M. Gupta, Jun Zhang [3] give an explicit fourth-order finite difference scheme for 3D convection diffusion equations in a highly efficient procedure for small to medium values of the grid Reynolds number in 2000.

Ewa Majchrzak, Łukasz Turchan [4] present the other algorithm based on the FDM for 1-dimension convection diffusion equation.

We will compare the explicit solution with numerical solution of Eq. (1) using FDM in the 1 - dimension and 2 dimensions cases and try to get 3 - situation.

3   Methodology

The FDM uses the finite difference in place of the derivative. Suppose $u(x) : R \to R$ is a real function. We approximate u' by calculate

$$D_+ u(x) \equiv \frac{u(x+h) - u(x)}{h} \tag{6}$$

where h is a small and positive value [5]. By the definition, the smaller h is, the closer $D_+ u(x)$ is to $u'(x)$. Similarly, we have many schemes to approximate $u'(x)$, such as

$$\text{backward approximation } D_-u(x) \equiv \frac{u(x) - u(x-h)}{h} \tag{7}$$

$$\text{centered approximation } D_0u(x) \equiv \frac{u(x+h) - u(x-h)}{2h} \tag{8}$$

We expand the function u about the point x in Taylor series

$$u(x+h) = u(x) + hu'(x) + \frac{1}{2}h^2u''(x) + O(h^4) \tag{9}$$

$$u(x-h) = u(x) - hu'(x) + \frac{1}{2}h^2u''(x) + O(h^4) \tag{10}$$

Then the errors of D_+, D_-, D_0 are

$$D_+u(x) - u'(x) = \frac{1}{2}hu''(x) + O(h^2) \tag{11}$$

$$D_-u(x) - u'(x) = \frac{1}{2}hu''(x) + O(h^2) \tag{12}$$

$$D_0u(x) - u'(x) = \frac{1}{6}h^2u'''(x) + O(h^4) \tag{13}$$

So centered approximation is more accurate than these formulas have different accuracy although all of them be used to approximate $u'(x)$

$$u(x+h) = u(x) + hu'(x) + \frac{1}{2}h^2u''(x) + O(h^4) \tag{14}$$

$$u(x-h) = u(x) - hu'(x) + \frac{1}{2}h^2u''(x) + O(h^4) \tag{15}$$

We call D_+, D_- are one order accuracy and D_0 is two order accuracy of approximation.

The second order derivative of u can be approximation by same way

$$D_0^2u(x) := D_+D_-u(x) \tag{16}$$

To sum up, the method of approximation of derivatives we need are enough. Then, let's discuss how to solve the equation by numerical method.

Let's start with the simplest case. There only one space dimension 'x' in the equation:

$$u_t + vu_x = \mu u_{xx} \tag{17}$$

We will express the equation as upwind scheme. First, The first order time derivative uses forward approximation

$$u_t = \frac{u(x, t + \Delta t) - u(x, t)}{\Delta t} \tag{18}$$

Then, first and second space derivatives use centered approximation

$$u_x = \frac{u(x + \Delta x, t) - u(x - \Delta x, t)}{2\Delta x} \tag{19}$$

$$u_{xx} = \frac{u(x - \Delta x, t) - 2u(x, t) + u(x + \Delta x, t)}{\Delta x^2} \tag{20}$$

3.1   1-Dim Case

If we plug the difference back into the Eq. (17), we obtain

$$\frac{u(x, t + \Delta t) - u(x, t)}{\Delta t} + v \frac{u(x + \Delta x, t) - u(x - \Delta x, t)}{2\Delta x}$$
$$= \mu \frac{u(x + \Delta x, t) + u(x - \Delta x, t) - 2u(x, t)}{\Delta x^2} \tag{21}$$

$$u(x, t + \Delta t)$$
$$= \left(1 - \frac{2\mu\Delta t}{\Delta x^2}\right) u(x, t) + \left(\frac{\mu\Delta t}{\Delta x^2} - \frac{v\Delta t}{2\Delta x}\right) u(x + \Delta x, t)$$
$$+ \left(\frac{v\Delta t}{2\Delta x} + \frac{\mu\Delta t}{\Delta x^2}\right) u(x - \Delta x, t) \tag{22}$$

Finally, we rewrite the equation as

$$U_i^{n+1} = \left(1 - \frac{2\mu\Delta t}{\Delta x^2}\right) U_i^n + \left(\frac{\mu\Delta t}{\Delta x^2} - \frac{v\Delta t}{2\Delta x}\right) U_{i+1}^n + \left(\frac{v\Delta t}{2\Delta x} + \frac{\mu\Delta t}{\Delta x^2}\right) U_{i-1}^n \tag{23}$$

This is an algebraic equation. We can calculate it by irritation method.

3.2   2-Dim Case

$$u_t + v(u_x + u_y) = \mu(u_{xx} + u_{yy}) \tag{24}$$

The 2-dim convection diffusion equation also could use upwind scheme. We can obtain that

$$
\begin{aligned}
&\frac{u(x,y,t+\Delta t) - u(x,y,t)}{\Delta t} \\
&+ v \left(
\begin{array}{l}
\dfrac{u(x+\Delta x,y,t) - u(x-\Delta x,y,t)}{2\Delta x} \\
+ \dfrac{u(x,y+\Delta y,t) - u(x,y-\Delta y,t)}{2\Delta y}
\end{array}
\right) \\
&= \mu \left(
\begin{array}{l}
\dfrac{u(x-\Delta x,y,t) - 2u(x,y,t) + u(x+\Delta x,y,t)}{\Delta x^2} \\
+ \dfrac{u(x,y-\Delta y,t) - 2u(x,y,t) + u(x,y+\Delta y,t)}{\Delta y^2}
\end{array}
\right)
\end{aligned}
\tag{25}
$$

Rewrite the equation as

$$
\begin{aligned}
U_{i,j}^{n+1} &= \left(1 - \frac{2\mu\Delta t}{\Delta x^2} - \frac{2\mu\Delta t}{\Delta y^2}\right) U_{i,j}^n + \left(\frac{\mu\Delta t}{\Delta x^2} - \frac{v\Delta t}{2\Delta x}\right) U_{i+1,j}^n \\
&+ \left(\frac{v\Delta t}{2\Delta x} + \frac{\mu\Delta t}{\Delta x^2}\right) U_{i-1,j}^n + \left(\frac{\mu\Delta t}{\Delta y^2} - \frac{v\Delta t}{2\Delta y}\right) U_{i,j+1}^n + \left(\frac{v\Delta t}{2\Delta y} + \frac{\mu\Delta t}{\Delta y^2}\right) U_{i,j-1}^n
\end{aligned}
\tag{26}
$$

3.3   3-Dim Case

$$
u_t + v\left(u_x + u_y + u_z\right) = \mu\left(u_{xx} + u_{yy} + u_{zz}\right)
\tag{27}
$$

$$
\begin{aligned}
&\frac{u(x,y,z,t+\Delta t) - u(x,y,z,t)}{\Delta t} \\
&+ v \left(
\begin{array}{l}
\dfrac{u(x+\Delta x,y,z,t) - u(x-\Delta x,y,z,t)}{2\Delta x} \\
+ \dfrac{u(x,y+\Delta y,z,t) - u(x,y-\Delta y,z,t)}{2\Delta y} \\
+ \dfrac{u(x,y,z+\Delta z,t) - u(x,y,z-\Delta z,t)}{2\Delta z}
\end{array}
\right) \\
&- \mu \left(
\begin{array}{l}
\dfrac{u(x-\Delta x,y,z,t) - 2u(x,y,z,t) + u(x+\Delta x,y,z,t)}{\Delta x^2} \\
+ \dfrac{u(x,y-\Delta y,z,t) - 2u(x,y,z,t) + u(x,y+\Delta y,z,t)}{\Delta y^2} \\
+ \dfrac{u(x,y,z-\Delta z,t) - 2u(x,y,z,t) + u(x,y,z+\Delta z,t)}{\Delta z^2}
\end{array}
\right) = 0.
\end{aligned}
\tag{28}
$$

It follows that

$$
\begin{aligned}
u(x,y,z,t+\Delta t) = {}& \left(1 - \frac{2\mu\Delta t}{\Delta x^2} - \frac{2\mu\Delta t}{\Delta y^2} - \frac{2\mu\Delta t}{\Delta z^2}\right) u(x,y,z,t) \\
&+ \left(\frac{\mu\Delta t}{\Delta x^2} - \frac{v\Delta t}{2\Delta x}\right) u(x+\Delta x, y, z, t) \\
&+ \left(\frac{v\Delta t}{2\Delta x} + \frac{\mu\Delta t}{\Delta x^2}\right) u(x-\Delta x, y, z, t) \\
&+ \left(\frac{\mu\Delta t}{\Delta y^2} - \frac{v\Delta t}{2\Delta y}\right) u(x, y+\Delta y, z, t) \\
&+ \left(\frac{v\Delta t}{2\Delta y} + \frac{\mu\Delta t}{\Delta y^2}\right) u(x, y-\Delta y, z, t) \\
&+ \left(\frac{\mu\Delta t}{\Delta z^2} - \frac{v\Delta t}{2\Delta z}\right) u(x, y, z+\Delta z, t) \\
&+ \left(\frac{v\Delta t}{2\Delta z} + \frac{\mu\Delta t}{\Delta z^2}\right) u(x, y, z-\Delta z, t)
\end{aligned}
\tag{29}
$$

$$
\begin{aligned}
U_{i,j,k}^{n+1} = {}& \left(1 - \frac{2\mu\Delta t}{\Delta x^2} - \frac{2\mu\Delta t}{\Delta y^2} - \frac{2\mu\Delta t}{\Delta z^2}\right) U_{i,j,k}^{n} \\
&+ \left(\frac{\mu\Delta t}{\Delta x^2} - \frac{v\Delta t}{2\Delta x}\right) U_{i+1,j,k}^{n} + \left(\frac{v\Delta t}{2\Delta x} + \frac{\mu\Delta t}{\Delta x^2}\right) U_{i-1,j,k}^{n} \\
&+ \left(\frac{\mu\Delta t}{\Delta y^2} - \frac{v\Delta t}{2\Delta y}\right) U_{i,j+1,k}^{n} + \left(\frac{v\Delta t}{2\Delta y} + \frac{\mu\Delta t}{\Delta y^2}\right) U_{i,j-1,k}^{n} \\
&+ \left(\frac{\mu\Delta t}{\Delta z^2} - \frac{v\Delta t}{2\Delta z}\right) U_{i,j,k+1}^{n} + \left(\frac{v\Delta t}{2\Delta z} + \frac{\mu\Delta t}{\Delta z^2}\right) U_{i,j,k-1}^{n}
\end{aligned}
\tag{30}
$$

4   Result

4.1   First Case

Let's take $v = 1, \mu = 0.5$, and equip suitable boundary condition. Then we can get a initial boundary value problem

$$
\begin{cases}
u_t + u_x = 0.5u_{xx}, x \in (0,1), t \in (0,1) \\
u(x,0) = e^x, x \in [0,1] \\
u(0,t) = e^{-0.5t}, t \in [0,1] \\
u(1,t) = e^{1-0.5t}, t \in [0,1]
\end{cases}
\tag{31}
$$

When we set $\Delta t = 0.01s, \Delta x = 0.05$, there is the irritation formula

$$
U_i^{n+1} = 0.45U_{i+1}^n + 0.55U_{i-1}^n
\tag{32}
$$

Through computer calculation by Matlab, we can get the solution and draw the figure of the equation (Fig. 1)

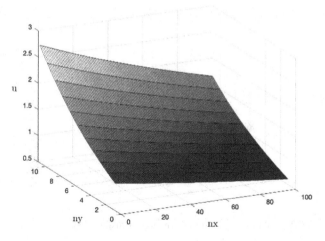

Fig. 1. Solution of 1-dim convection-diffusion equation

4.2 Case Two

When we take $v = -1$, $\mu = 0.05$, $\Delta x = 0.05$, $\Delta y = 0.05$, $\Delta t = 0.01s$, the 2-dimensional question become to (Figs. 2, 3, and 4)

$$\begin{cases} u_t = u_x + u_y + 0.05\left(u_{xx} + u_{yy}\right), (x, y) \in (0, 1) \times (0, 1), t \in (0, 1) \\ \quad u(x, y, 0) = e^{\frac{1}{2}(x+y)}, x \in [0, 1] \\ \quad u(x, 0, t) = e^{\frac{1}{2}x-t}, t \in [0, 1], x \in [0, 1] \\ \quad u(0, y, t) = e^{\frac{1}{2}y-t}, t \in [0, 1], y \in [0, 1] \\ \quad u(x, 1, t) = e^{\frac{1}{2}(1+x)-t}, t \in [0, 1], x \in [0, 1] \\ \quad u(1, y, t) = e^{\frac{1}{2}(1+y)-t}, t \in [0, 1], y \in [0, 1] \end{cases} \tag{33}$$

$$U_{i,j}^{n+1} = 0.2U_{i,j}^n + 0.1U_{i+1,j}^n + 0.3U_{i-1,j}^n + 0.1U_{i,j+1}^n + 0.3U_{i,j-1}^n \tag{34}$$

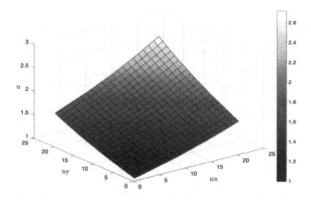

Fig. 2. Solution of 2-dim convection-diffusion equation $t = 0\,\mathrm{s}$

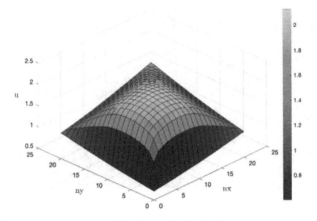

Fig. 3. Solution of 2-dim convection-diffusion equation $t = 0.5$ s

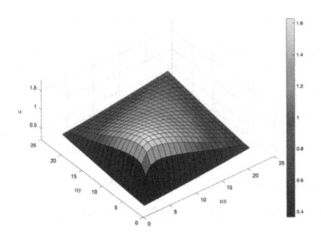

Fig. 4. Solution of 2-dim convection-diffusion equation $t = 1$ s

4.3   Case Three

We take $v = 1, \mu = 0.1, \Delta t = 0.01s, \Delta x = 0.1, \Delta y = 0.1$, then we get the equation

$$u_t = u_x + u_y + u_z + 0.1\left(u_{xx} + u_{yy} + u_{zz}\right). \tag{35}$$

we equip initial condition and boundary condition,

$$\begin{cases} u_t = u_x + u_y + u_z + 0.1\left(u_{xx} + u_{yy} + u_{zz}\right), (x,y,z) \in (0,1) \times (0,1) \times (0,1), \\ \qquad\qquad t \in (0,1) \\ u(x,y,z,0) = e^{\frac{1}{2}(x+y+z)}, x,y,z \in [0,1] \\ u(x,0,z,t) = e^{\frac{1}{2}(x+z)-t}, t \in [0,1], x,z \in [0,1] \\ u(0,y,z,t) = e^{\frac{1}{2}(y+z)-t}, t \in [0,1], y,z \in [0,1] \\ u(x,y,0,t) = e^{\frac{1}{2}(x+y)-t}, t \in [0,1], x,y \in [0,1] \\ u(x,1,z,t) = e^{\frac{1}{2}(1+x+z)-t}, t \in [0,1], x,z \in [0,1] \\ u(1,y,z,t) = e^{\frac{1}{2}(1+y+z)-t}, t \in [0,1], y,z \in [0,1] \\ u(x,y,1,t) = e^{\frac{1}{2}(1+x+y)-t}, t \in [0,1], x,y \in [0,1] \end{cases} \qquad (36)$$

The irritation is

$$U_{i,j,k}^{n+1} = 0.4U_{i,j,k}^{n} + 0.05U_{i+1,j,k}^{n} + 0.15U_{i-1,j,k}^{n} + 0.05U_{i,j+1,k}^{n} + 0.15U_{i,j-1,k}^{n} \\ + 0.05U_{i,j,k+1}^{n} + 0.15U_{i,j,k-1}^{n} \qquad (37)$$

Calculated by Matlab, we can obtain the solution of the problem (Figs. 5, 6, and 7).

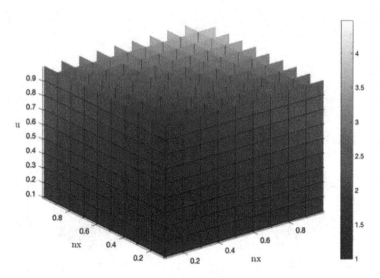

Fig. 5. Solution of 3-dim convection-diffusion equation $t = 0$ s

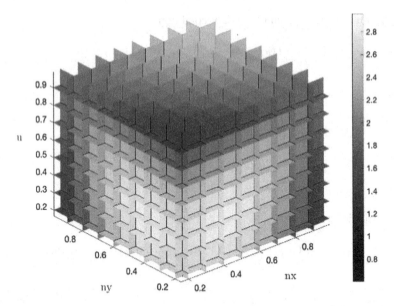

Fig. 6. Solution of 3-dim convection diffusion equation $t = 0.5$ s

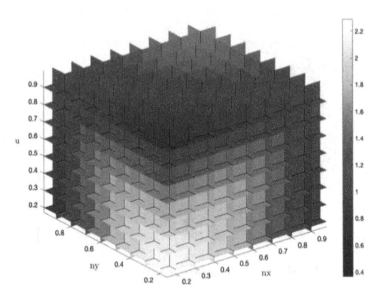

Fig. 7. Solution of 3-dim convection-diffusion equation $t = 1$ s

5 Discussion

In view of the above, we get some several picture of numerical solution of convection-diffusion with different dimension. We can compare 1-dim cases with its explicit solution. The observation that its numerical solution approach its explicit solution suggest us that the finite difference method is visible to solve the fixed coefficient convection-diffusion equation. In the other two cases, the high value domain move over time, which accord with convection physical phenomenon. The diffusion process also represented by the picture of the solution.

For 1-dim case, the numerical solution close with its explicit solution $e^{x-\frac{1}{2}t}$, and 2,3-dim cases display convection and diffusion phenomena.

In the case of improper coefficient setting, we find that there may be numerical oscillation. According to preliminary analysis, this may be caused by the positive and negative coefficients of the iterative formula. For convection-dominated problems these schemes have much smaller time-truncation errors than those of standard methods [6]. Improper coefficient may result in negative value of u, which violates the laws of physics. When you look at the coefficients of the 3-dimensional equation, the $1 - \frac{2\mu\Delta t}{\Delta x^2} - \frac{2\mu\Delta t}{\Delta y^2} - \frac{2\mu\Delta t}{\Delta z^2}$ term requires Δt to be small enough, the Δx to be large enough for the coefficient of $U_{i,j,k}^n$ to be positive, and the $\frac{\mu\Delta t}{\Delta x^2} - \frac{v\Delta t}{2\Delta x}$ term requires Δx to be small enough for it to be positive. So when we have numerical oscillations, we should pick the appropriate Δt and Δx, Δy, Δz.

6 Conclusion

Based on FDM, we derive the calculation format and iterative formula suitable for the convection-diffusion equation. Numerical experiments are carried out for the above three cases. The results are close to the theoretical solution and show the convection and diffusion phenomena.

References

1. Weidong, C.A.Z.: An economical difference scheme for convection-diffusion equations. Math. Numer. Sin. **3** (2000)
2. Saqib, M., Hasnain, S., Mashat, D.S.: Computational solutions of two dimensional convection diffusion equation using Crank-Nicolson and time efficient ADI. Am. J. Comput. Math. **07** (03), 208–227 (2017)
3. Gupta, M.M., Zhang, J.: High accuracy multigrid solution of the 3D convection–diffusion equation. Appl. Math. Comput. **113**(2–3), 249–274 (2000)
4. Majchrzak, E.: The Finite Difference Method for transient convection-diffusion problems. Sci. Res. Inst. Math. Comput. Sci. **11**(1), 63–72 (2012)
5. Leveque, R.J.: Finite Difference Methods for Ordinary and Partial Differential Equations
6. Douglas, J., Jr., Russell, T.F.: Numerical methods for convection-dominated diffusion problems based on combining the method of characteristics with finite element or finite difference procedures. SIAM J. Numer. Anal. **19**(5), 871–885 (1982)

A Review of Bayesian Posterior Distribution Based on MCMC Methods

Zijun Li[(✉)]

Free University Berlin, 14195 Berlin, Germany
zijun.li@fu-berlin.de

Abstract. Bayesian inference plays an essential role in the development of mathematical theory, as an important component of statistical methods. The prior distribution, the likelihood function and the posterior distribution are used in Bayesian inference. A combination of the prior distribution and the likelihood function will represent the posterior distribution, where the background information decides the prior distribution, and the background information and the observed data together form the likelihood function. This paper presents the background of Bayesian inference, the main developments, and the challenges of computing the posterior distribution. It focuses on six MCMC-based methods, such as the Metropolis-Hastings algorithm, Gibbs sampler, Reversible Jump MCMC, Hamiltonian Monte Carlo, Adaptive Metropolis, and preconditioned Crank-Nicolson. The advantages, limitations and applications of each algorithm are also briefly described.

Keywords: Markov chain Monte Carlo · Bayesian inference · Posterior distribution · Convergence

1 Introduction

In statistics, there are Frequentist and Bayesian. The Frequentist considers that parameters exist objectively and so can be determined by certainty optimization methods, such as the maximum likelihood function. While the Bayesian argues that the parameters are unknown random variables. In fact, the debates between these two schools of thought form a feature of the development process in modern mathematical statistics. Lindley [1] believed that the twenty-first century would be a world of Bayesian statistics, while Efron [2] held that there was only 15% probability that this situation occurred. Nevertheless, scholars of both schools believe that the discussion would have a positive effect on the evolution of statistical theory.

Bayesian statistics utilizes observed data to update the uncertainty in the prior distribution with respect to the model parameters, and to infer a more deterministic parameter posterior distribution. It stands for the process of accumulating research evidence. The prior distribution is an understanding of the parameter distribution before collecting observed data. In non-informative prior distributions, the distribution is flat and each possible parameter value has the same probability density. While in informative prior distributions, there are differences in the probability densities of each possible parameter value. The informative prior distribution is generated from previous

© Springer Nature Singapore Pte Ltd. 2021
W. Cao et al. (Eds.): CONF-CDS 2021, CCIS 1513, pp. 204–213, 2021.
https://doi.org/10.1007/978-981-16-8885-0_17

studies, relevant theories and professional judgment. The posterior distribution of parameters is calculated with the Bayes' theorem.

A full Bayesian inference can be divided into three layers. The top layer (the first layer) is the posterior probability of the hypothesis H. The second layer is the posterior probability of the hyperparameter α. The bottom layer (the third layer) is a posterior probability of the parameter θ. Specifically, the prior distribution is first performed to gain available knowledge of the given parameters in the model, then use the information in the observed data to determine the likelihood function, and finally the posterior distribution is derived based on Bayes' theorem.

This paper reviews Bayesian inference and discusses the research of Markov chain Monte Carlo (MCMC) in posterior distributions. The structure for this paper is illustrated as follows. Section 2 reviews how Bayesian inference has evolved. In Sect. 3, it presents six popular MCMC-based algorithms and their respective advantages, weaknesses and applicability. Limitations of Bayesian inference are summarized in Sect. 4.

2　Literature Review

The Bayesian theory originated from a paper by Reverend Tomas Bayes in 1763 [3], which proposed a method for estimating probabilistic inferences about the parameters of binomial distributions from their observed data. In general, Bayes assumed that the parameters are a uniform distribution over the unit interval. His method of parameter inference with binomial distributions is called the Bayesian theorem and has been extended to any statistical distribution. Many ideas in Bayesian methods can be traced back to the works of Bernoulli in 1713. In his monograph [4], Bernoulli not only developed the binomial theorem and proposed the commutative and associative laws, but also introduced the Bayesian inverse probability problem. However, Bernoulli did not formulate the mathematical structure of inverse probability. In 1812, Laplace [5] first presented Bayes' idea in the form of Bayesian theorem, i.e.,

$$P(A|B) = \frac{P(A)P(B|A)}{P(B)}. \tag{1}$$

However, in the 19th century, Bayesian statistics was controversial. The main reason was the lack of knowledge about how to deal with prior probabilities appropriately.

One of the methods for selecting the parameter prior distribution is Bayesian assumption, that is, the parameter's prior distribution $\pi(\theta)$ being a uniform distribution over the range θ. However, there is a contradiction in the Bayesian assumption. The uniform distribution generally does not satisfy the invariance when the parameters are transformed, which means that the transformed distribution is no longer a uniform distribution. In order to solve this problem, Jeffreys proposed a non-informative prior distribution, namely, Jeffreys prior [6].

Suppose $x = (x_1, x_2, \ldots, x_n)$ is a sample from a density function $p(x|\theta)$, where $\theta = (\theta_1, \theta_2, \ldots, \theta_p)$ is a p-dimensional parameter vector. Let $L(\theta|x) = \sum_{i=1}^{n} \log p(x_i|\theta)$ be the likelihood function, Jeffreys considered that the parameter prior distribution is proportional to $\sqrt{I(\theta)}$:

$$\pi\theta \propto I\theta = E\partial L\theta x \partial\theta 2 = E - \partial 2 L\theta x \partial\theta 2, \tag{2}$$

where $I(\theta)$ is Fisher information matrix. It has a key property that the Jeffreys prior is invariant under reparameterization. If $\pi(\theta)$ is the prior distribution with the parameter θ, and $\eta = h(\theta)$ is a parameter transformation, the Jeffreys prior for η is $\pi[h^{-1}(\eta)] \cdot \left| \frac{dh^{-1}(\eta)}{d\eta} \right|$.

Kass [7] showed that the Jeffreys prior approximately maintains the shape of the parameter posterior distribution. The Jeffreys prior is effective for the single-parameter case, but there may be some problems in multi-parameter cases. In many practical problems, sometimes only part of the parameters' information is considered, and the remaining parameters become nuisance parameters. In this case, there are two basic approaches to construct the prior distribution of nuisance parameters. One is the reference prior, suggested by Bernardo (1979, 1994) and Sun and Berger (1998). In contrast to Jeffreys' prior, the reference prior distinguishes between interest parameters and perturbation parameters. When deriving the posterior distribution, the conditional probabilities are applied to eliminate the information of the nuisance parameter. The other approach is known as the probability matching prior proposed by Stein (1985) and Tibshirani (1989). Its basic idea is that Bayesian probabilities are asymptotically matched to the corresponding frequency probabilities when the sample size tends to infinity.

The maximum likelihood estimate (MLE) was first proposed by C.F. Gauss and then refined by Fisher. Consider a random variable x with a probability density function of $f(x, \theta)$. If a sample of N observed values from independent identical distributions is $\{x_1, x_2, \ldots, x_N\}$, the likelihood function of the sample is

$$L(x_1, x_2, \ldots, x_N|\theta) = \prod_{i=1}^{N} f(x_i, \theta). \tag{3}$$

Since multiplication is likely to cause numerical underflow, the log-likelihood is maximized:

$$argmax_\theta \; LL(x_1, x_2, \ldots, x_n|\theta) = \log L(x_1, x_2, \ldots, x_n|\theta) = \sum_{i=1}^{n} \log f(x_i, \theta) \tag{4}$$

In the 1990s, Bayesian inference was hard to implement since the posterior distribution was difficult to compute in high dimensions, which greatly limited its application. However, with the development of computer software and the improvement of Bayesian methods, especially the development of MCMC methods, the originally complex numerical computations have now become simpler and more convenient.

The simulation of parametric posterior distribution also tends to be easier. Therefore, the Bayesian analysis theory and applications have been rapidly developed [8].

Currently, there are two major MCMC methods that are most widely used in Bayesian analysis: the Gibbs sampler and the Metroplis-Hastings (M-H) algorithm. In 1984, Geman [9] presented the Gibbs sampler which was initially utilized for analyzing large and complex data such as image processing analysis, artificial intelligence, and neural networks. Gelfand and Smith (1990) later applied it to Bayesian models to perform integration operations. Another MCMC method that is more general than Gibbs sampler is the Metroplis-Hastings algorithm. Metroplis (1953) proposed a transition kernel, and it was subsequently generalized by Hastings (1970) to form the Metroplis-Hastings (M-H) algorithm. For the complete flow of the M-H algorithm, see Table 1. In the M-H algorithm, the proposal distribution $q(x^*|x)$ represents the density function of the next value for x^* at the current value of x. The acceptance probability of x^* is

$$\alpha(x^*|x) = \min\left\{1, \frac{q(x|x^*)\pi(x^*)}{q(x^*|x)\pi(x)}\right\}. \tag{5}$$

The transition kernel of the M-H algorithm is

$$K_{MH}\left(x^{(i+1)}|x^{(i)}\right) = q\left(x^{(i+1)}|x^{(i)}\right)\alpha\left(x^{(i+1)}|x^{(i)}\right) + \delta_{x^{(i)}}\left(x^{(i+1)}\right)r\left(x^{(i)}\right) \tag{6}$$

where $r\left(x^{(i)}\right)$ is

$$r\left(x^{(i)}\right) = \int_\chi q(x^*|x^{(i)})\left(1 - \alpha\left(x^*|x^{(i)}\right)\right)dx^*. \tag{7}$$

The transition kernel K_{MH} fulfills the detailed balance condition

$$p\left(x^{(i)}\right)K_{MH}\left(x^{(i+1)}|x^{(i)}\right) = p\left(x^{(i+1)}\right)K_{MH}\left(x^{(i)}|x^{(i+1)}\right) \tag{8}$$

which ensures that $\pi(x)$ is invariantly distributed. Besides, M-H algorithm is convergent since it satisfies acyclic and integrable properties of Markov chains, for details referring to [10].

3 Discussion

Bayesian inference utilizes Bayesian formulas to update the probability of an event or hypothesis when more data are available. So, Bayesian inference can be interpreted as a parameter estimation problem. Before obtaining the observed data, the knowledge of the parameter $\theta \in \mathbb{R}^n$ is expressed by a probability distribution $p(\theta)$. Given the observed data $\mathcal{D} = \{x_1, \ldots, x_n\}$ in $\mathbb{R}^d$, and by Bayes' theorem, it follows that the posterior distribution is

$$p(\theta|\mathcal{D}) = \frac{p(\mathcal{D}|\theta)p(\theta)}{p(\mathcal{D})} \tag{9}$$

where $p(\theta)$ is prior distribution, $p(\mathcal{D}|\theta)$ is likelihood function, $p(\theta|\mathcal{D})$ is posterior distribution, and $p(\mathcal{D})$ is normalizing factor which is also called evidence.

Bayesian inference involves solving the following problems [8].

Problem 1. Computing the normalizing factor
Given a prior distribution $p(\theta)$ and a likelihood function $p(\mathcal{D}|\theta)$, the normalizing factor can be found in Bayesian theorem.

$$p(\mathcal{D}) = \int p(\mathcal{D}|\theta)p(\theta)d\theta \tag{10}$$

Problem 2. Computing the marginal likelihood
Given the joint posterior distribution $p(\mathcal{D}, \theta|\alpha)$, calculate the marginal likelihood.

$$p(\mathfrak{D}|\alpha) = \int p(\mathcal{D}, \theta|\alpha)d\theta \tag{11}$$

Problem 3. Computing expectations
Given a function $f : \mathbb{R}^n \to \mathbb{R}$, compute its expectation.

$$E_{p(\theta|\mathcal{D})}[f(\theta)] = \int f(\theta)p(\theta|\mathcal{D})d\theta \tag{12}$$

In real world, there are two challenges in posterior inference. First, there is no analytic expression for the normalizing factor. Therefore, the posterior distribution has no closed form, which means that it becomes impossible to infer the posterior distribution directly. Second, for Bayesian inference problems in image process or function space, the unknown parameters are high-dimensional. In this case, the cost of computation is extremely high whether using approximation methods or sampling methods. Hence, we need efficient inference methods [11]. MCMC method provides a useful tool for building statistical models, which can transform some complicated high-dimensional problems into a series of simple low-dimensional problems. So, it is suitable for Bayesian computation of complex statistical models. The research and application of Bayesian methods have improved dramatically since the MCMC methods were proposed in the 1980s [8, 12–15].

Table 1. Metropolis-Hastings algorithm.

Algorithm 1 Metropolis-Hastings algorithm

Initialize $x^{(0)} \sim q(x)$
for iteration $i = 1, 2, \dots$ do
Propose: $x^* \sim q(x^*\|x^{(i)})$
Acceptance Probability:
$\quad \alpha(x^*\|x^{(i)}) = \min\{1, \frac{q(x^{(i)}\|x^*)\pi(x^*)}{q(x^*\|x^{(i)})\pi(x^{(i)})}\}$
$u \sim$ Uniform $(u; 0,1)$
if $u < \alpha$ then
$\quad$ Accept the proposal: $x^{(i+1)} \leftarrow x^*$
else
$\quad$ Reject the proposal: $x^{(i+1)} \leftarrow x^*$
end if
end for

3.1 Algorithm 1: Metropolis-Hastings (M-H)

Critical points in the M-H algorithm are determining the proposal distribution of the parameters and processing the parameters' correlations, which allows sampling from complicated posterior distributions. There is no need for the normalizing constant in the target distribution for the M-H algorithm, namely, it is possible for M-H algorithm to perform sampling of samples even if the specific form of normalizing constant m(Y) in posterior distribution is unknown. Second, M-H algorithm works with a single chain, but several independent chains can be simulated in parallel. Finally, successful or unsuccessful results of M-H algorithm usually depends on the selection of the proposal distribution. M-H algorithm is suitable for evidence of posterior distribution expressions without explicit parameters. The algorithm is simple and can be used with arbitrarily complicated target distributions of any dimension to produce random samples.

3.2 Algorithm 2: Gibbs Sampler

One special case of the M-H algorithm is the Gibbs sampler, where the proposal distribution is the corresponding posterior conditional distribution, with a related acceptance probability of 100%. Gibbs sampler has the advantage that it utilizes the full conditional distribution to turn a complicated problem with multiple correlated parameters into a simpler task dealing with one parameter for each component. Gelfand and Smith (1990) [16] provided an outline and showed a method for Bayesian computation, that is, denoting the probability density of our interested unknown parameter θ as

$$p(\theta) = F'(\theta), \tag{13}$$

where $F(\theta)$ is the cumulative distribution function of θ. When the parameters are uncorrelated with each other, the sampling is efficient and easy to draw from the fully conditional distribution. However, although deriving conditional distributions is relatively easy, it is not always possible to find an efficient way to sample from these conditional distributions. The Markov chain of Gibbs sampler converges at a geometric rate under general regularity conditions.

3.3   Algorithm 3: Reversible Jump Markov Chain Monte Carlo (RJMCMC)

Reversible Jump Markov Chain Monte Carlo (RJMCMC) was introduced by Green (1995) [17]. The constructed Markov chain can not only transit within the parameter space of a model, but also jump between different models (the dimensions can be different), thus providing a powerful tool for Bayesian model selection. Richardson and Green (1997) applied RJMCMC to mixing estimation. Brooks, Giudici and Roberts presented a method to improve the efficient of transition in RJMCMC. Marin and Robert applied RJMCMC to variable selection. Since the samples obtained by the MCMC method are not independent samples that have autocorrelation, they cannot be used directly for parameter estimation, especially for directly estimating the standard errors of the parameters. In order to overcome autocorrelation, Hobert [18] et al. introduced an interval extraction to form a new sample sequence based on the original Markov transition kernel which allows to obtain parameter estimates and estimation errors.

3.4   Algorithm 4: Hamiltonian Monte Carlo (HMC)

Compared to traditional MCMC methods such as M-H and Gibbs, the major strengths of HMC are its high efficiency and high acceptance probability [19]. This algorithm is useful when there are difficulties in direct sampling, when there is a small sample size or when the autocorrelation is high. Also, HMC works well in the high-dimensional case [20]. There are two key points of HMC results. One is that it utilizes the information of target distribution, especially the gradient information, so that each step is accepted with high probability. It avoids the high rejection rate caused by random walk Markov chain. Another point is to make the target distribution correspond to the energy one by one through Gibbs canonical distribution (where the energy is low, the probability is high), and then introduce the virtual momentum so that the gradient information can be used by the Hamiltonian system in physics. An extension of the HMC is the No-U-Turn Sampler [21]. It is more effective since it helps to prevent tuning of the model. NUTS allows for efficient Bayesian posterior inference with limited human interference for wide classes of complicated high-dimensional models.

3.5   Algorithm 5: Adaptive Metropolis (AM)

To deal with the slow search speed of M-H algorithm, Haario (2001) [22] presented an adaptive Metropolis algorithm. The key aspects of AM are defining the proposal distribution of the i-th step parameters and defining the acceptance probability, i.e.,

$$\alpha = \min\left\{1, \frac{p(y|\theta^*)p(\theta^*)}{p(y|\theta_i)p(\theta_i)}\right\}. \tag{14}$$

Compared to the traditional M-H algorithm, AM is no longer needed to pre-determine the proposal distribution of the parameter; instead, it is evaluated by the covariance matrix of the posterior parameters, greatly enhancing computational efficiency. The covariance matrix of the posterior parameters is adapted after each iteration step, which accelerates the convergence rate.

3.6   Algorithm 6: Preconditioned Crank–Nicolson (pCN)

In function spaces, the acceptance probability of the M-H algorithm decreases to 0 with increasing discrete dimensionality [10, 11]. In order to solve this problem, Stuart introduced the Crank-Nicolson (CN) sampling algorithm that can be used in function spaces [23, 24]. The benefits of the CN algorithm are that it is dimension independent and its sampling efficiency is not affected by the discrete dimensions of the unknown variables. Thus, this method is well suited for sampling in function spaces. Hu [25] et al. suggested an adaptive pCN (ApCN) that approximates the actual covariance. The ApCN method requires that the covariance of the proposed distribution is diagonal. A drawback of ApCN is that it needs to compute the square root of large matrices, which has high computational complexity for non-diagonal matrices. A hybrid adaptive MCMC algorithm was introduced by Zhou [26] to deal with the problem of computational efficiency. Specifically, it performs the AM in a finite-dimensional subspace of the state space, and executes the standard pCN algorithm in its complementary space. In the hybrid adaptive MCMC method, the covariance of the proposal distribution is not restricted in form, and it uses the covariance of the proposal distribution to directly estimate the covariance of the posterior distribution. Reducing the restriction on the posterior covariance of the proposed distribution can lead to more efficient sampling. However, Wallin and Vadlamani [27] showed that regular estimation methods used in a finite-dimensional setting cannot be applied in an infinite-dimensional adaptive MCMC scheme.

4   Conclusion

Bayesian theorem and Bayesian inference are explicit and straightforward, and their applications are widely used, so they have been favored by many scholars. In addition to the choice of prior distribution, the biggest challenge in Bayesian analysis is the computation of the posterior distribution; especially for complicated and high-dimensional problems, the explicit posterior distribution by analytical methods is difficult to find. A symbol of the rapid advance of Bayesian inference is the appearance of Gibbs sampler. Since then, Markov chain Monte Carlo (MCMC) algorithms based on Monte Carlo simulation have gradually become well known in the statistical community. After the 1990s, due to the fast growth and widespread use of high-speed computers and MCMC algorithms, statisticians have been able to overcome the heavy computations and deal with more realistic and complex scientific problems by Bayesian methods. This paper reviews six classical MCMC-based methods for posterior inference, briefly describing their backgrounds, strengths, and drawbacks respectively.

Bayesian statistics has some advantages as follows.

1. An approach that incorporates information from prior distributions with the data, effectively avoiding information wastage.
2. It provides inference on data conditionally and precisely, without relying on asymptotic approximations. Small sample inference is carried out in the same way as that for larger sample sizes. Bayesian statistics can also directly estimate any function of the parameters.
3. It provides convenient settings for various models, such as hierarchical models and missing data problems.

Bayesian statistics also has its shortcomings.

1. Bayesian statistics does not provide a method on how to select a prior distribution. Without a proper method to choose the prior distribution, it may generate misleading results.
2. It usually has a high computational cost and time-consuming effort, especially in models that have large numbers of parameters and samples.

In conclusion, for traditional Bayesian statistics, a major problem is that Bayesian inference is usually slow; especially under the background of Big Data, it is hard to adapt to the requirements of new models. Therefore, how to perform large-scale Bayesian learning methods is one of the important challenges in the future. Enhancing the flexibility of Bayesian learning as well as speeding up its inference process, which makes it more adaptable to the era of big data, will be considered.

References

1. Efron, B.: Why isn't everyone a Bayesian? Am. Stat. **40**(1), 1–5 (1986)
2. Lindley, D.: Introduction to Probability and Statistics from a Bayesian Viewpoint. Part 1 Probability and Part 2 Inference. Cambridge University Press, Cambridge (1965)
3. Bayes, T.: LII: an essay towards solving a problem in the doctrine of chances. By the late Rev. Mr. Bayes, F. R. S. communicated by Mr. Price, in a letter to John Canton, A. M. F. R. S. Philos. Trans. Roy. Soc. London **53**, 370–418 (1763)
4. Bernoulli, J.: ARS conjectandi, Opus posthumum. Culture et Civilisation, Belgium (1968)
5. Laplace, P.: Essai Philosophique sur les Probabilités. Mme Ve Courcier, Paris (1814)
6. Jeffreys, H.: Theory of Probability, 3rd edn. Clarendon Press, Oxford (1961)
7. Kass, R.: Data-translated likelihood and Jeifreys's rules. Biometrika **77**(1), 107–114 (1990)

8. Andrieu, C., de Freitas, N., Doucet, A., Jordan, M.: An introduction to MCMC for machine learning. Mach. Learn. **50**(1/2), 5–43 (2003)
9. Geman, S., Geman, D.: Stochastic relaxation, Gibbs distributions, and the Bayesian restoration of images. IEEE Trans. Pattern Anal. Mach. Intell. PAMI **6**(6), 721–741 (1984)
10. Brooks, S., Gelman, A., Jones, G., Meng, X.: Handbook of Markov Chain Monte Carlo. CRC Press, New York (2011)
11. Robert, C., Casella, G.: Monte Carlo Statistical Methods. Springer, New York (2004)
12. Bishop, C.: Pattern Recognition and Machine Learning. Springer, New York (2007). https://doi.org/10.1007/978-0-387-45528-0
13. Haario, H., Laine, M., Mira, A., Saksman, E.: DRAM: efficient adaptive MCMC. Stat. Comput. **16**(4), 339–354 (2006)
14. Dellaportas, P., Forster, J., Ntzoufras, I.: On Bayesian model and variable selection using MCMC. Stat. Comput. **12**(1), 27–36 (2002)
15. Johannes, M., Polson, N.: MCMC methods for continuous-time financial econometrics. SSRN Electron. J. (2003)
16. Gelfand, A., Smith, A.: Sampling-based approaches to calculating marginal densities. J. Am. Stat. Assoc. **85**(410), 398–409 (1990)
17. Green, P.: Reversible jump Markov chain Monte Carlo computation and Bayesian model determination. Biometrika **82**(4), 711–732 (1995)
18. Hobert, J., Jones, G., Presnell, B., Rosenthal, J.: On the applicability of regenerative simulation in Markov chain Monte Carlo. Biometrika **89**(4), 731–743 (2002)
19. Duane, S., Kennedy, A., Pendleton, B., Roweth, D.: Hybrid Monte Carlo. Phys. Lett. B **195**(2), 216–222 (1987)
20. Neal, R.: MCMC Using Hamiltonian Dynamics. arXiv: Computation, pp. 139–188 (2011)
21. Hoffman, M.D., Gelman, A.: The no-U-turn sampler: adaptively setting path lengths in Hamiltonian Monte Carlo. J. Mach. Learn. Res. **15**, 1593–1623 (2014)
22. Haario, H., Saksman, E., Tamminen, J.: An adaptive metropolis algorithm. Bernoulli **7**(2), 223–242 (2001)
23. Cotter, S., Roberts, G., Stuart, A., White, D.: MCMC methods for functions: modifying old algorithms to make them faster. Statist. Sci. **28**(3), 424–446 (2013)
24. Stuart, A.: Inverse problems: a Bayesian perspective. Acta Numer. **19**, 451–559 (2010)
25. Hu, Z., Yao, Z., Li, J.: On an adaptive preconditioned Crank-Nicolson MCMC algorithm for infinite dimensional Bayesian inference. J. Comput. Phys. **332**, 492–503 (2017)
26. Zhou, Q., Hu, Z., Yao, Z., Li, J.: A hybrid adaptive MCMC algorithm in function spaces. SIAM/ASA J. Uncert. Quant. **5**(1), 621–639 (2017)
27. Wallin, J., Vadlamani, S.: Infinite dimensional adaptive MCMC for Gaussian processes. arXiv: Computation (2018)

RoboTutor: Predictions of Students' Answer Type

Randolph Zhao[✉]

Case Western Reserve University, Cleveland, OH 44106, USA

Abstract. *RoboTutor* is a successful intelligent tutor, a system that can teach students comprehension of stories without human teachers by generating four-choice cloze problems. In this paper, we predict the type of choices of each attempt on *RoboTutor* by using Naive Bayes and Logistic Regression. We collect us-age records of 295 students and questions from 79 Swahili stories. We implement data cleaning, standardization, normalization, feature selection to preprocess the data. We also adjust sample weights on observation of data distribution and adjust class weights by models' self-learning during training to improve the model. Since the number of students' trials varies greatly, to both guarantee the stability and similarity to the real-world application of performance measure, we use accuracy measure with 10-fold cross-validation. We achieve an average accuracy of 72.3% in prediction, com-pared to random-chose accuracy of 25% and the majority class of 57.7%.

Keywords: RoboTutor · Logistic Regression · Prediction to answer type · Item response theory · Naïve Bayes

1 Introduction

RoboTutor is an open-source Android tablet app that "enables children ages 7–10 with little or no access to schools to learn basic reading, writing, and arithmetic without adult assistance" [1]. While *RoboTutor* made excellent success in practice, there are still many improvements on the performance features of *RoboTutor* that could further maximize students' learning. For example, we may want to manipulate the question difficulty better for each student to reach a "desirable difficulty," which is a learning level achieved through a sequence of learning tasks and feedback that lead to enhanced learning and transfer [2]. To help to analyze performance features and control difficulty, we use machine learning models to predict the students' answer types. In other words, we are trying to explore what kind of choices or mistakes students will take.

We used data cleaning, normalization, and standardization to preprocess the data and adjusted sample weights and class weights to improve the model. We implemented accuracy measurement with 10-fold cross-validation as the performance measure for our model. Because of the limited *RoboTutor* usage records, we chose to train a Logistic Regression classifier and got an outstanding accuracy in cross-validation on the prediction.

© Springer Nature Singapore Pte Ltd. 2021
W. Cao et al. (Eds.): CONF-CDS 2021, CCIS 1513, pp. 214–227, 2021.
https://doi.org/10.1007/978-981-16-8885-0_18

2 Related Work

2.1 RoboTutor

RoboTutor is an open-source application of intelligent tutor, a system that can teach students basic literacy and numeracy [3] and has been used for multiple languages. In this experiment, we focus on the *RoboTutor* with Diagnostic Question Generator Lite (DQGen Lite), which is modeled after DQGen. Previous versions of *RoboTutor* with DQGen can adapt to each student by assessing the student performance automatically by AI algorithms [4]. *RoboTutor* with DQGen Lite, similarly, also can generate multiple-choice cloze questions to test children's comprehension of the given story [4] but adapts for Swahili instead of students. Basically, DQGen Lite adapts for Swahili and generates 4-choice questions to test students with the comprehension of Swahili stories. In this research, we used the *RoboTutor* data with Swahili stories.

2.2 Item Response Theory (IRT)

Item Response Theory (IRT), known as the latent response theory, is a test model that attempts to use discrete item responses as features to infer test performance. IRT model assumes that test scores are tested dependent and item and test parameters are sample dependent [5]. One of the IRT models is the third parameter (3PL) IRT model proposed by Birnbaum as Eq. 1, where a_i is the discrimination; b_i is the difficulty; θ is the student ability; and c_i is the pseudo-guessing, the probability of guessing the correct answer [6].

$$P_i(\theta) = c_i + (1 - c_i)\frac{1}{1 + \exp\{-a_i(\theta - b_i)\}} \tag{1}$$

This 3PL IRT model uses question discrimination of students, question difficulty, student ability to solve questions, and the guessing probability of questions to measure the probability that a student could pick the correct choice.

2.3 Naïve Bayes Classifier

Naïve Bayes is a classification algorithm that applies Bayes' theorem with independence assumptions between features. In our research, we implemented the Gaussian Naïve Bayes to deal with continuous data. Let μ_k be the mean of x with class k and σ_k^2 be the variance of x with class k, we have Eq. 2 to predict the $p(y = k|x)$ [7].

$$p(y = k|x) = \frac{1}{\sqrt{2\pi\sigma_k^2}}e^{-\frac{(c-\mu_k)^2}{2\sigma_k^2}} \tag{2}$$

2.4   Logistic Regression Classifier

Logistic Regression is a classification algorithm that attempts to learn a function about $P(Y|X)$. It uses the softmax function, a generalization of the sigmoid to compute $p(y = k|x)$ as Eq. 3.

$$p(y = k|x) = \frac{\exp(w_k \cdot x + b_k)}{\sum_i \exp(w_i \cdot x + b_i)}, \tag{3}$$

where and w is the weight vector, b is the bias [8].

To calculate the weights of features, the Logistic Regression model will minimize the negative log-likelihood loss as Eq. 4. To control overfitting caused by an extremely large weight of feature, Logistic Regression also includes a weight control term during optimization. In this research, we will use the L2 regularization as our weight control as Eq. 5.

$$min\, L_{CE}(\hat{y}, y = k) = -log\frac{\exp(w_k \cdot x + b_k)}{\sum_i \exp(w_i \cdot x + b_i)} \tag{4}$$

$$min\, L_{CE}(\hat{y}, y = k) = \frac{1}{2}\|w\|^2 + C\left[-log\frac{\exp(w_k \cdot x + b_k)}{\sum_i \exp(w_i \cdot x + b_i)}\right] \tag{5}$$

However, since we use L2 regularization, we need to pay attention to the scale of feature values because L2 regularization requires the scale of feature values should be similar.

3   Data Analysis

For our project, we collected three sources of data: the transactions of the *RoboTutor* app, information about 79 Swahili stories, and story word statistics. These transactions provide detailed records about the choices that students made for each attempt. The information about 79 Swahili stories includes the type of all possible choices and the information about the word and sentence. The story word statistics provides the level of words, or, to some degree, the difficulty of the word.

Since we extracted the data from the real-world raw data of the *RoboTutor* transaction records, we needed to be careful about the data distribution, data preprocessing, and even the necessary data cleaning process.

3.1   Class Distribution

In *RoboTutor* questions, there are four types of answers: "correct", "nonsensical", "plausible", and "ungrammatical". Intuitively, "nonsensical" and "ungrammatical" will be more recognizable and thus may have a low proportion for students to choose from. Thus, normally, the class distribution will not be balanced. As Fig. 1 shows, the attempts that took "correct" is 57.7% of the whole dataset, while the number of "nonsensical" and "plausible" is much lower. The classes of our dataset are not uniformly distributed.

Besides, our initial hypothesis of the class distribution is "correct" > "plausible" > "nonsensical" > "ungrammatical." Thus, it is surprising that "plausible" takes a such small proportion while "un-grammatical" takes such a high proportion of the dataset.

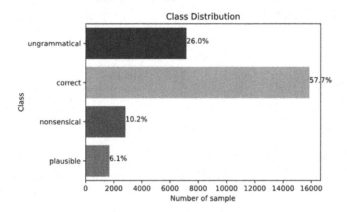

Fig. 1. Class distribution

3.2 The Number of Attempts

We used "the number of attempts" as one feature to represent the question difficulty to some degree. The number of attempts is how many attempts one student spends until making the correct choice or giving up. The more attempts spent on a question, the more difficult the question could be. Further, since there are four choices in each question, we expected that students spend at most four attempts on each question. However, Fig. 2 shows that some students still cannot pick the right choice after attempting four times, which probably represents that these students attempt more than 4 times just randomly choose the choice, not trying to solve the questions.

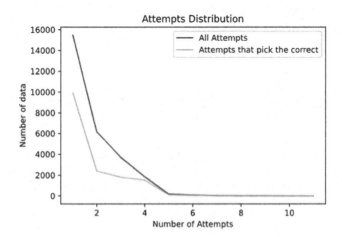

Fig. 2. Attempts distribution

3.3   Duration

Here, the "duration" represents the time a student spends on picking one choice for one question. Since the *RoboTutor* provides four choices for each question and each question is one sentence in a story, we will expect students to spend less than 5 min. However, as Figs. 3 or 4, the zoom-in version, shows, some students spend 0 s or more than 300 s (i.e., 5 min).

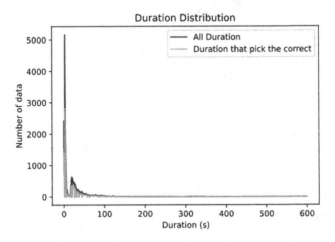

Fig. 3. Duration distribution

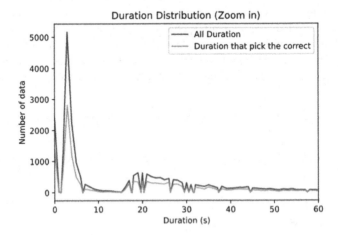

Fig. 4. Duration distribution (Zoom in)

3.4   Students Distribution

The student distribution refers to the distribution of the number of all trials of each student. In our transactions, there is a total of 295 students. Figure 5 display the distribution of the number of trials of students, sorted by the number of trials, where we can find that some students made a lot of attempts (e.g., 700+) and some students made a few attempts (e.g., 2).

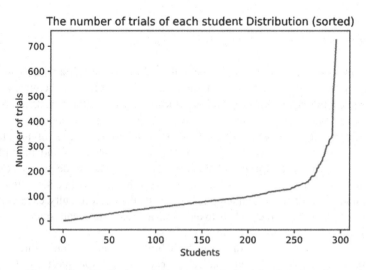

Fig. 5. The distribution of the number of all trials of each student

4   Algorithms

We implemented both the Naïve Bayes classifier and the Logistic Regression classifier for our project and then compared the performance by comparing the cross-validation accuracy. And then, we implemented several model improvement techniques to improve the performance of the better model.

4.1   Item Response Theory

As Eq. 1 shows, the Item Response Theory can estimate the probability that a student chooses the right answer to one question by considering the student's ability, question difficulty, question discrimination, and pseudo-guessing. It combines the question difficulty and student ability and thus is a good feature for predicting the student's answer type.

To measure the difficulty in our dataset, we figured out three different calculation methods of difficulty as Eqs. 6, 7, and 8:

$$difficulty_1 = 1 - \frac{\sum_i m_{i,correct} + 1}{\sum_i m_i + 2} \tag{6}$$

$$difficulty_2 = 1 - \prod_i \frac{m_{\leq i,correct} + 1}{m_i + 2} \tag{7}$$

$$difficulty_3 = 1 - \frac{m_{1,correct} + 1}{m_1 + 2}, \tag{8}$$

where m_i represents the number of samples which is the i'th attempts of students and $m_{i,correct}$ represents the number of samples which is the i'th attempts where the student picked the right choice. Similarly, the $m_{\leq i,correct}$ in the Eq. 8, represent the number of attempts that pick the right choice no larger than i'th attempt.

Equation 6 calculates the difficulty as (1 - the accuracy rate of all attempts). Equation 7 calculates the accuracy rate of the first i'th attempts and multiply them together. For each i, the algorithm calculates the number of students who chose the right answer using no more than i'th attempts. In Eq. 8, we calculate the difficulty as (1 - the accuracy rate of the first attempts). And for all three difficulty calculations, we used Laplace smoothing method to avoid zero accuracy rate and smooth the distribution of difficulty.

Then, we calculated three different probabilities based on these three difficulty calculations. Since there are four choices in each *RoboTutor* question, the pseudo-guessing is 0.25. The question of discrimination and student ability is dependent on the students. Thus, since we are trying to predict unseen students, we set these two parameters as 0.5, constantly.

4.2   Features

Since we are trying to predict the answer type, we want to collect some features to represent the question difficulty and student ability. In our model, we included 14 features totally.

From the transactions of the *RoboTutor* application, we extract or calculate the time that students spend on choosing an answer, the number of attempts, the correct rate of all attempts on one question, and the probability of picking the right choice by using Item Response Theory with three difficulty calculation methods: Eqs. 6, 7, and 8. From the information about 79 Swahili stories, we extract the length of the right word, story length, sentence length, and the position of the sentence in the story. The position of the sentence is represented by how many sentences precede the question sentence. From story word statics, we extract the word level of both right words and the max, min, and average of three distractors.

4.3   Validation

To better measure the performance, we implemented cross-validation to make the validation cases close to the real-world application in the future. Here, we used 10-fold cross-validation on n students. The reason is that if we separate the training and testing set by students, we create a case that our model tests on unseen students, which is close to the futural application where we will predict the answer type for the new, unseen student.

As Fig. 5 shows, the attempts of students may vary greatly, and some students made few attempts, which may result in the unstable of the accuracy measure. Thus, we implement the 10-fold cross-validation, instead of n-fold, where we use a tenth of 295 students (i.e., 29 students) as one fold. This guarantees the stability of the accuracy measure for each validation.

4.4   Preprocessing

Comparing Figs. 2 and 3, the range of attempts is [1, 11] while the range of duration is [0, 600]. This kind of large difference of feature values may result in a huge imbalance of feature weights in the Logistic Regression classifier which could result in poor performance after adding the L2 regularization term. Thus, we implement normalization and standardization to preprocess the data. Normalization is to convert all values into the range [0,1] as Eq. 9 and standardization is to convert all values to z-score as Eq. 10:

$$x' = \frac{x - x_{min}}{x_{max} - x_{min}} \tag{9}$$

$$x' = \frac{x - \mu}{\sigma}, \tag{10}$$

where μ is the mean of feature values and σ is the standard deviation of feature values.

4.5   Model Improvement

As discussed above, we expect that the number of attempts a student spends on one question should no more than 4 times and the time a student spends on one question should also no more than 5 min, but a small part of samples (Figs. 2 and 3) does not follow this expectation. To avoid those samples to mislead our model, we adjusted the weight of those unhelpful samples as weight = 0.2, which means these samples are less important for the model to learn during training.

Similarly, as Fig. 1 shows, the class distribution of our dataset is imbalanced. The majority class, the "correct" class, take 57.7% while the "plausible" class only takes 6.1%. Besides, the importance of each class during learning is also not equal. For example, "ungrammatical" may be much easy to learn because they are more recognizable, while "plausible" and "nonsensical" are difficult to learn and thus may have higher importance during learning. Thus, we let the model automatically adjust the class weight.

4.6   Feature Selection

To measure the importance and effectiveness of each feature and to avoid unhelpful features to mislead the model, we implemented feature selections for k-best features from k = 1 to k = 14 on the whole dataset. And then we plot the average accuracy with cross-validation of each feature selected model. If there is one feature combination with apparently better performance, we would modify our model to use that feature combination.

5   Experiments

5.1   Model Comparison

We implemented both the Naïve Bayes classifier and the Logistic Regression classifier. However, the Naïve Bayes classifier had relatively poorer performance than the Logistic Regression classifier as Table 1 shows. Thus, in the following research and experiments, we only used Logistic Regression as our model.

Table 1. Model comparison.

Model name	10-folds cross-validation accuracy		
	Max	Average	Min
Naïve Bayes	0.602	0.565	0.530
Logistic Regression	**0.744**	**0.721**	**0.697**

5.2   Preprocessing

Since the scales of feature values are largely different in our dataset, we implemented the standardization and normalization on the data before training. From Fig. 6, we can see there is a conspicuous improvement in accuracy from 0.6717 to 0.7198.

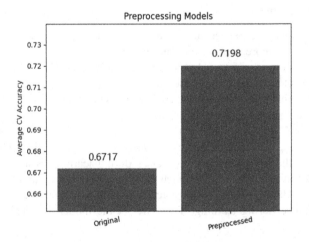

Fig. 6. Preprocessing model

5.3   Model Improvement

To decrease the misleading effect of some unhelpful samples, we decreased the sample weights of those data. As Fig. 7 shows, with adjusted sample weight, the average cross-validation accuracy increased from 0.7130 to 0.7166. To solve class imbalance and make use of different importance of classes, we adjusted class weights automatically. While training on the whole dataset, the final class weights are "correct": 6, "non-sensical": 1, "plausible": 6, "ungrammatical": 7 (Table 2). By adjusting the class weight, we increased the average cross-validation accuracy of our Logistic Regression model from 0.7130 to 0.7170 (Fig. 7). While both adjusting sample weights and class weights, we successfully improved the model from 0.7130 to 0.7203 (Fig. 7).

Table 2. Class weights (Automatically trained).

Class name	Class weights
Correct	6
Nonsensical	1
Plausible	6
Ungrammatical	7

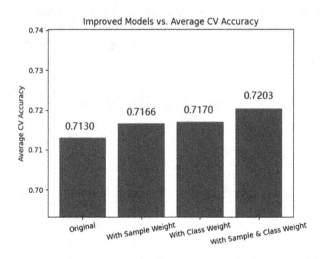

Fig. 7. Performance with/without sample weight and class weight

5.4   Feature Selection

To measure the importance of each feature and avoid misleading features in our model, we implemented feature selections on our model to measure the effectiveness of each feature. As Fig. 9 shows, there is a peak when there are two remained features, which are the number of attempts and IRT probability with difficulty method 1 (Eq. 1), and the other features just improved the min accuracy.

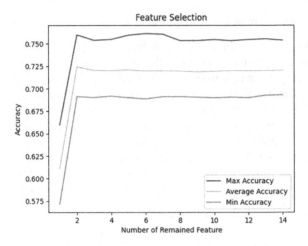

Fig. 8. Performance with/without sample weight and class weight

5.5   The Effect of the Training Size

To explore the effect of the size of the training set, we also plotted the relationship between the size of the training set and average cross-validation accuracy as Fig. 9 shows. We record the average cross-validation accuracy from training size = 514 to training size = 27514 with step = 1000. We can see the highest average accuracy appeared at training size = 8514, and then the average accuracy slightly decreases by the training size.

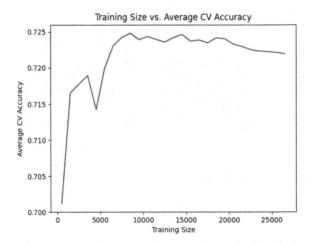

Fig. 9. Training size vs. average cross-validation accuracy

5.6   Performance of the Logistic Regression Model

With data preprocessing, adjusted sample weights, and adjusted class weights, Table 3 shows the performance of the final Logistic Regression Model.

Table 3. Final model performance (Logistic Regression).

Model name	Cross-validation accuracy		
	Max	Average	Min
Logistic Regression	**0.746**	**0.723**	**0.692**

6   Results Analysis

Since our data is directly extracted from the transactions, the records of human being activities, our data may include many cases, part of which may be useless or even misleading for our model. Figure 7 shows that by reducing the weights of some potentially misleading samples, the average accuracy improved. To solve the imbalanced class distribution and different class importance for the model to learn, we adjusted the class weights, which resulted in accuracy improvement from 0.7130 to 0.7170. The class weights automatically calculated display a combination of class distribution and class importance for learning. Since "correct" and "ungrammatical" take a large proportion of the dataset, it is reasonable that their weights are higher for the model to learn the high-proportion classes. And interestingly, our model shows a large tendency to learn "plausible," which is the lowest proportion of the dataset, which could be a signal that the "plausible" class contains some important properties that our model can learn to classify different classes.

Since one of our models is Logistic Regression and we use L2 weight penalty, the predictor is dependent on the scale of the features. However, our dataset contains features with greatly different scales. Thus, preprocessing such as standardization and normalization is necessary and also can improve the performance of our model. It is not surprising that there is an increase in accuracy from 0.6717 to 0.7198 by implementing preprocessing in Fig. 6.

In Fig. 8, we can see that when there are two remained features, the number of attempts and IRT with difficulty method 1 (Eq. 1), the performance achieved a peak. This means these two features are especially important to predict the answer type. The other features are not effective to improve the performance of the Logistic Regression model, but the other features do help to improve the min accuracy, which improves the robustness of our model.

Considering the complex prediction problem of choices of human beings, it is surprising that there is an accuracy decrease by the training size just after training size > 8514 in Fig. 9. There is an obvious drop at training size = 5514 and we believe there are some very misleading data that appeared between the 4514th to the 5514th, which caused the model to learn wrong information. Then, since the model sees more data, the model successfully corrects the wrong beliefs and thus the accuracy continues increasing. We can see the performance of the Logistic Regression model achieves its highest point at training size = 8514 and then starts to decrease. One potential explanation is that it is the result of overfitting because our dataset is relatively small with only 27514 samples. Another reason could be that there is much misleading or contradicted information in the datasets that we did not clean out or reduce the sample weights.

However, we still should notice that the performance of our final Logistic Regression model is outstanding. We achieved 0.723 (average), 0.746 (max), and 0.692 (min) cross-validation accuracy. If choosing randomly, the accuracy of a model should be 0.25. If always choosing the majority class "correct," the accuracy should be 0.577. The performance of our model, even the min accuracy, is much higher than the majority class or choosing randomly. Thus, our Logistic Regression model shows great accuracy in predicting students' answer types.

7 Conclusion

To predict the answer type of the *RoboTutor* questions for each student, we built the Naïve Bayes and the Logistic Regression model based on the information of *RoboTutor* transactions and Swahili stories. Since Logistic Regression shows better performance in our dataset, we continued to improve our model. The preprocessing, sample weight adjustment and class weight adjustment brought great benefits to our model. However, we should acknowledge that there may be more misleading information that we did not detect in our dataset. Besides, we collected only two effective features and other less helpful features.

In a conclusion, as we successfully achieved in 0.723 (average) accuracy of our model, compared to predicting randomly or using the majority class, we can predict students' answer type with better confidence in the future. With our predictor, researchers can further control the difficulty level of each question and reach the "desirable difficulty" to maximize students' learning. Education researchers also could further introduce more features to our predictor to analyze the effective factors that cause students to choose one kind of choice.

8 Future Work

As the data analysis and the results of our experiments show, there are many improvements we can do in the future to increase the performance of our model.

Our datasets may include much misleading, or at least unhelpful, data. As we show in the results of decreasing the unhelpful data in reducing the weights of some samples, we may want to clean or decrease the sample weight of more unhelpful information besides duration and the number of attempts. This may help our model to gain benefits from a larger training size.

Since we are trying to predict a complex situation where human beings are involved, the decision boundary may not be linear and maybe we should try nonlinear machine learning models, such as neural networks. However, the prerequisite of implementing nonlinear models is to have large enough training data.

Furthermore, we can include more effective features in our model. As Fig. 8 shows, although all features provide robustness to our model, most features are not very effective. However, in the transactions and stories, there is more potential information that we could use as a feature to improve our prediction models. One potentially effective feature is the semantic analysis about the context of the sentence since semantic analysis may provide the relationship information between context and choice type, such as "ungrammatical."

Acknowledgment. Randolph Z. thanks Prof. Jack Mostow for providing patient academic guidance and critical suggestions to the whole project.

References

1. RoboTutor. https://www.cmu.edu/scs/robotutor/index.html. Accessed 25 Feb 2021
2. Derks, D., Bakker A.: The Psychology of Digital Media at Work, p. 125. Psychology Press, East Sussex (2013)
3. What is RoboTutor. https://www.cmu.edu/scs/robotutor/what-is-robotutor/index.html. Accessed 25 Feb 2021
4. Mostow, J., Huang, Y., Jang, H., et al.: Developing, evaluating, and refining an automatic generator of diagnostic multiple choice cloze questions to assess children's comprehension while reading. Nat. Lang. Eng. **23**(2), 245–294 (2017)
5. Hambleton, R.K., Van der Linden, W.J.: Advances in item response theory and applications: an introduction. Appl. Psychol. Meas. **6**(4), 373–378 (1982)
6. van der Linden, W.J., Hambleton, R.K.: Handbook of Modern Item Response Theory, p. 13. Springer, New York (1997). https://doi.org/10.1007/978-1-4757-2691-6
7. Jahromi, A.H., Taheri, M.: A non-parametric mixture of Gaussian naive Bayes classifiers based on local independent features, pp. 209–212 (2017). https://doi.org/10.1109/AISP.2017.8324083
8. Krishnapuram, B., Carin, L., Figueiredo, M.A., Hartemink, A.J.: Sparse multinomial logistic regression: fast algorithms and generalization bounds. IEEE Trans. Pattern Anal. Mach. Intell. **27**(6), 957–968 (2005)

PM2.5 Density Prediction Based on a Two-Stage Rolling Forecast Model Using LightGBM

Zihao Liu[✉]

Beijing Haidian International School, No. 368-2 Hanhe Road,
Haidian, Beijing, China

Abstract. At present, air pollution is a primary issue of the world. Particularly, PM2.5 pollution can cause severe impact on economy and human health, so developing an accurate PM2.5 prediction model becomes a hot topic. Up to now, researchers had developed PM2.5 forecasting methods based on decision tree models, RNN models, and hybrid models. Previous works also discovered plentiful features, such as seasonal data and weather forecasting data that help increase the accuracy of PM2.5 prediction. To improve the model accuracy, we developed a LightGBM-based PM2.5 prediction model that has two innovations: 1) our model studies how special events (e.g., diplomatic visits, sport events, and government meetings) influence PM2.5 variation. 2) our model adopts the strategy of two-stage rolling forecasting so that it can achieve high accuracy without relying on weather forecasting data.

Keywords: Short-Time Fourier Transform · LightGBM · PM2.5 · Rolling forecast · Time series · What-if analysis

1 Introduction

Since the writing of Silent Spring in 1962, environmental protection has become a primary issue all over the world especially in developing countries. In particular, PM2.5 pollution is one of the environmental issues that have caused severe impact to people's daily life [1]. Although PM2.5 can directly cause health problems on the population, it also has impacts on economy. In fact, a study conducted by Xie *et al.* [2] indicates that health and economy issues at become substantial when PM2.5 concentrations are high at a provincial level. Specifically, it was projected that China will have to spend additional $25.2 billion on health expenditure for diseases brought by PM2.5 pollution. However, if PM2.5 is properly manipulated with air pollution control technology, by 2030 the number of patients due to PM2.5 will reduce by 75%, reducing PM2.5 health expenditure $6.5 billion. Accordingly, it is vital to develop solutions to the PM2.5 issues for their severe impacts in health and economy.

To minimize the damage of PM2.5, researchers in this field have developed various models based on the theory of time series to forecast air quality. Currently, most of the proposed models either use simple regression models, deep neural networks, or hybrid models that make use of both.

Typical regression models used for PM2.5 prediction include linear regression, decision tree, and random forest; but most authors adopt tree-based models to forecast

W. Cao et al. (Eds.): CONF-CDS 2021, CCIS 1513, pp. 228–248, 2021.
https://doi.org/10.1007/978-981-16-8885-0_19

future PM2.5 concentration. For example, Zhang *et al.* [3] proposed a LightGBM forecasting model that utilized past air quality data recorded by monitoring stations and meteorological data provided by weather forecasting. Similarly, Zhang *et al.* [4] suggested a PM2.5 forecasting model based on random forest algorithm. In fact, Lee *et al.* [5] analyzed the performance on PM2.5 prediction of all tree-based models such as XGBoost, LightGBM, and random forest and obtained promising results, explaining why tree-based prediction models are common in the field of PM2.5 forecasting.

Deep learning models include the traditional feed-forward neural networks, convolutional networks, and recurrent neural networks, but most deep-learning-based research done on PM2.5 forecasting make use of RNN-based networks. For instance, the STE (Spacial-Temporal Ensemble) model which makes use of temporal features, proposed by Wang and Song [6] is an LSTM-based algorithm. Likewise, Ong *et al.* [7] proposed an RNN-based PM2.5 quality prediction model with improved training methods. Particularly, they developed a new pre-training method that allows the model to make more accurate predictions. Essentially, researchers tend to use RNN-based networks to develop deep learning PM2.5 prediction models.

Not only did researchers developed model solely based on tree-based models or recurrent networks, but also created hybrid models that use both. For instance, Zheng *et al.* [8] proposed a hybrid PM2.5 forecasting model in which a specific mechanism is set up to combine predictions made by a linear regression model and a neural network. Similarly, Qi *et al.* [9] proposed a PM2.5 prediction model based on graph convolutional neural networks and LSTM. Furthermore, the methods Qi *et al.* [9] developed are also applicable to the prediction of other particles' densities. Likewise, Zhang *et al.* [10] proposed a hybrid prediction model that combines convolutional networks and recurrent networks. Particularly, Zhang *et al.* discovered that their model produces more accurate results than others when there are large fluctuations of values in the data.

Previous researches done on the field of PM2.5 forecasting have produced plenty of discoveries. For example, Zhang *et al.* [3] enhanced model accuracy by integrating the model with data obtained from weather forecasting stations. Likewise, Zhao *et al.* [11] discovered that seasonal data will improve the accuracy of their linear-regression-based PM2.5 prediction model. Similarly, Zhang *et al.* [4] proposed a random-forest-based PM2.5 prediction model that can effectively handle large-quantity data. Although these researches have already yielded remarkable results, their models require knowing weather forecast data and concentrations of pollutants other than PM2.5. In addition, current forecasting models did not take the impact of government's policy on PM2.5 concentration into account. Furthermore, previous works on PM2.5 prediction do not perform what-if analysis on their prediction models. As a result, we develop solutions to each of these issues.

In the face of the aforementioned potential improvements, we propose our own PM2.5 prediction model[1]. Similar to previous works, our model adopts the LightGBM framework for its efficiency and flexibility. [12] In our study, we use the PM2.5 data set published by Liang *et al.* [13] for its granularity: the data set contains hourly records of PM2.5 and other meteorological parameters between the year 2010 and 2015.

---

[1] The source code of our model is available at https://github.com/TravorLZH/pm25.

The density of this data set allows us to predict PM2.5 concentration in terms of hours. Nevertheless, the attributes in the original data set are not sufficient to train a prediction model with high accuracy, so we used a variety of techniques to generate more features. To let our model study the relationship between the attributes and their past states, we generate lagged features for PM2.5 concentrations and meteorological parameters. According to Zhang *et al.* [3], statistical features over rolling window are also helpful in PM2.5 prediction, so we generate them as well. In addition to the above time-domain features, we generate frequency-domain features via short-time Fourier transform on the time domain of the PM2.5 time series so that our model can study the seasonality of PM2.5 concentration, therefore improving its accuracy in prediction.

In their feature engineering process, Zhang et al. [3] generate a date-time feature called "is_weekend" which denotes whether the day predicted is weekend. This innovation motivates us to dig further in date-time feature generation. By tracking the government's event calendar, we are able to study the impacts of government's policies on PM2.5 since governments always make event-specific policies during these special time intervals. In fact, government's policies have substantial impacts on PM2.5 concentrations. For example, in 2013, the Chinese government imposes "Air Pollution Prevention and Control Action Plan," aiming to reduce PM2.5 concentrations of China's major cities by more than 10%, and investigation led by Zhang and Di [14] discovers that China's PM2.5 concentrations decreases substantially during 2013 and 2017. To track Beijing's special events, we manually collected date intervals during which special events occurred in Beijing from 2010 to 2015 using search engine and created a new data set. Not only does this "special event" data set contains the date intervals, but also labels the recorded special events by type. Types of recorded special events include celebration of special festivals (e.g., 2015 military parade to celebrate the allied victory over fascism), diplomatic visits (e.g., Michelle Obama's visit to China in 2014), and sport events that occurred in Beijing. Since governments often made special policies during these events, incorporating "special event" features into our data set allows the prediction model to learn how government's policies affect PM2.5 concentration.

Because our work is independent of weather forecasting, our testing set does not contain meteorological features. In order for our model to predict PM2.5 concentration, we use the following steps to handle this conflict: first, we use a separate model to predict meteorological features in the testing set. Then, we generate statistical and lagged features from the predicted meteorological parameters. Lastly, we use the technique of rolling forecasting to predict PM2.5 concentrations.

To test the effectiveness of our proposed new features, we perform control experiments. Particularly, we train two models: one with the new features and one without. Subsequently, we compare them using evaluation metrics such as mean absolute error, root mean square error, and symmetric mean absolute percentage error defined as in (1), (2), and (3).

To determine how influential governments' policies are during special event, we evaluate the performance of the two models during special event time intervals. In addition, we perform feature importance analysis on the PM2.5 prediction model to determine what features contribute most to our forecasting model.

$$MAE = \frac{1}{N} \sum_{i=1}^{N} |y_i - p_i| \tag{1}$$

$$RMSE = \sqrt{\frac{1}{N} \sum_{i=1}^{N} (y_i - p_i)^2} \tag{2}$$

$$SMAPE = \frac{1}{N} \sum_{i=1}^{N} \frac{|y_i - p_i|}{(|y_i| + |p_i|)/2} \tag{3}$$

2 Problem Setup

In this study, we aim to create a PM2.5 prediction model that guides local governments to make effective policies to improve PM2.5 quality while being independent of weather forecasting data. To implement, we develop a PM2.5 prediction model that requires knowledge of government's event calendar. Since governments make policies to control traffic and other aspects of a city when the city is holding special events, accessing government's event calendar allows our model to study the impacts of such policies. Not only do governments make special policies during special events but also enact policies during holidays, so we also incorporate "is_holiday" attribute denote whether the entry was recorded in a holiday. In order for our model to predict PM2.5 without weather forecasting data, we adopt the technique of rolling forecasting. As shown in Fig. 1, our model first predicts meteorological features of one future hour, and then predicts PM2.5 concentrations using these predicted values. Subsequently, we will compare the prediction results of the control group and the experimental group using evaluation metrics such as MAE, RMSE, and SMAPE.

3 Data Set

3.1 Data Description

In this study of PM2.5 forecasting, we used hourly recorded PM2.5 data provided by Liang et al. [13]. According to Table 1, the data set contains PM2.5 concentration measured from four different stations: Dongsi, Dongsihuan, Nongzhanguan, and U.S. diplomatic post. In addition to PM2.5 attributes, the data set also contains several hourly recorded meteorological attributes: wind speed, wind direction, precipitation, air pressure, humidity, dew point, and temperature. However, this data set contains redundant attributes, anomalies, and missing values [13]. As a result, we perform some preprocessing before conducting further analysis.

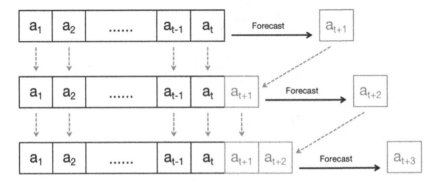

Fig. 1. Illustration of rolling forecasting

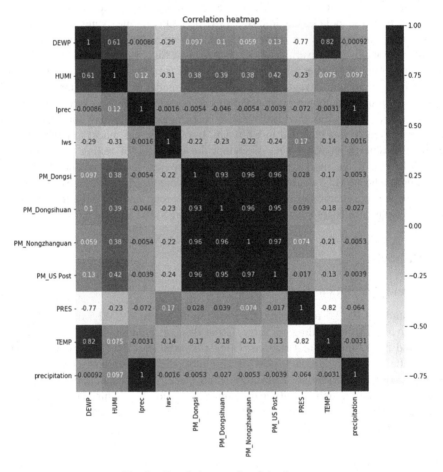

Fig. 2. Correlation matrix of the data set

Table 1. Attributes of the original data set

Classification	Attributes	Description
Date-time attributes	year, month, day, hour	The exact time of the data entry
	Season	Current season
Meteorological attributes	HUMI	Humidity
	TEMP	Temperature
	PRES	Atmospheric pressure
	precipitation, Iprec	Precipitation
	Iws, cbwd	Wind speed and wind direction
	Cbwd	Wind direction
PM2.5 concentration values	PM_Dongsi	PM2.5 from Dongsi observatory
	PM_Dongsihuan	PM2.5 from Dongsihuan observatory
	PM_Nongzhanguan	PM2.5 from Nongzhanguan observatory
	PM_US Post	PM2.5 from U.S. diplomatic post

3.2   Data Exploration

In truth, data preprocessing described in the next section allows us we can dig deeper into our data set since we have eliminated anomalies and imputed missing values. Exploring the data set allows us to discover various properties of PM2.5 concentrations and other meteorological attributes.

Relationship Between Dew Point and Humidity. Relationship between dew point and humidity. In our data set, dew point and relative humidity are stored as DEWP and HUMI, and according to Fig. 3, distribution of DEWP and HUMI appear to be very similar. In addition, correlation analysis in Fig. 4 reveals that there is a positive correlation between DEWP and HUMI. That is, dew point grows large as relative humidity increases, and dew point becomes low as relative humidity decreases. This explains why both dew point and relative humidity are often used to reflect the amount of moisture in the atmosphere [15].

Temperature Distribution in Beijing. The data set we use also contains a complete hourly record of Beijing's temperatures during 2010 and 2015. Studying its distribution allows us to discover some weather facts in Beijing. According to Fig. 3, there are two maxima in the distribution of temperature: one at approximately 22 °C above zero, the other at approximately 3 °C below zero. Since Beijing in the northern hemisphere, its temperature in summer is greater than that in winter. As a result, we conclude that Beijing is very cold in winter while not so hot in summer.

Distribution of PM2.5 in Beijing.   According to Fig. 5, Beijing's PM2.5 concentrations appear to follow an exponential distribution. That is, the frequency of PM2.5 records decrease exponentially as the PM2.5 values increase. This means that most of the PM2.5 concentrations are low, implying that Beijing experiences little PM2.5 pollution most of the time during 2010 and 2015.

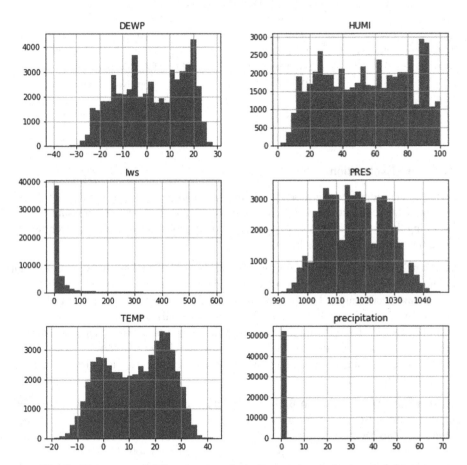

Fig. 3. Histograms of different meteorological parameters in the imputed data set

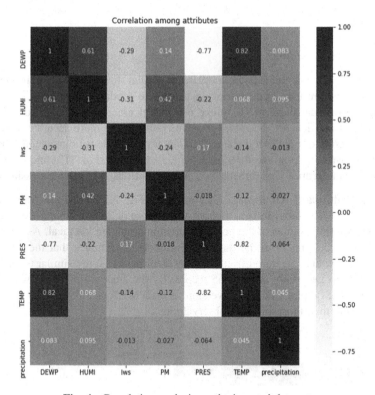

Fig. 4. Correlation analysis on the imputed data set

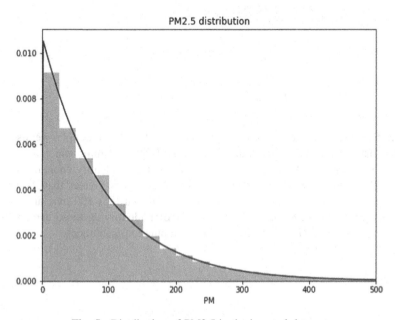

Fig. 5. Distribution of PM2.5 in the imputed data set

4   Methods

4.1   Data Preprocessing

In our study, we use regression models to predict future PM2.5 concentrations. Specifically, we are using our regression models to predict future PM2.5 values via studying the original data set. To make our model efficient, we need to reduce the dimensions of our data set. In order for our model to make more accurate predictions, we need to ensure our data set does not contain any anomalous or erroneous values. In this section, we scrutinize the data set provided by Liang *et al.* [13] and develop our own solutions to reduce data dimensions, process outliers, and impute missing entries.

Handling Redundant Attributes.   According to Fig. 2, "Iprec" and "precipitation" attributes are very similar. In fact, we perform a more definitive comparison, realizing that more than 95% values of "Iprec" and "precipitation" are identical. As a result, we detach "Iprec" column from the data set. Figure 1 also implies that the correlations among PM2.5 values measured from different stations are highly similar to each other, so we decide to keep only one PM2.5 record. By the analysis in Fig. 6, we decide to preserve the U.S. diplomatic post's version of the PM2.5 record since its data are the more complete than those of other observatories.

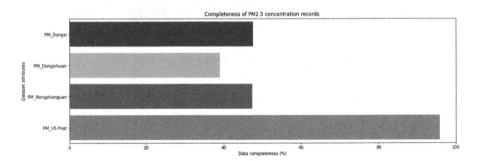

Fig. 6. Completeness of PM2.5 data

Outlier Removal.   The data set also contains anomalies. For Example, we discovered that the data set contains precipitation record of 999990 mm, which is certainly impossible to achieve. As a result, we set up a scheme to identify anomalous values. Similar to Zhang *et al.* [3], we regard PM2.5 data values greater than 500 ug/m^3, precipitation values exceeding 400 mm, wind speed that tops 500 m/s, and air pressures that go beyond 2000 kPa as anomalies. After identifying these anomalies, we replace them with NAN and refill them using imputation techniques.

4.2 Missing Values Imputation

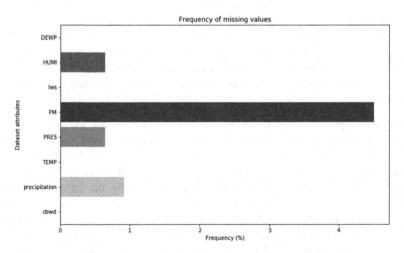

Fig. 7. Percentage of missing values in each attribute

Not only does the data set we use encompass anomalies, but also missing values [13]. According to Fig. 7, the number of missing values differ among each attribute, so we need to impute them separately. Since missing values are distributed randomly in the data set, we adopt different methods to handle them. Common methods for imputation include Next Observation Carry Backward (NOCF), Last Observation Carry Forward (LOCF), and linear interpolation [16]. Specifically, we use NOCF to impute missing values occurring at the beginning of the data set's record. For missing values at the tail of the record, LOCF is applied. At last, we handle missing values in between data entries with linear interpolation.

Processing Categorical Features. Not only does our data set contain numerical features but also categorical features. That is, some attributes of our data set can only have discrete values instead of continuous real numbers. For instance, date-time features can only have integer values. Although these categorical features can only be integers, they can be easily integrated into our regression model since integers are also numbers. However, the data set also contains categorical features that are not integers. For instance, wind direction attribute "cbwd" only stores string values (namely, NE for northeastern wind, SE for southeastern wind, etc.). As a solution, we map these string values to distinct integers so that wind directions can be integrated into our prediction model.

4.3 Feature Engineering

Liang *et al.* [13] have shown that PM2.5 concentrations are highly related to meteorological parameters, which motivates us to use meteorological parameters as one of the input variables for our PM2.5 prediction model. However, only using these attributes cannot produce high-accuracy prediction, and our means to improve model accuracy is to perform feature engineering. Time series itself can tell many information beyond the data values themselves. To study the relationship between PM2.5 concentrations and special occasions such as government meeting, holidays, diplomatic visits, and sport events, we generate additional date-time features with the help of external tools. To study the relationship between time series and itself, we extract lagged features and statistical features using sliding window mechanism. To study the seasonality of time series, we generate frequency-domain features via short-time Fourier transform. All features generated in our feature engineering process are listed in Table 3.

Holiday and Special Event Features. One main goal of our work is to study the influence of government's policies on PM2.5 concentration curve, and our means to investigate it is by creating date-time features. Motivated by Zhang et al.'s "is_weekend" features [3], we generate "is_holiday" attribute via using the external package "chinese-calendar"[2] so that our model can study the correlation between PM2.5 concentrations and holiday. In addition, we manually collected time intervals during which special events such as government meeting, sport events, and diplomatic visits occurred in Beijing during 2010 and 2015 from year tables provided by Baidu Baike. An excerpt of these collected events is available in Table 2. To integrate this special event data set into our feature data set, we create a Boolean column named "is_special_event" to denote whether the specific hour falls within any of the special event intervals of our special event data set.

Lagged Features and Statistical Features. Not only do we integrate features from external sources into our data set but also decompose the original data attributes to obtain new features. Correlation analysis in Fig. 4 reveals that time series in our data set are not completely independent of each other, and auto-correlation analysis in Fig. 8

Table 2. Selected samples from special event data set

Category	Event description	Starting date	Ending date
Meeting	First meeting of 12th National People's Congress	Mar 5, 2013	Mar 20, 2013
Visit	South Korea's President Lee Myung-bak visits China	Jan 9, 2012	Jan 11, 2012
Sport	Opening of 2010 Chinese Football Association Super League	Mar 27, 2010	Mar 28, 2010
Meeting	Second round of Sino-US military and economic dialogue	May 24, 2010	May 25, 2010

shows that time series are not independent of themselves either. To let our model study this relationship, we generate lag features with a period of 48 h. Zhang et al. [3] shows that statistical features are helpful in PM2.5 forecasting, so we also generate statistical parameters such as mean, minimum, and maximum over lagged features.

---

[2] It's an open source project at https://github.com/LKI/chinese-calendar.

Frequency-Domain Features. Time series varies with seasonality. A prediction model that understands the seasonality of PM2.5 time series may produce more accurate results than a model that does not study PM2.5's seasonality, and one way to extract seasonality of a time series is to analyze its spectrum. That is, we perform short-time Fourier transform on PM2.5 time series and incorporate the generated coefficients into each data entry. According to Fig. 9, Fourier coefficients of PM2.5 time series decay as the frequency increases, indicating that Fourier coefficients at high frequencies contain less useful information than those at low frequencies. As a result, we truncate the spectrum and only store Fourier coefficients of frequencies less than or equal to 0.02 units into our data set.

Features from "tsfresh" Package. In addition to the aforementioned features, we also considered incorporating features generated by a feature extraction package named "tsfresh." According to Christ et al. [17], this package extracts features from the data set using scalable hypothesis test. That is, a concrete mathematical method is used to determine whether a specific feature is relevant to (i.e., helpful for creating prediction on) the specified target variable. Examples of extractable features include lagged features, and wavelet features [18]. In our case, "tsfresh" extracts 122 relevant features for PM2.5 prediction. However, principal component analysis on these newly generated features reveals that the dimensions of "tsfresh" features can be virtually be reduced into 13. By analyzing these 13 principal components, we discovered that they are highly related to features that are already in our data set. For instance, as shown in Fig. 12, the largest principal component is almost identical to PM2.5 concentration trend. Therefore, we choose not to incorporate "tsfresh" features into our project.

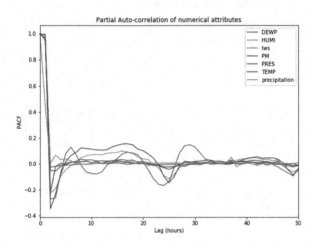

Fig. 8. Partial Auto-correlation analysis on the data set

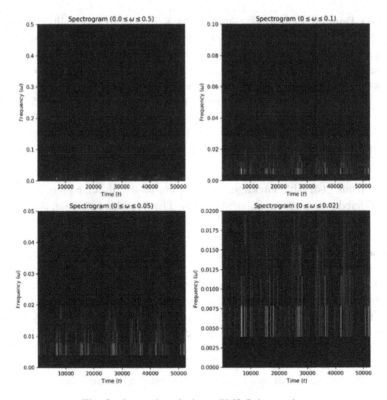

Fig. 9. Spectral analysis on PM2.5 time series

Table 3. List of newly generated features

Category	Feature	Description
Date-time features	is_holiday	Whether the entry is recorded during a holiday
	is_special_event	Whether Beijing held special events
Lagged features	{}_1, {}_2, {}_3... {}_48	Lagged meteorological and PM2.5 features with a size of 48 h
Statistical features	{}_mean, {}_min, {} _max	Local mean, minimum, and maximum on lagged features
Frequency-domain features	stft_1, stft_2, stft_3... stft_134	Truncated spectrum of PM2.5 time series

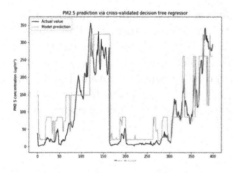

Fig. 10. PM2.5 prediction from decision tree

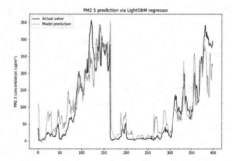

Fig. 11. PM2.5 prediction from LightGBM

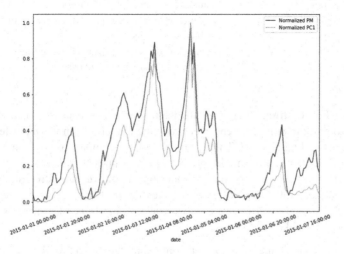

Fig. 12. Selection of normalized PM2.5 curve and normalized PC1 curve

4.4 Forecasting Method

Model Selection. Introduced by Ke et al. [12], LightGBM is a machine learning model based on gradient-boosting decision tree (GBDT) and XGBoost. Compared to traditional regression models such as decision tree, LightGBM is more efficient in training, especially when the amount and dimensions of the data are large. Particularly, LightGBM optimizes using bagging (i.e., trains tree models in parallel) and boosting (i.e., trains new models to minimize errors generated from the previous model). In fact, as shown in Figs. 10 and 11, LightGBM produces better prediction when the data contains many fluctuations. Therefore, we decide to build our prediction model using LightGBM as the basis for its efficiency and accuracy.

Configuration. To test whether rolling forecast helps the model provide more accurate PM2.5 prediction, we set up a baseline group that does not use rolling forecast. Instead, the baseline group uses data set features of the current day to predict PM2.5 on the next day. To verify how government policies affect the PM2.5 curve, we perform comparison on the control group and the experimental group. As shown in Table 4, the only difference between the control and experimental models is that the experimental group inputs holiday and special event features whereas the control group does not.

Table 4. Configuration of the experiment

Model	Input features
LightGBM without rolling forecast (baseline)	Features from original data set, lagged features, and statistical features. No rolling forecast
LightGBM (control)	Features from original data set, lagged features, and statistical features
LightGBM + holiday and special event (experimental)	Features from original data set, lagged features, statistical features, and holiday and special event features

Two-Stage Forecasting. For each model in our experiment, the same process is followed so that the only differences between the models are in the input features and whether using rolling forecast. To effectively verify the impact of government policies, we decide to let the control model predict PM2.5 values between Aug 20, 2015 and Sept 10, 2015. Because our study is independent of weather forecasting data, the prediction model itself needs to forecast meteorological parameters before predicting PM2.5 concentration values. Hence, a two-stage rolling forecast process is developed for the model to make predictions:

1 The model learns the training set containing the observed data and generated features
2 As illustrated in Fig. 13, the model first predicts meteorological features, then generate lagged features and statistical features, and, at last predicts PM2.5, and this process is executed for 24 times so that the hourly PM2.5 concentrations of the next day is predicted.
3 After one day, the model generates features from actual observation of meteorological features and PM2.5 data during the day and store them into the data set.
4 Retrain the model with the updated training set so that it becomes ready to predict PM2.5 of another new day.

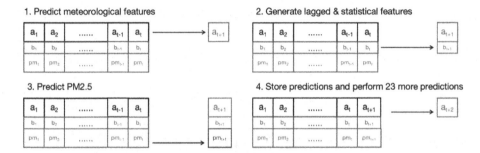

Fig. 13. Procedure for PM2.5 prediction

5 Performance Evaluation

After performing a series of experiments, we obtain three arrays of PM2.5 prediction: one from the baseline group that does not use rolling forecasting, one from the control group, and the other from the experimental group that incorporates holidays and special event features. As shown in Fig. 14, the control group is already able to make such an accurate prediction compared to the PM2.5 values actually recorded from the observatory, implying that the performance of our groups in the experiments cannot be solely determined by the visualizations. Consequently, we compare them using the evaluation metrics mentioned above in Eqs. (1), (2), and (3).

5.1 Model Comparison

In the study, we compare our prediction models with the LightGBM proposed by Zhang et al. [3] that uses weather forecasting data as inputs in addition to lagged features and statistical features. Although Zhang et al. used a different data set and configuration in their research. The comparison is still helpful on measuring how rolling forecast improves model accuracy. As Table 5 suggests, although incorporating weather forecasting indeed helps improve the accuracy of model prediction, the rolling-forecasting-based model we proposed yields substantially better results. In spite of the fact that the MAE scores worsen when comparing the baseline group and the control group, differences in RMSE and SMAPE scores between the baseline group and the control group reveals are substantially greater than those between Zhang et al.'s models. This phenomenon indicates that it is possible to make more substantial improvements on model accuracy without learning the weather forecasting data. In our case, we use rolling forecasting to fill in meteorological parameters and eventually achieve a more accurate prediction. Also illustrated in Table 5 is that the experimental group makes substantially more accurate PM2.5 prediction than does the control group. To determine how a change in government's event calendar, we perform what-if analysis on the experimental group (Figs. 15 and 16).

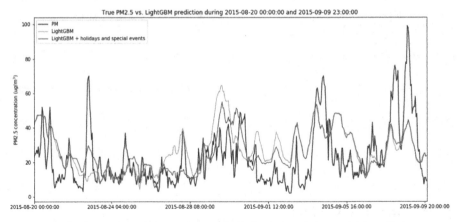

Fig. 14. Comparison between the true PM2.5 values and the models' predictions

Table 5. Comparison among the models

Model	MAE	RMSE	SMAPE
LightGBM without rolling forecast (baseline)	12.9255	18.1800	0.5695
LightGBM (control)	13.2621	17.1323	0.5453
LightGBM + holidays and special events (experimental)	11.7570	15.2813	0.4994
Zhang et al.'s model [3]	26.4359	32.8711	0.4229
Zhang et al.'s model without weather forecast [3]	26.6824	33.8922	0.4298

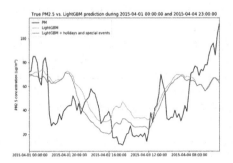

Fig. 15. PM2.5 prediction during April 1, 2015 and April 5, 2015

Fig. 16. PM2.5 prediction during June 1, 2015 and June 5, 2015

5.2 What-If Analysis

The term "what-if analysis" originally refers to detecting the impact of changing the cell values in a data sheet. In our study, we change the special event attribute to determine to which degree government event calendar assists PM2.5 prediction. In particular, we decide to compare the prediction results during two events: The IAAF

World Championships BEIJING 2015 during Aug 22, 2015 and Aug 30, 2015 and Military parade celebrating the 70th anniversary of victory over fascism from Aug 27, 2015 to Sept 3, 2015. As specified in Table 6, we let the aforementioned experimental model predict PM2.5 using an altered testing set that sets the special event flag to zero so that we can monitor how sensitive the model is to the nuance in government's event calendar.

Table 6. Configuration for what-if analysis

Model	Testing set setup
LightGBM + holidays and special events (normal)	Unchanged
LightGBM + holidays and special events (what-if)	All "is_special_event" are set to 0 (i.e., no special event occurring)

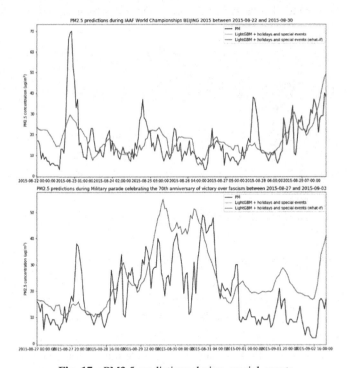

Fig. 17. PM2.5 predictions during special events

According to Fig. 17, the predicted curve of the control group and that of the experimental group completely overlap each other. Furthermore, as suggested in Table 7, it appears there were no differences between model scores. Therefore, the holiday and special event features did little in changing the model's performance. Further analysis in the next section offers a more detailed explanation.

Table 7. Model comparison during special events

Model	MAE	RMSE	SMAPE
IAAF World Championships BEIJING 2015			
LightGBM + holidays and special events (normal)	6.8482	9.5520	0.4019
LightGBM + holidays and special events (what-if)	6.8482	9.5520	0.4019
Military parade celebrating the 70th anniversary of victory over fascism			
LightGBM + holidays and special events (normal)	9.9296	12.4947	0.5006
LightGBM + holidays and special events (what-if)	9.9296	12.4947	0.5006

5.3 Feature Importance

One benefit brought by LightGBM other than efficiency and accuracy is that it allows users to study how much a specific feature of the data set contributes to the model prediction, and this functionality allows us to explain why there were no change in differences in accuracy between our normal group and what-if group.

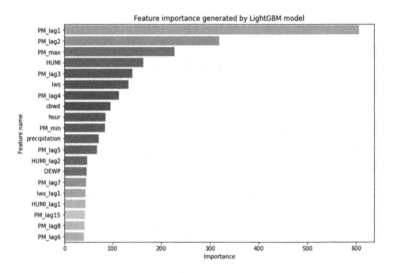

Fig. 18. Feature importance plot

As shown in Fig. 18, the key features that guide our LightGBM model to predict PM2.5 concentrations are lagged features and statistical features. This implies that nudges in holiday and special event features causes only little change in the prediction, which also means that lagged features and statistical features already compile sufficient information used for model prediction. Accordingly, using lagged features and statistical features alone can be already satisfactory to create accurate PM2.5 prediction models.

6 Conclusion

In our study, we propose a LightGBM model to produce PM2.5 prediction by processing high-dimensional data set. Specifically, we remove redundant attributes, filter out outliers, and impute missing values on this original data set created by Liang *et al.* [13]. Subsequently, we perform feature engineering on the preprocessed data set. For instance, we generate holiday and special event features using external packages and data sets to study how government policies impact PM2.5. In addition, we generate lagged features and statistical features using the sliding window principle. Furthermore, we generate frequency-domain features of the PM2.5 in order for the model to study the spectral characteristics of PM2.5 density values.

Following the feature integration, we conduct experiments on the model to testify the usefulness of holiday and special event features. Because our model does not use weather forecasting data, we adopt the two-stage rolling forecasting strategy to predict meteorological features and PM2.5 values. Additionally, for each 24 h, we retrain our models with newly observed features to prevent the model's prediction from deviating too much from the true PM2.5 curve.

After experimentation, we perform comparison among previous models and those we propose. An overview in evaluation metrics reveals that rolling forecast brings more substantial improvement to the prediction accuracy of the model than using weather forecasting data. A comparison between the control group and the experimental group in the overall testing set and special event intervals shows that holiday and special event features improves the model accuracy. Nevertheless, altering special event features in the testing set did not cause changes in predictions. In fact, this phenomenon is answered by the feature importance analysis. As LightGBM model's functionality suggests, what contribute most to the PM2.5 prediction are lagged features and statistical features, meaning that changes in holiday and special event features will not cause differences on the overall trend of the model prediction.

Although holiday and special event features in our study are unable to allow the prediction model to study the impact of government's policies on PM2.5 variation, the rolling forecasting technique put forward in this research creates a substantial improvement on the model accuracy, thus can be useful for future research in the field of PM2.5 prediction.

References

1. Wang, Y., et al.: Acute and chronic health impacts of PM2.5 in China and the influence of interannual meteorological variability. Atmos. Environ. **229**, 117397 (2020)
2. Xie, Y., Dai, H., Dong, H., Hanaoka, T., Masui, T.: Economic impacts from PM2.5 pollution-related health effects in China: a provincial-level analysis. Environ. Sci. Technol. **50**(9), 4836–4843 (2016)
3. Zhang, Y., et al.: A predictive data feature exploration-based air quality prediction approach. IEEE Access **7**, 30732–30743 (2019)

4. Zhang, C., Yuan, D.: Fast fine-grained air quality index level prediction using random forest algorithm on cluster computing of spark. In: 2015 IEEE 12th International Conference on Ubiquitous Intelligence and Computing and 2015 IEEE 12th International Conference on Autonomic and Trusted Computing and 2015 IEEE 15th International Conference on Scalable Computing and Communications and Its Associated Workshops (UIC-ATC-ScalCom), pp. 929–934 (2015)

5. Lee, J., et al.: Empirical analysis of tree-based models for PM 2.5 concentration prediction. In: 2019 13th International Conference on Signal Processing and Communication Systems (ICSPCS), pp. 1–7 (2019)

6. Wang, J., Song, G.: A deep spatial-temporal ensemble model for air quality prediction. Neurocomputing **314**, 198–206 (2018)

7. Ong, B.T., Sugiura, K., Zettsu, K.: Dynamically pre-trained deep recurrent neural networks using environmental monitoring data for predicting PM2.5. Neural Comput. Appl. **27**(6), 1553–1566 (2016)

8. Zheng, Y., et al.: Forecasting fine-grained air quality based on big data. In: Proceedings of the 21th ACM SIGKDD International Conference on Knowledge Discovery and Data Mining, pp. 2267–2276 (2015)

9. Qi, Y., Li, Q., Karimian, H., Liu, D.: A hybrid model for spatiotemporal forecasting of PM2.5 based on graph convolutional neural network and long short-term memory. Sci. Total Environ. **664**, 1–10 (2019)

10. Zhang, Q., Wu, S., Wang, X., Sun, B., Liu, H.: A PM2.5 concentration prediction model based on multi-task deep learning for intensive air quality monitoring stations. J. Clean. Prod. **275**, 122722 (2020)

11. Zhao, R., Gu, X., Xue, B., Zhang, J., Ren, W.: Short period PM2.5 prediction based on multivariate linear regression model. PLOS One **13**(7), e0201011 (2018)

12. Ke, G., et al.: LightGBM: a highly efficient gradient boosting decision tree. In: NIPS 2017 Proceedings of the 31st International Conference on Neural Information Processing Systems, pp. 3149–3157 (2017)

13. Liang, X., Li, S., Zhang, S., Huang, H., Chen, S.X.: PM2.5 data reliability, consistency and air quality assessment in five Chinese cities. J. Geophys. Res. **121**(17), 10220–10236 (2016)

14. Zhang, Q., Geng, G.: Impact of clean air action on $PM_{2.5}$ pollution in China. Sci. China Earth Sci. **62**, 1845–1846 (2019)

15. Lawrence, M.G.: The relationship between relative humidity and the dewpoint temperature in moist air - a simple conversion and applications. Bull. Am. Meteor. Soc. **86**(2), 225–233 (2005)

16. https://towardsdatascience.com/how-to-handle-missing-data-8646b18db0d4

17. Christ, M., Braun, N., Neuffer, J., Kempa-Liehr, A.W.: Time series feature extraction on basis of scalable hypothesis tests (tsfresh – A Python package). Neurocomputing **307**, 72–77 (2018)

18. Christ, M., Kempa-Liehr, A.W., Feindt, M.: Distributed and parallel time series feature extraction for industrial big data applications. arXiv Preprint arXiv:1610.07717 (2016)

A Spatial-Temporal Adaptive Video Denoising Algorithm

Shilong Lei[(✉)]

Department of Automation, Tsinghua University, Beijing, China
leisl18@mails.tsinghua.edu.cn

Abstract. Nowadays, video media is gaining increasing preference by the general public, and video denoising methods are paid lots of attention. In this paper, we present a novel Spatial-temporal Adaptive Denoising Algorithm, which adaptively changing denoising strategies according to the scene change of the micro block. The proposed method automatically chooses bilateral filter for a scene changing block and temporal filter for a relatively static block. Furthermore, our method adopts a fast motion estimation algorithm, which reduces the computational cost by adaptively adjusting the searching strategy based on the texture of micro blocks. Especially, the problem of the failure of temporal filter is alleviated with the scene changing frames. Experiments demonstrate that our method achieves satisfactory visual quality and PSNR (Peak Signal Noise Ratio) improvement.

Keywords: Video signal processing · Spatial filtering · Temporal filtering · White Gaussian Noise · Scene change

1 Introduction

Noise refers to unwanted random variations which can be added or multiplied with the video signal [1]. Video noise can be modeled as signal-independent or signal-dependent. Based on various spectral properties, video/image noise can be further classified as white or color noise. Video/image noise commonly includes Gaussian noise, Poisson noise, salt-and-pepper noise, etc. by their different models. In most research work, researchers are focused on white Gaussian noise and many denoise methods for Additive White Gaussian Noise (AWGN) were put forward, including image/video white Gaussian noise. In this work, our method will focus on white Gaussian noise.

In recent decades, great progress has been made in the area of image denoising. Typically, image denoising methods can be divided into three categories, including spatial denoising methods, frequency-domain denoising methods and CNN-based denoising methods [2]. The spatial denoising method removes noises by spatial domain filtering, which calculates the gray value of a pixel based on its correlation between the neighborhood. In [3], Bilateral filtering is proposed with its edge-preserving, noise-reducing and smoothing properties. By averaging the pixels in homogeneous regions and preserve edge information at the same time, it eliminates noise to a reasonable extent. However, the bilateral filter has a spatial domain kernel and a range domain

W. Cao et al. (Eds.): CONF-CDS 2021, CCIS 1513, pp. 249–259, 2021.
https://doi.org/10.1007/978-981-16-8885-0_20

kernel. When the radius of two kernels increases, the time costs become unacceptable. Based on the different characteristics of image information and noise in the transform domain, transform domain methods have developed a lot from the Fourier transform. In [4], an image denoising strategy was proposed based on an enhanced sparse representation in the transform domain. It is achieved by grouping similar 2D image blocks into 3D data arrays called "group" and then shrinking the transform spectrum of the 3D transformation of a group. This work preserves the essential unique features and fine details of blocks. Recently, CNN-based image denoising methods developed rapidly. The state-of-art denoising methods typically depend on CNNs. A fully blind video denoising method was proposed by [5], which is achieved by fine-tuning a pre-trained AWGN denoising network to the video with a novel frame-to-frame training strategy.

Typically, video denoising methods can be divided into traditional methods based on statistics and methods based on deep learning. The former uses spatial filters and temporal information, and is commonly based on statistical characteristics of noise, while the latter estimates noise models with the help of deep learning networks. In [6], a recursive video denoising method was proposed, which uses only the current frame and the previous denoised one. Each frame is modeled as a linear dynamic Gaussian model and denoised by a Kalman filter. This approach is mainly temporal. The results have a higher temporal consistency. However, it does not make good use of spatial information, which will help to achieve better performance in homogeneous regions. In [7], researchers presented a blind video denoising algorithm that adaptively measures noise level by the principal component analysis. Spatial and temporal information are both used to estimate the noise level. By texture-aware noise estimation, this method tries to achieve non-blind performance on the blind video sequence. It outperforms the state-of-art methods in most cases. From another perspective, deep learning has been widely used in the area of video denoising. A self-supervised approach for training multi-frame video denoising networks [8] has been proposed. This approach predicts each frame from the adjacent frames around it and benefits from the temporal consistency. It surpasses the performance of the state-of-art networks trained with supervision.

Generally, it can be seen that video/image denoising methods can be divided into two categories based on the usage of temporal information including traditional methods and deep learning methods. Methods mainly using spatial filters may lose edge information and blur texture region because of average operation for pixels around it. Methods mainly using temporal information could reduce noise on the whole frame but ignores spatial domain information. What's more, most methods are at the frame level, which means the denoising intensity or denoising approach is not appropriate. Without considering the characteristics of specific regions, some blocks can be lack filtering or over-filtered, which makes noise remained or the region blurred.

To solve the above problems, we present a novel video/image denoising algorithm in this paper. An adaptive block-level spatial-temporal video/image denoising algorithm, including 1) A fast adaptive motion estimation method based on AMMEA (Adaptive Multi-resolution Motion Estimation Algorithm) is introduced to search the best-matched block [9]. 2) A low complexity algorithm to detect scene changes. 3) A spatial-temporal joint filter is finally presented. Experiments show that the proposed method has good performance with PSNR up to 31.98 dB, which outperforms other traditional methods.

This paper is organized as follows. Section 2 presents the spatial-temporal adaptive video denoise algorithm and Sect. 3 shows the experimental results and analysis. Section 4 will conclude the paper.

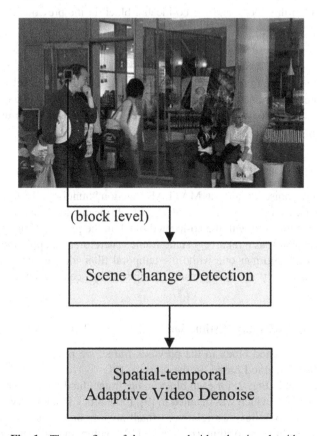

Fig. 1. The overflow of the proposed video denoise algorithm.

2 Spatial-Temporal Adaptive Video Denoise

The overall frame of the proposed denoising method is illustrated in Fig. 1. As frame level processing can lead to nonuniformity of denoising in different regions due to inappropriate filter intensity, we divide one frame into many adjacent and non-overlap 16 × 16 blocks. Thus, block-level adaptively denoising can be performed.

After dividing the frame into blocks, each block is fed into the Scene Change Detection module. In this module, we compare the current block with the co-located block in the previous frame to determine whether it is a scene-changing block.

Depending on whether it is a scene-changing block, the proposed algorithm will adaptively adjust the denoising strategy to obtain better results.

2.1 Scene Change Detection

For each block in the current frame, we calculate SAD (Sum of Absolute Differences) using (1) between this block and the co-located block in the previous frame.

$$SAD = \sum_{i=1,j=1}^{16,16} abs(C[i,j] - P[i,j]) \tag{1}$$

where $C[i,j]$ and $P[i,j]$ are the luminance values in the current block and the co-located block in the previous frame, respectively. Then we compare this SAD with a threshold TH, which is determined by different noise intensity. Empirically, we use Eq. (2) to estimate the threshold TH here.

$$TH = 118.56 \exp\left(2708.1\sigma_{noise}^2\right) \tag{2}$$

where σ_{noise}^2 is the noise variance in MATLAB function "imnoise". If SAD > = TH, we regard this block as a scene-changing block, which means this block has a relatively large difference compared with the co-located block in the previous frame. However, if SAD < TH, we treat it as a relatively static frame. Therefore, we apply the spatial filter to this block for the former one while the temporal filter for the later one. Thus, the whole frame adaptively denoising result is adjusted by scene detection at the block level.

2.2 Fast Adaptive Motion Estimation

To find the best-matched block in the previous frame, we propose the Fast Adaptive Motion Estimation method based on the work of [9].

As is illustrated in Fig. 2, for each block in the frame, firstly, we determine whether the block is stationary which was detailed in [9]. If the block is stationary, which means the best-matched block lies in a relatively small area around. Thus, we apply a full-search block matching algorithm (FSBMA) [12] within the search range (SR) of [SRx$_{static}$, SRx$_{static}$) × [SRy$_{static}$, SRy$_{static}$). However, if the block is not stationary, we will determine the degree of homogeneity to adaptively adjust the search strategy based on the texture complexity of the current region. According to the homogeneous regions detection method detailed in [9], we can make use of the Sobel edge operators to obtain the edge information and finally get the homogeneity size of the block denoted as $H(r, c)$. Therefore, according to $H(r, c)$, the block can be divided into three categories by two thresholds Thd1, Thd2. Experiments showed that Thd1 = 20000 and Thd2 = 16000 will achieve good performance. And each category corresponds to a search strategy as following.

If $H(r, c) \geq Thd1$, it means the current block shows highly complex texture and downsampling would result in non-negligible degradation. Hence, we apply FSBMA in the range of $[SRx^c_{L0}, SRx^c_{L0}) \times [SRy^c_{L0}, SRy^c_{L0})$ in the previous frame to search for the best-matched block.

If $Thd2 \leq H(r,c) < Thd1$, the current block is regarded as a modest complex texture region. Therefore, we adopt a 4:1 down-sampling search in the range of $[SRx^b_{L1}, SRx^b_{L1}) \times [SRy^b_{L1}, SRy^b_{L1})$ to find the so far best-matched block denoted M0. Then, we use the full-search method to search for the best-matched block in the range of $[SRx^b_{L0}, SRx^b_{L0}) \times [SRy^b_{L0}, SRy^b_{L0})$ centered in M0.

If $H(r,c) < Thd2$, it means that the current block contains homogeneous content and is suitable for down-sampling search in a wide range. So we first apply 16:1 down-sampling search in $[SRx^a_{L2}, SRx^a_{L2}) \times [SRy^a_{L2}, SRy^a_{L2})$ to find the best 3 matched blocks denoted as M1, M2, M3. The current block is denoted as C0. Then we apply four 4:1 down-sampling search in $[SRx^a_{L1}, SRx^a_{L1}) \times [SRy^a_{L1}, SRy^a_{L1})$ at the same time, which is centered in M1, M2, M3 and C0, respectively. Therefore, we get the so far best-matched block denoted M4 in these four regions. Centered in M4, we apply full-search within $[SRx^a_{L0}, SRx^a_{L0}) \times [SRy^a_{L0}, SRy^a_{L0})$ and finally get the best-matched block.

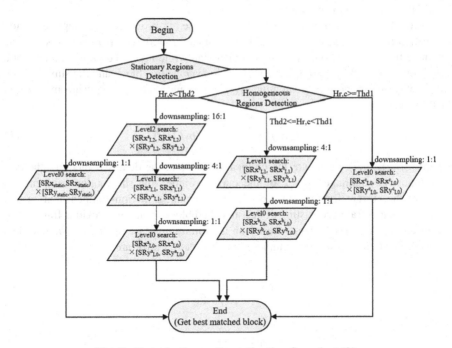

Fig. 2. Fast adaptive motion estimation flow chart [9].

2.3 Spatial and Temporal Adaptively Video Filter

Firstly, we consider the spatial filter method. Gaussian filtering is commonly used as a spatial filtering method. However, the Gaussian filter applies the same averaging operation to every pixel of the current block, which will blur the edge details in complex texture areas. To tackle this problem, we use Bilateral Filter to denoise the current block. It involves the ability to preserve edge information in the image. To apply Bilateral Filter, first, we calculate the weights as,

$$w(i,j,k,l) = \exp\left(-\frac{(i-k)^2 + (j-l)^2}{2\sigma_d^2} - \frac{\|I(i,j) - I(k,l)^2\|}{2\sigma_r^2}\right) \tag{3}$$

where σ_d and σ_r are smoothing parameters, and $I(i,j)$, $I(k,l)$ are the intensity of pixels (i,j) and (k,l) respectively.

After calculating the weights, we normalize them,

$$I_D(i,j) = \frac{\sum_{k,l} I(k,l) w(i,j,k,l)}{\sum_{k,l} w(i,j,k,l)} \tag{4}$$

where $I_D(i,j)$ is the intensity of the filtered pixel (i,j). In our experiment, we set $\sigma_d = 10$, $\sigma_r = 7$ with extensive experiments. The filter kernel size equals 3 as each pixel is filtered around the range of $[-1, 1]$.

Secondly, for the temporal filter method, we use our proposed fast adaptive motion estimation method to search a similar block called a motion-compensated block in the previous frame to filter out the temporal Gaussian white noise. To perform a temporal filter, for each block, we use special weights to average this block and the similar block in the previous frame after searching. By simplifying temporal denoising methods in [10], we can get,

$$I_D(i,j) = b_0 I(i,j) + b_1 I'(i,j) \tag{5}$$

where $I_D(i,j), I(i,j), I'(i,j)$ are the co-located pixels in the denoised block of the current frame, contaminated block of the current frame, and the motion-compensated block of the current frame, respectively. In particular, a motion-compensated current frame refers to a frame consisting of best-matched blocks from the previous frame. And b_0, b_1 are the filter coefficients. Based on the minimum least square's estimator [11], the optimal coefficients which minimize the estimation error are,

$$b_0 = \frac{\sigma_0^{-2}}{\sigma_{p(1)}^{-2} + \sigma_0^{-2}}. \tag{6}$$

$$b_1 = \frac{\sigma_{p(1)}^{-2}}{\sigma_{p(1)}^{-2} + \sigma_0^{-2}} \tag{7}$$

where σ_0^2 is the variance of undesirable noise in the current frame and $\sigma_{p(1)}^2$ is the variance of noise in the previous frame. According to [10], σ_0^2 can be obtained by dividing the frame into blocks with a size of 16×16, and then for each block, the variance is calculated and the average of the minimum 10 variances is used as σ_0^2. As for $\sigma_{p(1)}^2$, it can be calculated with the motion-compensated current frame and the contaminated previous frame. More details can be found in [10]. Thus, we can obtain $\sigma^2_{p(1)}$ by subtracting σ^2_0 from the block variance.

Thirdly, considering that scene changes can occur in some blocks, the denoising strategy of spatial and temporal adaptively filter would adjust to whether the scene changes or not. Therefore, the final filtering result is shown in (8),

$$
I_D(i,j) = \begin{cases} \dfrac{\sum_{k,l} I(k,l) w(i,j,k,l)}{\sum_{k,l} w(i,j,k,l)}, & \text{if } SAD \geq TH \\ b_0 I(i,j) + b_1 I'(i,j), & \text{if } SAD < TH \end{cases}
$$

(8)

Finally, we put the flow chart of the whole algorithm as follows (Fig. 3).

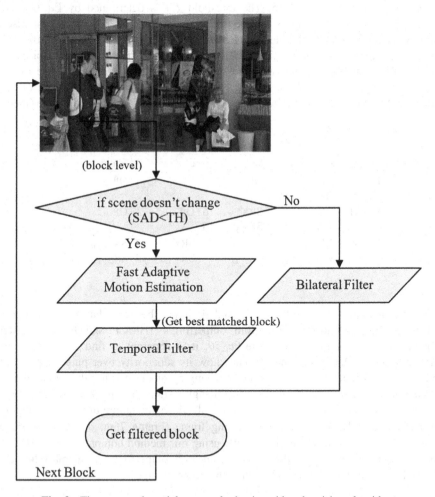

Fig. 3. The proposed spatial-temporal adaptive video denoising algorithm.

3   Experimental Results

We have conducted experiments to evaluate the performance of the proposed Spatial-temporal Adaptive Video Denoising Algorithm (SAVDA). We created several spliced video sequences for our test here. These spliced video sequences are all 200 frames with 832 × 480 resolution. *Pa&Ba_25* is obtained by splicing *PartyScene* and *BasketballDrill* every 25 frames. That is, 25 frames of *PartyScene* are followed by 25 frames of *BasketballDrill*, and then 25 frames of *PartyScene*, and so on. Similarly, *Pa&Ba_50* is obtained by splicing *PartyScene* and *BasketballDrill* every 50 frames and *Pa&BQ_25* is obtained by splicing *PartyScene* and *BasketballDrill* every 25 frames. We use the MATLAB function "imnoise" to add Gaussian noises with different variances to the luminance component of each frame. The variances used in "imnoise" are 0.0005, 0.0010, and 0.0015. The threshold *TH* is determined by Eq. (2). The proposed denoising algorithm is used to filter these video sequences. For comparison, the motion-compensated linear temporal filter with 1 hypothesis (1HMCF) [10] based on our Fast-Adaptive Motion Estimation, the Bilateral Filter [3] is used to denoise each noisy video sequences, respectively. For the Bilateral Filter, we set the size of two kernels are both 3 × 3 and $\sigma_d = 10$, $\sigma_r = 7$. Additionally, the search range of Fast Adaptive Motion Estimation (FAME) is set according to Table 1 in this experiment.

Table 1. The search range of FAME

Designs	a	b	c	Static
Level2	$SRx^a_{L2} = 128$ $SRy^a_{L2} = 96$	Off	Off	Off
Level1	$SRx^a_{L1} = 8$ $SRy^a_{L1} = 8$	$SRx^b_{L1} = 16$ $SRy^b_{L1} = 16$	Off	Off
Level0	$SRx^a_{L0} = 4$ $SRy^a_{L0} = 4$	$SRx^b_{L0} = 8$ $SRy^b_{L0} = 8$	$SRx^c_{L0} = 12$ $SRy^c_{L0} = 12$	$SRx_{static} = 12$ $SRy_{static} = 12$

As is tabulated from Tables 2, 3 and 4, it can be seen that Spatial-temporal Adaptive Video Denoising Algorithm outperforms 1HMCF and Bilateral Filter. Compared with *Pa&Ba_25* and *Pa&Ba_50*, it is apparent to find when the scene change is more intense, our method can show its superiority over pure temporal filtering better, as it adopts Bilateral Filter in changing blocks and use the temporal filter in stationary blocks. Particularly, at scene changing frame, our method will adaptively choose appropriate denoising strategy, which alleviates the failure of the pure temporal filter. For example, at one scene changing frame (Frame 76th, $\sigma^2_{noise} = 0.0005$) of *Pa&Ba_25*, the gain of PSNR is 2.55 dB using our method compared with 1HMCF. As is illustrated in Fig. 4, the proposed method outperforms Bilateral Filter and 1HMCF on *Pa&Ba_25*, especially when the scene changes.

Table 2. Noise variance = 0.0005

Video	PSNR(dB)			
	Unfiltered	1HMCF	BF	SAVDA
Pa&Ba_25	33.00	34.56	34.56	34.80
Pa&Ba_50	33.00	34.60	34.56	34.81
Pa&BQ_25	33.00	34.52	34.37	34.69

Table 3. Noise variance = 0.0010

Video	PSNR(dB)			
	Unfiltered	1HMCF	BF	SAVDA
Pa&Ba_25	29.99	31.82	31.24	31.90
Pa&Ba_50	29.99	31.87	31.24	31.92
Pa&BQ_25	29.99	31.82	31.12	31.85

Table 4. Noise variance = 0.0015

Video	PSNR(dB)			
	Unfiltered	1HMCF	BF	SAVDA
Pa&Ba_25	28.24	30.19	29.19	30.23
Pa&Ba_50	28.24	30.23	29.19	30.25
Pa&BQ_25	28.24	30.20	29.11	30.24

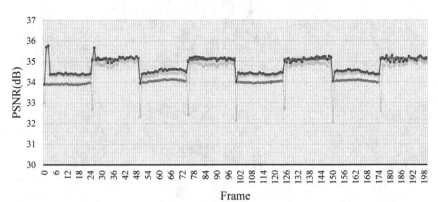

Fig. 4. Comparison of PSNR of each frame on *Pa&Ba_25* with σ_{noise}^2 = 0.0005 by BF, 1HMCF and SAVDA.

To evaluate the subjective quality of the filtered videos, two noisy consecutive scene changing frames of *Pa&Ba_25* (Frame 76th, $\sigma_{noise}^2 = 0.0015$) and its filtered result are shown in Fig. 5. As is illustrated in Fig. 5, the proposed algorithm has recovered more details and reduced more noise. Especially, the proposed algorithm is more robust between two consecutive fast scene changing frames.

(a) unfiltered: Frame 75th (left), Frame 76th (right)

(b) Bilateral Filter: Frame 75th (left), Frame 76th (right)

(c) 1HMCF: Frame 75th (left), Frame 76th (right)

(d) SAVDA: Frame 75th (left), Frame 76th (right)

Fig. 5. Two noisy consecutive scene changing frames of *Pa&Ba_25* with $\sigma_{noise}^2 = 0.0015$ and its filtered result.

4   Conclusion

In this paper, a novel Spatial-temporal Video Denoising Algorithm is proposed to better denoising video sequences, especially when the video has many scene-changing frames. Our method shows satisfactory denoising results by adaptively choosing appropriate denoising strategies. Furthermore, our method reduces computational cost in motion estimation module by adaptively changing searching strategies based on different textures. Finally, our method outperforms pure temporal filter and pure spatial filter with more PSNR improvements and better visual quality.

References

1. Ghazal, M., Amer, A., Ghrayeb, A.: A real-time technique for spatio–temporal video noise estimation. IEEE Trans. Circ. Syst. Video Technol. **17**(12), 1690–1699 (2007). https://doi.org/10.1109/TCSVT.2007.903805
2. Fan, L., Zhang, F., Fan, H., Zhang, C.: Brief review of image denoising techniques. Vis. Comput. Ind. Biomed. Art **2**(1), 1–12 (2019). https://doi.org/10.1186/s42492-019-0016-7
3. Tomasi, C., Manduchi, R.: Bilateral filtering for gray and color images. In: Abstracts of the Sixth International Conference on Computer Vision, pp. 839–846. IEEE, Bombay, India (1998)
4. Dabov, K., Foi, A., Katkovnik, V., Egiazarian, K.: Image denoising by sparse 3-D transform-domain collaborative filtering. IEEE Trans. Image Process. **16**(8), 2080–2095 (2007). https://doi.org/10.1109/TIP.2007.901238
5. Thibaud, E., et al.: Model-blind video denoising via frame-to-frame training. In: Proceedings of the IEEE/CVF Conference on Computer Vision and Pattern Recognition (2019)
6. Thibaud, E., Morel, J.-M., Arias, P.: Non-local Kalman: a recursive video denoising algorithm. In: 2018 25th IEEE International Conference on Image Processing (ICIP), pp. 3204–3208. IEEE (2018)
7. Xiao, J., Tian, H., Zhang, Y., Zhou, Y., Lei, J.: Blind video denoising via texture-aware noise estimation. Comput. Vis. Image Underst. **169**, 1–13 (2018). ISSN 1077–3142. https://doi.org/10.1016/j.cviu.2017.11.012
8. Valéry, D., Anger, J., Davy, A., Ehret, T., Facciolo, G., Arias, P.: Self-supervised training for blind multi-frame video denoising. In: Proceedings of the IEEE/CVF Winter Conference on Applications of Computer Vision, pp. 2724–2734 (2021)
9. Jie, L., et al.: Adaptive multi-resolution motion estimation using texture-based search strategies. In: 2014 IEEE International Conference on Consumer Electronics (ICCE). IEEE (2014)
10. Guo, L., et al.: A multihypothesis motion-compensated temporal filter for video denoising. In: 2006 International Conference on Image Processing. IEEE (2006)
11. Brown, R.G., Hwang, P.Y.C.: Introduction to Random Signals and Applied Kalman Filtering. Wiley, New York (1997)
12. Chen, T.C., et al.: Analysis and architecture design of an HD720p 30 frames/s H.264/AVC encoder. IEEE Trans. Cir. Syst. Video Tech. **16**(6), 673–688 (2006)

You Are What You Eat: Predictive Model of Eating Habits and Health Outcomes

Xiumin Chi[✉]

Shanghai Pinghe School, Shanghai, China

Abstract. Overweight/obesity and associated chronic disease have become a major global challenge for overall well-beings. This research adopts a large-scale purchase data set (including foods' corresponding energy and nutrition) of 420 million pieces collected from 1.6 million users of 411 Tesco supermarkets in London [7, 8], and the health data published by the local government of the same area (including child overweight and obesity [9], and adult diabetes [10]). Spearman correlation is used to identify the linear relationship between supermarket purchase data and health outcomes. Linear regression model is further utilized to explore the relationship between food consumption (total energy and fat energy, saturated fat energy, sugar energy, protein energy, carbohydrate energy, fiber energy, energy density and nutrition diversity) and first grade children (5–6 years old) overweight and obesity, sixth grade children (10–11 years old) overweight and obesity, and estimated adult diabetes prevalence. Finally, the research uses machine learning models to predict the health outcome.

The research results show that the food consumption data is related to children overweight and obesity and adult diabetes with statistics significance. Machines learning models can efficiently predict the incidence of children overweight and obesity and adult diabetes. Random forest model performed the best regarding first grade children overweight and obesity with an accuracy score of 0.73, and adult diabetes with an accuracy rate of 0.86. Logistics regression and gradient boosting model performed the best predicting sixth grade children overweight and obesity with an accuracy score of 0.89. The research conducted in this paper is beneficial for the government to inquire citizens' health conditions through the new data source of big supermarkets. Also, the government could promote or discourage the consumption of some food through issuing related policy to improve citizens' health conditions. Food companies could also develop new products that are beneficial for people's health based on the information discovered within the research, leading to a lower rate of chronic diseases such as diabetes among citizens.

Keywords: Food consumption · Machines learning models · Health

1 Introduction

Overweight and obesity become increasingly serious public health crisis across the world. One of the major diseases that is brought about by obesity and overweight is diabetes. In United Kingdom (UK), it is estimated that more than 1 in 16 people who

© Springer Nature Singapore Pte Ltd. 2021
W. Cao et al. (Eds.): CONF-CDS 2021, CCIS 1513, pp. 260–270, 2021.
https://doi.org/10.1007/978-981-16-8885-0_21

has diabetes, totaled 3.9 million people. As diabetes nowadays is considered mostly chronic disease, the burden on medical costs for critical continued treatment and medication would follow the patient for his or her entire lifetime. For each patient, the medication costs per month is estimated around $30. Thus, costs for treatment of diabetes for the entire country is aggregated to the number of $1.4 billion per month. As such, accurate estimation of the future diabetes prevalence would great benefit the society to initiate preventive measure that could be taken in advance to alter the health conditions of the people and save the cost. In particular, regarding the relationship between people's eating behavior and their health, there has been a theory about "you are what you eat" [1–3]. People's health is directly affected by the food and nutrition they ingest. Medical studies have proven the correlation between various single nutrient elements and health problems [4–6].

"Determinants of American food choice" explores how environmental changes would affect the choice of food through investigating immigrants' daily food purchases. The paper proves that there is a strong stability in people's food choice despite different environments they live in. "Resistance towards economic recession" proposed that for low-income people, even during economic recessions, the ratio of them eating at home and outside is still stable. Meanwhile, the ratio of eating at home is larger than that of eating outside despite race and gender.

However, from the perspective of real life, the specific impact of comprehensive intake of various foods and nutrients on health has not been studied in depth Based on the food purchase data from large supermarkets and the data on the health status of residents in the same area released by the health department, this paper attempts to explore food consumption patterns as an alternative perspective to understand how people's grocery purchase may affect them develop obesity-related diseases from what they eat.

2 Data

This research adopts a large-scale purchase data set (including foods' corresponding energy and nutrition) of 420 million pieces collected from 1.6 million users of 411 Tesco supermarkets in London [7, 8], and the health data published by the local government of the same area (including child overweight and obesity [9], and adult diabetes [10]). The research utilizes the accumulative data upon ward level (administrative area unit) to analyze the correlation between food consumption data (total energy and fat energy, saturated fat energy, sugar energy, protein energy, carbohydrate energy, fiber energy, energy density and nutrition diversity) and first grade children (5–6 years old) overweight and obesity, sixth grade children (10–11 years old) overweight and obesity, and adult diabetes (Table 1).

Table 1. Variable, definition, and value.

Term	Definition	Mean	Std
Total energy	Amount of energy from nutrients in total in the average product, in kcals	180.06	8.14
Saturated fat energy	Amount of energy from saturated fat in the average product, in kcals	31.88	1.63
Fat energy	Amount of energy from fat in the average product, in kcals	81.26	3.52
Protein energy	Amount of energy from protein in the average product, in kcals	21.07	0.9
Sugar energy	Amount of energy from sugar in the average product, in kcals	41.01	3.99
Carbohydrate energy	Amount of energy from carbohydrate in the average product, in kcals	73.03	6
Fiber energy	Amount of energy from fiber in the average product, in kcals	3.05	0.13
Energy density	Concentration of calories in the area's average product, in kcals/gram	0.49	0.07
Nutrition diversity	Density (entropy) of energy from nutrients, normalized in [0,1]	0.68	0.01
Female ratio	Ratio of female in total population of residents in the area. Calculated by female population	0.5	0.02
Average age	Average age of residents according to the 2015 census	36.24	3.14
Median income	The median income of households in a ward after log transformation	38793.33	6601.37
Children (aged 5–6) overweight and obesity prevalence	The total percentage of overweight and obese children when measured at the year of reception (aged 5–6)	0.331	0.072
Children (aged 10–11) overweight and obesity prevalence	The total percentage of overweight and obese children when measured at the sixth year (aged 10–11)	0.584	0.112
Adult diabetes prevalence	The estimated prevalence of adult diabetes	0.0636	0.0191

3   Data Analysis

First, Spearman correlation is used to explore the linear relationship between super-market food purchase data and health results, its statistics significance, and existing positive or negative correlation. Primarily investigate related factors.

We compare all nutrition data with children (aged 5–6 and aged 10–11) overweight and obesity prevalence and adult diabetes prevalence to select the statistically significant data (Table 2).

Table 2. Health condition data, food purchase data, correlation coefficient, significance

Children (aged 5–6) overweight and obesity prevalence	Saturated fat energy	0.1142	0.0089
	Protein energy	−0.1539	0.000
	Carbohydrate energy	0.1629	0.000
	Fiber energy	−0.5770	0.000
	Nutrition diversity	−0.2743	0.000
Children (aged 10–11) overweight and obesity prevalence	Protein energy	−0.2188	0.000
	Carbohydrate energy	0.1323	0.0024
	Fiber energy	−0.6181	0.000
	Nutrition diversity	−0.2932	0.000
Adult diabetes prevalence	Total energy	0. 5444	0.000
	Fat energy	0.3215	0.000
	Saturated fat energy	0.3411	0.000
	Sugar energy	0.4990	0.000
	Protein energy	−0.5050	0.000
	Carbohydrate energy	0.6532	0.000
	Fiber energy	−0.4831	0.000
	Nutrition diversity	−0.7585	0.000

Nutritional factors related to all three types of disease includes protein energy, carbohydrate energy, fiber energy, and nutrition diversity. Among them, carbohydrate energy demonstrates a positive correlation, which means that the more carbohydrate is in food purchased, the higher the ratio of overweight and obese children and adults with diabetes is. The other 3 factors all demonstrate a negative correlation, which means that the more protein or fiber is in food purchased, or the higher nutrition diversity is in food purchased, the higher the ratio of overweight and obese children and adults with diabetes is.

Among the other nutritional factors, saturated fat energy is related to two types of diseases with a positive correlation, which means that the more saturated fat is in food purchased, the higher the ratio of overweight and obese children and adults with diabetes is.

Among all three types of diseases, adult diabetes has a highest correlation with supermarket food purchase data, with 8 nutritional factors having statistical significance, demonstrating a correlation. Children (aged 5–6) overweight and obesity prevalence has 5 related nutritional factors. Children (aged 10–11) overweight and obesity prevalence has the least of 4 related nutritional factors.

The Spearman correlation exploration demonstrates that protein energy, carbohydrate energy, fiber energy, and nutritional diversity most prevalently suits the three different diseases belonging to different age groups, have a stable correlation with the diseases. Adult diabetes prevalence is the most reflective through supermarket food purchase data since it has the highest correlation with the nutritional data. It is due to that household purchasing behavior is usually controlled by adults. Thus, the food purchase data reflects adults' eating habits better than that of children. Although children have some impact on food purchased through influencing the adults, they do not have the control over purchasing behaviors.

Then we tried to identify the main factors from correlation exploration as independent variables of the linear regression models. The efficiency of the models was examined through comparing the coefficients of the model with proven health outcomes and identify the features with statistical significance.

Since some of the grocery purchase data have interrelationships, it is necessary to find a suitable combination of data that would work together and lead to the final outcome instead of contradicting and influencing each other. We use nutritional factors with significant correlation in the Spearman correlation investigation as independent variable and the three types of diseases as dependent variables to construct a linear regression model. Meanwhile, energy density was added to reflect the actual energy density distribution condition when all energies are average values (Tables 3, 4 and 5).

Table 3. Children (aged 5–6) overweight and obesity prevalence

	No. observations	Coefficient	Standard error	Significance
Total energy	475	−6.9189	1.042	***
Fat energy	475	7.8642	1.047	***
Saturated fat energy	475	−2.361	0.395	***
Sugar energy	475	0.3598	0.234	None
Protein energy	475	7.7301	1.063	***
Carbohydrate energy	475	6.942	1.035	***
Fiber energy	475	−26.6446	2.381	***
Energy density	475	−16.8144	7.994	*
Nutrition diversity	475	176.8799	21.335	***

Table 4. Children (aged 10–11) overweight and obesity prevalence

	No. observations	Coefficient	Standard error	Significance
Total energy	475	−10.081	1.549	***
Fat energy	475	12.3164	1.555	***
Saturated fat energy	475	−3.9173	0.587	***
Sugar energy	475	0.3507	0.348	None
Protein energy	475	9.7957	1.58	***
Carbohydrate energy	475	9.9671	1.539	***
Fiber energy	475	−40.917	3.538	***
Energy density	475	−37.6822	11.878	*
Nutrition diversity	475	284.4546	31.704	***

Table 5. Adult diabetes prevalence

	No. observations	Coefficient	Standard error	Significance
Total energy	475	−0.7069	0.201	***
Fat energy	475	0.6873	0.202	**
Saturated fat energy	475	0.287	0.076	***
Sugar energy	475	−0.181	0.045	***
Protein energy	475	−0.0712	0.205	None
Carbohydrate energy	475	0.9915	0.2	***
Fiber energy	475	−0.7849	0.459	None
Energy density	475	−6.1525	1.542	***
Nutrition diversity	475	15.7867	4.115	***

As shown by the three charts above, sugar energy demonstrated the same result as the Spearman correlation exploration, showing now statistical significance with children (aged 5–6 and 10–11) overweight and obesity prevalence. It demonstrated a negative correlation with adult diabetes prevalence, which is contradictory to the common medical knowledge that sugar leads to overweight and diabetes. The cause of the phenomenon may be the low influence of children on household purchasing behavior discussed before. Also, carbohydrates are transformed into sugar after entering the body. Thus, it is also considered as the main cause of overweight. The coexistence of these two factors within the linear regression model causes a cross-effect, making the significance and positiveness of sugar energy's correlation to be absorbed by carbohydrate energy.

However, protein energy and fiber energy which demonstrated a stable negative correlation within the Spearman correlation exploration also demonstrated insignificant correlation within this linear regression model with adult diabetes prevalence. Also, protein energy demonstrates a positive correlation within the model of the children overweight and diabetes, which is a mismatch with prediction of Spearman correlation. Thus, the model needs to be adjusted and improved.

Based on the problems summarized from the first model, part of the factors were adjusted, deleted and added.

Firstly, all nutrition energy factors were scaled to the range of [0,1] in order to remove the instability brought by the difference in the absolute values of the nutrition energies. For example, fiber energy is usually a lot smaller than other nutrition energies since fiber do not commonly exist in large amounts in foods.

Secondly, sugar energy and saturated fat energy were removed since these two factors may have a cross-effect with carbohydrate energy and fat energy. Total energy is removed since it may have a cross-effect with all of the other factors.

Thirdly, gender (female ratio), age (average age), and economic well-being (median income) [11] were added. Among them, median income went through logarithms calculation procedure to stabilize its standard deviation. According to prediction, adding the income factor could stabilize the problem occurred within the children overweight and obesity prevalence model since it is a variable reflecting children's influence on the household's purchasing behaviors.

The result of the new model is shown below (Table 6):

Table 6. Improved model of children (aged 5–6) overweight and obesity prevalence

	No. observations	Coefficient	Standard error	Significance
Fat scaled energy	475	−0.0226	0.037	None
Carbohydrate scaled energy	475	0.3344	0.048	***
Protein scaled energy	475	−0.0125	0.037	None
Fiber scaled energy	475	−0.3360	0.044	***
Energy diversity	475	31.0988	4.116	***
Female ratio	475	0.9464	1.602	None
Average age	475	−0.0398	0.012	***
Median income	475	−1.9000	0.269	***

Fat scaled energy, protein scaled energy, and female ratio are statistically insignificant. Carbohydrate scaled energy, fiber energy, average age and median income demonstrate a negative correlation. Nutrition diversity demonstrates a positive correlation.

Among them, the insignificance of protein scaled energy are inconsistent with the result of steady negative correlation demonstrated by the previous Spearman correlation exploration and already established medical research (Table 7).

Table 7. Improved model of children (aged 10–11) overweight and obesity prevalence

	No. observations	Coefficient	Standard error	Significance
Fat scaled energy	475	0.0849	0.034	**
Carbohydrate scaled energy	475	0.2248	0.045	***
Protein scaled energy	475	−0.0814	0.035	**
Fiber scaled energy	475	−0.3369	0.041	***
Energy diversity	475	32.0823	3.846	***
Female ratio	475	−3.2323	1.497	**
Average age	475	−0.0575	0.011	***
Median income	475	−1.7150	0.251	***

Fat scaled energy, carbohydrate scaled energy, and nutrition diversity demonstrate a positive correlation.

Protein scaled energy, fiber scaled energy, female ratio, average age, and median income demonstrate a negative correlation.

Among them, the positive correlation of nutrition diversity is inconsistent with the result of steady negative correlation demonstrated by the previous Spearman correlation exploration and already established medical research (Table 8).

Table 8. Improved model of adult diabetes prevalence

	No. observations	Coefficient	Standard error	Significance
Fat scaled energy	475	0.0765	0.033	**
Carbohydrate scaled energy	475	0.6063	0.043	***
Protein scaled energy	475	−0.4005	0.033	***
Fiber scaled energy	475	−0.1853	0.039	***
Energy diversity	475	27.2025	3.672	***
Female ratio	475	−5.1736	1.429	***
Average age	475	0.0348	0.010	***
Median income	475	−1.6106	0.240	***

Fat scaled energy, carbohydrate scaled energy, nutrition diversity, and average age demonstrates a positive correlation.

Protein scaled energy, fiber scaled energy, female ratio and median income demonstrates a negative correlation.

All factors except nutrition diversity corresponds with already known medical research.

It can be summarized from the three models above that the accuracy of the model has greatly enhanced after adjustments. The inconsistency of nutrition diversity may be due to the new factor added of median income. Improvements in economic conditions usually bring improvements in nutrition values provided by foods as the households have more options and care more about healthy. Thus, there may be a cross-effect.

Comparing the three models, adult diabetes prevalence model outperforms the children (aged 10–11) overweight and obesity prevalence model while there are still several insignificant factors within the children (aged 5–6) overweight and obesity prevalence model. It represents that children's influence on household purchasing is improved by the newly added factor of median income, but still has a impact on the models, which is consistent with the results demonstrated by the literature review. Thus, analyzing nutrition and health condition through the perspective of supermarket food purchase data is a reliable and realistic angle. The reliability and reality of the previous results are again proven.

4 Predictive Models

This research further utilized 5 different machine learning models to predict the prevalence of children overweight and obesity and adult diabetes through the sci-kit package in Python. The adopted models include Decision Tree, Logistics Regression, Random Forest, AdaBoost, and Gradient Tree Boosting.

Prediction accuracy of different models:
We divided the entire data set into two parts. 80% of the data is used to train the models while the rest 20% is used to evaluate the accuracy of the models. We categorized the outcome variables as high/low diabetes/overweight by separating the median value of each outcome. For example, the median value of children (aged 5–6) overweight and obesity prevalence is 32.5. If the predicted/actual result is over or equal to 32.5, the result would be categorized as high overweight and obesity. Otherwise, it would be categorized as low overweight and obesity. After all health result variables were transformed into the binary form, machine learning models would be trained based on training data. The entered variables included fat scaled energy, carbohydrate scaled energy, protein scaled energy, fiber scaled energy, energy diversity, female ratio, average age, and median income, which were the independent variables of the improved linear regression model. The predicted variable is the corresponding health outcome. Then, the model would predict the result of the rest 20% of data. Predictions were compared with actual results, and thus gave an accuracy rate of the model based on F1-score.

Table 9. F1-score model accuracy

	Children (aged 5–6) overweight and obesity prevalence	Children (aged 10–11) overweight and obesity prevalence	Adult diabetes prevalence
Decision Tree	0.67	0.8	0.81
Logistics Regression	0.72	0.89	0.82
Random Forest	0.75	0.87	0.86
Ada Booster	0.73	0.83	0.81
Gradient Boosting	0.69	0.89	0.85

Hyperparameters of all models are fine-tuned through grid-search. As shown by Table 9, Random Forest model performed the best at predicting children (aged 5–6) overweight and obesity prevalence with an accuracy rate of 0.73, and adult diabetes prevalence with an accuracy rate of 0.86. Logistics regression and gradient boosting model perform the best predicting children (aged 10–11) overweight and obesity prevalence with an accuracy rate of 0.89.

Again, out of the three different health result variables, adult diabetes prevalence can be most accurately predicted while the accuracy decreases with the decrease in patients' age.

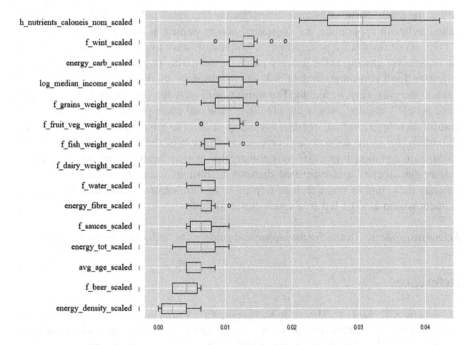

Fig. 1. Most important features ranked by importance scores

As Random Forest is the most suitable model in our case, we can further explore what factors in it are more predictable and discriminative for making the predictions. We adopt the permutation importance that is a model inspection technique. We calculated the importance of features within the random forest model suitable for adult diabetes. Figure 1 shows the most important features based on the sequence of its importance score. As expected, nutrition diversity, carbohydrate scaled energy, and median income are important features of determining adult diabetes. The interesting fact is that wine energy is also an important feature ranked high on the list. A possible interpretation for the fact is that wine, as a more expensive and high-end type of liquor, is more generally consumed by households with higher income. Medical research showed that the social economic well-being may be the determining factor for adult diabetes.

5 Conclusions

The research successfully completes and proves the 3-step connection of human shopping behavior, i.e., food consumption habits and health condition outcome. The theory that what people eat determines their health outcomes has long been established, and there exists an overarching relationship between what people bought and what they eat. However, this is a relatively novel perspective to establish between groceries purchase and people's health outcomes. Thus, it opens up a new pathway to develop further research about consumer consumption and health. Behavioral economics is linked to health economics, are connected and examined in this case.

Given our results, for government, it is relatively easy to predict health condition of the citizens by looking at the grocery purchase data. This requires less effort compared to getting food consumption data, asking citizens door by door about what they have eaten in the past week or month. The result would have the possibility to be unreliable since people's memory would not hold over time and some people tend to not disclose truthful diet due to various reasons including distrust to government investigators. By controlling for more accurate and precise information of the citizens, the government could initiate tailored policies to stabilize the overall health condition, preventing overweight, obesity and estimated diabetes to turn into actual diseases. With more accurate data, further research based on these health outcomes published by the government would also be led to a result closer to reality.

Acknowledgement. Thanks for the support and guide of Dr. Weiqi Han regarding the data set!

References

1. Bryden, K.S., Neil, A., Mayou, R.A., Peveler, R.C., Fairburn, C.G., Dunger, D.B.: Eating habits, body weight, and insulin misuse. A longitudinal study of teenagers and young adults with type 1 diabetes. Diabet. Care **22**, 1956–1960 (1999)
2. Savoca, M.R., Miller, C.K., Ludwig, D.A.: Food habits are related to glycemic control among people with type 2 diabetes mellitus. J. Am. Diet. Assoc. **104**, 560–566 (2004)
3. Flegal, K.M., Kruszon-Moran, D., Carroll, M.D.: Trends in obesity among adults in the United States, 2005 to 2014, vol. 315, pp. 2284–2291 (2016)
4. Lodefalk, M., Aman, J.: Food habits, energy and nutrient intake in adolescents with Type 1 diabetes mellitus. Diabet. Med. **23**, 1225–1232 (2006)
5. Toeller, M., Buyken, A.E., Heitkamp, G., Cathelineau, G., Ferriss, B.: Nutrient intakes as predictors of body weight in European people with type 1 diabetes. Int. J. Obes. **25**, 1815–1822 (2001)
6. Liese, A.D., Weis, K.E., Schulz, M., Tooze, J.A.: Food intake patterns associated with incident type 2 diabetes. Diabet. Care **32**, 263–268 (2009)
7. Aiello, L.M., Quercia, D., Schifanella, R., Prete, L.D.: Tesco Grocery 1.0, a large-scale dataset of grocery purchases in London. Sci. Data **7** (2020)
8. Aiello, L.M., Schifanella, R., Quercia, D., Prete, L.D.: Large-scale and high-resolution analysis of food purchases and health outcomes. EPJ Data Sci. **8** (2019)
9. The NHS National Child Measurement Programme. https://digital.nhs.uk/data-and-information/publications/statistical/national-child-measurement-programme/2015-16-school-year
10. London DataStore, Obesity in Adults. https://data.london.gov.uk/dataset/obesity-adults
11. London DataStore, Household Income Estimates for Small Areas. https://data.london.gov.uk/dataset/household-income-estimates-small-areas

Using Co-evolution of Artefacts in Git Repository to Establish Test-to-Code Traceability Links on Method-Level

Yichao Xu$^{(\boxtimes)}$

University College London, Gower Street, London WC1E 6BT, England, UK
`yichao.xu.19@ucl.ac.uk`

Abstract. Test-to-code traceability links describe the test relationship between the test codes and the product codes. It is beneficial for maintaining the test codes during developing, but to manually create and manage such links are time-consuming and fragile. The automatic link establishing strategies can properly solve such an issue.

Our works analyse the feasibility of using the co-evolution relationship in the code repositories to establish links between test and tested codes. Because the performance of such an idea depends on how the developers maintain their test codes, we mined six projects to observe how their developers did. The results demonstrated the rareness of such a relationship, which implies the bad performances of the idea.

We still implemented the Co-Evolution and the three optimisations: co-creation relations, the commits filters, and the APRIORI algorithm. Then, we applied all these approaches to three large, well-studied open-source Java projects. The precision, recall and f1 score were used as performance measures during the experiments. Although all of them performed worse results than the previous approaches, the Co-Evolution approach shown a significant boost after these optimisations. That implies the potential of such kind of idea that to use the information from version control tools to establish the test-to-code traceability links.

Keywords: Test-to-code traceability link · Codes co-evolution · GitHub repository mining

1 Introduction

Test-to-code traceability link is a way to model the relationship between tests (i.e. test codes) and functions (i.e. product codes). This kinds of links are helpful for developing, maintaining, and testing. As for the developing, a unit test is a continuously updating document of a certain function for its common user stories [1]. The test-to-code traceability links imply them test relationships between functions and tests, which make the codes more understandable. As to the maintaining, the unit tests may need to be refactored or even be re-engined after changing the tested functions [1], so the possible issues will occur if the developers unexpectedly forget to change some of them. Well-maintained traceability

© Springer Nature Singapore Pte Ltd. 2021
W. Cao et al. (Eds.): CONF-CDS 2021, CCIS 1513, pp. 271–287, 2021.
https://doi.org/10.1007/978-981-16-8885-0_22

links can help to avoid this kind of problems because these links precisely indicate the tests of each function. Regarding testing, these links provide the developers with a more specific view about the validation of the software [2], compared with the line or the branch coverage.

It is time-consuming to maintain such links manually during development. Hence, a better way is to automatically establish them when needed. There has already been some widely-used technique. The most common ones are String-Based approaches like the "Naming Convention" (i.e. NC). In NC, the tests and functions are linked if their names following a simple pattern. For example, the function "A" and test "testA" will be linked. There still are Invocation-Based approaches. One example is "Last Call Before Assert" (i.e. LCBA), which will establish links if a function is invoked at the end of a test. Except for the two, many Statistical Call-Based approaches were also proposed in previous researches. All of them base on own assumption to the developers of a project. Specifically, the String-Based ones rely on that the developers named the tests and functions following specific patterns. The Invocation-Based and Statistical ones assume the particular invoking locations or frequency of functions in the tests. Because not all developers follow these assumptions, their performances fluctuated in different projects. Even if the current approaches have shown high performance in many projects, it is still valuable to investigate the possible new approaches. Because they may be more suitable in some cases. The idea of the CoEv focuses on the changes in the project's repository instead of the codes. It is potential to find out the hidden links from the co-evolution relationship. Moreover, White [3] implemented the TCtracer, which uses different approaches to score links and then choose the links with high scores. The idea addresses the issues from the unexpected programming customs by mixture results of different approaches. The tools like TCtracer demand more approaches based on various assumptions. Therefore, our research on the CoEv is valuable to it.

As to our works, we implement the CoEv on the method-level and three optimised approaches. Our research questions are about the feasibility of the co-evolution-based idea and the performances of the implemented approaches. To investigate the usability, we analyse how the developers maintained the tests in six open-source Java projects. For measuring the performances, these approaches are applied to the repositories of three widely-used open-source projects. The precision, recall and f1-score are used to evaluate their performance. The main contributions of the paper are:

- An analysis of the test maintenance for six open-source Java projects.
- An tool for establishing test-to-code traceability links between the test methods and tested functions by the CoEv approach.
- An evaluation for the performances of these strategies on the method-level to three open-source Java projects.

The remained parts of the paper is based on the structure below: Sect. 2 discusses the previous the related research about the co-evaluations; Sect. 3 demonstrates all techniques used and the implementation of them in the tool; Sect. 4 discusses the experimental design, the experimental implementation and the findings from the experiments; Sect. 5 compares the co-evaluation methods with other strategies; And Sect. 6 concludes the whole paper.

2   Background

Regarding the previous works, the most straightforward idea to establish a test-to-code traceability link is to manually identify the links after creating tests and also manually update them after changing. The idea was actually suggested by many standards and papers [2,4,5], but the manually-maintained links are fragile, error-prone and time-consuming [2,3,6,7]. Various automatic approaches have already been proposed for solving these issues. The most classic ones are "Naming Conventions" (NC) and "Last Call Before Assert" (LCBA): NC assumes that the name of a tested function is similar to the names of its tests, like the 'functionA()' and the 'testFunctionA()'; LCBA believes that a tested function is always invoked at the end of its tests. In addition to the two common approaches, there are "Statistical Call-based Techniques" (SCTs) and the "Co-Evolution" (CoEv) approaches. SCTs uses the statistical data to calculate scores for the possible links and then filter invalid ones out by a predefined threshold. White [3] has implemented such kind of approaches based on the Tarantula fault localisation and Term-Frequency-Inverse Document Frequency (TFIDF). CoEv mines the repository of the target software to find out all functions and tests changed in the same commits, and links all of them. It was implemented by Rompaey on the class-level [7], but the approach performed with worse precision and recall than others.

In terms of the related works, our approaches are enlightened by the research approaches and the findings from the papers about the co-evolution of the software artefacts. As to their approach, both Marsavina [8] and Vidacs [9] used the APRIORI algorithm to find out the association rules for the changes occurred on linked functions and tests. We "reverse" such an idea and apply the algorithm directly to all tests and functions in a project. After that, the association rules between tests and functions are identified as the traceability links. Besides, Zaidman [10] analyse the test behaviours in three open-sources projects by the co-evolution of test and product code. We partly redo their experiments by using a visualised technique, "Change History View", to analyse how the developers in six open-sources Java projects maintained their test codes. As for the result, Marsavina [8] released a series of co-evolution patterns between test codes and product codes. We use the co-creation pattern to establish the traceability links. Such a pattern implies that a tested function is frequently co-created with its tests in most projects.

3   Approach

Our works focus on the CoEv approach on tests-level. We divided it into two steps: The first one is to mine the code repository to obtain the changes in each commit; The second one is to establish the links from the co-evolution of tests and functions. In the following parts of the section, we discuss the two steps respectively.

3.1 Repository Mining

Figure 1 shows a process for repository mining. We extract the changes on each commit from the Git repository, and then stores them into a database. Three different programs are used:

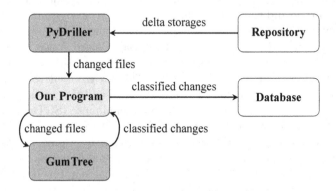

Fig. 1. Processes for changes mining

PyDriller.[1] It is used to mine the changes on each commit of a repository, including changed files, tests and functions. However, the tool cannot identify the specific types of these change, which makes impossible to track them after renaming.

GumTree.[2] It is used for identifying the type of changes. The tool is similar to the DIFF, but it can provide us with more information such as adding new local variables, removing a test invocations, or modifying the value of a certain field [11]. In our approach, we classify changes into the following four categories:

- *ADD*: A new test or a new function is created.
- *MODIFY*: The codes of a test or a function are changed.
- *RENAME*: The signature of a test or a function is changed.
- *OTHERS*: The changes to global variables, the class variables, or the interface etc.

Our Program. It handles the interaction between the *PyDriller* and the *GumTreeDiff*. After *PyDriller* finds out the changed files in a commit, these files will be sent to our program, and then the *GumTreeDiff* will be invoked to extract the fine-grained changes from these files. Then, our program classifies all of these changes and puts results into a database.

---

[1] PyDriller:https://github.com/ishepard/pydriller.

[2] GumTreeDiff:https://github.com/GumTreeDiff/gumtree.

3.2 Link Establishing

"Co-Ev" approach links tests and functions changed in single commit, which relies on the intuition that the tests and the functions are evolved together. Because of its bad recall and precision value comparing with others, we also implement the following three optimised approaches.

Co-create Pattern. As we discussed in previous sections, Marsavina [8] and Vidacs [9] find out a co-creation pattern which implies a strong relationship between the creating of a function and its tests. According to the pattern, it is reasonable to deduct that a function is typically created with its tests in the same commit. Therefore, we link all tests and functions, which are created in single commits.

Commits Filters. During the researching process, we find that hundreds of or even thousands of unrelated tests and functions are changed in some commits. It is a common situation during developing. For example, the developer added the keyword final to nearly all tests at a single commit in the repository of the Commons-Lang. Understandably, such kind of commits can lead to a broad set of mistaken links, so we applied a set of filters to find out these abnormal commits and ignore them during link establishing.

APRIORI Algorithm. The last one comes from the testology in [8] and [9]. The original version of the algorithm is used to mine the association rules for items from a large number of transactions [12]. In the case that two entities are associated, it is reasonable to believe that they will occur again in future transactions. In our optimisation, the changes to codes and commits are seen as the items and the transactions, respectively. We apply the algorithm to find out the association rules between the changes to both of the tests and the functions. Such a kind of rules implies a strong co-evolution relationship between the tests and the functions. According to our previous assumption, we believe that the test and the function in a traceability link are frequently changed, so it is reasonable to link tests and functions which are associated together.

Figure 2 illustrates how the algorithm predicts a link. Specifically, there are four different steps: Firstly, the algorithm finds out all frequently changed tests (FCT) and frequent changed functions (FCF). Two thresholds, *"min test changes support"* and *"min function changes support"* are used in here to define the FCT and FCF. A test (or a function) will be classed as frequently-changed ones, if the number of commits where it was changed is larger than the *"min test changes support"* (or the *"min function changes support"*). In Fig. 2, there are three tests and two of them are FCTs (t_{01} and t_{02}). There are two functions and all of them are FCFs (f_{01} and f_{02}). Secondly, the algorithm constructs a series of combinations by joining each FCT and FCF together, which is similar to the Cartesian product for a set of FCTs and a set of FCFs. In Fig. 2, there are four combinations, $(t_{01}, f_{01}), (t_{01}, f_{02}), (t_{02}, f_{01}), (t_{02}, f_{02})$, because of the two FCFs

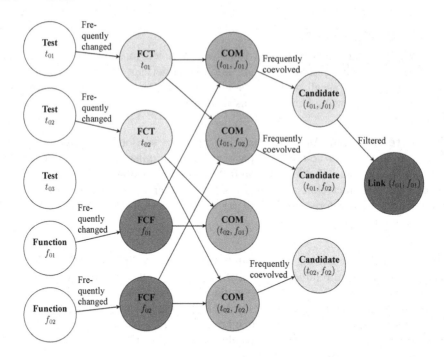

Fig. 2. Illustration for APRIORI Algorithm

and the two FCTs. Thirdly, the algorithm finds out all combinations in which both the FCF and FCT are frequently changed. These combinations are seen as candidates for the links. We use a threshold, *"min coevolution support"*, to identify whether a combination is a candidate or not. If it is, the number of the commits, where both FCF and FCT in the combination were changed, should be larger than the threshold. Finally, the algorithm will output any candidate link whose confidence value is greater than the *"min confidence"*. The number is a threshold to limit the confidence value of the predicted links, and we use the following equation to calculate the confidence of a candidate link.

$$Confidence = \frac{\#OfCoEvolvedCommits}{\#OfFunctionEvolvedCommits}$$

The numerator is the number of commits where both the FCF and FCT in the candidate link were changed. And the denominator is the number of the commits in which the FCF was changed. In Fig. 2, there is only one remained candidate which satisfies the limit for min confidence, so the algorithm will only outputs the (t_{01}, f_{01}) as a predicted link. The algorithm uses total four thresholds, and Table 1 shows the values of these thresholds that we used during the experiments. Specifically, as for three *support_numbers*, the median are used, because it filter out the lower half from the dataset. As to the confidence, we simply use the 0.5 as universal threshold for all projects.

Table 1. Values for all thresholds

Threshold	Value
$min\_function\_change\_support$	$Median_{functions}$
$min\_test\_change\_support$	$Median_{tests}$
$min\_coevolution\_support$	$Median_{coevolution}$
$min\_confidence$	0.5

4 Evaluation

In this section, we discusses the research questions, experiments design, and their result.

4.1 Research Questions

Our first research question focuses on how developers maintained the tests. As we mentioned, CoEv is based on the assumption for co-evolution, which is directly affected by the developers' behaviours when they maintain the tests. Specifically, suppose they always change the product codes and the test codes in different phases. In that case, the approach will undoubtedly show a bad performance. It is reasonable to estimate that the approach will perform with high precision and recall if the developer continually updates or creates the tests with the functions together. The second one is about the performance of all approaches that we implemented.

In conclusion, the two research questions are list as below:

- **RQ01**: How the developers typically maintain the tests in the real-world projects? Is the tests co-evolve with the functions frequently?
- **RQ02**: What are the performance of the co-evolution, co-creation, commits-filtered co-evolution and APRIORI approach in method-level?

4.2 Experiments Design

Tests Maintenance Behaviour Analysing. For investigating the research question, we first counted the number of different commits. These figures numerically demonstrates the frequency of the co-evolution. And then, we used the *"Change History View"*. It was used by Zaidman [10] for analysing developers' behaviours when they maintain test codes. Such a diagram provides us with a visualised and general view about the changes of tests and functions based on commits. Figure 3 shows the example for such a view. Its x-axis is the id for each commit, and y-axis is the id for each method. The shape of point means different types of changes: $+$ is *ADD-METHOD*, Δ is *MODIFY-METHOD* and $\star$ is *RENAME-METHOD*. Besides, the different color can be used to identify the changes to the tests and the tested function: red points are for the functions, and the blue ones are for the methods.

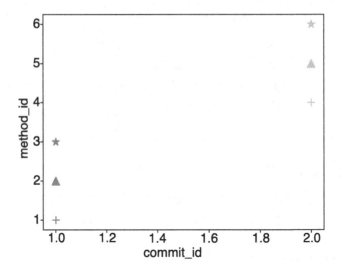

Fig. 3. Example for change history view

Approaches Performance Measuring. In the experiments for the performance of different approaches, we use the ground-truth data from White [3] and there are total 138 oracle links on the method-level. These links were manually identified by three different judges respectively, and then the disagreements were inspected collectively. In order to evaluate the performance of link establishing approaches, the following three measures are used: The first one is the *"Recall"* value, which is used for analysing how many expected links are successfully predicted, by a approach. The following equation is used to calculate the measures:

$$Recall = \frac{TruePositive}{TruePositive + FalseNegative} = \frac{\#OfValidPredicts}{\#OfGroundTruthLinks}$$

The next one is the *"Precision"*, which is used to describe the relationship of how many predicted links are expected. The formula below is used to calculate the measure.

$$Precision = \frac{TruePositive}{TruePositive + FalsePositive} = \frac{\#ofValidPredicts}{\#ofAllPredicts}$$

"F1-Scores" is used to balance the value of the *"Precision"* and *"Recall"*. The formular for *"F1-Scores"* is:

$$F1Score = 2 \times \frac{Precision \times Recall}{Precision + Recall}$$

Experiments Subjects. As to the first research question, we select the following six open-source Java projects on GitHub: *Guava, Argouml, Apache-Ant, Commons-Lang, Commons-IO, JFreeChart.* As for the second research question, the following three projects are used: *Commons-Lang, Commons-IO, JFreeChart*. We select these projects as our subjects because they are famous, the widely-used in many projects, continuously and frequently maintained on the GitHub website.

4.3   Experimental Setup

In the projects, we use various different parameters, so this section discusses all of them on each projects.

Table 2. Paths for the tests and functions in six projects

Project name	Tested path	Test path
Commons-IO	src/main/	src/test/
Commons-Lang	src/main/	src/test/
JFreeChart	source/	tests/
Guava	guava/src/	guava-tests/
Apache-Ant	src/main/	src/tests/
ArgoUML	src/argouml-*/src/	src/argouml-*/tests/

Pathes. In the experiments, the paths of source codes are used to distinguish the tests and functions. Table 2 shows the two paths for the six projects that are used in our experiments. In the four projects, *Commons-Lang, Commons-IO, JFreeChart* and *Guava*, all tests and functions are stored in two separate directories. In *Apache Ant*, it is slightly different, but the number of the tests and the functions in the two directories occupy about 95% of the total number. The most of the remained ones are those for the tutorials or the example codes etc., so it is reasonable to only consider the codes in the two directories. Regarding *ArgoUML*, the project structure is relatively-complex, because the test and the product codes are put into many different directories. Fortunately, the directories for both test codes and product codes follow two patterns. We demonstrate the two patterns in Table 2, in which the character ∗ is the wildcard.

Parameters. As to the Commits-Filtered Co-evolution approach, there are four filters in the and these filters base on the the values of the Min, $Q1$, $Q3$ and Max to the number of each types of changes in a project. Figure 4 shows the box-plot for the number of each type of changes in three projects, which also demonstrates all parameters that we used in the approach. Specifically, there are 12 boxes: the top four are for the "*JFreeChart*", the middle and the bottom boxes are for the "*Commons IO*" and "*Commons Lang*" respectively.

The different colours means different types of changes: the black is for all changes, the red is for "ADD-METHOD", the blue is for "MODIFY-METHOD" and the green is for "RENAME-METHOD". Therefore, in the first two filters, we focus on the IQR and the length of whisker for black boxes in the diagram. For the other two, we find out the these values from the boxes in other three colours. As for the APRIORI algorithm, there are four parameters. The value of the $min\_confidence$ is universal for all projects, but the remained three are depended by the project. Table 3 shows their values. Specifically, the column 2 is the median for the number of commits in which at least one test was changed. The column 3 is for commits where at least one function was changed. The column 4 is for the commits where at least one test and one function changed.

Table 3. Counts for the *co-evolved commits* and *evolved commits*

Projects	Functions	Methods	CoEvolution	Confidence
Commons-Lang	1	3	2	0.5
Commons-IO	1	3	2	0.5
JFreeChart	2	1	1	0.5

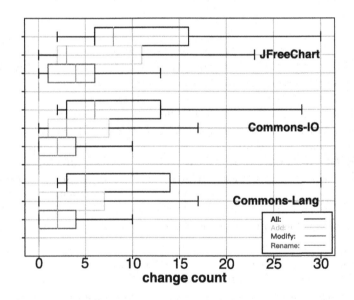

Fig. 4. Changes to tests per commits

4.4   RQ01: Tests Maintenance Behaviour Analysing

For the first research question, we investigated the test maintenance behaviours of the developers in six open source projects.

Table 4. Counts for the *co-evolved commits* and *evolved commits*

Projects_Name	NoC_Test	NoC_Func	NoC_T&F	NoC_T‖F	T&F_Rate
Commons IO	562	558	251	869	28.88%
Commons Lang	1342	1590	698	2234	31.24%
JFreeChart	287	1333	81	1539	5.26%
Guava	1830	2201	1022	3009	33.96%
Argouml	703	6153	147	6709	2.19%
Apache-Ant	289	4933	137	5085	2.69%

Commits Count. Table 4 demonstrates the counting results. Specifically, from left to right, the five columns record: $Projects\_Name$[3]; NoC_Test[4]; NoC_Func[5]; $NoC\_T\&F$[6]; $NoC\_T\|F$[7]; $T\&F\_Rate$[8]. According to the table, we obtain three findings:

Finding01. In half of the subjects, the number of commits, where tests changed, are significantly less than those where functions changed. Especially in the Apache-Ant, the value of NoC_Func is even around twenty times as many as that of NoC_Test. The ratios are also about eight in the ArgoUML and JFreeChart.

Finding02. In all subjects, the frequency of commits, where both of the tests and the functions were changed, is small. It can be proven by the values of $T\&F\_Rate$. The figures are very low in all projects. In those three with frequent test maintenance, the value is only about 30%. Regarding to other three projects, the number is less than 5%.

Finding03. The function codes were unmodified in around half of commits where tests changed. Worst case is JFreeChart where the developers changed test codes in 287 commits and function codes were co-changed in only thirty percent of them.

Change History View. Figure 5 is the *"Change History View"* for the six project. The id of each method bases on their order of creation, and that of commit is also chronological. Our program removes all changes about deleted tests and functions from the database. Therefore, there will be a gap in the diagram if too many methods are deleted. Compared with the counted results, such a diagram shown us the distribution for changes to the test codes.

---

[3] The name of each project.

[4] The number of commits with at least one changed test.

[5] The number of commits with at least one changed function.

[6] The number of commits with at least one changed test **and** function.

[7] The number of commits with at least one changed test **or** function.

[8] The ratio of the commits when tests changed to those when codes changed (i.e. the value of column 4 divided by column 5 in each row).

Finding04. In half of these projects, the modifications to the test codes are clustered in certain period instead of whole life-cycle. One example is the commits of the *"JFreeChart"* with an id number about 2,700, where almost all tests changed. The similar patterns also occurred in the commits of *"Guava"* with id about the 4,300 and the commits of *"Common IO"* with id about 1,500 etc.

Takeaways Message. These findings answer our first research question that *How the developers typically maintain the tests in the real-world projects? Is the tests co-evolve with the functions frequently?*.

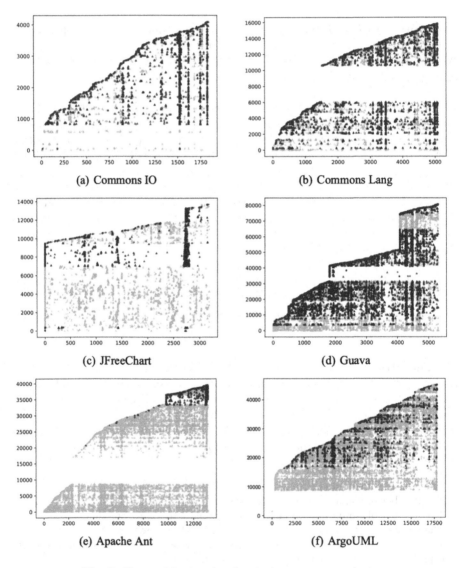

Fig. 5. Change history view for six open-source projects

Based on our experiment results, the test codes were not well-maintained in half of these subjects. In addition, most subjects are modified in some periods instead of the whole life cycle. In all of them, the developers typically modified the functions and the tests in different commits. Therefore, the co-evolution of their tests and functions are indeed a rare circumstance. Such an answer implies a bad performance for the co-evolution approach in most projects, which is also proven in the following section.

4.5 RQ02: Performance Evaluation

Table 5. Performance for Co-evolution approach

Projects	Precision	Recall	F1 score
Commons-Lang	0.43%	65.38%	0.87%
Commons-IO	0.22%	80.95%	0.45%
JFreeChart	0.02%	24.32%	0.04%

Co-Evolution. Table 5 shows the result of the co-evolution approach on the three projects. It demonstrates the precision, recall, and f1 score. The result is similar to that in the previous research in classes level, in which the precision and recall are very low. Specifically, the precision values are less than 1% on all of the three projects. The recall values are more reasonable in the *Commons IO* and *Commons Lang*, but the figure is only 24.32% on the JFreeChart, which implies that only around a quarter of tests were co-evolved with their functions. Besides, the approach performs a relatively better result on the "*Commons IO*" and "*Commons Lang*" than on the "*JFreeChart*". Such differences show that the projects depend on the approach, and to be more specific, by the behaviours of the developers for maintaining the tests.

Table 6. Performance for the Co-creation approach

Projects	Precision	Recall	F1 score
Commons-Lang	8.06%	48.72%	13.84%
Commons-IO	8.15%	45.23%	13.82%
JFreeChart	0.02%	24.32%	0.04%

Co-Creation. Similarly, Table 6 shows the values of the three measures for the three projects. As to the "*Commons IO*" and "*Commons Lang*", their precision increase from less than 1% to about 8%, but they are still very low. The values of recall moderately reduce to around 45%, and that of f1 score improve to about 14%. As for the "*JFreeChart*", it performs the same values for the precision, recall and f1 score on the three projects to that on the co-evolution approach, so the tests and the functions are only co-created in the project.

Table 7. Performance for the APRIORI algorithm approach

Projects	Precision	Recall	F1 score
Commons-Lang	10.26%	5.12%	6.84%
Commons-IO	9.66%	33.33%	14.97%
JFreeChart	0.02%	10.81%	0.04%

APRIORI Algorithm. Table 7 shows the performances of the approach, in which the precision, recall and f1 score is about 10% for precision in the "*Commons IO*" and "*Commons Lang*", the recall values are different in three projects. Besides, the approach performs the terrible result in the "*JFreeChart*", which is similar to other approaches.

Table 8. Performance for the CoEv with a filter for the number of changes in each commit

Repository	Filter range	Precision	Recall	F1 score
Commons-Lang	[Min, Max]	20.30%	34.62%	25.59%
	[Q1, Q3]	35.71%	25.64%	29.85%
Commons-IO	[Min, Max]	16.05%	30.95%	21.13%
	[Q1, Q3]	21.43%	21.43%	21.43%
JFreeChart	[Min, Max]	20.00%	2.70%	4.76%
	[Q1, Q3]	20.00%	2.70%	4.76%

Table 9. Performance for the CoEv with a filter for the number of each type of changes in each commit

Repository	Filter range	Precision	Recall	F1 score
Commons-Lang	$[Min, Max]$	35.84%	24.35%	29.01%
	$[Q1, Q3]$	33.33%	10.26%	15.69%
Commons-IO	$[Min, Max]$	22.22%	19.05%	20.51%
	$[Q1, Q3]$	30.43%	16.67%	21.54%
JFreeChart	$[Min, Max]$	20.00%	2.70%	4.76%
	$[Q1, Q3]$	20.00%	2.70%	4.76%

Commits-Flitered Co-evolution. Table 8 shows the performance of the approach with two different general filters. Specifically, the "*Commons Lang*" and the "*Commons IO*" perform the similar precision and recall in about [15%, 35%]. And besides, when using the second filtering range, it performs better precision, recall and f1 score. Regarding the "*JFreeChart*", the values of measures when using the first range equal that when using the second one. The values for precision are 20%, but the recalls are only about 2% so that for the f1 score are also less than 5%.

Table 9 shows the performance of the approach with more specific filters on different types of changes. The result is mixed, and it shows better values for precision but lower values for the recall. The f1 scores for the two filters are similar. As to the *"JFreeChart"*, it is completely same with previous.

Takeaways Message. The precision of CoEv approach is as bad as the similar approach on class-level occurred in the previous research of Rompaey [7]. However, the precision moderately grew up after the optimisations. The best result is in the Commits-Filtered CoEv approach, in which the value for the precision is about thirty-five per cent and that for the recall is about twenty-four per cent. Such an improvement implies the potential to use that information not related to the source codes for establishing the test-to-code traceability links.

5   Related Work

Zaidman [10] has investigated the similar research question about the co-evolution relationship for the test methods and tested functions, in which they used *"Change History View"*, *"Growth History View"* and *"TestCoverage Evolution View"* to analyse whether the methods and functions are evolved synchronously or in phases. Their paper mined the repositories from *CVS*, but our research question focuses that from *GitHub*. And besides, they did not analyse the projects that we used in the experiments. Therefore, the outcomes of this paper cannot completely address our first research question.

Levin [13] has implemented a tool, *CodeDistillery*, which is also able to traverse a Git repository and to identify the different types of changes in a file. The main difference between the two tools is their purpose: Their tool focuses on the repository mining and the changes classifying; By contrast, our tool more cares about the test-to-code traceability links. There also certain differences in the design and implementation of the two tools.

Rompaey [7] has implemented a similar idea for test-to-code link establishing by the CoEv approach. Their works focus on the classes-level, and their purpose is to compare the performance for different approaches. By contrast, our work implements that idea on the methods-level with three optimisations, and the research purpose focuses on the feasibility for the co-evolution approaches.

White [3] analyses several different links establishing approaches on both the method-level and the class-level. The results of these approaches are used to calculate a score. After that, they compare these scores with a predefined threshold to find out the possible links. Our works use the ground-truth oracle links from White's works. Compared with the predicted links from the TcTracer, those from our works show relatively low precision and low recall on the method level in three open-source projects.

6   Conclusion

This paper focuses on the CoEv approach that can use the co-evolution relationship between the tests and the functions to establish the test-to-code traceability link.

We mined six open-source Java projects to analyse how their developer maintained the test codes. In half of these widely-used projects, the test codes were not well-maintained. Besides, test codes of most subjects are modified in some periods, and the tests are typically changed individually. All of these prove that the co-evolution of their tests and functions are indeed a rare circumstance.

We still implemented the CoEv approach on the method level whose performance is as bad as that on the class level. However, the optimised approaches demonstrated a significant improvement for both recall and precision, which implies the potential of such an idea.

References

1. Hayes, J.H., Dekhtyar, A., Janzen, D.S.: Towards traceable test-driven development. In: Proceedings of the 2009 ICSE Workshop on Traceability in Emerging Forms of Software Engineering, TEFSE 2009, pp. 26–30. IEEE (May 2009)
2. Qusef, A.: Test-to-code traceability: why and how? In: 2013 IEEE Jordan Conference on Applied Electrical Engineering and Computing Technologies (AEECT), pp. 1–8. IEEE (Dec 2013)
3. White, R., Krinke, J., Tan, R.: Establishing multilevel test-to-code traceability links. In: Proceedings of the International Conference on Software Engineering (2020)
4. Mens, T., Demeyer, S.: Software Evolution, p. 347. Springer, Heidelberg (2008). https://doi.org/10.1007/978-3-540-76440-3
5. ISO. ISO/IEC 15504-5 Information technology - Process assessment - Part 5: An exemplar software life cycle process assessment model (2006)
6. Sneed, H.M.: Reverse engineering of test cases for selective regression testing. In: Proceedings of Eighth European Conference on Software Maintenance and Reengineering, CSMR 2004, vol. 8, pp. 69–74. IEEE (2004)
7. Rompaey, B.V., Demeyer, S.: Establishing traceability links between unit test cases and units under test. In: 2009 13th European Conference on Software Maintenance and Reengineering, pp. 209–218. IEEE (2009)
8. Marsavina, C., Romano, D., Zaidman, A.: Studying fine-grained co-evolution patterns of production and test code. In: 2014 IEEE 14th International Working Conference on Source Code Analysis and Manipulation, pp. 195–204. IEEE (Sep 2014)
9. Vidacs, L., Pinzger, M.: Co-evolution analysis of production and test code by learning association rules of changes. In: 2018 IEEE Workshop on Machine Learning Techniques for Software Quality Evaluation (MaLTeSQuE), pp. 31–36. IEEE (Mar 2018)
10. Zaidman, A., Rompaey, B.V., Deursen, A.V., Demeyer, S.: Studying the co-evolution of production and test code in open source and industrial developer test processes through repository mining. Empirical Softw. Eng. 16(3), 325–364 (2011)

11. Falleri, J.-R., Morandat, F., Blanc, X., Martinez, M., Monperrus, M.: Fine-grained and accurate source code differencing. In: ACM/IEEE International Conference on Automated Software Engineering, ASE 2014, pp. 313–324. Vasteras, Sweden (September 15–19 2014)
12. Agrawal, R., Ramakrishnan, S., et al.: Fast algorithms for mining association rules in datamining. Int. J. Sci. Technol. Res. **2**(12), 13–24 (2013)
13. Levin, S., Yehudai, A.: Processing large datasets of fined grained source code changes. In: 2019 IEEE International Conference on Software Maintenance and Evolution (ICSME), pp. 382–385. IEEE (Sep 2019)

Convergence Media Related Information Production Platform Based on Kalman Filter Video Target Tracking

Li Luo[(✉)]

Communication University of China, Chaoyang, Beijing, China

Abstract. This paper summarizes the current status and needs of the development of media convergence, adopts a Kalman filter-based video target tracking. Moreover, this paper studies the in-depth information of the video content, designs a specification for related information, and uses this specification to develop a related information production platform. Target tracking, as a key module of the related information production platform, detects and tracks a single target selection hot spot in the video screen, and can update the selected target template. The design and module implementation of the platform are introduced here. Through test data analysis, the platform can automatically and all-timely add the related information of the video screen; the stored related information conforms to the media metadata format. The platform takes practicability and innovation as the standard, effectively setting up an application demonstration for the radio and television industry to explore new models.

Keywords: Kalman filter · Target tracking · Associated information · Media metadata format

1 Introduction

With the rapid development of the Internet, traditional media and new media are gradually converging. In order to adopt new media and web technologies, major traditional TV platforms have fully changed their business concepts.

Turn TV viewers into users. The basic business model of traditional TV stations have been advertising, but TV stations actually did not have any information about their audiences. Through the establishment of a complete user system through video APP products, the user's viewing behavior, habits, preferences, personal information and other information have been mastered. The future TV will provide users with a personalized program experience while also provide precision advertising, online transactions and other business models [1].

Turn channels into platforms. After the programs of traditional TV stations have been produced and broadcasted, channels such as cable TV networks, satellite TV networks, and terrestrial TV networks did have responsibility for transmitting the programs to the audience. While TV stations in transition must have the content of the programs through network TV, interactive TV, mobile TV, website. It has also

W. Cao et al. (Eds.): CONF-CDS 2021, CCIS 1513, pp. 288–301, 2021.
https://doi.org/10.1007/978-981-16-8885-0_23

published on the mobile terminal APP to watch TV and participate in TV interaction through multiple screens.

Transform communication into operations. The Internet has eliminated information asymmetry, but it has also resulted in information fragmentation. The functions and advantages of TV stations dissemination no longer exist. Operating products, operating users, and operating businesses have become necessary for the transformation of TV stations. This requires the internal optimization of the TV station's organization, content production and distribution mechanism, and achieves accurate user analysis and advertising [2].

Some innovative TV media convergence technologies have been developed, generally showing the characteristics of two-way interaction, multi-channel transmission, and multi-screen reception. In the process of program production, the application of these technologies can present content in new forms and produce new forms of television programs.

The convergent media related information production platform is the application of internet technology to traditional radio and television. It reconsiders the production of program content and business design from the needs of users. Through the integration of innovations in media production and release methods, the platform conducts secondary production of multimedia resources generated in the production of traditional TV programs. The platform deeply mines the associated information of the material, uses video image detection and tracking technology, and tracks the video target based on the Kalman filter algorithm. This algorithm replaces the manual extraction of related information. It can automatically detect the target and add its related information, and update the selected target template during the entire video process. After completion, it generates XML media metadata files, as well as media assets such as materials and related multi-media information and uploads to the back-end service system of the TV station. With the video related information provided, the mobile terminal can interact with the TV screen in real time, and correlate the program content with the mobile phone application, so that the mobile phone and the TV complement each other, and provide users with online and offline interaction.

This paper studies the production of converged media related information, so the organization structure of the thesis is divided into the following four parts. In the second chapter, the methods are introduced, which are a brief introduction to the Kalman filter algorithm, related information rules, and software system technology. The third chapter introduces system design, specifically the overall design of the system function and the key module of the system. The fourth chapter system introduces the implementation, data analysis and the output of related information; The fifth chapter concludes, summarizes the full text, and looks forward to the application of the system platform.

2 Method Introduction

2.1 Target Tracking Algorithm

Kalman filter was proposed by Rudolf E. Kalman in 1960. It is a highly efficient recursive filter and a linear method based on minimum variance estimation. Based on the estimation theory, Kalman filter puts forward the concept of state equation. Through the system state transition equation, the current state of the system can be input and the next state of the system can be output. So as to realize the estimation of the target state [3]. The main body of the Kalman filter is composed of two parts: the state equation and the observation equation. Suppose the state vector of the state equation is n-dimensional, and the observation of the observation equation is p-dimensional. U_k is the input vector, W_{k-1} is the noise vector, X_k is the n-dimensional state vector, and the state equation of the system is:

$$X_k = FX_{k-1} + BU_k + W_{k-1} \tag{1}$$

Where F is a state transition matrix of size n $\times$ n, which is used to describe the state change of the system from time k-1 to time k, and B is an input control matrix of n $\times$ 1 dimension, which is used to control the input quantity U_k, W_{k-1} is the input noise, generally zero-mean Gaussian noise, and its covariance matrix is Q, which is used to express the error between the predicted state and the real state, that is, the error of the system state equation. The observation equation of the system can be expressed as:

$$Z_k = HX_k + V_k$$

Among them, H is the observation matrix, which is mainly used to extract the elements of X_k in the state vector, and V_k is the noise, which is used to describe the noise during observation. It is generally zero-mean Gaussian white noise, and its covariance matrix is R, which is not correlated with Q. Under normal circumstances, we set it as a constant.

Knowing the state at time $k - 1$, then the prior state estimate at time k is defined as $\hat{X}_{k|k-1}$, when the observation value Z_k at time k is known, the posterior state estimate of the system is defined as $\hat{X}_k$, the posterior estimated covariance of the system is P_k, and the system covariance prediction equation is:

$$\hat{P}_{k|k-1} = FP_{k-1}F^T + Q \tag{2}$$

The formula for calculating the posterior state estimate $\hat{X}_k$ is:

$$\hat{X}_k = \hat{X}_{k|k-1} + K_k(Z_k - H\hat{X}_{k|k-1}) \tag{3}$$

In the formula, the n $\times$ m matrix K_k is the gain matrix, and its value can be obtained according to the prior estimation error covariance obtained before:

$$K_k = \frac{\hat{P}_{k|k-1}H^T}{H\hat{P}_{k|k-1}H^T} \tag{4}$$

The update equation for calculating the covariance is:

$$P_k = \left(\hat{P}_{k|k-1} - K_kH\right)\hat{P}_{k|k-1} \tag{5}$$

Through the above five main iterative formulas of (1)–(5) Kalman filter work, it can be understood that Kalman filter mainly uses the feedback of system state observation to realize the motion estimation of the system state, which includes two main steps: system state prediction and system state update. The prediction procedure refers to the prior estimation of the system state for the next moment after error correction on the state prediction of the system. The update procedure refers to using the obtained observations to update the prior estimation value of the system prediction and then get the posterior estimate of the system. By repeating these two recursive operations, the working process of Kalman filtering is realized.

2.2   Related Information Rules

For the related information of video target tracking, the format stored by the system must comply with the standards for audiovisual media transmission and exchange [4]. Related information rules refer to the following domestic and foreign media metadata description specifications.

The domestic audio-visual media metadata description has mainly adopted the following two specifications. One has been the Dublin core element set used by traditional TV station audio-visual materials cataloging and most Internet audio-visual media network companies. This specification has defined the core standards followed by the web resource system structure, with less content and high versatility, and more comprehensively summarizes the main characteristics of electronic resources. Based on the core element set of Dublin, the State Administration of Radio, Film and Television has formulated GYT202.1-2004 "Radio and TV Audiovisual Materials Cataloging Specification Part 1: Television Materials" [5]. This specification has defined the metadata framework for the cataloging of TV program materials, and used 15 metadata items of Dublin Core Metadata to allocate cataloging items. According to the characteristics of the TV program material itself, the cataloging has been divided into four levels from top to bottom, which have been program layer, segment layer, scene layer, and lens layer in turn.

Another type of media metadata specification has borrowed the metadata definition standard adopted by foreign network operators for similar services, that is, the VOD standard for video-on-demand services and the asset distribution interface ADI definition standard developed by Cable Television Laboratories in the United States. Under the construction of the broadcast and television network video on demand system platform, this specification has absorbed the advantages of foreign ADI specifications and formulated GYT259-2012 "Next Generation Broadcasting Network Video on Demand System Metadata Specification" [6]. This specification has aimed at the transformation of two-way services of the broadcast and television network, including interactive settings for on-demand services, such as content markings such as dismantling information and management information. The disadvantage is that the definition of foreign cataloging metadata is quite different from the actual application of domestic business operations. Thus it cannot meet the data exchange business with major domestic Internet audio-visual media.

Both standard metadata exchanges have adopted XML format uniformly. This kind of markup is suitable for data transmission and exchange on various heterogeneous platforms such as traditional media and Internet media.

2.3 Software Development Technology

The related information production software is developed based on the WPF4.0 technology of the .NET platform. The main advantages of introducing WPF technology into the editing subsystem are as follows.

First, WPF separates interface design and logic programming. The front-end interface design uses XAML as the interface language, and the back-end program control uses high-level languages such as C# as the control language, allowing developers easy to use graphical user interfaces when designing programs. Second, WPF has its own video processing controls, which shortens the time for video processing development. Third, WPF's DevExpress control development is powerful and easy to operate. It can be used directly without secondary development. The layout controls are simple and generous, and you can change different skins and colors. Fourth, WPF's unique graphics and image programming, super support for vector graphics, and compatible support for 2D drawing, such as rectangles, custom paths, bitmaps, etc. The graphic control can also adapt to different resolution displays [7].

3 System Design

3.1 Function Design

Related information production software is a software designed and developed as a video editing subsystem. Introduce the main functions implemented by the software and description of requirements [8–10]:

1. Video target tracking. The research object of this paper is single target tracking. The editors can select a specific area of the video frame as a hot zone. In the video target tracking, the Kalman filter is used to obtain the moving target and the center point position is extracted; if the target shape changes or a new target appears, re-select the hot area of the new scene as a template and then perform target tracking [11, 12].
2. Add related information. The related information types in the video screen include pictures, text, video, audio, and hyperlinks. Editors collect related information materials in advance, and add the related materials to hot areas of different video frames. This process is called "secondary production" of the video.

3. Generate metadata files. It is mainly to generate metadata format files of related information, including time point, object location, object description, and collected related information data. The data is transmitted and stored in XML Extensible Markup Language. It is necessary to design the logical structure, elements, content and naming rules of the output file, and the production software uses this rule to generate the output file.

According to the research and analysis of the related information of TV programs in traditional TV stations, this paper designs a related information format describing the metadata of video files. The main ideas are as follows:

- Apply the idea of DC and extend the DC element to describe the video file metadata;
- Add an element of "video object" and modifiers (tags) of various related information;

In this paper, the metadata describing the related information of the video file borrows the idea of the video-on-demand system on tagging the information and dismantling information of the video program to supple the deficiencies of the four-layer cataloging system of traditional TV stations. In the analysis of the program layer, segment layer, scene layer, and lens layer of the traditional TV station cataloging system, the description of the video frame is lacking, so an element "video object" is added, and its modifiers are added to describe related information. Modifiers include time, coordinates, remarks, links, content descriptions, pictures, videos and audios. The specific definition is shown in the Table 1.

Table 1. Define "video object" elements and modifiers

Element	Modifier (label)	Definition
Video object	time	The time point when the video object appears
	coordinate	The spatial extent of the video object
	remark, link	The category and related link of the video object
	content description, picture	The text description of the video object, the related picture
	video, audio	Video and audio related with the video object

4. Media assets are bound to the backend system. Media asset binding and storage mainly include media asset packaging, media asset storage, media asset content binding and task completion notification. The platform migrates the local media assets in the production task to the back-end service subsystem, and bind the media assets files to generate an excel form, which is used to insert into the media-asset database of the back-end service subsystem, and finally send the task completion notification to complete the media asset storage.

The overall process of making related information is shown in the Fig. 1 below.

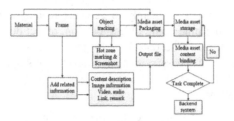

Fig. 1. The overall process of related information production

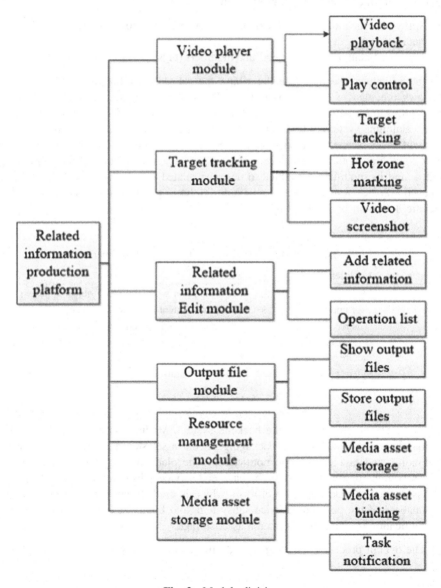

Fig. 2. Module division

3.2   System Module

The designed and developed related information production software has a relatively comprehensive function. It is applied to the broadcasting and television converged media publishing service platform, as an editing subsystem to provide rich related information resources other than TV program content. Here the platform is mainly build through WPF, which is mainly divided into six modules: video playback module, target tracking module, related information editing module, output file module, resource management module and media asset storage. See Fig. 2.

The video playback module is used to open, play, and control playback of video files in a specific format, as shown in logo 1 below; the related information editing module is the core of the software operation, by adding, modifying, deleting, automatically importing and view the related information materials, as shown in logo 3 and logo 4; the target tracking module, as shown in Fig. 5, select the hot zone example on the video frame, click the left button below the video to correspond to the hot zone label, and the right button below the video is a screenshot; the resource management module is to view the local media asset database and the back-end mapping media asset database, as shown in logo 3 below; the generated metadata file module is to save, load and validate the metadata file of the related information. See Fig. 3.

Fig. 3. Modules of related information production platform

4 System Implementation and Data Analysis

The system is divided into three major modules by function, namely, video playback and target tracking module, related information editing module, media data storage and management module.

4.1 Video Playback and Target Tracking Module

The video playback and target tracking module is the most basic module of the system, with playback control video and target tracking and tracking. This module provides operation sources for the related information editing module, media asset file module and other modules.

1. The realization of video playback mainly uses the System.Windows.Controls class provided by WPF. The item of MediaElement adds media playback controls to the application to complete the basic functions of video playback, audio and playback control [12].
2. The target tracking module detects and tracks the specified target after marking the hot zone on the video [13, 14]:

The target detection process is to use the background subtraction method to detect the foreground by converting the labeled video frame into a gray image, and then use the Canny operator to detect the frame, extract the labeled target object, and record the center point position. By comparing the center point of the desired target and the center point of the detection target with the color histogram of the targets, the tracking algorithm calculates the minimum square difference distance as the cost function, and uses the Hungarian algorithm to allocate the expected target to obtain the optimal cost value, and then uses the Kalman filter to update the state of the target, Results and tracking trajectory.

4.2 Realization of Related Information Editing Module

The related information editing module is the most important module of the editing subsystem, responsible for generating all kinds of related information. The main process includes three parts: hot zone labeling, adding related information, and operation list. There is a row of toolbars at the top of the related information editing module, including adding a blank row of records, deleting a row of records, marking hot area rectangles, saving output files, adding picture information, adding text information, adding video files, adding audio files, batch button for importing related information materials; in the middle is the related information editing area, which can edit the specific content of the related information, including the time, id, coordinates, remark, link, text editing box and multimedia editing area of the video object; the bottom is the output file list column, which displays each record of related information and save it as a output file after editing.

4.3 Data Analysis

The experiment in this section is to make a comprehensive test and check on the algorithm proposed by the target tracking module, which detect and track a single target, and finally analyze the data results and influencing factors. The target detection process performs background subtraction detection, Canny edge extraction, and color histogram feature matching on the hot areas marked by the video to obtain the center position of the target. The target tracking algorithm uses Kalman filtering to update the target state and trajectory.

Parameter Influence: Target Threshold. Because the marked area is a rectangle, the width and height of the target body must be larger than the threshold, and the threshold parameter is modified according to the size of the tracking target, so as to improve the accuracy of detection. The selected video target changes from far to near from small to large from the initial position, and the thresholds are set to 5 pixels, 10 pixels, and 20 pixels. The results are shown in the following table.

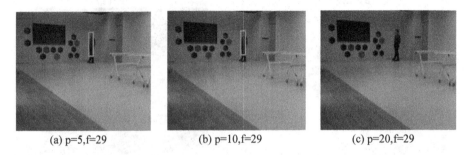

(a) p=5,f=29   (b) p=10,f=29   (c) p=20,f=29

Fig. 4. .

The above Fig. 4 (a), (b) (c) show the tracking results of the 29th frame with the thresholds of 5 pixels, 10 pixels, and 20 pixels. It can be seen that since the Fig. 4 (c) has a larger threshold and a smaller target, he target cannot be detected; and when the threshold is 5 pixels or 10 pixels in Fig. 4 (a) (b), the target can be tracked well.

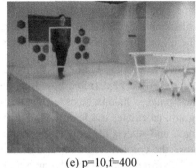

(d) p=5,f=400   (e) p=10,f=400

Fig. 5. .

The above Fig. 5 (d), (e) show the tracking results of the 400th frame with a threshold of 5 pixels and 10 pixels. It can be seen that the target position drifts due to the small threshold value in the Fig. 5 (d), and it is tracked as a local small block when the background area is incorrectly detected. Obviously, the threshold of Fig. 5 (e) is 10 pixels, the target can still be tracked well.

(a)f=29

(b)f=177

(c)f=400

(d)f=600

Fig. 6. (a) (b) (c) (d) different frames when threshold is 10 pixels

The above Fig. 6 (a), (b), (c) (d) show the tracking results of different video frames when the threshold is 10 pixels. It can be seen that the initial position of the target is smaller, and then the target becomes larger. The target can be accurately tracked at frames 29, 400, and 600. But in the 177th frame, because the background TV wall area is black and the light is relatively dark, the target is only tracked to the lower half. In general, the threshold tracking result is the best in the entire video process.

Feature Influence: Color Histogram. The Kalman filter algorithm predicts the target position in the next frame based on the target displacement within the threshold distance range. On this basis, using the target feature matching, that is, the color histogram, calculates the feature similarity between the target template and the candidate target, and selects the area that best matches the target template. The following Fig. 7 shows the color histograms of multiple video frames.

The rise of the rectangular area represented by the solid star-shaped line in the 29th frame is because the selected initial frame target template area itself contains a part of

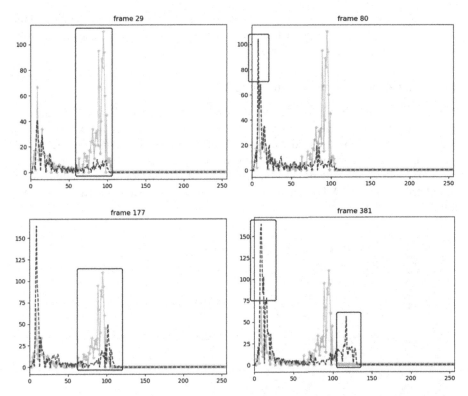

Fig. 7. Color histogram of different frames. The dotted line in the two curves represents the candidate target area, and the solid star line represents the target template area. (Color figure online)

the pixel background, which is a light white wallboard, corresponding to the number of pixels of about 100 grayscale. While the background of candidate target area is close to black color, and it is not tracked.

The rise of the rectangular area indicated by the dotted line in the 80th frame is due to the black area in the background of the target object in the video screen, so some pixels with a black background are used as candidate target areas.

The rise of the rectangular area indicated by the dotted line in the 177th frame is due to the fact that the legs of the target object are moving in the video frame, and a part of the background of the light white area is leaked in the middle, so part of the background is used as the candidate target area.

The rise of the rectangular area indicated by the dotted line on the left in frame 381 is because of the increase of pixels in the black area due to the presence of a black TV in the background behind the target object. The rise of the rectangular area indicated by the dotted line on the right is due to the fact that the background floor brightness of the lower part of the target is higher than the wall brightness during movement of the target. Thus, the candidate area indicated by the dotted line on the corresponding histogram is brighter than the template area of the solid line table. The dotted line is to the right of the solid line area and the height is smaller than the solid line area.

It can be seen that the pixels are inconsistent due to the background change and the target scale change, but the color histogram distribution of the candidate area and the target template are basically the same.

4.4   Related Information Module Output

The target area of each frame of target tracking output is automatically filled into the coordinate data of the related information editing module, namely x1, x2, y1, y2. In addition, heterogeneous related information of the target hot zone can be added, including links, descriptions, texts, multimedia files etc., as shown on the left side of the figure below. After the production of the related information of the entire video is completed, the file in XML metadata format is output, as shown on the right side of the following Fig. 8.

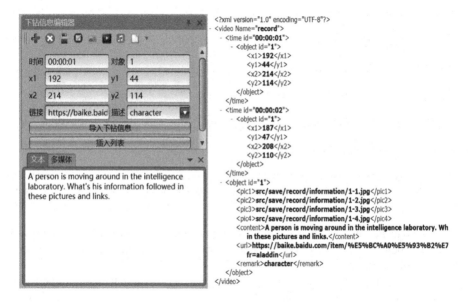

Fig. 8. Related information module output

5   Conclusion

This paper first introduces the background and purpose of the subject research, summarizes the current situation of the development of media convergence, and introduces the main research content of this paper. Secondly, according to the research order, the video target tracking algorithm, that is, Kalman filter for tracking moving objects is introduced. Then, in the research process of metadata cataloging, this paper proposes the standard design of related information by borrowing the existing standard description specifications to store the in-depth video information and to provide users with the related information of the video content. This realizes the personalization of the media content recommend. Based on the Kalman filter target tracking algorithm, this paper mines the deep information of the video screen, designs and implements the related information production platform, which includes the functions of adding related information and generating output files (format conforming to the related information specification) to store media assets. In conclusion, the related information production platform based on Kalman filter video target tracking realizes the association of video and heterogeneous data, and the intelligent and automated production of video related information. Of course, there are some shortcomings in this paper, including the lack of accuracy for multiple target tracking and detection in complex backgrounds, which need follow-up research and improvement.

References

1. Wang, Y.: Research on the development of my country's radio and television all-media under the background of media convergence. Dalian University of Technology (2013)
2. Xiong, B.: Research on China's TV industry development in the new media era. Wuhan University (2013)
3. Liang, Z.: Video target tracking method based on position prediction and double matching. Dalian University of Technology (2016)
4. Luo, L., Miao, F., Wu, M.: Research on association and aggregation of video content under convergent media. In: Video Engineering (2015)
5. State Administration of Radio, Film, and Television.: GYT202.1–2004 Catalogue specifications of radio and television archives Part 1: Television archives (2004)
6. State Administration of Radio, Film, and Television: GYT259–2012 Metadata Specification for Video on demand system of NGB (2012)
7. Wang, Z.: Design and implementation of image processing system based on WPF. Jilin University (2012)
8. Lu, H., Peixia, L., Dong, W.: Overview of target tracking algorithms. Pattern Recogn. Artif. Intell. (2018)
9. Fu, C.: Research on content-based video structure mining method. National University of Defense Technology (2008)
10. Gong, S.: Research on moving target recognition and tracking system. Harbin Institute of Technology (2014)
11. Tang, B.: Research on target tracking algorithm based on template matching. Changsha University of Science & Technology (2013)
12. Chen, Y.: Design and implementation of a multi-touch intelligent multimedia display system based on WPF. Beijing University of Technology (2013)
13. Mallikarjuna Rao, G., Satyanarayana, Ch.: Object tracking system using approximate median filter, Kalman filter and dynamic template matching. Int. J. Intell. Syst. Appl. 6(5) (2014)
14. Sun, M., Xiao, J., Lim, E.G., Zhang, B., Zhao, Y.: Fast template matching and update for video object tracking and segmentation. In: IEEE Conference on Computer Vision and Pattern Recognition (2020)

Supervised Sliding Window Smoothing Loss Function Based on MS-TCN for Video Segmentation

Timing Yang[✉]

Dalian University of Technology,
Dalian, Liaoning Province 116024, People's Republic of China
yangtiming@mail.dlut.edu.cn

Abstract. Recently, more and more videos have been uploaded to the network, so that video analysis task has been one of the most important applications in various fields. At present, video analysis methods can be divided into two kinds: weakly supervised video action segmentation and supervised video action segmentation. The former uses a sliding window or Markov model, while the latter uses the TCN model. In this paper, we introduce the Supervised Sliding Window Smooth Loss Function (SSWS) into the TCN baseline, which is a complement to MS-TCN smoothing loss function TMSE. In this method, three discriminant frames are selected from the video prediction sequence and combined into an adaptive sliding window to selectively smooth the whole prediction sequence. In particular, it doubles the penalty when it slides to the wrong place in the category. Compared to TMSE, our method effectively increases the receptive field of smoothing loss function. And, the proposed new supervised loss function only penalizes error frames. The experiment shows that compared with the Smoothing loss function TMSE of MS-TCN, SSWS has significantly improved in the three datasets: 50Salads, GTEA and the Breakfast Dataset.

Keywords: Video segmentation · Supervised sliding window · Smooth loss · MS-TCN

1 Introduction

In recent years, video analysis has become increasingly important as more and more videos are exponentially uploaded to the Internet. The huge growth in the number of uploads has allowed video analytics tasks to be fully developed in many industries. The task of video analysis is to classify and segment a video simultaneously. Although the task of video analysis has been successful in classifying short clips of video [1], it remains challenging to detect and locate action clips over long stretches of untrimmed video. Temporarily locating and cataloguing action clips is crucial for many applications in long videos, such as robotics and surveillance. While traditional video analysis methods employ a two-stream approach by generating probabilities between frames and then feeding them into an advanced time model, the more recent approach uses time convolution to classify video frames directly.

© Springer Nature Singapore Pte Ltd. 2021
W. Cao et al. (Eds.): CONF-CDS 2021, CCIS 1513, pp. 302–314, 2021.
https://doi.org/10.1007/978-981-16-8885-0_24

There are two methods of video action segmentation: weakly supervised video action segmentation and supervised video action segmentation. In weakly supervised video action segmentation, it can be divided into two categories. One is based on sliding window [2], which uses different temporal windows to detect action segments. The other is the hybrid method using Markov model with a coarse temporal modeling on the frame classifier [3]. Although they all achieved good results in accuracy, they spend a lot of expensive computing power and train very slowly. So they are not suitable for long videos. With the development of video analysis task technology, supervised video motion segmentation is rising gradually. Just like temporal convolutional networks (TCNs), it has achieved success in action segmentation. It has obvious advantages, such as flexible sensing field, stable gradient, low memory resources and so on. Because of its advantages, a large number of researchers have started to study video motion segmentation tasks based on TCNs models. TCN has achieved an overall lead in almost all tasks, which fully demonstrates the effectiveness of this network structure in sequence modeling tasks. In recent work, Colin Lea and his team have proposed encoder-decoder based TCN (ED-TCN) and Dilated TCN [4]. ED-TCN uses pooling and up-sampling to effectively capture remote time patterns. Yazan Abu Farha and Juergen Gall have presented a Multi-Stage Temporal Convolutional Network for Action Segmentation (MS-TCN) [5]. On the basis of MS-TCN, Shijie Li et al. have improved it and proposed MS-TCN++ [6].

In the current method, although MS-TCN++ improves MS-TCN on the network structure, it still uses smoothing loss function TMSE. The core idea of TMSE is to use the subtraction between the previous frame and the frame to prevent the difference between the two adjacent frames from being too large. Though TMSE has achieved certain results, it has obvious shortcomings. Its receptive field is too small, and it still punishes the correct segmentation. In order to solve these problems, we propose a method: supervised sliding window smoothing loss function (SSWS), which is to use sliding window method. The main contributions of SSWS are as follows: 1. It effectively increases the receptive field of smoothing loss function. 2. It only punishes error frames. 3. It is a supervised smoothing loss function. Compared with the baseline model MS-TCN, SSWS improves F1@10 by 6.60% on 50Salads [7], 8.16% on Breakfast [8] and 0.94% on GTEA [9]. The experimental results fully show the excellence of SSWS.

In this paper, we will first introduce baseline MS-TCN and our method SSWS. And then, in Experiments, Experimental Setting, Ablation Study and Performance Evaluation will be introduced. Finally, this paper will be summarized in conclusion.

2 Method

In this section, we will introduce a method named a supervised sliding window smoothing loss function (SSWS) to mitigate over-segmentation errors in MS-TCN. Given the frame $x_{1:T} = (x_1, \ldots, x_T)$ and the number of video categories GT for a video, our aim is to surmise the class label $c_{1:T} = (c_1, \ldots, c_T)$ for each frame, where T is the length of the video. First, describe the baseline model MS-TCN. Second, explain

SSWS. SSWS is combined with the smoothing loss function of the baseline model MS-TCN, so we define our loss function as:

$$\mathcal{L}_s = \mathcal{L}_{cls} + \lambda(\mathcal{L}_{T-MSE} + \mathcal{L}_{ssws}) \tag{1}$$

where, $\mathcal{L}_{cls}$ is Cross Entropy Loss Function, $\mathcal{L}_{T-MSE}$ is Truncated Mean Squared Error (TMSE), $\mathcal{L}_{ssws}$ is Supervised Sliding Window Smoothing Loss Function (SSWS).

2.1 Baseline Model

MS-TCN is the baseline model of SSWS. In this paper of baseline model, the author combines classification loss function and smoothing loss function. For the loss function of classification, the author uses the cross entropy loss function, the formula can be defined as:

$$\mathcal{L}_{cls} = \frac{1}{T}\sum_t - \log\left(y_{t,c}\right) \tag{2}$$

Where $y_{t,c}$ is the predicted probability for the ground truth label at time t.

However, although the cross entropy loss function has performed well, the authors find that there are some over-segmentation errors in the predicted video. In order to improve the quality of prediction, they add a supplementary smoothing loss function to alleviate the over-segmentation error. They use truncated mean squared error in frame logarithm probability. The formula can be expressed as follows:

$$\mathcal{L}_{T-MSE} = \frac{1}{TC}\sum_{t,c} \tilde{\Delta}_{t,c}^2 \tag{3}$$

$$\tilde{\Delta}_{t,c} = \begin{cases} \Delta_{t,c} & : \Delta_{t,c} \leq \tau \\ \tau & : \text{otherwise} \end{cases} \tag{4}$$

$$\Delta_{t,c} = \left|\log y_{t,c} - \log y_{t-1,c}\right| \tag{5}$$

Where C is the quantity of classes, T is the length of the video, and $y_{t,c}$ is the probability of class c at time t.

The final loss function of a single stage is a combination of the above losses. The formula can be expressed as follows:

$$\mathcal{L}_s = \mathcal{L}_{cls} + \lambda\mathcal{L}_{T-MSE} \tag{6}$$

Where λ is a model hyper-parameter, which determines the contribution of the different losses.

Finally the author minimize the sum of the losses over all stages to train the complete model

$$\mathcal{L} = \sum_s \mathcal{L}_s \tag{7}$$

2.2   Loss Function for SSWS

SSWS is integrated into the loss function of MS-TCN, which is a supplement to the $\mathcal{L}_{T-MSE}$ function. SSWS smoothes Pred Feature, which is the output of input X that enter multi-layer TCN. It can be expressed as shown in Fig. 1.

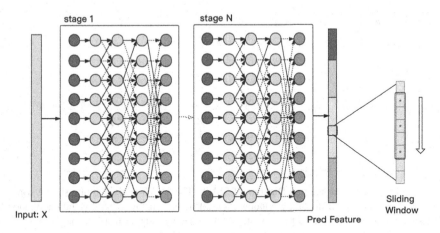

Fig. 1. The Figure of Combination of SSWS and MS-TCN. Input X enter the multi-layer TCN, and output the Pred Feature. And then, Sliding window smooths the Pred Feature.

The SSWS flow chart is shown in Fig. 2.

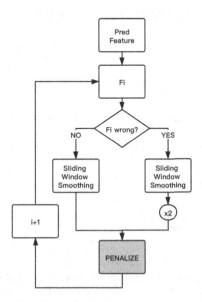

Fig. 2. Work flow chart of SSWS. Fi represents frame i of the video. When Fi frame is incorrect, SSWS doubles the penalty.

The SSWS model is illustrated in Fig. 3.

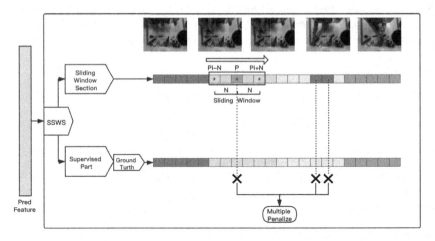

Fig. 3. The Model Interpretation Diagram of SSWS. The SSWS is divided into sliding window part and supervised part. In sliding window part, all frames are smoothed by sliding Windows. The supervised part punishes a frame with double times by judging if it is wrong

Let's take the i frame in the video as an example, and take it as a reference frame P, whose category is set as $C_i \in c_{1:T}$. Then two discrimination frames P_{i-N} and P_{i+N}, are selected at the front and back ends of the reference frame, where N is set as the distance between the two selected frames and P, and their categories are $C_{i-N} \in c_{1:T}$ and $C_{i+N} \in c_{1:T}$. Three frames can be combined into eight situations. Before explaining each situation, all situations can be listed in Fig. 4 firstly.

NUM	$|C_i - C_{i-N}|$	$|C_{i+N} - C_i|$	$|C_{i+N} - C_{i-N}|$	PUNISHMENT
1	0	0	0	NO
2	0	0	1	
3	0	1	0	
4	0	1	1	NO
5	1	0	0	
6	1	0	1	NO
7	1	1	0	YES
8	1	1	1	YES

Fig. 4. In the right part, '0' means that the two categories are the same categories, and '1' means that they are different categories. 'No' means no punishment for them. 'Yes' is the opposite. Diagonals indicate that this situation does not exist. In the left part, these sliding windows correspond to the visualization of different situations. Different colors represent different categories.

In Fig. 4, the eight situations can be combined into three cases, these can be listed as:

Case 1, situations don't exist: There is no exist of serial number 2, 3, 5. It's not hard to find out from the table that they all have two '0'. Through transitivity, it can see that if $a \cong b$ and $b \cong c$, then $a \cong c$, where $a, b, c \in C_k, \mathrm{k} = i, i \pm N$ and a, b, c are different from each other.

Case 2, situations don't need to be punished: It can be seen from the serial number 1 that the sliding window is in the whole segment, and there is no error frame in the segment, so there is no need to punish. From serial number 4 and 6, it is known that they are at the junction of the two fragments, so they don't need to be punished. Take serial number 4 as an example. Because there are $\begin{cases} C_i = C_{i-N} \\ C_{i+N} \neq C_i \\ C_{i+N} \neq C_{i-N} \end{cases}$, then P_{i-N}, P belong to the same segment, P_{i+N} is in different segments with P_{i-N}, P. This situation corresponds to the time when the sliding window crosses the boundary between the two segments, so there are no penalties.

Case 3, situations require to be punished: By observing serial number 7 and 8, from $|C_i - C_{i-N}| = 1$ and $|C_{i+N} - C_i| = 1$, it can be seen that the reference frame P is not equal to the two discrimination frames. This case shows that error frame appears at this time, and it needs to be punished.

Based on the Fig. 4 and the analysis of all situations, it can conclude that the function of the sliding window are as follows:

$$\mathcal{L}_{SWS} = \frac{1}{TC} \sum_{t,c} \psi_{t,c} \tag{8}$$

$$\begin{cases} \varphi_l = \left| \log y_{m,c} - \log y_{n,c} \right|^2, l = 1, 2, 3; \\ (l, m, n) = (1, t, t - N); (2, t - N, t - 2N); (3, t, t - 2N) \end{cases} \tag{9}$$

$$\phi_l = \begin{cases} 1 & : \frac{1}{TC} \sum_{t,c} \varphi_l \leq \varphi_l, \; l = 1, 2 \\ 0 & : \text{otherwise} \end{cases} \tag{10}$$

$$\psi_{t,c} = (\varphi_1 + \varphi_2 + \varphi_3)(\phi_1 \cap \phi_2) \tag{11}$$

Where C is the quantity of classes, T is the length of the video, and $y_{m,c}$ and $y_{n,c}$ are the probability of class c at time m and n respectively.

Then the prediction category $PRED_{1:T} = (p_1, \ldots, p_T)$ of each frame is compared with the real class label GT of each frame to find out error frame. If a frame is error, supervised part is to double the penalty. The formula can be expressed as follows:

$$\mathcal{L}_{sup} = |p_i - g_i| \tag{12}$$

Finally, it can get a supervised sliding window smoothing loss function SSWS:

$$\mathcal{L}_{ssws} = \mathcal{L}_{sws}(1 + \mathcal{L}_{sup}) \tag{13}$$

3 Experiments

We use three benchmark actions to segment the dataset: GTEA, 50Salads and Breakfast to analyze our proposed SSWS.

The GTEA Dataset: It contains 28 videos, all of which are recorded by cameras mounted on the actors' heads. On average, each video has 20 actions and 7 daily kitchen activities, such as making a cup of tea, making a cup of coffee, making a sandwich, etc. The video resolution is 1280×720 pixels. The video frame has 11 action class annotations including the background. Every video lasts about one minute and has a frame rate of 15 frames per s.

The 50Salads Dataset: It has 17 action classes in 50 videos. Among the 50 videos, 25 people prepare two mixed salads. It includes 30 FPS RGB video data and depth maps data. Each video takes about 5–10 min. Each video lasts 6.40 min and contains 20 action instances on average. The 3-axis accelerometer data at 50 Hz device is connected to a knife, a stirring spoon, a glass, a bottle of oil, a peeler, and a pepper dispenser. Video and accelerometer data align and synchronize parameters.

The Breakfast Dataset: It is bigger than the other two datasets, which is one of the largest fully annotated datasets. There are 1712 videos in the dataset with a total duration of 77 h. The video has a resolution of 320×240 pixels and a frame rate of 15 fps. The dataset is more complicated than The GTEA dataset and the 50Salads dataset. The number of cameras used for data recording varies from location to location. Camera not calibrated. The position of the camera changes according to the position. All these reflect the real situation. In 18 different kitchen environments, 52 participants participated in 10 different cooking activities, such as preparing coffee, fruit salad, orange juice, chocolate milk, tea, cereal, etc.

Evaluation Metrics: For effective evaluation, we use frame-wise accuracy (Acc), segment edit distance and the segment F1 score under three different overlap thresholds (10%, 25%, 50%), which are expressed as F1 @ {10,25,50}. Acc is the most commonly used measure of motion segmentation, but it can't capture the underlying time structure of prediction output. This will contribute to different qualitative results for models with similar frame accuracy, and in reverse, these same models will create a lot of over-segmentation errors.

For more effective evaluation, we use the segment edit distance and F1 score as the measurement criteria of prediction quality. Segment edit distance describes the offset distance of segmented segments, and measures the performance of the model independent of slight time change in predicting the sequence of action segments. It quantifies the similarity between the prediction sequence and the target sequence by calculating the Levenshtein Distance between them. Levenshtein Distance is the minimum number of editing operations required between two strings to change from one to the other. The operations that can be used are: insert, delete and replace. Generally speaking, the smaller the editing distance, the greater the similarity between two strings. The segmental F1 score compares the model segment with the real segment, and then judges it according to the overlap threshold (IOU). a. Punish the error of excessive subdivision; b. The small time offset between predictions is not penalized; c. The score depends on the number of operands, not on the duration of each operation instance. This indicator is alike to map with IOU threshold, but the difference is that it does not need to determine the confidence for each prediction. Its model can be expressed as:

$$F1-score = \frac{2 \times recall \times precision}{recall + precision}$$

3.1 Experimental Setting

GPU 2080ti was used in the experiment. The MS-TCN model is based on the network framework of Pytorch. Model is composed of 4 dilated layers. The data sets are GTEA, 50Salads and Breakfast. The feature map of each layer in the model is 64, The dilated-n-layers of each layer is 10, the proportion of smoothing loss function λ set to 0.6,the batch size of each input training video is 1, the in channel of the input feature channel is set to 2048. The thresholds for calculating F1 score were [0.1, 0.25, 0.5], the number of workers is set to 4, training max epoch is set to 50. The learning-rate is set to 0.0005. Optimizer is Adam, and optimizer parameters are consistent with MS-TCN. Sliding window size 2N is set to the minimum segment length divided by the number of segments, it can be expressed as:

$$N = \frac{\min(\text{Length of each segment of pred})}{2 \times (\text{the number of segments})}$$

3.2 Ablation Study on SSWS

So as to evaluate the replacement effect of SSWS loss function module and the effect of different values of super parameter of SSWS loss function, we have carried out two ablation experiments. We take 50Salads as an example to carry out the ablation experiment.

Replacement Effect of Loss Function Module: The supervised sliding window smoothing loss function (SSWS) is divided into supervised part and sliding window part. Compared with baseline, each module has a certain improvement. Table 1 shows three parts: Su-only, SWS and SSWS.

Table 1. Comparing the effects of different parts on 50Salads

Parts	F1@ {10,25,50}	Edit	Acc
MS-TCN [5]	76.30 74.00 64.50	67.90	80.70
Su-only	79.96 77.51 69.43	72.12	82.06
SWS	80.36 78.37 69.94	73.52	82.05
SSWS	**81.34 78.41 70.47**	**74.14**	**82.10**

It can be seen from Table 1 that the SSWS on the 50Salads dataset is improved by 6.60%, 5.96% and 9.26% on F1 @ {10,25,50}, 9.19% on edit distance and 1.73% on accuracy respectively. In contrast, the effect of Su-only is much better than that of baseline, but the improvement is not obvious compared with SWS and SSWS. SSWS performs better than either of them.

The Effect of Different Values of the Parameter of Loss Function: We set the hyper- parameters as follows: $\lambda = 0.6$ in all experiments. In order to analyze the influence of parameter λ, different parameters λ are used for training the same dataset, which is 50Salads. The final results are shown in Table 2. It shows that parameters have little effect on performance. By contrast $\lambda = 0.6$, if $\lambda < 0.6$, the punishment is small. The performance is very good, but it is not as good as $\lambda = 0.6$; if $\lambda > 0.6$, the penalty is too large. The change of frame direction label will be seriously destroyed. If λ is too large, it will affect to detect boundary between action segments. So it's not as good as $\lambda = 0.6$.

Table 2. Comparing the effects of different parameters λ on 50Salads

λ	F1@ {10,25,50}	Edit	Acc
0.15	79.39 77.51 68.89	72.74	**82.45**
0.50	80.44 78.16 69.90	73.24	81.69
0.55	80.59 **78.69 70.74**	73.42	81.36
0.60	**81.34** 78.41 70.47	**74.14**	82.10
0.65	80.22 78.28 69.84	72.89	81.87
0.70	79.80 77.57 68.95	72.62	81.89

3.3 Performance Evaluation on SSWS

In this section, SSWS is compared to some existing excellent methods in three datasets: 50Salads, GTEA and Breakfast. Comparison in the qualitative results can be visualized in Fig. 5. The comparative results were presented in Table 3, Table 4 and Table 5 respectively. It is noted that we use the configuration of parameters for best visualization in Fig. 5 instead of that at the highest score.

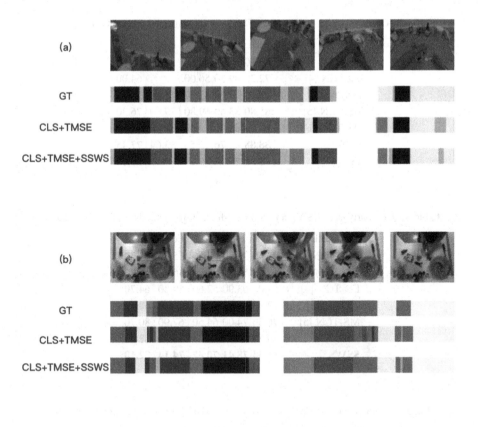

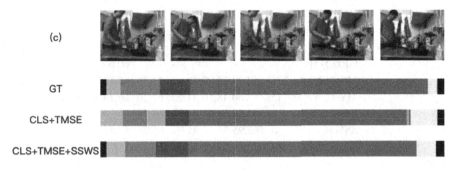

Fig. 5. (a) is the visual representation on the GTEA dataset; (b) is the visual representation on the 50Salads dataset; (c) is the performance on the Breakfast dataset. The selected parameter $\lambda = 0.15$, and N = min(Length of each segment of pred).

Table 3. Comparison of SSWS and SWS with existing methods on GTEA dataset.

GTEA	F1@ {10,25,50}	Edit	Acc
Bi-LSTM [10]	66.50 59.00 43.60	–	55.50
ED-TCN [4]	72.20 69.30 56.00	–	64.00
TDRN [11]	79.20 74.40 62.70	74.10	70.10
MS-TCN [5]	85.80 83.40 69.80	79.00	76.30
MS-TCN (FT) [5]	87.50 85.40 **74.60**	81.40	**79.20**
SWS	**88.88** 85.76 72.56	83.64	77.45
SSWS	88.32 **86.76** 73.19	84.37	76.65

Table 4. Comparison of SSWS and SWS with existing methods on 50Salads dataset.

50SALADS	F1@ {10,25,50}	Edit	Acc
IDT + LM [12]	44.40 38.90 27.80	45.80	48.70
Bi-LSTM [10]	62.60 58.30 47.00	55.60	55.70
ED-TCN [4]	68.00 63.90 52.60	59.80	64.70
TDRN [11]	72.90 68.50 57.20	66.00	68.10
MS-TCN [5]	76.30 74.00 64.50	67.90	80.70
SWS	80.36 78.37 69.94	73.52	82.05
SSWS	**81.34 78.41 70.47**	**74.14**	**82.10**

Table 5. Comparison of SSWS and SWS with existing methods on Breakfast dataset.

BREAKFAST	F1@ {10,25,50}	Edit	Acc
ED-TCN [4]	– – –	–	43.30
HTK [13]	– – –	–	50.70
TCFPN [14]	– – –	–	52.00
HTK (64)[3]	– – –	–	56.30
GRU [15]	– – –	–	60.60
MS-TCN (IDT) [5]	58.20 52.90 40.80	61.40	65.10
MS-TCN (I3D) [5]	52.60 48.10 37.90	61.70	**66.30**
SWS	**63.56 56.63 42.27**	**66.20**	65.20
SSWS	62.95 56.12 41.97	65.78	64.54

It can see from Table 3 that SSWS and SWS are equivalent in performance on GTEA dataset. The gap between them and the baseline model MS-TCN is small. Except that F1 @ {50} and Acc were slightly lower than MS-TCN (FT), the scores were slightly improved on the whole. It can conclude from Table 4 that both SSWS and SWS are better than some excellent existing methods. In addition, SSWS performs better than SWS on 50Salads dataset. At this time, the supervision part reflects its superiority. SSWS is in F1@ {10,25,50} increased by 6.60%, 5.96%, 9.26%, in edit distance increased by 9.19% and in accuracy increased by 1.73%. From the Table 5, both SSWS and SWS makes great progress in Breakfast. In addition to a slight decrease in accuracy, SSWS is increased by 8.16%, 6.10%, 2.87% in F1@ {10,25,50} and 7.14% in edit distance compared with the baseline model MS-TCN. What's more, SWS is slightly better than SSWS. In F1@ {10,25,50}, edit distance and accuracy, it enhanced by 9.22%, 7.05%, 3.60%, 7.81%, 0.15%.

In a word, it can conclude that SSWS is improved in these three datasets in F1@ {10,25,50} and edit distance. On Acc, except for 50 salads, there was a slight decrease. In a large and complex Breakfast dataset, the unsupervised sliding window smoothing loss function SWS is slightly better than the supervised sliding window smoothing loss function SSWS. However, in the GTEA dataset, SSWS is comparable to SWS. And in the medium size 50Salads dataset, SSWS fully showed the advantage of supervision, and it performed better than SWS.

4 Conclusion

In this paper, we proposed the Supervised Sliding Window Smooth Loss Function (SSWS), which is an adaptive sliding window size. It selectively smoothed the entire prediction sequence and doubled the penalty for error frames. And it effectively complemented the vacancy and shortage of the original smoothing loss function TMSE. Compared with the original smoothing loss function in MS-TCN, it not only changed from unsupervised to supervised loss function, but also enhanced the receptive field and only carried out targeted punishment for the wrong category. All of these helped the network improve the burr situation and improve the prediction quality to some extent on the three benchmark datasets. The prediction quality of MS-TCN network assisted by SSWS had been significantly improved, but the parameter selection of the sliding window size is still an open problem worth discussing in the future work.

References

1. Carreira, J., Zisserman, A.: Quo vadis, action recognition? A new model and the kinetics dataset. In: IEEE Conference on Computer Vision and Pattern Recognition (CVPR), pp. 4724–4733 (2017)
2. Rohrbach, M., Amin, S., Andriluka, M., Schiele, B.: A database for fine grained activity detection of cooking activities. In: IEEE Conference on Computer Vision and Pattern Recognition (CVPR), pp. 1194–1201 (2012)
3. Kuehne, H., Gall, J., Serre, T.: An end-to-end generative framework for video segmentation and recognition. In: IEEE Winter Conference on Applications of Computer Vision (WACV) (2016)
4. Lea, C., Flynn, M.D., Vidal, R., Reiter, A., Hager, G.D.: Temporal convolutional networks for action segmentation and detection. In: IEEE Conference on Computer Vision and Pattern Recognition (2016)

5. Farha, Y.A., Gall, J.: MS-TCN: multi-stage temporal convolutional network for action segmentation. In: Proceedings of the IEEE/CVF Conference on Computer Vision and Pattern Recognition, pp. 3575–3584 (2019)
6. Li, S.J., AbuFarha, Y., Liu, Y., et al.: MS-TCN++: multi-stage temporal convolutional network for action segmentation. In: IEEE Transactions on Pattern Analysis and Machine Intelligence (2020)
7. Stein, S., McKenna, S.J.: Combining embedded accelerometers with computer vision for recognizing food preparation activities. In: ACM International Joint Conference on Pervasive and Ubiquitous Computing, pp. 729–738 (2013)
8. Kuehne, H., Arslan, A., Serre, T.: The language of actions: recovering the syntax and semantics of goal- directed human activities. In: IEEE Conference on Computer Vision and Pattern Recognition (CVPR), pp. 780–787 (2014)
9. Fathi, A., Ren, X., Rehg, J.M.: Learning to recognize objects in egocentric activities. In: IEEE Conference on Computer Vision and Pattern Recognition (CVPR), pp. 3281–3288 (2011)
10. Singh, B., Marks, T.K., Jones, M., Tuzel, O., Shao, M.: A multi-stream bidirectional recurrent neural network for fine-grained action detection. In: IEEE Conference on Computer Vision and Pattern Recognition (CVPR), pp. 1961–1970 (2016)
11. Lei, P., Todorovic, S.: Temporal deformable residual networks for action segmentation in videos. In: IEEE Conference on Computer Vision and Pattern Recognition (CVPR), pp. 6742–6751 (2018)
12. Richard, A., Gall, J.: Temporal action detection using a statistical language model. In: IEEE Conference on Computer Vision and Pattern Recognition (CVPR), pp. 3131–3140 (2016)
13. Kuehne, H., Richard, A., Gall, J.: Weakly supervised learning of actions from transcripts. Comput. Vis. Image Underst. **163**, 78–89 (2017)
14. Ding, L., Xu, C.: Weakly-supervised action segmentation with iterative soft boundary assignment. In: IEEE Conference on Computer Vision and Pattern Recognition (CVPR), pp. 6508–6516 (2018)
15. Richard, A., Kuehne, H., Gall, J.: Weakly supervised action learning with RNN based fine-to-coarse modeling. In: IEEE Conference on Computer Vision and Pattern Recognition (CVPR) (2017)

Statistics and Machine Learning for Behavioral Prediction of Operational Transconductance Amplifiers with Focus on Regression Analysis

Malinka Ivanova[✉], Petya Petkova, and Nikolay Petkov

Technical University of Sofa, Sofia, Bulgaria
{m_ivanova, petya.petkova}@tu-sofia.bg, ntoshevp@abv.bg

Abstract. The goal in this paper is to present a method for predictive analysis of Operational Transconductance Amplifiers behavior in frequency domain applying regression algorithms. The exploration is performed applying linear regression, additive regression and transformed regression algorithms for solving regression tasks and linear and logistic regression for deciding classification problems. The evaluation of developed predictive models show the advantage of linear regression in comparison to others.

Keywords: Regression analysis · Operational transconductance amplifier · Machine learning · Statistics

1 Introduction

Nowadays, artificial intelligence and data science methods are in progressive development, giving huge possibilities for predictive modeling and analysis. Machine learning algorithms as part of artificial intelligence in combination with statistics techniques for data processing are used to outline, study and understand events, processes, phenomena. Such approach is also applicable in domain of electronics for design, analysis and optimization of circuits' behavior as well as for fault diagnosis and risk evaluation [1, 2]. Regression analysis is classified to the area of statistics, but in many cases it is utilized with some machine learning algorithms to predict a variable of interest taking into account one or several other variables [3]. These allow in depth to be explored some circuit features that are not so obvious as well as to give understandable explanation about occurring events and processes. Several engineering tasks could be automated in order to save time, efforts, usage of any additional resources and also to achieve higher accuracy and better engineering performance. One good example is the work of Ghai et al. who combine polynomial regression with genetic algorithm to optimize the design of analog circuits [4]. The applied constrained multi-objective optimization leads to faster design process and to the optimized values of the target parameters.

In the scope of research in this paper is application of regression analysis for prediction the electrical behavior of Operational Transconductance Amplifiers (OTAs).

W. Cao et al. (Eds.): CONF-CDS 2021, CCIS 1513, pp. 315–324, 2021.
https://doi.org/10.1007/978-981-16-8885-0_25

OTAs are realized in practice through usage of operational amplifiers or in the form of integrated circuits. Their function is related to conversion the differential voltage input into the current output. OTAs could be designed to amplify or to integrate current or voltage signals. Among the specific OTAs features are: large input and output resistances, wide bandwidth, high working frequency, high transconductance. Currently, the design and implementation of OTAs is extensively explored by researchers from academy and experts from industry, because of their applications in filters [5, 6], biomedical devices [7], mobile devices [8], sensors [9]. The further research goals are focused on improvement the OTAs parameters and characteristics as well as on improvement their design and simulation process through predictions and analysis.

The aim of the paper is to present a method for predictive analysis of OTAs based on regression techniques. For this purpose several predictive models are created and evaluated applying linear regression, additive regression and transformed regression algorithms for solving regression tasks and linear and logistic regression for deciding classification problems.

2   Bibliometric Study

To grasp the general view and different aspects about the progress of development and application of machine learning and particularly regression methods in electronics the bibliometric approach is used [10]. The bibliographic information is taken from the scientific database Scopus regarding the key words: *regression analysis* and *electronics*. The exploration is performed on 3 June 2021 and 1664 documents are obtained as result. The created bibliographic map (Fig. 1) through the VoSviewer [11] points out the complex connections between the domains of regression analysis and electronics. The most utilized regression technics are linear, logistic and multiple regression that are combined with support vector machines algorithm, time series prediction algorithms, data envelopment analysis, factor analysis for prediction, optimization, performance and reliability analysis of electronic products.

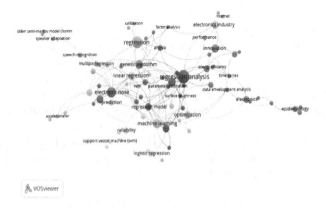

Fig. 1. The constructed bibliometric map regarding the keywords regression analysis and electronics

More detailed analysis of the published scientific production shows that this area of research is in its early stage, but also presents the increased interests to the topic as for 2008 – 91 documents are indexed in Scopus, 2010 – 74, 2012 – 82, 2014 – 92, 2016 – 57, 2018 – 91 and 2020 – 102. The authors with the biggest number of articles are from USA, China, Japan, India, Taiwan, Germany, South Korea, United Kingdom, Canada and Malaysia. The analysis of the subject area outlines that 29,7% of the published papers are in the engineering fields, 12,9% - in computer science, 8,3% - medicine, 5,6% - physics and astronomy, 4,8% - business, management, chemistry, etc.

3   Regression Methods

Regression algorithms are part of supervised machine learning and they are created to learn from cases that consists of input-output pairs. Different regression methods exist in order to solve simple or more complex predictive problems.

Simple linear regression is applied to point out the linear dependence between two continuous variables X and Y, where coefficients β_0 and β_1 present respectively the intercept and slope of the regression line and ε_i is a random error or noise [12]:

$$Y_i = \beta_0 + \beta_1 X_i + \varepsilon_i, i = 1, 2, \ldots, n \qquad (1)$$

For achieving a "best fitting" regression line, the estimates $\hat{\beta}_0$ and $\hat{\beta}_1$ of coefficients β_0 and β_1 is more often found through the least squares method. Then, the predicted estimated mean response $\hat{Y}_{pr}$ at $X = X_{pr}$ is calculated through estimated regression formula:

$$\hat{Y}_{pr} = \hat{\beta}_0 + \hat{\beta}_1 X_{pr}. \qquad (2)$$

"Best fitting" of the regression line according to the least squares method is found through minimization of the residual sum of squares (RSS):

$$RSS(\beta_0, \beta_1) = \sum_{i=1}^{n} [Y_i - (\beta_0 + \beta_1 X_i)]^2. \qquad (3)$$

At *multiple linear regression* more than one variables of interest $X_1, X_2, \ldots$ could be examined. Equation with two predictors X_1 *and* X_2 is as follows:

$$Y = \beta_0 + \beta_1 X_1 + \beta_2 X_2 + \varepsilon. \qquad (4)$$

If interaction between predictors X_1 *and* X_2 exist, then a product of variables X_1 x X_2 is added:

$$Y = \beta_0 + \beta_1 X_1 + \beta_2 X_2 + \beta_3 X_1 X_2 + \varepsilon. \qquad (5)$$

Logistic regression is suitable when a binary response has to be predicted concerning one or several predictors. Simple logistic regression takes into account one predictor X and it is calculated through logit transformation equation:

$$g(X) = \ln\left[\frac{p(X)}{1 - p(X)}\right] = \beta_0 + \beta_1 X, \tag{6}$$

where $p(X)$ is the probability of the response and more often is presented with S-shaped curve:

$$p(X) = \frac{e^{\beta_0 + \beta_1 X}}{1 + e^{\beta_0 + \beta_1 X}}. \tag{7}$$

At *multiple logistic regression* the predicted binary response is based on several predictors:

$$p(X) = \frac{e^{\beta_0 + \beta_1 X_1 + \ldots + \beta_n X_n}}{1 + e^{\beta_0 + \beta_1 X_1 + \ldots + \beta_n X_n}}. \tag{8}$$

Polynomial regression is preferred when nonlinear dependence between a predictor X and a response Y has to be modeled:

$$Y = \beta_0 + \beta_1 X + \beta_2 X^2 \ldots + \beta_n X^n + \varepsilon. \tag{9}$$

Additive regression model is obtained from multi-dimensional parametric linear regression (Eq. 4) replacing linear parts $X_i \beta_i$ with nonlinear ones $r_i(X_i)$:

$$Y = \beta_0 + r_1(X_1) + \ldots + r_n(X_n) + \varepsilon. \tag{10}$$

Its advantage is possibility complex nonlinear relations with big number of predictors to be modeled. That allows some new patterns to be discovered, which cannot be find with linear regression.

Transformed regression model is utilized for linearization of nonlinear relations through appropriate transformation. The functions for linearization could be in the form:

$$Y = \beta_0 X^{\beta_1}, Y = \beta_0 + \beta_1 \log X, etc. \tag{11}$$

4   Predictive Modelling

The goal in this work is to explore the capabilities of regression techniques for building predictive models in support of design and analysis of electronic circuits. The used workflow is depicted on Fig. 2 and it consists of data set preparation through circuit simulation, data pre-processing, development of a predictive model through applying regression algorithms, evaluation the model performance and model improvement.

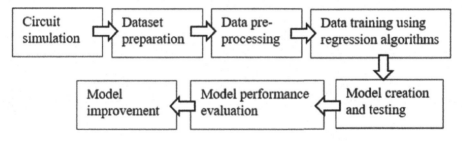

Fig. 2. The used workflow

The chosen electronic circuit for experimentation is CMOS OTA with 13 transistors [13] (Fig. 3). The input differential stage is with current mirror and consists of PMOS transistors M1 and M2 and NMOS transistor M2 and M3. This stage is characterized with big amplification, good reduction of common mode signals. The bias current source is implemented through NMOS transistors M5–M9 as M6–M9 form cascode mirror. It contributes to high output impedance and lower transfer errors. Transistors M10–M12 organize another current mirror and M13 is common source amplifier. It can be said that the most of the OTA's parameters and characteristics depend on the length L and width W of the channel of included MOS transistors [13–15]. In practice the engineers are interested in finding the optimal solution that points out the best combination among important parameters like: signal magnitude (Mag), phase margin (Phasemarg), unity gain bandwidth (UGB), cut-off frequency (Fcutoff). The proposed method could save much efforts, working hours and simulation resources, as all as to automate the engineering tasks related to design and analysis of electronic circuits. The method involves utilization of predictive model that has possibility to outline the optimal variant. The predictive model is created through data collected from simulation of AC analysis in LTspice of presented on Fig. 3 OTA circuit. The changing variables are coefficients $k_i = W_i/L_i$, $i = 1,\ldots13$ as the basic channel parameters are taken from [13]: $k_{M1} = k_{M2} = 32$, $k_{M3} = k_{M4} = 14$, $k_{M5} = k_{M6} = k_{M7} = k_{M8} = k_{M9} = 14$, $k_{M10} = k_{M11} = 41$, $k_{M12} = 220$, $k_{M13} = 148$. The OTA circuit is simulated to examine its behavior in the frequency domain. Its magnitude and phase characteristics are presented on Fig. 4 and the values of Mag, Phasemarg, UGB, Fcutoff parameters are obtained. The gathered data set is pre-processed and formatted in .csv and .arff files. 70% of data is used for training and 30% for testing. The environment of RapidMiner Studio is used for generation the predictive models applying linear regression, additive regression and transformed regression algorithms for solving regression tasks and linear and logistic regression for deciding classification problems.

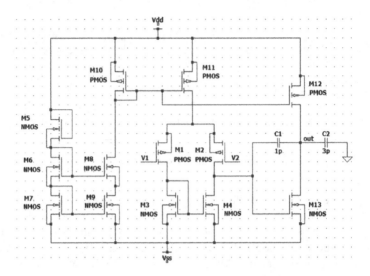

Fig. 3. Operational Transconductance Amplifier [13]

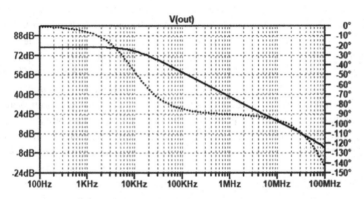

Fig. 4. Magnitude-frequency and phase-frequency characteristics

The regression algorithms for regression tasks are evaluated according to the following parameters (Table 1):

- Root Mean Square Error (RMSE) – it is the squared root of the averaged value between observation and prediction.
- Absolute error – it is the averaged absolute deviation between observation and prediction.
- Relative error – it is the averaged absolute deviation between observation and prediction divided by the observation.
- Squared error – it is the averaged squared error.
- Correlation – it shows the relationship straight between observation and prediction.
- Squared correlation – it is the squared correlation.

Table 1. Evaluation the regression algorithms for regression tasks

Parameters	Linear regression for regression tasks	Additive regression Decision Tree	Transformed regression Decision Tree
RMSE	2.241	5.184	6.332
Absolute error	1.007	2.315	3.000
Relative error	1.68%	3.95%	5.10%
Squared error	5.024	26.874	40.097
Correlation	0.989	0.945	0.947
Squared correlation	0.978	0.893	0.896

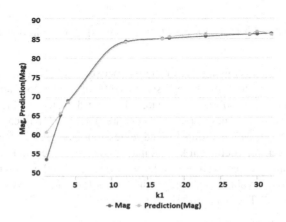

Fig. 5. Dependence between k1 and Mag/prediction(Mag) for linear regression

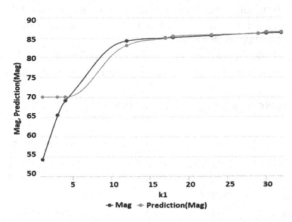

Fig. 6. Dependence between k1 and Mag/prediction(Mag) for additive regression

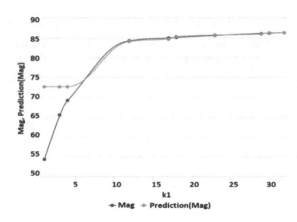

Fig. 7. Dependence between k1 and Mag/prediction(Mag) for transformed regression

The visual results, showing the deviation between the observed and predicted values of magnitude for linear regression, additive regression and transformed regression algorithms for solving regression tasks are depicted on Fig. 5, Fig. 6 and Fig. 7. It can be said that more precise results are obtained for linear regression and then for additive regression and transformed regression. One presented example for the dependence between the coefficient k1 and magnitudes (observed and predicted) points out that the deviation is received at smaller values of the coefficient k1.

The results from evaluation the regression algorithms for classification tasks are presented in Table 2. The main criteria are following:

- Accuracy – it shows the percentage of predictions that are correctly classified.
- Classification error – it is the percentage of incorrectly classified predictions.
- Kappa – it presents the correctly classified predictions that are taken by chance.
- Precision – it is the proportion between all observations from one class to all observations classified as this class.
- Recall – it gives the proportion between all observations from one class to the sum of all observations from this class and incorrectly identified that are not from this class.
- F-Measure – it presents how precise is a classifier.

Table 2. Evaluation the regression algorithms for classification tasks

Parameters	Logistic regression for binary classification task	Linear regression for classification task
Accuracy	75.00%	85.71%
Classification error	25.00%	14.29%
Kappa	0.467	0.000
Precision	80.00%	85.71%
Recall	80.00%	100%
F-Measure	80.00%	92.31%

5 Conclusion

This work is focused on exploration regarding application of regression analysis for facilitating the predictions in solving some engineering tasks at design and analysis of electronic circuits. The examined OTA is simulated in frequency domain as the aim is to understand whether regression techniques could be used for analysis and prediction the magnitude, phase margin, unity wideband and cut-off frequency according to the channel parameters (length L and wide W) of CMOS transistors. The findings indicate the applicability of regression algorithms for deciding regression tasks as the RMSE is smaller for linear regression in comparison to additive and transformed regression. The accuracy of linear regression for classification task is better than the accuracy of logistic regression for binary classification task.

Acknowledgment. This research is supported by Bulgarian National Science Fund in the scope of the project "Exploration the application of statistics and machine learning in electronics" under contract number KΠ-06-H42/1.

References

1. Zhao, S., Blaabjerg, F., Wang, H.: An overview of artificial intelligence applications for power electronics. IEEE Trans. Power Electron. **36**(4), 4633–4658 (2021). https://doi.org/10.1109/TPEL.2020.3024914
2. Rutkowski, J., Grzechca, D.: Use of artificial intelligence techniques to fault diagnosis in analog systems. In: Proceedings of the 2nd Conference on European Computing Conference, ECC'08, pp. 267–274 (2008)
3. Guerra-Gomez, I., McConaghy, T., Tlelo-Cuautle, E.: Study of regression methodologies on analog circuit design. In: 16th Latin-American Test Symposium (LATS), pp. 1–6 (2015). https://doi.org/10.1109/LATW.2015.7102504
4. Ghai, D., Mohanty, S.P., Thakral, G.: Fast analog design optimization using regression-based modeling and genetic algorithm: a nano-CMOS VCO case study. In: International Symposium on Quality Electronic Design (ISQED), pp. 406–411 (2013). https://doi.org/10.1109/ISQED.2013.6523643
5. Soni, B.H., Dhavse, R.N.: Design of operational transconductance amplifier using 0.35 μm technology. Int. J. Wisdom Based Comput. **1**(2), 28–31 (2011)
6. Kamat, D.V., Mohan, P.V.A., Prabhu, K.G.: Current-mode operational transconductance amplifier-capacitor biquad filter structures based on Tarmy-Ghausi Active-RC filter and second-order digital all-pass filters. IET Circuits Devices Syst. **4**(4), 346–364 (2010). https://doi.org/10.1049/iet-cds.2009.0213
7. Bautista, F., Martinez, S.O., Dieck, G., Rossetto, O.: An ultra-low voltage high gain operational transconductance amplifier for biomedical applications (2007)
8. Katolkar, P., Dahigaonkar, D., Wakde, D.G.: Low noise CMOS transconductance amplifier for GPS applications. In: Proceedings of International Conference of Electrical, Automation and Mechanical Engineering (EAME 2015), Advances in Engineering Research Series, pp. 518–521 (2015). https://doi.org/10.2991/eame-15.2015.145

9. Hijazi, Z., Caviglia, D., Chible, H., Valle, M.: Design of operational transconductance amplifiers for voltage to current conversion in gas sensing applications. In: Proceeding of AEIT International Annual Conference, pp. 1–5 (2016). https://doi.org/10.23919/AEIT. 2016.7892798

10. Ellegaard, O., Wallin, J.A.: The bibliometric analysis of scholarly production: how great is the impact? Scientometrics **105**, 1809–1831 (2015). https://doi.org/10.1007/s11192-015-1645-z

11. Perianes-Rodriguez, A., Waltman, L., Jan van Eck, N.: Constructing bibliometric networks: a comparison between full and fractional counting. J. Informet. **10**(4), 1178–1195 (2016). https://doi.org/10.1016/j.joi.2016.10.006

12. Ciaburro, G.: Regression Analysis with R: Design and Develop Statistical Nodes to Identify Unique Relationships Within Data at Scale. Packt Publishing (2018). ISBN-13 : 978 – 1788627306

13. Laajimi, R., Gueddah, N., Masmoudi, M.: A novel design method of two-stage CMOS operational transconductance amplifier used for wireless sensor receiver. Int. J. Comput. Appl. **39**(11), 1–11 (2012)

14. Palmisano, G., Palumbo, G., Pennisi, S.: Design procedure for two-stage CMOS transconductance operational amplifiers: a tutorial. Analog Integr. Circ. Sig. Process. **27**, 179–189 (2001). https://doi.org/10.1023/A:1011229119071

15. Baharudin, S.N.S., Jambek, A.B., Ismail, R.C.: Design and analysis of a two-stage OTA for sensor interface circuit. In: 2014 IEEE Symposium on Computer Applications and Industrial Electronics (ISCAIE), pp. 88–92 (2014). https://doi.org/10.1109/ISCAIE.2014.7010215

Comparative Study of Loss Function Based on Neural Network

Hongyi Du[✉]

The High School Affiliated to Renmin University of China,
Beijing 100086, China

Abstract. With the increase of road mileage, the complexity of road conditions and the increasing demand for real-time update of road data, more accurate and efficient road detection methods are gradually put on the agenda. Among them, the road detection method based on deep learning has the greatest potential at present. In order to improve the efficiency of the neural network, this paper introduces the definition of the loss function, the main classification of the loss function, the advantages and disadvantages of the corresponding and the application of the loss function from the perspective of the loss function.

Keywords: Edge detection · Loss function · Comparisons

1 Introduction

Road detection is a powerful application of edge detection of roads, by applying image processing and computer vision methods [1]. The timely and accurately updating of road's database is crucial for diversified social functions such as urban planning, navigation, traffic commanding, and e-maps. The traditional methods of road detecting are artificial vectorization, vehicle-mounted road detection or hand-held road detection to achieve manual update or semi-automatic update [2]. However, with the economic boom, the mileage of road increased rapidly. Using the traditional manual or semi-automatic methods to update the road's database timely and accurately is not realistic any more. It is essential to develop a new method to improve detecting efficiency. The development of high-resolution remote-sensing technology offers more reliable resources for road detection. The detection based on remote sensing images has higher detecting efficiency than traditional process. However, manual-based detection not only cannot save resources but also could not ensure the accuracy of detection. Therefore, utilizing computers to detect roads from remote sensing images becomes the research hotspot.

In recent years, with the rapid development of computing power, DL (Deep Learning) has achieved supervising results in many fields such as target recognition, object detection and image classification. Researchers began to try DL technology to process high-resolution remote sensing images with massive features. By using the layered mechanism of convolutional neural network for information processing, we can learn the road data features obtained from massive high spatial resolution remote sensing images, so as to obtain better road detection results.

© Springer Nature Singapore Pte Ltd. 2021
W. Cao et al. (Eds.): CONF-CDS 2021, CCIS 1513, pp. 325–334, 2021.
https://doi.org/10.1007/978-981-16-8885-0_26

The training of deep neural networks is very important to the performance of neural network. Within the complex structure of deep neural networks, the loss function plays an important role in the feedback of training results. It calculates the error between the predicted value and the ground truth value during the training, feeds back the training results to the neural network through the backpropagation algorithm, and adjusts the parameters of each neuron. Therefore, choosing appropriate loss function for convolutional neural network plays an important role in network training. At present, the loss function of the mainstream deep neural networks includes hinge loss function, cross entropy loss function and exponential loss function. This paper focuses on the analysis of road detection algorithms, discusses the selection of loss functions based on different problems, analyzes the main problems in the field of image segmentation, and analyzes the applicable loss functions for various problems.

2 Brief on Loss Function

A loss function is a function that evaluates the risk of an event. In supervised learning problem, model F is selected as the decision function f in hypothesis space F. For given input X, loss function $L(Y, f(x))$ is used to measure the difference between the output value calculated by decision function f and the true value Y of the sample [3]. The greater the output value of the loss function, the greater the difference between $f(x)$ and the real value Y. Therefore, the value of the loss function can directly reflect the prediction performance of the model. The smaller the value of the loss function, the better the accuracy of the model. At the same time, the loss function can be used to express the relationship between the predicted value and the actual value. If the loss value is less than a threshold, then the sample is similar, otherwise, it is not similar.

In practical problems, the choice of loss function is subject to many constraints, such as the choice of machine learning algorithm, whether there are outliers, the complexity of gradient descent, the difficulty of derivation and the confidence of predicted value. There is no single loss function that can handle all types of data perfectly. If the loss function can enlarge the distance between classes and reduce the distance within classes, the accuracy of model prediction will be higher. Therefore, in the same model, a loss function matching the solution problem plays a great role in improving the model performance. As a result, if the characteristics of each loss function can be correctly understood, the applicable scenarios can be analyzed, and the appropriate loss function can be selected for specific problems, the prediction accuracy can be further improved.

Specifically, loss function plays an important role in many fields of research such as computer science, finance, etc. In the financial field, the loss function mainly plays the role of risk assessment. Better use of appropriate loss functions can improve the reliability of the model. For example, Li et al. [4] constructed the reliability premium with special dependence effect by using the Buhlmann-Straub model under MLNEX loss function. In the field of computer, the loss function is mainly applied to the result feedback of deep neural network. Using appropriate loss function can improve the accuracy of neural network recognition. For example, Sun and Zhang [5] used the deep learning network constructed by triple loss function to improve the accuracy of objectified dialectical tongue image in 18.34% of tumor patients.

3   Different Forms of Loss Function

After years of development, there are more and more types of loss function, and the range of use of loss function is more and more wide. Different types of loss functions should be selected according to different requirements. This section will introduce the mainstream loss functions, and analyze their advantages and disadvantages and their applicable scope.

3.1   Loss Function of Square Deviation

The square error loss function is a loss function fitted according to the Euclidean distance between the expected value and the actual value of the residual. Its standard form is

$$C(w,b) = \frac{1}{2n}\sum_x \|y(x) - a^L(x)\|^2$$

where C represents the cost, x represents the sample, $a^L(x) = f(w \cdot x + b)$ (w and b are parameters) represents the output value, $y(x)$ represents the actual value, and n represents the total number of samples. $y(x) - a^L(x)$ represents the residual, and the purpose of training the neural network is to minimize the output of the loss function by adjusting the weight and bias, that is, to minimize the sum of squares of the residual.

For simplicity, the same sample is illustrated as an example. At this point, the square error loss function will be simplified as

$$C(w,b) = \frac{(y-a)^2}{2}$$

When using the loss function of square deviation, several issues should be noted. When the loss function of square deviation is used, it usually converges slowly. This leads to slower learning speed and higher learning cost of the neural network. The reason for this phenomenon is that the partial derivatives of the loss function of squares with respect to w and b are proportional to the slope of the activation function:

$$\frac{\partial C}{\partial w} = (a-y)\sigma'(Z)x = a\sigma'(Z)$$

$$\frac{\partial C}{\partial b} = (a-y)\sigma'(Z)x = a\sigma'(Z)$$

Normally, the activation function used by the neural network is the Sigmoid function, shown as Fig. 1.

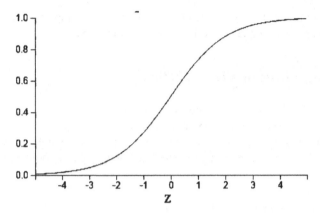

Fig. 1. Sigmoid activation function.

It can be seen that as the input value increases, the slope of the sigmoid activation function gradually decreases. Since the learning rate of the loss function of square error is directly proportional to the slope of the activation function, the gradient descent rate of the function will be slower when the input value of the function is larger.

Therefore, when using the loss function of square deviation to construct the neural networks, it should avoid using the loss function in combination with sigmoid, tanh and other nonlinear activation functions. On the contrary, when used in combination with linear activation function, the loss function of square deviation can converge quickly. When the convergence rate of the squared error loss function is slow, the activation function can be changed into a linear activation function, or the input value range can be adjusted so that the slope of the activation function value of the input value mapping is in a larger range. If the results are not good, other loss functions (such as the cross entropy loss function) are usually used.

3.2 Cross Entropy Loss Function

According to Shannon's concept of information entropy [6], cross entropy is a method developed on the basis of Kullback-Leibler distance to measure the difference between two elements. The expression of cross entropy is as follows:

$$H(p,q) = D(P||Q) + H(p,q) = -\sum_{x \in X} P(x) \cdot log_2 P(x)Q(x) \qquad (1)$$

The cross entropy is used to measure the information difference between elements [7]. The cross entropy can be regarded as the expected value of the change of system information when the distribution P replaces bits as the probability distribution of a single system. It can also be regarded as the information difference between the two probability systems P and bit. Therefore, the cross entropy minimum criterion [8] can be used to estimate or approximate the probability distribution of the system. in the form of

$$C = -\frac{1}{N}\sum_{i=1}^{N}[y_i ln_a + (1 - y_i)\ln(1 - a)] \qquad (2)$$

The gradient formula of the function with respect to the weight w is

$$\frac{\partial C}{\partial w_j} = -\frac{1}{N}\sum_{i=1}^{N} x_j(\sigma(z) - y) \qquad (3)$$

There is no derivative of the activation function in the gradient formula of the cross entropy loss function. Therefore, the learning speed of the cross entropy loss function is independent of the derivative of the activation function. When the nonlinear activation function such as sigmoid/softmax is used to process the output data together with the cross entropy loss function, and the solution is solved by the gradient descent method, the problem of learning rate reduction in the iteration process of the loss function of square deviation can be avoided due to the decline of the derivative of the activation function.

The cross entropy loss function is applicable to the construction of most neural networks. The cross entropy loss function can enlarge the distance between different classes, make the difference between classes bigger, and facilitate the learning of neural network [9].

But similarly, the cross entropy loss function also has some limitations. When sigmoid/softmax-cross-entropy combination is used, the loss function only cares about the accuracy of prediction probability for correct tags because it adopts the inter-class competition mechanism, ignoring the difference of other incorrect tags, resulting in the looser learned features. This phenomenon can be improved by using activation functions such as L-softmax, M-softmax, AM-softmax, etc. in conjunction with the cross entropy loss function.

3.3   Intersection Over Union in the Target Detection

The IOU (Intersection over Union) is a kind of reference to measure the degree of box coincidence. The basic idea of IOU is to determine the degree of overlap by analyzing the ratio between the overlapping area and the total area occupied by the two frames. In the field of target detection, the main function of loss function is to measure the difference between the prediction box and the real box, and return the loss value for further learning. The crosscutting ratio can meet the requirement of target detection algorithm for loss function. Therefore, the crossover ratio has become an important index to measure the detection accuracy in the field of target detection.

The basic idea of IOU loss function is to measure the degree of overlap between the two frames according to the overlapping area and the total covered area. As shown in Fig. 2, the overlapping area of the blue box and the yellow box is B, and the total area covered is A + B + C, then the value of IOU is the ratio of B and (A + B + C).

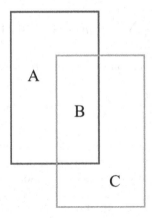

Fig. 2. The basic idea of IOU

Different Forms of IOU. The results obtained from IOU model can well evaluate the difference between the prediction box and the real box, so as to return more accurate loss value for the neural network [10]. At the same time, IOU also has scale invariance. Since the value obtained by IOU algorithm is a fraction, when the upper and lower values are simultaneously enlarged or reduced, the output value of IOU remains unchanged. However, IOU is not suitable for direct use as a loss function. It also has two limitations, 1) If there is no intersection between the prediction box and the real box, then the return value of IOU is 0, and the gradient is also 0. This prevents the function from further learning; and 2) IOU cannot accurately judge the coincidence degree of the two boxes. As shown in the Fig. 3 below, the return value of classical IOU only refers to the area of intersection and union, but the overlapping shape cannot be well judged. The IOU return values of the three figures are all the same, but it is obvious that the regression effect of the left figure is the best among the three figures. Therefore, in this case, the classical IOU loss function cannot correctly judge the differences between the three learning effects, so further learning cannot be carried out.

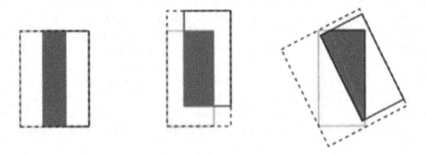

Fig. 3. Three cases in which the classic IOU returns the same value

Because of two defects shown above of classic IOU, the improved GIOU (generalized IOU), DIOU (distance IOU) and CIOU (compete IOU) are proposed. Specific comparison is shown in the Table 1.

GIOU. GIOU [11] also refers to the two-box minimum closure region as a loss function. If the prediction box is A, the true box is B, and the minimum closure region of the two boxes is C, then the definition of GIOU is

$$GIOU = IOU - \frac{|C \backslash A \cup B|}{|C|}$$

GIOU has following advantages:

1. GIOU has the ability to judge the coincidence degree of two boxes and has the basic conditions for using it as a loss function;
2. GIOU is not sensitive to scale changes. The change of scale has little effect on the return value of GIOU;
3. GIOU is a very good distance metric. This solves the problem that when the two boxes of IOU function do not coincide, the gradient of the function is always 0 and the next step of learning cannot be carried out [12];
4. GIOU not only pays attention to boxed areas, but also pays attention to other non-coincidence areas, which can better reflect the coincidence degree relationship between the two frames and improve the learning effect [13].

Also, GIOU has drawback. If the horizontal or vertical directions of the prediction box overlap, or the two boxes contain, the difference between the two boxes and the minimum closure region is 0, that is, $GIOU = IOU$. This slows down the convergence rate of the GIOU in the case of the above.

DIOU. In view of the problems of small gradient and slow convergence of IOU and GIOU in the training process, DIOU puts forward corresponding improvement measures on the basis of GIOU. If b and b^{gt} represent the center points of the prediction box and the real box respectively, then

$$DIOU = IOU - \frac{\rho^2(b, b^{gt})}{c^2}$$

Where ρ is the Euclidian distance of two points, and c is the minimum closure area of the prediction box and the true box.

The advantages of DIOU are as follows, 1) DIOU is scale invariant; 2) when the prediction box and the true box do not overlap or are not in the horizontal or vertical direction, DIOU can normally learn and give a loss value; and 3) when the prediction box and the real box are overlapped, or in the same horizontal or vertical direction, the DIOU learns faster than GIOU and IOU in this situation.

DIOU improves on GIOU by adding the second factor of the three elements of border regression, that is, the distance from the center point, into consideration. DIOU has no obvious shortcomings in learning, which makes it the first relatively perfect loss function in the series of IOU loss functions. All problems that can be solved by GIOU can be solved by DIOU function as well. However, since the aspect ratio of the three elements of the box regression is still not within the consideration range of the function, the loss function of IOU series still has room for further improvements.

CIOU. In the previous discussions, three factors are considered to describe the degree of overlap between the two boxes: the overlapping area of the two boxes, the distance between the center points of the two boxes, and the length-width ratio of the two boxes. A better overall performance of the regression location loss function needs to take these three factors into account. Therefore, an improved CIOU based on DIOU model is proposed.

The three measurement factors of CIOU are the same as the three elements mentioned above, and CIOU is defined as following.

- $CIOU = DIOU - \alpha v$
- $v = \frac{4}{\pi^2} \left(arctan \frac{w^{gt}}{h^{gt}} - arctan \frac{w}{h} \right)^2$
- $\alpha = \frac{v}{1 - IOU + v}$

  Where w and h represents the width and height of two boxes.

The CIOU loss function has the following advantages:

1. CIOU is scale invariant;
2. regardless of the position relationship between the prediction box and the actual box (no overlap, complete inclusion, the same horizontal position, the same vertical position, etc.), CIOU has a good convergence effect; and
3. the convergence speed and effect of CIOU is further improved.

   The CIOU loss function is the one with the fastest regression speed and the best comprehensive effect among the IOU series of loss functions. The αv parameter, the aspect ratio of the two boxes, is taken into account to make the regression effect reach the highest level of the existing function.

IOU series functions are still in the development stage at present, each update can solve and replace the use of the previous generation of loss functions. Under the current situation, CIOU function is the one with the best comprehensive performance, and can well replace the other three loss functions in practical applications. In the future, parameters may be adjusted based on the idea of CIOU function according to the actual situation, so as to achieve better results under specific circumstances.

Table 1. Different forms of IOU

	IOU	GIOU	DIOU	CIOU
Formula	$IOU = \frac{|A \cap B|}{|A \cup B|}$	$GIOU = IOU - \frac{|C \backslash A \cup B|}{|C|}$	$DIOU = IOU - \frac{\rho^2(b, b^{gt})}{c^2}$	$CIOU = DIOU - \alpha v$
Advantages	Scale invariance; basic ability to determine coverage	Insensitive to scale changes; ability to learn without coincide; better ability to determine coverage, compared with IOU	Scale invariance; better ability to determine coverage, compared with GIOU, and have better performance when boxes are at same horizontal or vertical position	Scale invariance; High performance learning regardless of the position relationship between two boxes; highest learning efficiency
Drawbacks	0 gradient when two frames have no coincide; cannot accurately determine coverage	Limited ability of learning when two boxes have same horizontal or vertical direction	No obvious drawbacks, but still have potential to improve	No obvious drawbacks
Application	Not a practical loss function	Serves as loss function in target detection, for instance, Faster R-CNN or YOLO-v3	Serves as loss function in target detection; and DIOU NMS	Almost all applications of IOU can be used

4 Conclusion and Discussion

In order to improve the accuracy and efficiency of road test, proceed from the Angle of loss function, this paper first introduces the definition of loss function and loss function in the application of neural network, and the common principle and properties of several kinds of loss function are introduced, by discussing the advantages and disadvantages of the present in the neural network and using range. In the future, with the further development of remote sensing technology, images with higher definition and larger data volume will bring new challenges to deep learning-based road detection algorithms. Therefore, the loss function with faster convergence and wider applicability will be the development trend of the loss function in the future. Now the mainstream loss function is a single model. The combined application of multiple models, such as IOU and cross-entropy thought, may be able to meet new requirements in new environments.

References

1. Liu, R.: Research and Improvement of High Resolution Remote Sensing Image Road Extraction Algorithm. Xidian University (2019)
2. Hong, Z.: Road extraction from high spatial resolution remote sensing images based on deconvolution network. China University of Geosciences, Beijing
3. Deng, J., Zhang, S., Zhang, J., et al.: Research on loss function and its application in supervised learning. Big Data 000(001), 60–80 (2020)
4. Li, X., Wu, L.: Reliability model with risk dependent effect under MLINEX loss function. J. Jiangxi Norm. Univ. Nat. Sci. Edn. **1**, 17–19 (2020)

5. Sun, M., Zhang, X.: Study on tongue image classification method based on loss function of TripleLoss. Beijing Biomed. Eng. **39**(02), 25–31 (2020)
6. Shannon, C.E.: A mathematical theory of communication. Bell Syst. Tech. J. **27**(3), 379–423 (1948)
7. Mitchell, T.M., Carbonell, J.G., Michalski, R.S.: Machine Learning. China Machine Press (2003)
8. Liu, W., Pokharel, P.P., Principe, J.C.: Correntropy: properties and applications in non-
9. Gaussian signal processing. IEEE Trans. Signal Process. **55**(11), 5286–5297 (2007)
10. Guo, Y., Alimujiang, A., Nurbiya, Y., Zhu, Y., Kuerban, W.: Multi-country face classification and recognition based on MobileNet network. Image Signal Process. **9**(3), 146–155 (2020)
11. Rezatofighi, H., Tsoi, N., Gwak, J.Y., et al.: Generalized intersection over union: a metric and a loss for bounding box regression (2019)
12. Generalized intersection over union: a metric and a loss for bounding box regression (2019)
13. Rezatofighi, H., Tsoi, N., Gwak, J.Y., Sadeghian, A., Savarese, S.: Generalized intersection over union: a metric and a loss for bounding box regression. In: 2019 IEEE/CVF Conference on Computer Vision and Pattern Recognition (CVPR). IEEE (2019)

Research on the Prediction of Logistics Demand for Emergencies Based on BP Neural Network

Kang Ming, Zhao Ying, and Zhang Jing[✉]

Beijing University of Posts and Telecommunications, Beijing 100876, China
zhangjing@bupt.edu.cn

Abstract. Logistics demand forecasting is a prerequisite and an important part of logistics system planning and optimization, especially in emergencies, where short-term, massive and multi-discipline material demands put forward extremely high requirements on the guarantee capacity of logistics systems. In this paper, a logistics demand prediction model based on time series is constructed for the logistics demand characteristics of emergency events. Since the BP neural network method has the advantages of non-linear mapping capability, self-learning and self-adaptive capability, the BP neural network method is used to solve the model, and finally the model is verified and improved by practical cases. The results show that the model and method used in this study can better predict the logistics demand under unexpected events, which meets the need for rapid prediction of logistics demand in the early stage of unexpected events and is of great significance to improve the efficiency of logistics under unexpected events.

Keywords: Logistics · Demand forecasting · Time series · BP neural network

1 Introduction

There are four broad categories of emergencies in China: natural disasters, accidents, public health and social security incidents. The impact on society and families of economic and casualty losses caused by major emergencies is difficult to estimate, such as SARS in 2002 and COVID-19 that continues to this day last year. Logistics demand forecast is a premise and an important part of logistics system planning and optimization, especially in emergencies, short-term, a large number of real-time rescue needs, logistics demand forecast accuracy and timeliness put forward higher requirements. Traditional logistics demand forecasting methods require high data integrity and quality, complex model structure and poor timeliness, which make it difficult to meet the needs of rapid logistics demand forecasting in the early stage of emergencies. Therefore, this paper constructs a time series-based logistics demand forecasting model for the logistics demand characteristics of emergencies, solves it using BP neural network method and conducts case validation, which is important for improving the response efficiency of logistics system under emergencies and reducing disaster losses.

© Springer Nature Singapore Pte Ltd. 2021
W. Cao et al. (Eds.): CONF-CDS 2021, CCIS 1513, pp. 335–348, 2021.
https://doi.org/10.1007/978-981-16-8885-0_27

2   Literature Review

Liu Hui [1] Science and Technology Management Research used BP neural networks to price the IPO in order to overcome the disadvantages of existing valuation methods such as insufficient information and subjective pricing process. This is because compared with the traditional IPO pricing methods, BP neural networks still have the superior ability to deal with nonlinear relationships in the presence of insufficient information; Zhao Minglan [2] advantages of BP neural networks to build an IPO pricing model for the GEM; Wen Ke [3] used dynamic parameters to optimize the traditional BP neural network in building a risk warning model for securities companies, further improving its accuracy in this application. It can not only keep the network training error small enough, but also make the network weights and thresholds smaller; Yang Limin [5] et al. selected some risk indicators by studying the risk early warning of securities companies, and used the L-M algorithm to optimize the BP neural network to some extent; Zhang Guozheng [6] used BP neural network to build a model for risk early warning, and venture investors or venture capital institutions can predict investment risks well when selecting investment projects; Hu Yanjing [7] et al. improved the traditional BP neural network and predicted risk indicators; Guo Peng [8] et al. established a risk prediction model by BP neural network. After verification, compared with other models, the model prediction used in this paper is more comprehensive and objective, and has a good development prospect; Li Haitang [9] first performed principal component analysis, and then optimized it by combining the optimization algorithm of particle swarm with BP neural network to achieve the short-term accurate prediction of grain pile temperature; Ye Fei [10] combined three algorithms of genetic, BP network and particle swarm to predict the Si content in blast furnace iron; Song Bo [11] used BP neural network method to optimize the clinical path modeling and conducted simulation experiments with actual data; Huang Xiaolong [12] introduced the genetic algorithm and used it to optimize the BP neural network to form a non-holiday intercity passenger flow prediction model; Zhao Fanghui [13] used the collected sample data to construct a PSO-BP neural network and used the model to predict the residential demand in Hefei city in the next three years.

3   BP Neural Network Algorithm

3.1   Basic Concepts

BP (Back Propagation) neural networks are divided into two processes.

1) Work signal forward-transmission sub-process
2) Error signal back-transmission sub-process

In a BP neural network, a single sample has m inputs and n outputs, and there are several hide layers between the input and output layers. A three-layer BP network can complete an arbitrary m-dimensional to n-dimensional mapping. These three layers are the input layer, the hide layer and the output layer, as shown in Fig. 1.

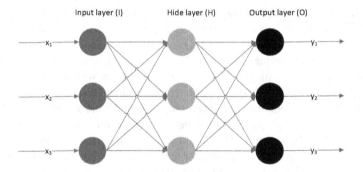

Fig. 1. BP neural network layers

The input variables are first passed as nodes in the input layer to the nodes in the intermediate layer, the implicit layer. The number of layers of the hide layer should be determined according to the problem under study. It can be designed as multiple hide layers or a single hide layer. Different levels of hide layers will form networks of different complexity and accuracy. The hide layers can transform and process the information from the input layer and finally get the result. The error can be gradually reduced by adjusting the weights and thresholds of the input layer-hide layer and hide layer-output layer nodes. The above steps are repeated several times to train the network. The training can be ended when the number of training times reaches a set value or the output error is within the set range.

3.2 Calculation Steps

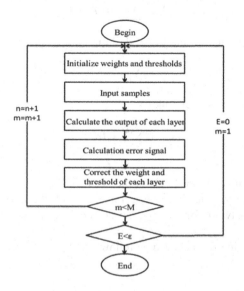

Fig. 2. Flowchart of BP neural network algorithm

The training process of BP neural network is as follows: the first stage is forward-propagation. The data is first transferred from the input layer to the hide layer, and then to the output layer after relevant calculations and processing are performed at that layer. At this point, the output value is obtained. By this time, the error between the calculated value and the expected value is calculated. If the value is within a reasonable range, training will be stopped, otherwise error retransmission occurs. The sample data is replaced by the main median error of back-propagation. Errors go from the output layer to the hide layer, then propagate to the input layer. In this propagation process, the network can adjust the weight and threshold value of each layer of nodes until the error gradually reduces to an acceptable range or reaches the training times. The following is the detailed description process of the algorithm [14] (Fig. 2).

1) Input sample data
2) First start the calculation of forward-propagation
   The output of the i-th node in the input layer is as follows:

$$Y_i = f(x_i) \tag{1}$$

The input of the h-th node in the hide layer is as follows:

$$I_h = \sum_n \omega_{hi} I_i + \theta_i \tag{2}$$

The output of the h-th node in the hide layer is as follows:

$$Y_h = f(I_h) \tag{3}$$

3) Calculate the input of the j-th node of the output layer as follows:

$$I_j = \sum_n \omega_{jh} Y_h + \theta_j \tag{4}$$

The actual output value of the j-th node in the output layer is as follows:

$$Y_j = f(I_j) \tag{5}$$

4) Calculate the output error as follows:

$$E_k = \frac{\sum_{(j=1)}^{M} (d_j - Y_j)^2}{2} \tag{6}$$

5) Modify all weights and thresholds in the network:
6) Judge whether all samples have been trained, if not, the new sample data is then provided to the network for training, repeat step 2); if all the training is completed, start step 7).
7) The total error value is calculated as follows:

$$E = \sum_{k=1}^{K} E_k = \frac{1}{2 \sum_{k=1}^{K} \sum_{j=1}^{M} \left(T_j^k - Y_j^k \right)^2} \tag{7}$$

Judge whether $E < \varepsilon$ is satisfied, if so, stop training, otherwise go to step 8).

8) Judge whether the training times have reached the set value. If the training has been completed, stop the training; if not, go back to step 2) and start training again.

4 Model Establishment

The model constructed in this paper predicts the material demand based on time series, and deduces the unknown quantity of material demand in the next few days by the known material demand in the previous days [15].

4.1 Determine the Network Layers

Determine the Number of Network Layers and the Nodes of Input Layer and Output Layer. This model is a three-layer model. Using the materials of the first 7 days of the earthquake disaster as input data, the material demand of the 8th day is predicted by running the BP model b of the MATLAB program. Then the data of the 8th day is put into the database, and the material demand of the 9th day is predicted by the material demand of the 2nd–8th days, and so on. So the number of nodes in the input layer is 7 and the number of nodes in the output layer is 1.

Determine the Number of Hide Layer Nodes. Same as BP model a, this model has only one hide layer. Based on the above empirical formula, this model conducts experiments on BP neural network and determines that the interval of the number of hide layer nodes is [5], [17]. And then the number of nodes is increased sequentially to train the network starting from the minimum number of nodes in this range.

By using trial-and-error method in this paper, we determine the number of nodes in the hide layer corresponding to 16 when the minimum network error is 0.0049.

Determine the Samples. According to the random function of RANDPERM, the training samples are [1–3, 5–8, 11] and the test samples are [4, 9, 10].

4.2 Set the Network Parameters

When setting network parameters for this model, the following parameters need to be considered:

Function Select. Function selection of this model is the same as BP model a.

Learning Rate. After several training sessions with this model, the learning rate was finally set to 0.03.

Expected Error. After several training sessions of this model network, the expected error of this model was determined to be 0.001, where the number of training sessions was set to 20 and the error metrics were RMSE and MEAP. Once the parameters are set, the samples can be trained, and the execution code is shown in the attached page.

5   Case Analysis

The vegetable demand at the time of the Jiuzhaigou earthquake is selected here as the data source needed for the material demand forecasting model, as shown in Table 1. The empirical case data are mainly obtained through the statistical data from the statistical bureau of the region.

Table 1. Total demand for vegetable materials (unit: g) in a region from 8 to 25 days

Date	Aug. 8	Aug. 9	Aug. 10	Aug. 11	Aug. 12	Aug. 13
Demand	1251514.5	1419551	1613274.5	1380102.5	1076933	1248046.5
Date	Aug. 14	Aug. 15	Aug. 16	Aug. 17	Aug. 18	Aug. 19
Demand	990989.5	1331856.5	1377008.5	1851725	1069538	1918305.5
Date	Aug. 20	Aug. 21	Aug.22	Aug.23	Aug. 24	Aug. 25
Demand	1649501.5	1540871.5	1257320	1632867	2210255	1292586.5

First observe the size [sample size, number of indicators] by Size function, here set to [8, 11], that is, the sample size is 11, the number of indicators is 8, of which 7 are input indicators, 1 is output indicators, meaning that inputting the first 7 days of the demand for supplies in the disaster area, and then predicting the number of supplies needed on the 8th day by running the BP model of MATLAB program (Tables 2 and 3).

Table 2. Input data

Dataset	Serial number	Input data					
		Xi	xi + 1	xi + 2	xi + 3	xi + 4	xi + 5
Training set	1	1251514.5	1419551	1613274.5	1380102.5	1076933	1248046.5
	2	1419551	1613274.5	1380102.5	1076933	1248046.5	990989.5
	3	1613274.5	1380102.5	1076933	1248046.5	990989.5	1331856.5
	4	1380102.5	1076933	1248046.5	990989.5	1331856.5	1377008.5
	5	1076933	1248046.5	990989.5	1331856.5	1377008.5	1851725
	6	1248046.5	990989.5	1331856.5	1377008.5	1851725	1069538
	7	990989.5	1331856.5	1377008.5	1851725	1069538	1918305.5
	8	1331856.5	1377008.5	1851725	1069538	1918305.5	1649501.5
Test set	1	1377008.5	1851725	1069538	1918305.5	1649501.5	1540871.5
	2	1851725	1069538	1918305.5	1649501.5	1540871.5	1257320
	3	1069538	1918305.5	1649501.5	1540871.5	1257320	1632867

Table 3. Output data

Dataset	Serial number	Output value	
		xi + 6	xi + 7
Training set	1	990989.5	1331856.5
	2	1331856.5	1377008.5
	3	1377008.5	1851725
	4	1851725	1069538
	5	1069538	1918305.5
	6	1918305.5	1649501.5
	7	1649501.5	1540871.5
	8	1540871.5	1257320
Test set	1	1257320	1632867
	2	1632867	2210255
	3	2210255	1292586.5

The input and output data are normalized between [0,1], as Tables 4 and 5.

Table 4. Input data normalization

Dataset	Serial number	Input Data					
		Xi	xi + 1	xi + 2	xi + 3	xi + 4	xi + 5
Training set	1	0.3027	0.4622	0.6711	0.4196	0.0927	0.2772
	2	0.4979	0.6711	0.4196	0.0927	0.2772	0.0000
	3	0.7230	0.4196	0.0927	0.2772	0.0000	0.3676
	4	0.4521	0.0927	0.2772	0.0000	0.3676	0.4163
	5	0.0998	0.2772	0.0000	0.3676	0.4163	0.9282
	6	0.2986	0.0000	0.3676	0.4163	0.9282	0.0847
	7	0.0000	0.3676	0.4163	0.9282	0.0847	1.0000
	8	0.3960	0.4163	0.9282	0.0847	1.0000	0.7101
Test set	1	0.4485	0.9282	0.0847	1.0000	0.7101	0.5930
	2	1.0000	0.0847	1.0000	0.7101	0.5930	0.2872
	3	0.0913	1.0000	0.7101	0.5930	0.2872	0.6922

Table 5. Output data normalization

Dataset	Serial number	Output value	
		xi + 6	xi + 7
Training set	1	0.0000	0.2300
	2	0.2796	0.2695
	3	0.3166	0.6857
	4	0.7059	0.0000
	5	0.0644	0.7441
	6	0.7606	0.5084
	7	0.5401	0.4132
	8	0.4510	0.1646
Test set	1	0.2184	0.4938
	2	0.5264	1.0000
	3	1.0000	0.1955

Training and testing the input and output, running MATLAB yields the following results (Fig. 3):

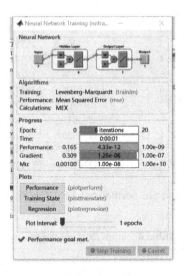

Fig. 3. Training results

Model D was trained 6 times and stopped, with regression evaluation metric mse1.00e−08 and performance indicators = 4.33e−12. Figure 4 is the training process diagram, the image shows that the error decreases gradually with the number of training sessions (Fig. 5).

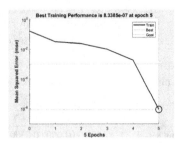

Fig. 4. Training process diagram

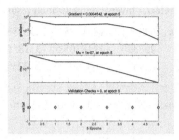

Fig. 5. Training status diagram

Figure 6 shows that the horizontal and vertical axes are fitted to a linear image when they are very similar (Table 6).

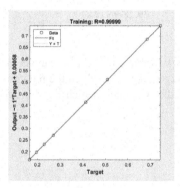

Fig. 6. Exporting object values

Table 6. Network output value

Training sample predicted values	0.5084	0.6857	0.1955	0.4132
	0.1646	0.7441	0.23	0.2695
Test sample predicted values	0.5202	0.655	0.0094	
Final overall predicted values	0.23	0.2695	0.6857	0
	0.7441	0.5084	0.4132	0.1646
	0.4938	1	0.1955	

The results were back-normalized as in Table 7.

Table 7. Inverse normalization results

Training samples	1649501.5	1851725	1292586.5	1540871.5
	1257320	1918305.5	1331856.5	1377008.5
Test samples	1069538	1632867	2210255	

The results of the root mean square and relative errors are calculated in Table 8.

Table 8. Validation results

Root mean square of the training data	Root mean square of the test data	Root mean square of all samples
2.37436028	744475.8894	388789.8533
Relative error of the training samples	Relative error of the test sample	Relative error of all samples
7.7624E−05	39.28789194	10.71493607

Finally, a graph is drawn to make the result analysis more intuitive: Fig. 7 shows the scatter plot of the training samples, in which the red cores are the actual values and the blue circles are the predicted values, which overlap when they are very close to each other.

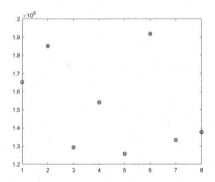

Fig. 7. Scatterplot of actual and predicted values of training samples

In order to see it more intuitively, we subtract the actual value from the predicted value, and the following is the result of the specific value of the subtraction (Fig. 8).

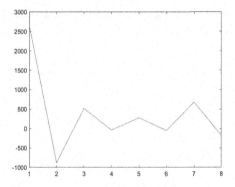

Fig. 8. Difference between actual and predicted values of training samples

The graphs of the results generated from the test samples are as follows (Figs. 9 and 10):

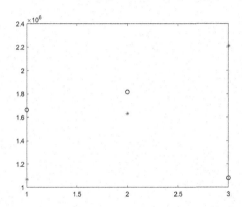

Fig. 9. Scatter plot of actual value predicted value of the test sample

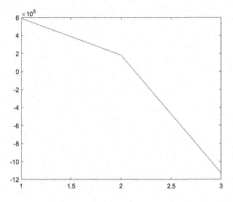

Fig. 10. The difference between the actual and predicted values of the test samples

The results of the analysis of the actual and predicted values of the overall sample are as follows (Figs. 11 and 12):

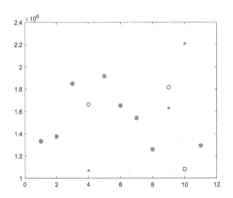

Fig. 11. Overall sample scatter plot

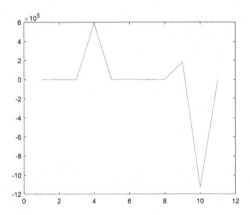

Fig. 12. Difference between the actual and predicted values of the overall sample

Percentage error (Fig. 13):

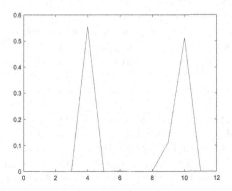

Fig. 13. Error percentage graph

6 Conclusion

The BP neural network model constructed in this paper is a direct prediction model, by inputting the actual amount of materials in the days before the disaster and then making analysis and prediction of the amount of materials in the next few days, so that it can further modify and improve the accuracy of emergency materials on the basis of the initial demand prediction and improve the prediction accuracy. The model is validated by actual cases, and it is concluded that the predicted material requirements under the contingency scenario are basically the same as the actual occurrence of the requirements, so the application of this model can reasonably forecast the material requirements under the contingency.

Acknowledgement. Supported by the National Key Research and Development Program of China (Grant No. 2018YFB1403101) and the Fundamental Research Funds for the Central Universities (Grant No. 2020RC22).

References

1. Liu Hui, F.: The Research on IPO with BP Neural Network. Wuhan University of Technology, China (2008)
2. Zhao Minglan, F.: A study on IPO pricing of GEM listed companies based on BP neural network. Lanzhou J. 77–80 (2010)
3. Wen Ke, F.: Investment bank risk prediction model of dynamic parameters of the neural
4. Network. Sci. Technol. Bull. **31**(09), 192–195 (2015)
5. Yang Limin, F.: Investment banks risk early warning based on BP neural network. J. Anhui Univ. Technol. (Nat. Sci. Edn.) 96–100 (2006)
6. Zhang Guozheng, F.: Research on early warning of venture capital risk based on neural network. Sci. Technol. Manag. Res. 182–184 (2006)

7. Hu Yanjing, F.: BP artificial neural network model: a new visual angle of the financial risk early-warning. J. Chongqing Technol. Bus. Univ. (West. Econ. Forum), 68–71 (2003)
8. Guo Peng, F.: Research of BOT project risk assessment based on BP neural network. Sci. Technol. Manag. Res. 210–214 (2015)
9. Li, Haitang, F.: Research on grain pile temperature prediction model based on improved BP neural network. Henan University of Technology, China (2019)
10. Ye Fei, F.: Prediction Method of Silicon Content in Blast Furnace Hot Metal Based on Improved BP Neural Network. Anhui University of Technology, China (2019)
11. Song Bo, F.: Clinical path optimization based on BP neural network. Comput. Technol. Dev. **30**(04), 156–160 (2020)
12. Huang Xiaolong, F.: Study on passenger flow prediction of intercity passenger line based on improved BP neural network. Harbin Institute of Technology, China (2019)
13. Zhao Fanghui, F.: Research on Housing Demand Forecast Based on PSO-BP Neural Network in Hefei City. Hebei University of Engineering, China (2020)
14. Fan Rui, F.: Research on Demand Prediction of Large Earthquake Emergency Materials Based on PSO-BP Neural Network. Beijing Jiaotong University, China (2020)
15. Kang Lijun, F.: Application of Particle Swarm Optimization BP Neural Network in Emergency Material Demand Forecasting. Lanzhou Jiaotong University, China (2013)

Advances in Natural Language Processing

Research on Twitter Data Crawling and Data Visualization Analysis Based on Python

Ziyuan Ma[✉]

Dalian University of Technology, Dalian 116033, China
zml08@student.le.ac.uk

Abstract. In this era of rapid development of the Internet, there will always be a large amount of new and innovative information. For Internet users, it is very tedious and impractical for them to filter out interesting and high-quality information. Therefore, a good-performance recommendation system that can intelligently screen and recommend users is necessary in the Internet era, and the essence of a good-performance recommendation system is a reliable recommendation algorithm.

With the development of the Internet, the generation and storage of data are everywhere, and it is of great significance to analyze social reality responses based on user behavior data. The article mainly uses python user comments to crawl, and use python for text data mining and analysis, by using more than 100,000 sets of captured data to form multi-party visualization including line graphs, histograms, and tag clouds to promote conclusions.

In that case, the automatic collection of people's search data to determine the weight of the index solves the problem of the lack of persuasiveness of the traditional expert method of determining the weight. Finally, it helps people effectively draw conclusions from extensive and complex data.

Keywords: Twitter · Data analysis · Data crawling · Data visualization · Tag cloud

1 Introduction

As the era of big data and artificial intelligence comes, network and information technology begin to permeate all aspects of human daily life, and the amount of data generated also shows an exponential growth trend. At the same time, the existing data order of magnitude has far exceeded the current human [1]. In this context, data analysis has become a new research topic in the field of data science.

By importing text data to establish a corpus, and performing Chinese word segmentation, word frequency statistics [2], and word cloud generation processes to realize user evaluation word frequency statistical analysis, obtain user reactions to current affairs hotspots, and give different perspectives based on news hot search words A macro perspective on social hot events. The analysis of the risk level uses the advantages of the current Internet search data. The automatic collection of people's search data determines the weight of the index, which solves the problem of the lack of persuasiveness in the traditional method of determining the weight by experts.

© Springer Nature Singapore Pte Ltd. 2021
W. Cao et al. (Eds.): CONF-CDS 2021, CCIS 1513, pp. 351–362, 2021.
https://doi.org/10.1007/978-981-16-8885-0_28

In the era of big data, in our lives, most of the information that can be obtained is stored in text databases in the form of text, such as web pages, news documents, research papers, emails, digital libraries and books, etc. Due to the rapid development of the Internet, text information in the real world is more electronically presented, and text mining has also become a research hotspot and learning focus in the information field. Using computers to realize the recognition and analysis of massive texts has become the focus of research. Text mining technology has also been widely used in many fields, and many problems have been solved prominently. Many scholars in China have also put forward their own opinions and applications in different fields regarding text mining. Luo Yiwei, Zhang Kewei [4] in his article "Analysis of Internet Hotspot Public Opinion Based on Text Mining", they used python and data mining algorithms to realize the word frequency statistical analysis of the hot issues of school bullying, and obtained the public's negative attitude towards this issue. Feng Lina In her article comparative study of Confucius and Yan Zhitui's educational thought based on word frequency statistics, through the word frequency statistics and comparison of "The Family Instructions of Yan Family" [5] and "The Analects", they revealed the differences in educational thoughts between the two in the 1990s, Professor Qian Xuesen pointed out that society is a special, open and complex giant system. Traditional research methods are not enough to comprehensively and systematically study social issues. The comprehensive integrated methodology is proposed to solve this kind of open and complex giant system problems. Under the guidance of the integrated methodology and based on the characteristics of the era of big data, this paper starts with the development of an analysis system for social hotspots and social risk levels of social issues from the Internet search data.

The latest research progress at home and abroad shows that there is a high correlation between web search data and many social and economic behaviors. Search data can reflect users' concerns and needs, and map user behavior trends and laws in real life. In addition, compared with traditional data, network search data can relatively eliminate statistical "time lag"; it can also eliminate users' "privacy" concerns, so as to obtain more authentic data.

In this article, we will capture the data and send it to form a visual chart, so as to intuitively analyze the changes in people's emotions, and finally help people to efficiently draw conclusions from the wide and complex data.

2   Twitter Hot Search Word Collection Process and Data Set Search

To access Twitter data programmatically, we need to create an application that interacts with Twitter API. For real-time data collection, we need a user key and a user secret: these application settings should always remain private. From your application's configuration page, you can also ask for a secret to access tokens and tokens. Similar to consumer keys, these strings must also remain private: they provide permission for the application to access Twitter on behalf of your account. The default permission is read-only, which is what we need in this example, but if you decide to change your permission to provide write features in your application, you must negotiate a new access token. Then we can do the next step [6].

To start building a code framework, we need to import a large number of libraries and packages, and here we intercept some of them as a display. These imports include json libraries, requests methods, and so on. However, some problems may arise in the process of import according to computer differences. I had some problems during the installation requests. The installation process, because the pip version is too low to update, so cannot be requests installation. But the method given by the command prompt for automatic system updates cannot be updated, so you can find a mirror source to install.

After the construction of the requirements code, we can log in to the key obtained just now.

Then search for API. Twitter's search API provides an endpoint to search for tweets related to queries related to terms, accounts, hashtags, languages, locations, and date ranges. The rate limit for this API endpoint is 180 requests every 15 min, 100 states per request, or 18,000 states per window or 72,000 states per hour.

You can explore some search functions through Twitter's advanced search interface. Please note that in the past 7 days, the standard search API has only provided limited access to tweet samples, and you will have to pay more to access the historical API.

3 Twitter Graph Visualization

After completing the data set search, we can build the graph. This data set search time range 28 days, finally according to crawling data, I obtained the following timeline (Fig. 1).

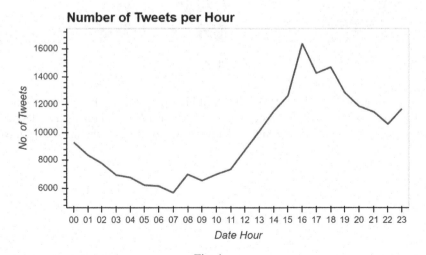

Fig. 1 .

Here we can clearly see the number of Twitter users changing within a day, starting from zero and falling asleep with most people until five or six in the morning. Then, with the start of the new day's work and study, until after four or five o'clock in the evening, the number of tweets changed similarly to the number of users. It can be seen from the figure that the minimum time period for posting twitter in a day is between 2 am and 6 am. At this time, most of us are in the sleeping stage, so the number of twitter will naturally be relatively small. However, after 6 in the morning, the number of twitter posts obviously increased, and it began to slowly decrease at around 9 and 10 o'clock. The editor believes that this is somewhat different from when most people start formal work after 9 to 10 o'clock. Related, and before that, office workers would use the time on the way to work to browse or post on twitter. At ten o'clock in the evening, there will be a small peak. After ten o'clock in the evening, the number of twitter begins to decrease. At this time, many people probably start to sleep and rest.

Of course, we can also count the total amount of data to form a histogram (Fig. 2).

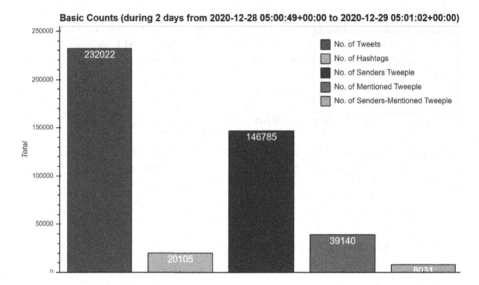

Fig. 2 .

You can also make statistics on data with high frequency of keyword references.

Here we count the number of occurrences more than 100, and finally use these data to form a word cloud map, the higher the frequency of the font the thicker (Fig. 3).

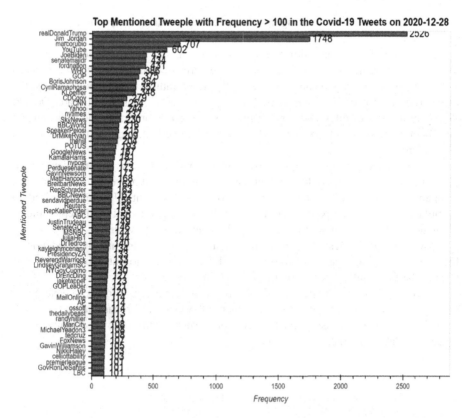

Fig. 3 .

Label cloud (word cloud): arranged by words or labels with high frequency, mainly used for data mining. Clearly show the connection, connotation and frequency of each keyword (Fig. 4).

Fig. 4 .

These tables are two visual figures that extract popular words in the dataset about the election.

During the Democratic primaries, opponents of Joe Biden criticized him for focusing on charisma over policy. He is now the party's candidate and has put forward a detailed program that contains some of the most radical proposals made by the Democratic nominee in recent years. Since the former vice president leads Donald Trump in the polls, individuals and businesses are more concerned about the impact that Biden may have on them as president. Medical treatment: More active response to the epidemic.

If Biden is elected president, his first challenge will be to deal with the new crown epidemic. Biden promised to conduct large-scale free testing and force insurance companies to bear the full cost of prevention and treatment. He also promised to formulate an emergency paid vacation system for workers affected by the epidemic as the first step to allow all workers to enjoy the paid vacation system.

However, the biggest difference from Trump's attitude toward the epidemic is likely to be the transmission of information-Biden promised to put public health officials at the forefront of formulating policy responses.

In the long run, Biden has vowed to implement health care reforms to ensure that more people are covered under the Obama-era affordable health care law.

Of course, we can also extract other topics, such as the following figure is the epidemic related graphics (Figs. 5 and 6).

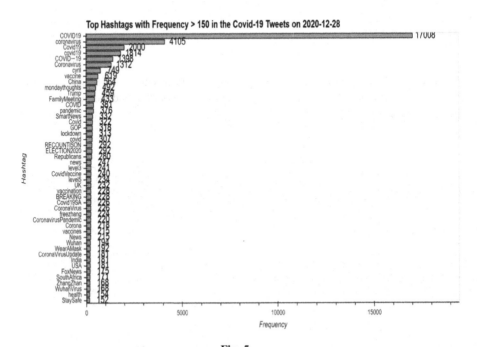

Fig. 5 .

Fig. 6 .

At that time, a very important reason for these three words on Twitter was that Trump, Vice President Mike Pence and other US officials were all vaccinated with the newly approved COVID-19 vaccine. Part of a sexual plan. According to sources, important members of the White House and all specific staff at the three levels of the government will be vaccinated within the next 10 days.

Trump was previously infected with the new coronavirus and later recovered. Many employees of the White House are infected with COVID-19, which may hinder the need for rapid vaccination.

Before Trump tweeted, the spokesperson of the National Security Council, administrative agency, parliament, and judicial officials said that the US government has plagues or disasters in order to ensure that the designed protocol is vaccinated in accordance with the protocol. Even if it is an emergency, it can continue to act.

"U.S. citizens should believe that, based on the advice of public health experts and national security leaders, they, like U.S. government officials, have received a safe and effective vaccine."

It is unclear whether Joe Biden, Kamala Harris and other members of the Biden transition team will receive the vaccination.

4 The Internal Connection Between Twitter Users and Hot Search Words Shows Emotional Orientation

Crawling data, often we want to know not only the number and frequency of keywords, we want to find out the internal relationship between them.

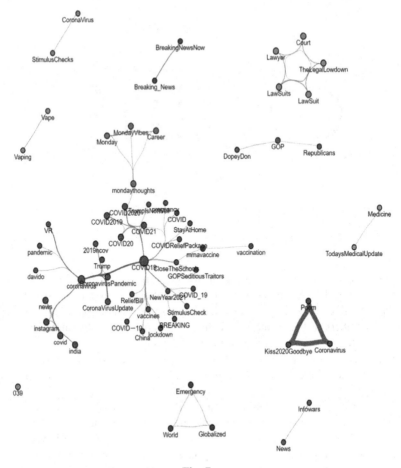

Fig. 7 .

From the Fig. 7, we can see a dense spherical connection, which shows that starting from a central word, people continue to derive discussions on this topic. Let's zoom in and look at this key word.

We see that the center of this word is the epidemic and then spread to related words such as vaccines, masks, etc. The end points are connected between the related words, and finally the relationship diagram is presented. We can see that some graphs start with a large central keyword and then form multiple small branches, and some are connected by two or three. The connection means that the different keywords as independent points are connected, and the individual points that do not have a relationship can be diffracted from one point, progressive layer by layer, and intersecting in pairs (Fig. 8).

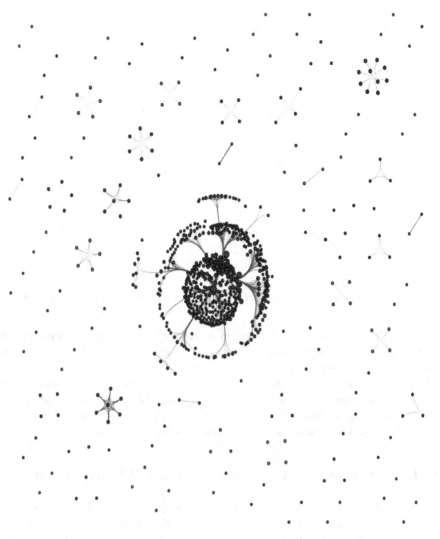

Fig. 8 .

Of course, in addition to watching the relationship between different keywords, we can also see the relationship between Twitter users in different regions (Fig. 9).

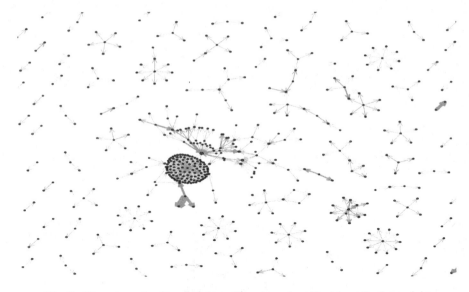

Fig. 9. The cut graph of top mention-edging tweeple with at least 5 edge weight

Through the statistics of the location of twitter users, it can be found that the number of twitter users in coastal city far exceeds the number of twitter users in other provinces. The number of twitter users in coastal areas is generally higher than that in inland areas. It can be explained that the first reason: Because the economy and education in the coastal areas are relatively developed, and people's knowledge level is generally high, the number of people using twitter is relatively large. The second reason is that the coastal area has a large population, and the inland area.

5   Intrinsic Connection Reaction Between Hot Search Words

RefIn the three visualizations, we extract and visualize two different topics, new coronavirus and general election, respectively, but often, what we need to analyze the data is to see the relationship and relationship between different topics. Below we will combine these two topics (Fig. 10).

Fig. 10 .

Thus, we realize the interaction between data. According to a report on the "Forbes" website on the 9th, according to Google's 2020 hot search list announced that day, Biden topped the character trend list and became the most popular search figure this year. According to reports, Biden's search volume peaked between November 1 and November 7, and this week coincided with the US general election.

US Vice President-elect Harris ranked third in the character trend list, while the current President Trump did not enter the top ten. He was the person with the most twitter in 2016. However, Forbes said Trump became the person who tweeted the most this year, followed by Biden, and Harris was the woman who tweeted the most on Twitter.

Most of the most popular search terms on twitter in 2020 are related to the US election, the new crown virus pandemic, and the lives of black people. The most popular search term is "election results", followed by "new crown virus."

6 Conclusions

Data visualization is the scientific and technical study of the visual representation of data. The visual representation of this data is defined as information extracted in summary form, including the various attributes and variables of the corresponding information unit.

It is a concept that is evolving and whose boundaries keep expanding. They are essentially relatively advanced technological approaches that use graphics, image processing, computer vision and user interfaces for visual interpretation of data, through representation, modeling and presentation of data objects, surfaces, attributes and animations. Data visualization techniques [7] involve much broader technical approaches than special technical approaches such as stereomodelling. Essentially, data mining is the basis of machine learning and artificial intelligence. Its main purpose is to extract information about subsets from various data sources. This information is then merged together so you can find patterns and relationships you never imagined. This means that data mining is not a way to prove hypotheses, but rather to construct different hypotheses.

This article mainly uses python user comments for crawling, and python for text data mining and analysis. It uses more than 100,000 sets of captured data to form multi-party visualizations including line graphs, histograms, and tag clouds to facilitate conclusions. As well as the word cloud generation process, it realizes statistical analysis of user evaluation word frequency, obtains users' reactions to current affairs hotspots, and provides a macro perspective of social hotspot events based on different perspectives of news hotspot search terms.

Of course, there are many shortcomings. For example, the amount of data extracted is not large enough, only a certain day does not reflect the problem of a stage, and it is limited to only one platform, which also provides a direction for future research.

Data mining is not intended to replace traditional statistical analysis techniques. Instead, he is an extension and extension of statistical analysis methodologies. Most statistical analysis techniques are based on perfect mathematical theory and superb skills. The accuracy of prediction is satisfactory, but the requirements for users are very high. With the continuous enhancement of computer computing power, it is possible to use the powerful computing power of the computer to accomplish the same function only by relatively simple and fixed methods. Some emerging technologies have also achieved good results in the field of knowledge discovery, such as neural networks and decision trees. With enough data and computing power, they can accomplish many valuable functions without human care. Data mining is an application that uses statistics and artificial intelligence technology. It encapsulates these sophisticated technologies so that people can do the same without mastering them themselves. And more focused on the problems they have to solve. In the future, data mining will become more and more important.

References

1. Xu, B., Shang, H., Ma, C., et al.: Visual analysis based on Movielens movie data. Comput. Eng. Sci. **11**, 2086–2094 (2017). https://doi.org/10.3969/j.issn.1007-130X.2017.11.017
2. Zhang, D.: The multi-dilemma of contemporary Chinese new media culture development. News Lovers **4**, 30–33 (2016). https://doi.org/10.3969/j.issn.1003-1286.2016.04.006
3. He, Q., Wang, Z.: Analysis of the influence of Internet companies' film layout on the film industry. Contemporary Film **7**, 11–18 (2015)
4. Whitney, P., Nowell, L., Hetzler, E., Havre, S.: ThemeRiver: visualizing thematic changes in large document collections. IEEE Trans. Vis. Comput. Graph. **8**(1), 9–20 (2002). https://doi.org/10.1109/2945.981848
5. Keywords Anonymity. Python data analysis: from data collection to data visualization to complete house price data analysis. https://ke.qq.com/course/424495
6. Public Number: Major in Transport Planning and Management; Python data analysis. https://zhuanlan.zhihu.com/p/234983632
7. Anonymity; Data Visualization. https://baike.baidu.com/item/data visualization/1252367

The Survey of Joint Entity and Relation Extraction

Sai Wang[(⊠)]

School of Mechanical Engineering, Northwestern Polytechnical University,
Xi'an, China

Abstract. In general, people use the pipeline method for named entity recognition and relationship extraction, which, though, cannot take full advantage of the benefits in between. To solve this problem, people turned their attention to the method of joint entity and relation extraction. This review surveys several ways in joint entity and relation extraction based neural networks. It systematically summarizes the advantages and disadvantages of the models. After comparing these models' performance of various datasets, this paper found that the model using BERT achieve the state-of-the-art result. The reasons and possible future development directions are analyzed and discussed.

Keywords: NLP · Joint entity and relation extraction · Relation extraction · Named entity recognition · Neural networks · BERT

1 Introduction

Entity recognition and relation extraction aims to find entities and discover the connections in between. Due to the large amount of text appearing now, they are useful for many NLP tasks, for example, the question answering [1], as well as knowledge base population [2].

Named Entity Recognition (NER) [17] is a method that can determine the entity boundaries then classify entities into predetermined categories including person, location and organization [3]. For instance, NER needs to identify that Jack in "Jack is my friend." is a person. There are some difficulties in the NER: first, few supervised training data can be used for a great amount of the languages and domains. Second, the training dataset contains only a few of all entity types, so the model does not recognize these types well. So, CRFs [4] and SVMs [5], and other hand-crafted features and additional NLP tools, are used in many methods [39]. Recently, many neural networks have been used in NER, for example CNN and RNN. The most common and useful model now is LSTM-CRF [17]. These methods [6–8] get state-of-the-art results in public datasets.

Relationship extraction aims at identifying pairs of related entities from unstructured text, classifying the relationships, and finally storing them in triples (e_1, r, e_2). Taking "Jobs is an employee of Apple" as an example, it is extracted as (Jobs, *the_Member_of*, Apple). Because relational extraction extracts useful information from a variety of texts, it is a vital part of many applications. The traditional relational extraction methods have various manually extracted characteristics. As neural networks

W. Cao et al. (Eds.): CONF-CDS 2021, CCIS 1513, pp. 363–381, 2021.
https://doi.org/10.1007/978-981-16-8885-0_29

are developing rapidly, relational extraction models no longer need to rely on manual extraction features [9, 10]. More and more models use neural networks for relation extraction tasks (e.g. CNN [11, 12, 18] and RNN [13–15]) and achieve good results. Now, this field has attracted much attention.

The traditional method is to divide entity and relation extraction into two separate tasks: 1) Named Entity Recognition (NER) [17], which aim at obtaining a target entity pair, and 2) Relationship Extraction (RE) [18], the task of which focuses on figuring out the relationship between the target pairs. However, this method has some disadvantages: 1) error propagation: the errors of NER can affect the result of relation extraction, and 2) useful information cannot be shared. To overcome the above shortcomings, the joint learning method is developed to find the entity and relationship. Moreover, by using the neural network, the joint learning method can get state-of-the-art results.

Although previous models have achieved good results, they didn't take full advantage of in-text information. The transformer [29] solves this problem by attention mechanism. Because the self-attention mechanism has the ability to represent, the transformer structure can better understand the hidden information in the text than the previous CNN and LSTM structures. Recently, with the application of the BERT [19] language model, the effect of the joint learning method using BERT is better than using the transformer, because it is a multi-layer bidirectional Transformer encoder [19]. Unlike previous language models [20–23], BERT can together extract left and right text information. By using BERT language model, people can obtain word vectors that can better represent hidden relationships between words (such as referential relationships). Named entity recognition and relationship extraction tasks can both gain benefits from this information. So, BERT can improve the effectiveness of models for these tasks.

In Sect. 2, we introduce some common tools and methods for named entity recognition and relation extraction, consisting of NER, Relation Extraction, and Pipeline methods, where the LSTM + CRF structure for NER is described in detail. This section also introduces a method using Bert for relation extraction. In the final of the chapter, we discuss some disadvantages of pipeline and the future direction. In Sect. 3, we summarize the methods of recent joint entity as well as relation extraction. In the beginning, we introduced the model using multiple neural networks. To improve efficiency, we summarize a method in which relationship extraction is used for multi-head selection. Finally, on the basis of the attention mechanism and BERT, we introduced various models. Section 4 lists common datasets and evaluation metrics, as well as the comparison of the results of methods. We conclude this survey in Sect. 5.

2 Common Tools and Methods for Named Entity Recognition and Relationship Extraction

2.1 Named Entity Recognition

NER usually comes the first in the pipeline method.

BIO (Beginning, Inside, Outside) encoding scheme is common in NER: B-type is the first token of the entity; the I-type is every other word of the entity, and O is the token outside the entity.

In general, the input of NER is a sentence $s = (W_1, W_2, \ldots, W_l)$. In order to enable the computer to process sentences, we convert each word W_i into a vector E_i, and there is the following formula:

$$E_i = W^{word} V^i \tag{1}$$

W^{word} is a parameter that can be learned through learning. Such a sentence becomes $emb_s = (E_1, E_2, \ldots, E_l)$, input it to the next layer.

Many manually extracted features are used in various methods [5, 45] for NER. Lately, NER tasks have been solved with neural networks. These methods using neural networks are also state-of-the-art for datasets.

Bekoulis et al. [39] developed a BiLSTM+CRF model for NER to solve the problem that the previous neural network does not perform well in a long text. The principle of LSTM [25] is as follows:

$$\begin{bmatrix} i_t \\ f_t \\ o_t \\ \hat{c}_t \end{bmatrix} = \begin{bmatrix} \sigma \\ \sigma \\ \sigma \\ tanh \end{bmatrix} W \cdot [h_{t-1}, e_t] \tag{2}$$

$$c_t = f_t \odot c_{t-1} + i_t \odot \hat{c}_t \tag{3}$$

$$h_t = o_t \odot \tanh(c_t) \tag{4}$$

BiLSTM extracts both forward sequence text and backward sequence text, so the output is:

$$H_t = \left[\vec{h}_t \oplus \overleftarrow{h}_t \right] \tag{5}$$

The use of CRF also improves the effect. In the NER task, the general method is to take the highest probability of each word into the final prediction of each word. In general, the above way can get the right result. But in some cases, the above strategy does not get the correct results. This is why we need to input the result of the LSTM into the CRF layer to get better results. In short, the role of the CRF layer is to develop an optimal strategy: in the case of knowing the probability of each word's various predictions, we choose the best forecast for the overall text. Then the label corresponding to each word is the final result. There are calculation details:

For an input sentence:

$$X = (x_1, x_2, \ldots, x_n) \tag{6}$$

The final output is:

$$Y = (y_1, y_2, \ldots, y_n) \tag{7}$$

y in the above formula is the label for each word. We aim to find the best combination of labels. The rating for each word is:

$$S(X_i, Y_i) = \sum\nolimits_{i=0}^{n} A_{y_i, y_{i+1}} + \sum\nolimits_{i=1}^{n} P_{i, y_i} \tag{8}$$

A is the transition score, which is the probability of the label from the label of the i_{th} word to the label of the $(i+1)_{th}$ e word. This probability is not processed by additional tools. It automatically obtained from the training data and is continually optimized as the training progresses. In order to facilitate the calculation, two packages (start and end) are added on the first and last sides of the sentence. P is the probability that the i_{th} word is labeled y_i, and the LSTM layer output can obtain this data. So the total score is:

$$S = \sum\nolimits_{i}^{n} S(X_i, Y_i) \tag{9}$$

Finally, the CRF layer uses softmax as the classifier. Assuming that the prediction structure of the sentence has k possibilities, the loss function can be defined as:

$$LossFunction = \frac{e^{S_{real}}}{e^{s_1} + e^{s_2} + \ldots + e^{s_k}} \tag{10}$$

Substituting all the results into the above loss function to find out the maximum loss function is the prediction result.

In summary, adding a layer of CRF after the LSTM structure can give better prediction results. For example, the LSTM network sometimes predicts the label at the beginning of I- (such as I-person) as the first word of the sentence. But joining the CRF layer can effectively reduce this error.

Simultaneously the CRF layer relies on the transition score, which is randomly initialized at the beginning of the training and is continuously updated as the training progresses, achieving better results. Therefore, whether the CRF layer can be effective is influenced by the training set quality: if the training set can provide useful information about the connection between word sequences, it can achieve excellent results.

2.2   Relation Extraction

The relationship extraction task is to extract information of relationship from the text. Different from traditional methods (feature-based and kernel-based), the neural network method can better finish the extraction with better results.

Recently, people [41] proposed a model for relational classification tasks on the basis of pre-trained Bert, which results good with some public datasets.

Here, the authors want to make the model get the location information of the entity. $ is added before and after the first entity, and # is added at the same place of the second entity. Moreover, [CLS] is added at the beginning of the sentence to indicate a start. For example: [CLS]$Jobs$ work in #Apple#.

The core of the model is the use of a pre-trained Bert [19] model so that it represents the relation between tokes better in the text. After a series of processing of Bert's output, the classifier (e.g.: softmax) is used to obtain the relationship result.

The pre-trained BERT model is a multi-layer bidirectional Transformer encoder [29]. Its one advantage is that it can simultaneously represent a pair of sentences as input. For relationship extraction, the feature vector can more reflect the relationship between each word of the text and other words after the processing of the Bert language model. So the final classification effect is optimized a lot.

Bert trains model parameters through the masked language model (MLM), which optimizes the parameters by randomly masking some of the tokes and then predicting the original id of the words by textual information. Unlike the left-to-right language model, MLM can use both left and right text information.

There are the calculation details of the method:

$$H_1' = W_1 \left[tanh \left(\frac{1}{j-i+1} \sum\nolimits_{t=i}^{j} H_t \right) \right] + b_1 \qquad (11)$$

The final hidden state output form Bert model is vector H. An entity contains the i_{th} to j_{th} tokes in the sentence and H_i to H_j is the output of the vector by the entity e_1 at the last layer of Bert.

$$h'' = W_3 \left[concat \left(H_0', H_1', H_2' \right) \right] + b_3 \qquad (12)$$

$$p = softmax(h'') \qquad (13)$$

[CLS] and e_2 are processed to obtain H_0' and H_2', then H_0', H_1', H_2' are connected, and then classified by softmax classifier (Fig. 1).

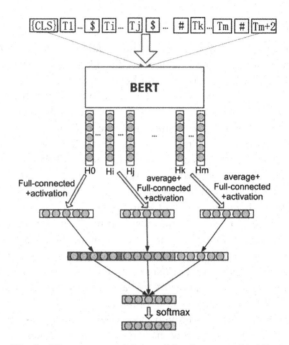

Fig. 1. The structure of the model using pre-trained Bert

2.3   Pipeline Methods

The traditional approach is to divide this problem into two pipeline subtasks: NER and Relation Extraction. Generally, with NER completed, relationship extraction is performed on the target entity pair. But in the early days, the completion of these two tasks required a lot of artificial features, which made the model costly in time and money. As neural networks developing, people gradually use CNN, RNN, LSTM, etc. to complete tasks. These methods [15, 43, 44] have achieved excellent results in the public data set, but have the following problems:

- Error propagation: Errors in upstream tasks can propagate to downstream tasks, resulting in poor results. For example, the NER recognition entity error can cause the relationship extraction task to be ineffective.
- Information that is mutually beneficial between tasks cannot propagate with each other, leading to the loss of information which, as a result, affects the final output.
- It may generate unnecessary operations and increase costs. The model also extracts relationships between more pairs of entities that have no relationship, wasting time.

3   Joint Entity and Relation Extraction Methods

To solve the difficulties of pipeline methods, people have turned their attention to the joint learning method of Zhou et al. [38]. It uses a joint learning approach by using a hybrid neural network, making good use of the relationship between each other. For the improvement the result of NER and the efficiency of relation extraction, the model [39] use CRF and multi-head strategy. But these methods can't extract hidden information of the text. For solving the problem, the models [40, 42] use attention mechanism and Bert to understand the text better (Fig. 2).

3.1   Joint Extraction of Multiple Relations and Entities by Using a Hybrid Neural Network

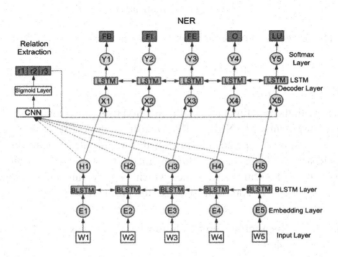

Fig. 2. The structure of the model using a hybrid neural network

To have a better effect, more attention has been paid to joint entity and relation extraction. Zhou et al. [38] proposed the joint learning method by using LSTM and CNN hybrid neural network for entity recognition and relationship extraction tasks. With the neural network method, features can be automatically extracted. The step of manually extracting features is not needed, and the cost is saved. The use of the LSTM network overcomes the problem: previous methods (CNN, RNN) can't get the dependencies information of long texts. Because the number of pairs of entities in a general sentence is much larger than the number of relationships between pairs of entities in a sentence. Therefore, this paper first extracts the relationship and then uses the result of the relationship extraction for entity identification, which not only reduces the complexity of the calculation but also improves the accuracy of entity recognition.

- **Relation Extraction**
  Here, BLSTM has an output H_t, which is processed as input to CNN to get:

$$z = (c_1, c_2, \ldots, c_l) \tag{14}$$

  Then put it into the sigmoid classifier for relationship classification:

$$p = (y|s) = sigmoid(W_R \cdot z + b_R) \tag{15}$$

- **Named Entity Recognition**
  In NER task, this model combines the relationship vector from relational extraction model with the vector H_t obtained by BLSTM, and then put it into the LSTM layer as input:

$$y_t = LSTM(\text{concat}(H_t, r)) \tag{16}$$

  Put the above vector into the softmax layer to predict the entity class:

$$p = (y|s) = softmax(W_T \cdot y_t + b_T) \tag{17}$$

- **Summary**
  Compared with the pipeline method, this method using joint learning can reduce the error of the upstream task (NER) to the downstream task (RE) to improve the effect. And, it is possible to spread information that is useful to each other in the two subtasks to achieve better results. But this method can only extract the relationship between a pair of entities at a time, which is very time-consuming. Next, we introduce a multi-head approach to solve this problem.

3.2 Joint Entity Recognition and Relation Extraction as a Multi-head Selection Problem

Bekoulis et al. [39] raised a joint learning method for entity recognition and relational extraction without any additional NLP tools and manual extraction of features. This model extracts features from the input using the BiLSTM neural network and adds the CRF layer for named entity recognition to optimize the results. Finally, the BiLSTM output and label embeddings are simultaneously used as inputs for relationship extraction. The relationship is extracted from the model as a multi-head selection problem. With the method, relationship existing between one target entity and several other entities can be simultaneously extracted from the model, which significantly improves the computational efficiency.

- **Named entity recognition**
  In the named entity recognition task, every word in the sentence should be mapped into a feature vector by word embedding. It's processed into a vector pattern which is understandable for the computer. Then, processed feature vector should be input into a bidirectional LSTM. The result of the final output is the probability that each word is of various types. CRF layer is used in this model and it improves the result of NER (Figs. 3 and 4).

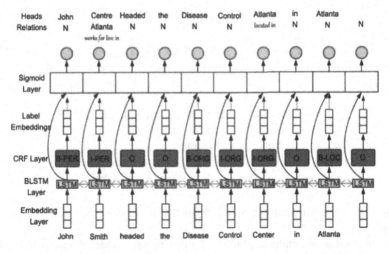

Fig. 3. The structure of the method using the multi-head selection

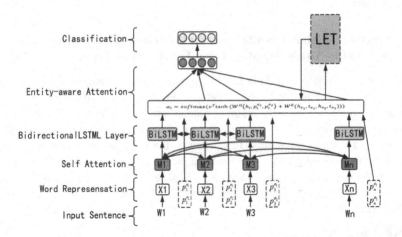

Fig. 4. The structure of the model using attention

- **Relation extraction as a multi-head selection problem**

  As for the subtask, relational extraction is treated in this model as a multi-head problem [26, 27]. There can be multiple heads for each token in a sentence: one toke can have multiple relationships with other tokes. In this task, the choice of the head and the extraction of the relationship are performed simultaneously. For a given input W and relationship labels $\mathcal{R}$, we aims at finding the most likely head $w_j \in W$ and the most likely relationship $r \in \mathcal{R}$ between them for each toke w_i. Define the score function as:

$$S(z_j, z_i, r) = V \cdot f(U \cdot z_j + W \cdot z_i + b) \qquad (18)$$

Where z contains the output of BiLSTM and label embedding, and f is the activation function (for example, relu and tanh). Then put score into the sigmoid classifier:

$$P(head = w_j, \text{label} = \text{r}|w_i) = sigmoid(S(z_j, z_i, r)) \qquad (19)$$

We minimize the loss function in training:

$$\mathcal{L}_{rel} = \sum_{i=0}^{n} \sum_{j=0}^{m} -\log P(head = y_{i,j}, \text{label} = r_{i,j}|w_i) \qquad (20)$$

Since it is a joint learning model, our final goal is to calculate $\mathcal{L}_{rel} + \mathcal{L}_{NER}$.

- **Summary**
  This method uses a multi-head method for improving model efficiency and achieves a good result on public dataset. But LSTM can't effectively mine the correlation information in the text. With the use of self-attention mechanisms, the result has been improved.

3.3 Semantic Relation Classification via Bidirectional LSTM Networks with Entity-Aware Attention Using Latent Entity Typing

In the past models, people did not find enough hidden relationships in the text, such as referential relationships. A model developed by Lee et al. [40] uses the attention mechanism to take further advantage of hidden information in the text.

In practical applications, we find that even without text data, we can infer the relationship between two words. For instance, the relationship between this pair of entities being *Cause-Effect* can be found higher than *Component-Whole*, even other words in the text have not been taken into consideration except for crash and attack. This paper proposes the Latent Entity Typing (LET) model in order to solve this problem (Fig. 5).

- **Self Attention**
  Many neural network models do not solve long-term dependency problems [28] well. To understand the positional information of each word in the sentence and its relevance to other words, we adopted the Self Attention mechanism.

The model proposed here adopts a multi-attention mechanism [29], belonging to one of the attention mechanisms. The process is shown in the figure. An important process of the multi-attention mechanism relies on scaled dot-product attention, whose calculation method is as follows:

$$\text{Attention}(Q, K, V) = softmax\left(\frac{QK^{\mathrm{T}}}{\sqrt{d_w}}\right) \qquad (21)$$

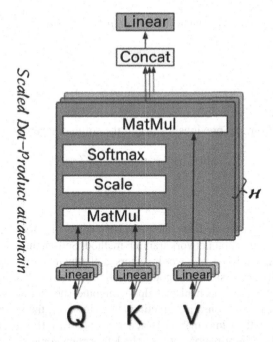

Fig. 5. Illustration of the self-attention mechanism

The multi-attention mechanism combines the results of r the scaled dot-product attention and then processes it through a linear transformation and enters the next part. The formula is as follows:

$$MultiHead(Q, K, V) = W^M(head_1, \ldots, head_r) \tag{22}$$

$$head_i = Attention(Q_i, K_i, V_i) \tag{23}$$

- **Entity-aware Attention**
  Although some NLP tasks have good results of the attention mechanism, problems still exist in the relationship extraction task. Because we don't know the target entity pair in advance, we can't extract the information between the target entity pair and other entities well. This model uses the entity-aware attention method, which includes the following two aspects: 1. Relevant location features [31]: information between the target entity pair and each other word in the sentence; 2. entity characteristics with LET: use the information of the type of the entity pair to improve accuracy, the formula is as follows:

$$a_i^j = softmax((h_{e_j})^\mathrm{T} c_i) \tag{24}$$

$$t_{j \in \{1,2\}} = \sum_{i=1}^{K} a_i^j h_i \tag{25}$$

$$\alpha_i = softmax\big(v^T \tanh\big(W^H(h_i, p_i^{e_1}, p_i^{e_2}) + W^E(h_{e_1}, t_{e_1}, h_{e_2}, t_{e_2})\big)\big) \qquad (26)$$

$$Z = \sum\nolimits_{i=1}^{n} \alpha_i h_i \qquad (27)$$

- **Classification**
  Put the input from the previous layer into the softmax layer to classify:

$$p(y|S, \theta) = softmax(W^q Z + b^q) \qquad (28)$$

- **Summary**
  Different from the past methods: the input sentence is directly word embedded and then input into the neural network training method. Self-attention mechanism mines the relationship between the word vectors and obtain more information that is beneficial to the next task in this model, which improves its effectiveness. The novel entity-aware attention mechanism helps overcome shortcomings of self-attention mechanism in the relationship extraction task. However, the order of the attention mechanism to extract information is generally one-way (from left to right or the opposite), and the information between the left or right contexts cannot be extracted well simultaneously. Future models should also take this problem into consideration.

3.4   Span-Based Joint Entity and Relation Extraction with Transformer Pre-training

The model mentioned by Wu et al. [41] takes advantage of the pre-trained BERT model for relationship extraction, but it must have the entities in the data labeled in advance, costing much time and money. Markus et al. [42] raised a span-based joint learning model with Bert, solving some problems in the previous models and its output in joint entity and relation extraction was state-of-the-art.

- **Span classifier**
  Select any spans as input:

$$S = (e_i, e_{i+1}, \ldots, e_{i+k}) \qquad (29)$$

When the span is too large, the calculation is difficult. In order to increase the calculation rate, the max-pooling process is usually performed (Fig. 6):

$$S' = maxpool(e_i, e_{i+1}, \ldots, e_{i+k}) \qquad (30)$$

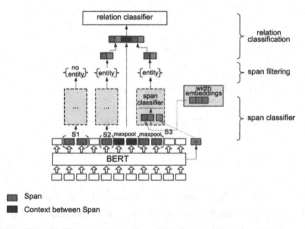

Fig. 6. The structure of span-based model using Bert

Sometimes there is a requirement for the width of the span. For instance, if the span reaches 10, it is probably not an entity. So width embeddings [32] is used to constrain the width:

$$e(s) = maxpool(e_i, e_{i+1}, \ldots, e_{i+k} \circ w_{k+1}) \qquad (31)$$

Finally, a toke c is added to represent all the text information.
The final input to the span classifier is:

$$X = e(s) \circ c \qquad (32)$$

Finally, enter the softmax classifier:

$$y = softmax(W \cdot X + b) \qquad (33)$$

- **Span Filtering**
  It is predicted by softmax which type each span belongs to. For span exclusions that do not contain entities. At the same time, spans over 10 tokes are removed by width embedding.

- **Relation Classifier**
  To represent two pairs of target entities, we use BERT/width embedding $e(s_1), e(s_2)$ as the input to the classifier. Certain words in the text can express a potential type of relationship. But for long sentences, it is too difficult to express all the text. We use c to express the text of the entity to the surrounding part. And in general, the relationship is not equal, so we need $c(s_1, s_2)$, $c(s_2, s_1)$: at the same time:

$$X_1^r = e(s_1) \circ c(s_1, s_2) \circ e(s_2) \tag{34}$$

$$X_2^r = e(s_2) \circ c(s_2, s_1) \circ e(s_1) \tag{35}$$

Then put the representation into the sigmoid:

$$Y_{\frac{1}{2}}^r = \sigma\left(W^r \cdot X_{\frac{1}{2}}^r + b^r\right) \tag{36}$$

- **Summary**
  Because Bert can mine the correlation between tokes in text, the result is state-of-the-art. Span-based methods can better detect the boundaries of entities and solve the problem of overlap well. For instance, the model can identify Siberian from the Siberian tiger. Compared with the one developed by Wu et al., this model adds fine-tuning operations to make it perform better on specific tasks. Although the effect has been improved, it is not enough to put into practical use. So improving the effect of the model is still the future direction.

4 Experiences

4.1 Datasets

In entity and relationship extraction, same models have different results in different data sets. So to compare the quality of different models, people build some public datasets. At the same time, these datasets can also be used as a standard training set to help with future work.

CoNLL04 [33]: There are a total of 1,441 sentences, and every sentence contains at least one relationship. This dataset defines four named entity categories and five relationships. Zhou et al. and Markus et al. use 1153 sentences as training data and 288 sentences as test data.

ACE04: The data set contains seven named entity categories. Seven relationship categories are also defined. Giannis et al. removed the DISC when using the data set.

ADE: The ADE dataset [35] was compiled from medical reports. This task aims at finding out drug entity types and relationship between the drug and the disease. A total of 6821 instances are in the dataset. There are two types – drugs and diseases. It only contains one kind of relationship type Adverse-Effect.

SemEval-2 Task 8: This dataset [36] contains 10,017 annotated examples. It includes ten relationship categories. It should be noted that there are two very similar relationship categories (Entity-Origin/Entity-Destination and Content-Container/Component-Whole/Collection-Collection) that can evaluate the model ability to be fine-grained.

4.2 Evaluation Index

In different situations, a unified evaluation index is needed to measure the model quality. Under the classification problem, common indicators are Precision, Recall, and F-measure.

- **Confusion matrix**

  Suppose there is a two-category problem of positive and negative. While the instance and the prediction result are the same, it is true, and otherwise, the case is False, so there is the following Table 1:

Table 1. Confusion matrix

	Instance: positive	Instance: negative
Prediction: positive	TP (True Positive)	FP (Negative Positive)
Prediction: negative	FN (False Negative)	TN (True Negative)

- **Precision, Recall, F-score**

  Precision indicates the probability that the instance is also positive if the prediction is positive. It reflects the probability that the result is correct.

$$Precision = \frac{TP}{TP + FP} \tag{37}$$

Recall indicates the probability that the prediction is also positive if the instance is positive. It reflects the probability that positive is detected.

$$Recall = \frac{TP}{TP + FN} \tag{38}$$

In general, we want Precision and Recall to be as large as possible at the same time. But if one of them gets bigger, the other one will get smaller. So to better evaluate the model, introduce F-measure:

$$\frac{1}{F - measure} \times \left(1 + \frac{1}{a^2}\right) = \frac{1}{Precision} + \frac{1}{Recall} \tag{39}$$

Generally, let a = 1:

$$F1 = \frac{2 \times Precision \times Recall}{Precision + Recall} \tag{40}$$

- **Comparison**

  The method based on hybrid neural networks [38] performed better than the feature-based entity and relationship joint learning method [37], which increased by 9.6% in F1. Because the method [38] uses LSTM and CNN neural networks to better extract features without relying on external tools. This not only reduces the steps of manually extracting features but also avoids the propagation of errors caused by external tools. In terms of the task order, the method first performs relationship extraction because the number of relationships in a sentence is often less than the number of entities. So this can increase efficiency.

  The method proposed by Bekoulis et al. [39] has achieved good results on named entity recognition tasks. Because the way adopts the structure of LSTM-CRF to realize the function of entity recognition and this structure considers the optimal result for the overall text, so that the type of the corresponding entity is given for this optimal result. This overall optimal strategy effect is significantly better than the optimal local strategy.

  The F1 in the method [40] reached 85.2, a better result than that of Miwa et al., Zhou et al., and Bekoulis et al., the main difference is the use of attention mechanisms. The use of attention mechanisms allows the model to understand the hidden relationship between pairs of entities better, but the general attention mechanism is one-way. In this way, the relationship between the word and text is not well obtained at the same time.

  The method [41] uses BERT, which is better than other methods and gets a score of 89.25% on F1. The method proposed by Eberts et al. [42] uses BERT for joint learning at a time, and the method has been state-of-the-art on ADE dataset. Using BERT is supposed to be the core of these methods. BERT uses the Masked Language Model (MLM) so that BERT can better mine the relationship between contexts and get better results. The method proposed by Eberts et al. also uses the Span method to detect the boundaries of the entity better (Table 2).

Table 2. Data sets and evaluation criteria for different models

The way of relation extraction	NO.	Model	Dataset	Evaluation index	Evaluation value	Year
Pipeline method	1	RNN [44]	SemEval-2 Task 8	F1	79.4	2013
	2	SDT-LSTM [15]	SemEval-2 Task 8	F1	83.7	2015
	3	CR-CNN [43]	SemEval-2 Task 8	F1	84.1	2015
Joint method	4	Table representation [37]	CoNLL04	F1	71	2014
	5	LSTM + CNN [38]	CoNLL04	F1	80.6	2017
	6	LSTM-CRF [39]	ADE	F1	80.49	2018
			CoNLL04	F1	72.97	
			ACE04	F1	54.15	
	7	LSTM with attention [40]	SemEval-2 Task 8	F1	85.2	2019
	8	Span-based BERT [42]	ADE	F1	84.06	2019

Because joint learning methods enable useful information to spread effectively between named entity recognition and relation extraction, it can easily be seen that the joint entity and relation extraction method has achieved better results than pipeline methods on datasets. So the joint learning method is the direction of future development.

But these methods have some problems with the dataset: Getting labeled data is expensive, and some types of data are difficult to obtain. In the future, we can consider using distant supervision and training with similar data to solve these problems.

In summary, from experience, the effect of named entity recognition and relationship extraction has a high impact on the downstream tasks of NLP. Hence we want to be able to preserve the advantages and improve the effectiveness of the existing model.

References

1. Kumar, A., Irsoy, O., Ondruska, P., et al.: Ask me anything: dynamic memory networks for natural language processing (2015)
2. Shin, J., Wu, S., Wang, F., et al.: Incremental knowledge base construction using DeepDive. VLDB J. **8**(11), 1–25 (2015)
3. Nadeau, D., Sekine, S.: A survey of named entity recognition and classification. Lingvisticae Investigationes **30**(1), 3–26 (2007)
4. Yao, L., Sun, C., Li, S., et al.: CRF-based active learning for chinese named entity recognition. In: IEEE International Conference on Systems. IEEE (2009)
5. Tsochantaridis, I., Hofmann, T., Joachims, T., et al.: [ACM Press Twenty-first International Conference - Banff, Alberta, Canada (2004.07.04–2004.07.08)] Twenty-First International Conference on Machine learning - ICML 2004 - Support vector machine learning for interdependent and structured output spaces. Machine Learning, p. 104 (2004)
6. Collobert, R., Weston, J., Bottou, L., et al.: Natural language processing (almost) from scratch. J. Mach. Learn. Res. **12**(1), 2493–2537 (2011)
7. Ma, X., Hovy, E.: End-to-end sequence labeling via bi-directional LSTM-CNNs-CRF (2016)
8. Lample, G., Ballesteros, M., Subramanian, S., et al.: Neural architectures for named entity recognition (2016)
9. Zelenko, D., Aone, C., Richardella, A.: Kernel methods for relation extraction. J. Mach. Learn. Res. **3**(3), 1083–1106 (2003)
10. Rink, B., Harabagiu, S.: UTD: classifying semantic relations by combining lexical and semantic resources. In: International Workshop on Semantic Evaluation (2010)
11. Xu, K., Feng, Y., Huang, S., et al.: Semantic relation classification via convolutional neural networks with simple negative sampling. Comput. Sci. **71**(7), 941–949 (2015)
12. Bin, H., Yi, G., Rui, D.: Classifying medical relations in clinical text via convolutional neural networks. Artif. Intell. Med. **93**, 43–49 (2018)
13. Socher, R., Chen, D., Manning, C.D., et al.: Reasoning with neural tensor networks for knowledge base completion. In: International Conference on Neural Information Processing Systems. Curran Associates Inc. (2013)
14. Zhang, D., Wang, D.: Relation classification via recurrent neural network. Comput. Sci. **1**(3), 234–244 (2015)
15. Yan, X., Mou, L., Li, G., et al.: Classifying relations via long short term memory networks along shortest dependency path. Comput. Sci. **42**(1), 56–61 (2015)

16. Mintz, M., Bills, S., Snow, R., et al.: Distant supervision for relation extraction without labeled data. In: ACL 2009, Proceedings of the 47th Annual Meeting of the Association for Computational Linguistics and the 4th International Joint Conference on Natural Language Processing of the AFNLP, 2–7 August 2009, Singapore. Association for Computational Linguistics (2009)

17. Huang, Z., Xu, W., Yu, K.: Bidirectional LSTM-CRF models for sequence tagging. arXiv preprint arXiv:1508.01991 (2015)

18. Zeng, D., Liu, K., Lai, S., et al.: Relation classification via convolutional deep neural network (2014)

19. Devlin, J., Chang, M.W., Lee, K., et al.: BERT: pre-training of deep bidirectional transformers for language understanding. arXiv preprint arXiv:1810.04805 (2018)

20. Dai, A.M., Le, Q.V.: supervised Sequence Learning. Adv. Neural Inf. Process. Syst. **28**, 3079–3087 (2015)

21. Peters, M.E., Ammar, W., Bhagavatula, C., Power, R.: Semi-supervised sequence tagging with bidirectional language models. CoRR abs/1705.00108 (2017). arXiv:1705.00108

22. Radford, A., Narasimhan, K., Salimans, T., Sutskever, I.: Improving language understanding with unsupervised learning. Technical report, OpenAI (2018)

23. Ruder, S., Howard, J.: Universal language model fine-tuning for text classification. In: Proceedings of the 56th Annual Meeting of the Association for Computa-tional Linguistics, ACL 2018, Melbourne, Australia, 15–20 July 2018, Volume 1: Long Papers, pp. 328–339 (2018)

24. Devlin, J., Chang, M.-W., Lee, K., Toutanova, K.: BERT: pre-training of Deep Bidirectional Transformers for Language Understanding. CoRR abs/1810.04805 (2018). arXiv:1810.04805

25. Hochreiter, S., Schmidhuber, J.: Long short-term memory. Neural Comput. **9**(8), 1735–1780 (1997)

26. Zhang, X., Cheng, J., Lapata, M.: Dependency parsing as head selection. In: Proceedings of the 15th Conference of the European Chapter of the Association for Computational Linguistics: (Volume 1, Long Papers), pp. 665–676, Valencia, Spain (2017)

27. Bekoulis, G., Deleu, J., Demeester, T., Develder, C.: An attentive neural architecture for joint segmentation and parsing and its application to real estate ads. Expert Syst. Appl. **102**, 100–112 (2018). https://doi.org/10.1016/j.eswa.2018.02.031

28. Bengio, Y., Simard, P., Frasconi, P.: Learning long-term dependencies with gradient descent is difficult. IEEE Trans. Neural Netw. **5**, 157–166 (1994)

29. Vaswani, A., et al.: Attention is all you need. In: Advances in Neural Information Processing Systems, pp. 5998–6008 (2017)

30. Graves, A., Schmidhuber, J.: Framewise phoneme classification with bidirectional LSTM and other neural network architectures. Neural Netw. **18**, 602–610 (2005)

31. Zhang, Y., Zhong, V., Chen, D., Angeli, G., Manning, C.D.: Position-aware attention and super- vised data improve slot filling. In: Proceedings of the 2017 Conference on Empirical Methods in Natural Language Processing, pp. 35–45 (2017)

32. Lee, K., He, L., Lewis, M., Zettlemoyer, L.: End- to-end neural coreference resolution. In: Proceedings of EMNLP 2017, pp. 188–197. ACL, Copenhagen, Denmark (2017)

33. Roth, D., Yih, W.-T.: A linear programming for-mulation for global inference in natural language tasks. In: Proceedings of CoNLL 2004 at HLT-NAACL 2004, pp. 1–8. ACL, Boston, Massachusetts, USA (2004)

34. Luan, Y., He, L., Ostendorf, M., Hajishirzi, H.: Multi-task identification of entities, relations, and corefer-ence for scientific knowledge graph construction. In: Proceedings of EMNLP 2018, pp. 3219–3232. ACL, Brussels, Belgium (2018)

35. Gurulingappa, H., Rajput, A.M., Roberts, A., Fluck, J., Hofmann-Apitius, M., Toldo, L.: Development of a benchmark corpus to support the automatic extraction of drug-related adverse effects from medical case reports. J. Biomed. Inform. **45**(5), 885–892 (2012)

36. Hendrickx, I., Kim, S.N., Kozareva, Z., et al.: Semeval-2010 task 8: multi-way classification of semantic relations between pairs of nominals. In: Proceedings of the Workshop on Semantic Evaluations: Recent Achievements and Future Directions. Association for Computational Linguistics, pp. 94–99 (2009)

37. Miwa, M., Sasaki, Y.: Modeling joint entity and relation extraction with table representation. In: EMNLP, pp. 944–948 (2014)

38. Zhou, P., Zheng, S., Xu, J., Qi, Z., Bao, H., Xu, B.: Joint extraction of multiple relations and entities by using a hybrid neural network. In: Sun, M., Wang, X., Chang, B., Xiong, D. (eds.) CCL/NLP-NABD -2017. LNCS (LNAI), vol. 10565, pp. 135–146. Springer, Cham (2017). https://doi.org/10.1007/978-3-319-69005-6_12

39. Bekoulis, G., Deleu, J., Demeester, T., et al.: Joint entity recognition and relation extraction as a multi-head selection problem. Expert Syst. Appl. **114**, 34–45 (2018)

40. Lee, J., Seo, S., Choi, Y.S.: Semantic relation classification via bidirectional LSTM networks with entity-aware attention using latent entity typing. Symmetry **11**(6), 785 (2019)

41. Wu, S., He, Y.: Enriching pre-trained language model with entity information for relation classification. arXiv preprint arXiv:1905.08284 (2019)

42. Eberts, M., Ulges, A.: Span-based joint entity and relation extraction with transformer pre-training. arXiv preprint arXiv:1909.07755 (2019)

43. Santos, C.N., Xiang, B., Zhou, B.: Classifying relations by ranking with convolutional neural networks. arXiv preprint arXiv:1504.06580 (2015)

44. Hashimoto, K., Miwa, M., Tsuruoka, Y., et al.: Simple customization of recursive neural networks for semantic relation classification. In: Proceedings of the Conference on Empirical Methods in Natural Language Processing, pp. 1372–1376 (2013)

45. Taskar, B., Guestrin, C., Koller, D.: Max-margin markov networks. In: Proceedings of the 16th International Conference on Neural Information Processing Systems, pp. 25–32. MIT Press, Bangkok, Thailand (2003)

Music Recommendation Algorithm Through Word2vec Embeddings

Siyi Gu[1], Jinxi Zhang[2], Xinyu Qiu[3], Fengzuo Du[4],
and Haoxinran Yu[5(✉)]

[1] College of Arts and Sciences, Emory University, Atlanta, GA 30322, USA
[2] Xi'an Tie Yi High School, Xi'an 710054, Shaanxi, China
[3] Faculty of Electrical Engineering and Informatics, Budapest University
of Technology and Economics, Budapest 1117, Hungary
[4] Chongqing University of Technology, Yubei, Chongqing 400054, China
[5] Baylor School, Chattanooga, TN, USA

Abstract. Music recommendation has received increasing attention with the development of online music industry. Modern music recommendation systems offer new songs to users mainly based on collaborative filtering and content-based recommendation. However, both methods have their shortage. To alleviate the disadvantages, this paper presents a music recommendation algorithm that hybridizes both content and user information through word2vec embeddings. Lyrical information and playlist data are separately vectorized to determine the similarities between individual musical tracks and to calculated a similarity score through cosine distance formula. While evaluation to the accuracy is provided in the end, future study is necessary to improve the current recommendation system.

Keywords: Music recommendation system · Collaborative filtering · Content-based recommendation · Lyrics analysis · Playlist similarity · word2vec embedding

1 Introduction

The Internet has become a social network that links "people, organizations, and knowledge" [1]. Due to the robust development of technology and the Internet, people have access to a vast amount of online data. Zhang showed that recommendation system analyzes users' historical behaviors to create a user preference model and recommend information that meets users' needs. [2] System of recommendation will collect data and send a lot of information to users. People use social networks frequently nowadays, so understanding their behaviors would be useful for several applications [3]. With the rise of need for behavior analysis, recommender systems become unavoidable in our daily life, from e-shopping to online advertisement. Due to the vast amount of online users' browsing behaviors, companies have been able to harness these behaviors to make accurate recommendation systems (Fig. 1).

© Springer Nature Singapore Pte Ltd. 2021
W. Cao et al. (Eds.): CONF-CDS 2021, CCIS 1513, pp. 382–392, 2021.
https://doi.org/10.1007/978-981-16-8885-0_30

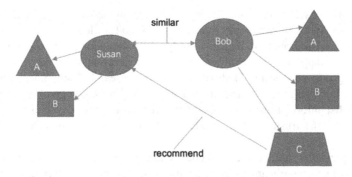

Fig. 1. A very simple illustration of how recommender systems works in the content of an e-commerce site

Collaborative Filtering is one of the most popular recommendation algorithms, especially for data scientists to build custom recommendation systems [4]. There are two methods of collaborative filtering algorithms: user-based and item-based recommendation. Shao et al. showed that both algorithms have their own disadvantages: collaborative filtering method needs a amount of user data while content-based method lacks the capacity of understanding users' personal preferences [5].

Music has been an integral part of life as a means of expressing emotions [6]. Andjelkovica et al. leveraged collaborative filtering for music recommendations using KNN-based methods have been harnessed to make pop music recommendations and research has shown a positive correlation between users' favorite music and what is recommended by the algorithms. [7] Bulger showed that music recommendation is however a very challenging task, and the quality of current recommendations is still not always satisfying [8]. For instance, the size of pool of tracks from which to make recommendations can be quite huge.

Previous studies have focused on similarities by either analyzing audio tracks of artists, or relying on cultural information or a combination of both [9–11]. Similarly, Logan considered how user-selected songs would be used to recommend songs with similar properties based on solely audio analysis. Researches have indicated a significant semantic gap between characteristics of a song that affects user preferences and corresponding audio signals [12]. However, lyrics information is more effective than audio features when categorizing music, implying that lyrics might perform better in music recommendation [8]. Therefore, recommendation algorithms based on content of lyrics may be a breakthrough.

Nevertheless, it is not feasible to recommend with only content information. Focusing on content information only leads to low variety of music, repeating songs from same artists and albums and results in little surprise for new songs [8]. In some situations, because users may have different preferences in different contexts, not taking into account users' current situation can result in significantly lower recommendation performance [13]. It is also impossible to recommend some similar songs while users have few listening records, and the number of users is very high. People generally only consider user-specific characteristics at a very basic level.

Therefore, it seems necessary to take into account both content and user information. Since lyrics proves better than traditional audio files, when hybridizing both content and user information, focus on the lyrics content along with the music playlist information by applying the word2vec embeddings, a recent technology in the field of natural language processing. It distinguishes this research from more conventional sound-based or hybrid recommendation methods. This research employ the lyrics and users' playlist information as factors in this recommendation system, attempting to mimic actions of a trusted friend or expert and producing a personalized collection of recommendations [14].

From previous studies, music recommendations solely based on lyrics or user preferences have significant defects, so this research would hybridize both to find similarities among songs then to recommend them to users. Using lyrics together with playlist as user data, aim to improve recommendation accuracy of conventional recommendation system by applying new technology into this research (e.g. word2vec embedding).

2 Data

The dataset is obtained from Kaggle, which contains over more that 18,000 Spotify music tracks and their relative information, as described in Table 1. Each song is accompanied with its unique Spotify ID and features such as title, artist, release date, genre and lyrics, as demonstrated by Table 2.

According to Fig. 2, the genre distribution of the music tracks is relatively even. Their percentage ranges from 11%(edm) to 22%(pop). Those genres are further split into twenty four subgenres.

Table 1. General information

Number of songs	Number of artists	Number of main genre	Number of sub-genre
18194	5946	6	24

Table 2. Dataset content

Track_id	Song unique ID from Spotify
Track_name	Title
Track_artist	Artist
Lyrics	Song lyrics
Track_popularity	Song popularity
Track_album_name	Song album name
Track_album_release_date	Date of release
Playlist_name	Playlist name
Playlist_id	Playlist ID
Playlist_genre	Genre

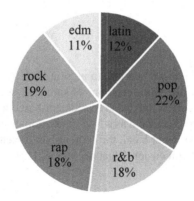

Fig. 2. Genre distribution

The data is processed as follows:

1. Delete missing values. All null values were deleted to prevent intervention from missing information.
2. Filter out non-English musical tracks. Since the work will include natural language processing, limiting the language to English will makes the vectorization process more accurate.
3. Delete the stop words of lyrics. Stop words are meaningless words in lyrics. Deleting them will prevent clustering of music due to useless information.
4. Take stem body of lyrics. Words with different tenses have the same meaning and sentiment. Therefore, converting all the words into stem will further improve the matching of words.
5. Data splitting. The dataset after preprocessing includes 14505 lines. The team splits the dataset randomly with 80% as train set and 20% as test set.

Example of the dataset after processing is shown in Table 3.

Table 3. Processed dataset

Track _id	Track_name	Track_artist	Lyrics	Language	Playlist_genre	Clean_lyrics	Stem _body
004s3t0ONYlzxII9PLgU6z	I Feel Alive	Steady Rollin	The trees, are singing in the wind The sky blue, only as it can be And the angels, smiled at me I saw you, in that lonely bench At half past four, I kissed your soft soft hands and at 6 I kissed your lips and the angels smiled…	en	rock	The trees singing wind The sky blue And angels smiled I saw you lonely bench At half past four I kissed soft soft hands I kissed lips angels smiled…	The tree sing wind the sky blue and angel smile I saw you lone bench At half past four I kiss soft hand I kiss lip angel smile…

3   Methodology

3.1   Problem

To obtain a hybrid system, it is important to present both user and content data in the same modeling. However, the representations of similarity scores and user preferences are different between the collaborative and the content-based method. The collaborative method represents a user preference u as a NM-dimensional vector that contains ratings of all the song data. On the other hand, the content-based method represents the music preference as a set of NT-dimensional feature vectors [15].

3.2   Word2vec

One of the potential solution is word2vec embeddings. It has been widely used in the field of recommendation system and text classification recently in the field of NLP (natural language processing). Its function is to capture the meaning of semantic and syntactic similarity between words. The key principle behind word2vec is the notion that the meaning of a word can be implied from its context–the words around it. Such distributed representation of words as embedded vectors offers many possibilities for NLP applications.

The key components of the model are two weight matrices. The rows of the first matrix (W1) and the columns of the second matrix (W2) are embedded with input words and target words respectively. The product of these two vectors is then used to obtain the probability that a given input word becomes the target word. Gradient descent is used to optimize these embedded vectors to maximize the probability of the real target. The word2vec model mainly has two parts: building the model and finding the embedded word vector. To put it simply, a neural network will be constructed based on the training data at first. And then the parameters learned through the training data will be used to calculate the similarity score of the test set. In Fig. 3, W1 and W2 are the metrices that would return the most similar tracks with the input track. This offers an example to illustrate the application of the word2vec algorithm in the field of music recommendation.

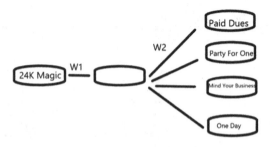

Fig. 3. Illustration of music recommendation through Word2vec

In word2vec, there are two widely used training algorithms: continuous bag of words (CBOW), and skip-gram (SG). The main difference is that CBOW uses context to predict the target word while SG uses a word to predict the target context. As for the music recommendation, the SG model is more efficient since it can catch multiple semantics for a single word [15].

There are also several important parameters in genism that needs to be evaluated. While most of the parameters stays the same as the default value, we alter some values to improve the performance of our model as follows:

Min word count: The parameter ignores words with frequency lower than this value. For this recommendation system, since the words are generally scattered, the value is set to 1.

Size: The size parameter reflects the dimension of vectors with a default value of 100. A higher number will increase accuracy but requires more data. We set this value to 50 and 100 with respective to the lyrics and playlist dataset due to the difference of the data size.

Window: The window parameter sets the maximum distance between given and predicted words and its default value is 5. Due to the complexity of the dataset, this value is set to 10 to allow more space for further visualization [15].

Since the desired outcome is a hybridized system that analyzes lyrics and playlist information separately, these two datasets are processed respectively. First, the lyrics dataset is used to train the data through word2vec and each lyrics will be turned into a vector of 50 dimensions. On the other hand, for the playlist data, since there is no actual user data such as listening record and frequency, we treated each playlist as an individual user, and the songs in the playlist be the music that the user would prefer. In such playlist, the songs in each music playlist are modeled into an vector with dimension of 100.

Afterwards, T-SNE is conducted to reduce the dimensionality and visualize the data separately. Lyrical and playlist information are converted into two-dimensional vectors and visualized in a two-dimensional scatter plot separately. The similarity score for each dataset is calculated according to the cosine distance formula. Finally, an average between these two values will be used to get the final similarity score.

4   Results

4.1   Visualization Model

In this project songs are converted into a two-dimensional vector. Step is repeated twice with lyrics and playlist information as the vectorization factor, and obtained two separate visualization graphs as shown below.

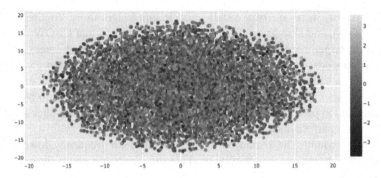

Fig. 4. Visualization scatter plot of Word2Vec embedding of playlist information

Note: Fig. 4 represents all the songs given their coordinates calculated from T-SNE dimensionality reduction. Each point represents a single musical track and the distance is derived from their similarity of playlist information (Fig. 5).

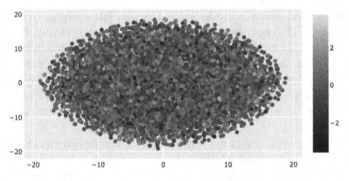

Fig. 5. Visualization scatter plot of Word2Vec embedding of lyrics information

Note: This figure represents all the songs given their coordinates calculated from T-SNE dimensionality reduction. Each point represents a single musical track and the distance is derived from their similarity of lyrics information.

4.2   Recommendation Model

In order to increase accuracy, these two models are combined at a scale of 50% each to acquire a better prediction on user preference as content based and user-based data have some drawbacks. Model returns five most similar songs with respect to the given music track and their similarity score. Below is an example of our hybridized method of recommendation (Fig. 6).

index	track_artist	rec1	sim1	rec2	sim2	rec3	sim3	rec4	sim4	rec5	sim5
1	Bell Biv DeVoe - Poison	Nas - Bridging Gap	0.999	Queen - Flick Of The Wrist - Remastered 2011	0.999	Maurice West - The Kick	0.9986	Tom Petty and the Heartbreakers - Mary Jane's ...	0.998	Major Lazer - Lean On (feat. MØ & DJ Snake)	0.997
2	CeeLo Green - Baby It's Cold Outside (feat. Ch...	David Bowie - Heat	1	Old School Freight Train - Superstition	1	Mickey Cho - Thoughts (feat. Sam Ock & J. Han)	0.9981	Marilyn Manson - God's Gonna Cut You Down	0.997	The Velvet Underground - The Black Angel's Dea...	0.996

Fig. 6. Hybrid recommendation algorithm model

4.3 Artist Variety Comparison

To evaluate the feasibility of model, artist variety is counted by using the several distinct artists of the recommended songs. The artist variety for each individual song is computed as:

$$Artist\ Variety\ =\ Number\ of\ Distinct\ Artists/5\ (N)$$

A higher result means the model is more effective [5].

4.4 Genre Accuracy Comparison

Genre accuracy is treated as a factor that determines the effectiveness of our model. It compares the genre of the recommended song with that of the given music track and compute the probability if they match. A higher number means that they're categorically more like each other. Genre accuracy is computed as:

$$Genre\ Accuracy\ =\ Number\ of\ Identical\ Genre/5\ (N)$$

The method is identical to the artist Variety, yet this project utilized the method differently because of the unique feature of music: different artist have similar music, yet genres are used to recognize different songs.

4.5 Result

Two different methods of assessment are introduced. The first method compares the genres of target songs and recommended songs with top 5 similarity scores to assess recommendation's accuracy. The second method compares artists of target songs and recommending songs with top 5 similarity scores to determine the artist variety of the recommendation. The result for artist variety is significant; the average score turns out to be 1, indicating all 5 recommended songs are from different artists. The accuracy of genre comparison is 0.28, indicating that only 1.4 recommending songs of the 5 songs shares the genre with the target song (Tables 4 and 5).

Table 4. Model evaluation

	Average artist variety	Average genre accuracy
Hybridized model	1	0.28

Recommendation system also took the accuracy of playlist only model and lyrics only model to compare with hybridization model, which is shown below:

Table 5. Genre accuracy comparison

	Playlist	Lyrics	Hybrid	Random
Genre accuracy	0.26	0.27	0.28	0.2

The genre accuracy score for hybridized model is 0.28, the highest among all the models. Hybridized model has a much higher accuracy compared with randomized model, indicating that the model does recommend music within similar genres more frequently than the randomized model. Also, the score of the hybridized model is slightly higher than that of the playlist and lyrics only models which shows average score improves the effectiveness of the recommendation system at a small amount.

5   Conclusion

This paper presents a recommendation system through word2vec embeddings of lyrics and playlist data to make music recommendations. Comparing lyrics similarities and playlist information, system recommend TOP five similar songs of input music regarding both lyrics and playlist information. This method mainly uses lyrics to recommend similar songs to users. However, low accuracy of this system can be explained by multiple factors.

The first issue with model is that evaluation method only compares basic information about the genre and artist and lacks user data. Therefore, to evaluate if the user would like the songs that recommended to them is impossible. To solve this problem, a survey for music listeners in the future is needed. In the survey, it will automatically give recommendations to the volunteers by using their favorite song lyrics and ask them to rate system. By this way, a useful evaluation of our recommendation algorithm comes out.

Recommendation system also need more data to improve its training of code. For now, because of copyright issue, there is no way to get a dataset that consists of all required data. Datasets with complete information of both lyrics and user data provided by large companies like Metrolyrics cannot find on the internet. In the future, we need to crawl some real data from some music application to develop a more organized algorithm. This system will not only focus on lyrics but also on audio tracks, genre, and artist information. Lyrics may not be the best reflection of the music and needs to be accompanied with several other factors.

Besides, current model is relatively immature for simply taking an average score from the two approaches. Further studies should be done to weight these two similarity scores (the lyrics similarity score and playlist similarity score) through modeling and find out how to weight them.

Overall, since the effectiveness of assessment method is unknown and the dataset has several problems, further research on similar recommending algorithms are needed to make some improvements on current music recommendation system.

References

1. Wellman, B.: Computer networks as social networks. Science **293**, 2031–2034 (2001)
2. Zhang, L.: The definition of novelty in recommendation system. J. Eng. Sci. Technol. Rev. **6**(3), 141–145 (2013)
3. Fong, A.C.M., Zhou, B., Hui, S.C., Hong, G.Y., Do, T.A.: Web content recommender system based on consumer behavior modeling. IEEE Trans. Consum. Electron. **57**(2), 962–969 (2011)
4. Korbut, D.: cube.js, 6 July 2017. Retrieved from Recommendation System Algorithms: https://blog.statsbot.co/recommendation-system-algorithms-ba67f39ac9a3
5. Shao, B., Wang, D., Li, T., Ogihara, M.: Music recommendation based on acoustic features and user access patterns. IEEE Trans. Audio Speech Lang. Process. **17**(8), 1602–1611 (2009)
6. Sloboda, J.A., Juslin, P.N.: Psychological perspectives on music and emotion. In: Juslin, P.N., Sloboda, J.A. (eds.) Series in Affective Science. Music and emotion: Theory and research, pp. 71–104. Oxford University Press (2001)
7. Andjelkovic, I., Parra, D., O'Donovan, J.: Moodplay: interactive mood-based music discovery and recommendation. In: User Modeling, Adaptation and Personalization, vol. 54. ACM (2016)
8. Bulger, D.: Music data analysis: foundations and applications. In: Weihs, C., Jannach, D., Vatolkin, I., Rudolph, G. (eds.) CRC press, Boca Raton, Florida (2017). 675 p. aud$94.99 (hardback). ISBN 97898756. Aust. New Zealand J. Stat. **60**, 405–406. https://doi.org/10.1111/anzs.12244
9. Pachet, F., Westermann, G., Laigre, D.: Musical data mining for electronic music (2001)
10. Aucouturier, J.J.: Representing musical genre: a state of the art. J. New Music Res. **32**(1), 83–93 (2003)
11. Whitman, B., Smaragdis, P.: Combining musical and cultural features for intelligent style detection. In: Paper Presented at the Third ISMIR, Paris, 13–17 October 2002
12. Oord, A.V.D., Dieleman, S., Schrauwen, B.: Deep content-based music recommendation. In: NIPS Distribution. International Conference on Web Delivering of Music, pp. 2643–2651. IEEE (2013)

13. Celma, O.: Music recommendation. Music recommendation and discovery, pp. 43–85. Springer, Heidelberg (2010)
14. Zhang, Y.C., et al.: Auralist: introducing serendipity into music recommendation. In: Proceedings of the Fifth ACM International Conference on Web Search and Data Mining (2012)
15. Ozsoy, M.: From word embeddings to item recommendation (2016)

A Review of End-to-End Chinese – Mandarin Speech Synthesis Techniques

Wenzhuo Gong[(✉)], Yang Hong, Hancheng Liu, and Yutong He

School of Cyber Science and Engineering, Sichuan University,
Chengdu 610207, China
gwz@stu.scu.edu.cn

Abstract. Text-to-speech (TTS) is currently a significant research field of speech synthesis. It has been used in intelligent conversational artificial intelligence (AI), chatbot, speech interaction, and a large variety of other application scenarios. Credit to the application of deep learning and end-to-end technology in speech synthesis, the current advanced TTS system is able to synthesize speech close to the real human voice. However, its application in Chinese Mandarin is hindered by the diversity of pronunciation of Chinese characters and the complexity of Chinese grammar. This article will follow the development of speech synthesis technology to elaborate on the research and development of Mandarin speech synthesis and discuss the existing problems of current research. This work is anticipated to further improve the performance of the Chinese-Mandarin end-to-end system and point out some valuable research directions which can bring the research of Mandarin speech synthesis into a new stage.

Keywords: Mandarin speech synthesis · Review · End to End · Text analysis

1 Introduction

Speech synthesis technology [1–3] aims to transform text information into clear and natural speech by computer, which involves phonetics, digital signal processing, and computer science. In the field of information processing, It is cutting-edge technology which has a wide application prospect. At present, the research on speech synthesis technology mainly focuses on text to speech (TTS), which transforms text information into audio data and then plays it out by voice. People who have visual impairment can be helped to receive the information on the computer. It can also increase the readability of text documents. Today's TTS applications can often be useful in voice-driven email, voice sensitive systems, and voice recognition programs.

Speech synthesis has been widely studied in the last century. Speech synthesis systems for French, German, English, Japanese and other languages have been successfully developed [4–7] in the early 1990s. Since the 1980s, Chinese speech synthesis technology has attracted wide attention of speech synthesis researchers and developed rapidly [8–15]. A series of Chinese speech synthesis systems emerged, such as Lenovo Jiayin (1995) and Tsinghua University TH_SPEECH (1993), China University of science and technology KDTALK (1995), iFLYTEK Interphonic 5.0

© Springer Nature Singapore Pte Ltd. 2021
W. Cao et al. (Eds.): CONF-CDS 2021, CCIS 1513, pp. 393–435, 2021.
https://doi.org/10.1007/978-981-16-8885-0_31

(2009), etc. These systems, which can be applied to different scales of voice service platforms and create huge social and economic benefits, can synthesize any text into continuous and natural voice, and have the characteristics of multi-language and multi-tone. As the continuous development of the field of deep learning, especially the recent study on speech synthesis based on the technology of deep learning and end-to-end, the speech synthesized by the most advanced speech synthesis system became comparable to the real voice. However, its extension to the Mandarin speech synthesis system is still a big obstacle [16–19].

Mandarin is not only one of the oldest languages in the world, but also the most widely used language in the world. It has been a momentous research direction in the field of speech synthesis to construct an advanced Mandarin speech synthesis system and promote the development of this. Compared with phonetic characters like English, Chinese Mandarin has the following characteristics [19]:

- The Chinese-Characters have almost no acoustic characteristics;
- The semantic information of sentences is complex;
- There is no clear separator between words;
- There is a lot of polyphonic tone sandhi.

To solve the above problems, researchers have proposed various solutions and achieved gratifying performance improvement [16–19]. Therefore, it is necessary to summarize the speech synthesis technology for Chinese at this stage, which will be helpful to researchers to clarify the research fronts in this field.

This article will follow the development of speech synthesis technology, focusing on the technical research of Mandarin speech synthesis, elaborating the technical research characteristics of different stages, comparing the merits and demerits of different models, and discussing the latest research-based on Mandarin speech synthesis. In the end, this article looks forward to the future research directions in this field, hoping to provide new ideas for researchers. The article's main content will be organized as follows: Sect. 2 outlines the development of Chinese speech synthesis, which includes basic concepts, history, and technology. Section 3 introduces the most advanced speech synthesis technology based on end-to-end. Section 4 discusses the research of end-to-end speech synthesis based on Chinese-Mandarin. Section 5 summarizes the research work and provides a discussion about new research directions. Section 6 Conclusions.

2 Mandarin Speech Synthesis Overview

2.1 Early History of Speech Synthesis

Basic Concepts of Speech Synthesis. Joint Synthesis, Parametric Speech Synthesis, and Concatenative Speech Synthesis are three basic methods of speech synthesis. Joint synthesis employs computational model by simulating human vocal organs (tongue, lip, etc.) so that the model can simulate human joint motion and calculate the acoustic characteristics of vocal cord shape. However, its high complexity prevents its commercial feasibility.

Parametric speech synthesis is a method of synthesizing speech from the text by using digital signal processing technology, which uses the sound source to excite time-varying digital filter with vocal tract resonance characteristics, to simulate human voice generation. Compared with joint synthesis, parametric speech synthesis directly extracts acoustic features from language representation through a set of well-designed rules, thus avoiding the complexity of modeling. But for the huge human language system, designing a set of language feature rules is also a difficult task.

Concatenative speech synthesis is based on the speech waveform Library in series to output a continuous speech stream. The basic principle is to analyze the context information from the text input, using the information to select the appropriate voice units from the pre-recorded and marked voice database, and finally connect the selected voice units in series. Because of this characteristic, compared with the first two methods, concatenative language synthesis bypasses the most complex problems. Moreover, the method is based on the real human voice unit, so the speech synthesized in series has obvious naturalness for a single word. However, there are still some problems to be solved, including connect the serial units naturally, keep the prosodic features of each series unit conform to the context, and design a huge speech database.

Early Mandarin Speech Synthesis. In the 1990s, the research on Mandarin synthesis attracted widespread attention, and many studies have proposed various types of high-quality Mandarin speech synthesis systems.

Mandarin speech synthesis based on the concatenative synthesis model can be traced back to the research of Lei [20] Huang [21] and Zhou [22, 23] in the early 1980s. The focus of this research is to adapt the system to the speed and capability of the machine at that time, so the number of units of synthesized speech at that time is often small. Subsequent research by Qin et al. [24] and Shi et al. [25]. increased the number of synthesized speech units to about 60, but this model lacks the processing of the boundary effect of adjacent speech units, so the naturalness of its synthesized speech is poor. Furthermore, Cai [26], Chu [27], and Hwang [28] studied the consonance of syllable boundaries and found that the list of Mandarin types based on syllables alone cannot simulate the consonant effect of syllable boundaries. How to deal with unnatural pauses in syllable boundaries became a thorny issue at that time.

Mandarin synthesis based on the parametric synthesis model is earlier than the concatenative system. It can be traced back to 1976 when Suen [29] used the VOTRAX synthesizer to generate Mandarin speech from speech transcription, with five tonal contours in the form of simple citations. Later, many rule-based syntheses are based on this principle, using rule generation parameters to synthesize a single syllable, and then connect these syllables. Therefore, like concatenative systems, these systems cannot handle the natural transition of syllable boundaries.

In 1996, Bell Labs [30] proposed a relatively complete Mandarin speech synthesis system. The whole system consists of about ten modules, which is a pipeline model. Every module in the pipeline is encapsulated and is in contact with the next module through a unified interface. The model can process different modules relatively independently, enabling researchers to perform modular analysis. The system is a Linear

Predictive Coding (LPC) based concatenative system, and the synthesizer is based on the male voice corpus of Beijing Mandarin. For the first time, this system uses phonemes as concatenative units instead of traditional syllable units and ultimately produces highly intelligible speech. However, the generated speech was still very mechanical, and there were problems common to synthesizers of any language at that time, such as poor text analysis capabilities, difficulty in predicting phrase boundaries, and inability to select appropriate unit prosodic structures. To solve these problems, the concatenative speech synthesis system based on the Corpus is gradually on the main stage.

2.2 Unit Selection Based on Corpus

Corpus refers to a large-scale electronic text bank that has been scientifically sampled and processed, which stores the language materials that have appeared in the actual use of language. Having the ability to process a large number of corpora increasing, all parts of the speech database can be utilized as synthesis units. Theoretically, giving an infinite speech corpus and an effective index, the model can generate almost the same synthetic speech as human speech. However, this is an idealized situation. The initial stage of this study is based on medium-sized corpora, using well-designed models to cover most speech units and language changes.

Earlier study, by Chou [31] in 1998, introduced a corpus-based Mandarin concatenative synthesis model. Based on a designed speech corpus, they selects concatenation units of syllables online, and optimized the tonal resonance by additionally incorperated prefixes and suffixes. Finally, the system generates the most natural speech output by selecting the best segment from the corpus. However, due to the lack of accurate and complete rules for the use and extraction of corpus information, synthesized speech is still very mechanical. In order to fully use of the information of the speech database and make the synthesized speech more natural, many efforts were devoted. Tseng [32] has researched how to use the frequency of words and syllables that are frequently used in spoken English to provide useful clues for correct word selection when the size of the speech database is limited, which means the available acoustic information is insufficient. Gu et al. [33] believes that in the corpus-based unit selection system of Putonghua, the key factor affecting the fluency of synthesized speech is the discontinuity of formant trace on the syllable boundary. They proposed to integrate acoustic knowledge (spectrum distance measurement) and pronunciation knowledge (restriction rules defined in phoneme pronunciation knowledge) into the algorithm based on dynamic programming (DP), and used the DP based algorithm to select the global optimal composite unit sequence.

Based on these studies, the fluency and naturalness of synthesized speech have been significantly improved, but for the synthesis of Mandarin Chinese, the precise conversion of characters to syllables (G2P) and the problem of polysyllabic ambiguity are still great challenges.

Since Chinese is a syllable language, syllables are usually selected as the phonetic unit in the Mandarin Text-to-Speech System (TTS), represented by the standard Chinese Pinyin. However, the G2P conversion of Chinese is to convert the polyphonic characters of input text into the corresponding pinyin. In 2004, Xu [34] proposed a statistical framework for Chinese G2P, which is based on the statistical method of hidden Markov model (HMM), which can effectively implement word segmentation, part of speech tagging (POS tag), and character to Pinyin conversion. In the meantime, the framework proposes that in the conversion from character to Pinyin, POS marking is particularly effective for eliminating multi-tone ambiguity. POS marking can significantly increase the performance of Chinese G2P which was show by experiments. At the same time, researchers have also raised a new problem. When dictionaries from different sources are inconsistent with the test data set, some errors might be caused. In particular, there are still many unpredictable errors in the current standard test corpus, which have a profound impact on the test results [34]. It has become an significant research path to construct an excellent corpus that can adapt to the current advanced Chinese TTS system.

The construction of the corpus acts an momentous role in the corpus-based speech synthesis system. Thus, the small and medium-sized speech corpus can not meet the needs of the advanced Mandarin TTS system at this time. It is of great importance and practical value to establish a reasonably designed and high-quality speech corpus. In 2008, Zhang [35] summarized the construction method of the Mandarin comprehensive speech database and designed several standards for rapid selection from a large number of original texts, speaker selection, and data annotation. At the same time, the corpus provides all the basic unit and context information for the TTS system. The published corpus has been successfully used in the comprehensive evaluation of Mandarin speech in the blizzard Challenge 2008. TH-CoSS [36] is a corpus designed and produced by the Tsinghua University team for Mandarin speech synthesis. The balance of corpus and the richness of segmental and prosodic information are considered in the design. In addition to text and voice data, the corpus also contains segment segmentation marks, and the annotation file is in XML format. The design of the corpus, a speech analysis basing on the decision tree which has fully considered the influence of context features on prosodic features and analyzed the relative weights of different contextual features provides a useful reference for the new corpus's construction.

With the help of advanced corpus technology and the PSOLA algorithm, the concatenative speech synthesis system based on the corpus has made remarkable progress in the naturalness and comprehensibility of synthesized speech. However, with the extensive application of synthetic speech technology in our daily life, people have higher requirements for synthesized speech, that is, they want the synthesized speech to have rhythm and emotional changes, and to construct an advanced expressive speech synthesis system. For data-driven methods such as corpus, the quality of emotional speech synthesis largely depends on the size of the emotional speech corpus, and it will cost a huge number of manpower and material resources to construct a corpus with different emotions and different prosody. At this time, the statistical parametric speech synthesis system (SPSS) began to be favored by researchers, because it can easily modify the prosodic parameters of synthesized speech, and overcome the shortcomings of traditional models that are difficult to change the way speaker speak.

2.3   Statistical Parametric Speech Synthesis

SPSS method is essentially a data-driven synthesis method. Its basic principle is based on the idea of machine learning. It performs statistical modeling on the data in the training set to obtain a statistical model of acoustic parameters, and Based on this model, a corresponding speech synthesis system is constructed.

The SPSS system usually consists of the following three modules:

- **Text Analysis Module:** By preprocessing the original text (text normalization, automatic word segmentation, and G2P conversion, etc.), it is converted into language features that can be read by the speech synthesis system.
- **Parameter Prediction Module:** It predicts the corresponding acoustic feature parameters based on the feature information output by the text analysis module.
- **Speech Synthesis Module:** The characteristic parameters output by the parameter prediction module are used as input to generate the target voice.

The process of the statistical parametric speech synthesis is mainly divided into two parts: training and synthesis. At the training end, the frequency spectrum, fundamental frequency F0, and duration extracted from the training corpus are trained on statistical parameter models, and a trained model is obtained. In the synthesis process, text analysis is performed on the original input text, and then the previously trained statistical parameter model is used for parameter prediction, and finally, the speech is synthesized by the parameter synthesizer.

The early SPSS system is mainly based on Hidden Markov Model (HMM) for modeling, and to solve the problem of insufficient long-term relevance of speech context information in HMM, researchers have proposed parameters based on Deep Neural Network (DNN) Prediction methods, next, we will briefly introduce the development of the above two methods in Mandarin speech synthesis.

Speech Synthesis Based on Hidden Markov Model. At the beginning of the 21st century, the synthesized speech had made significant progress with its naturalness and intelligibility. The focus of research has shifted to how to deal with the expression of prosody and emotion in synthesized speech, and build an advanced prosody prediction model.

Speech synthesis based on Hidden Markov Model (HMM) has been proving to be an excellent system, which can simultaneously model short-term frequency spectrum, fundamental frequency (F0), and duration. The speech generated by the HMM-based TTS model is quite smooth. Unlike the corpus-based system, it is based on statistical modeling, so it is terser and more flexible. The system has been successfully applied to TTS systems for many languages (such as Japanese, English and Mandarin [37]).

However, researchers focus on the research direction of the HMM-based TTS system in the field of expressive speech synthesis, which has three major defects [38, 39].

- Firstly, The prosodic feature parameters predicted by the HMM model are usually too smooth, making the synthesized speech very mechanical and unnatural.
- Secondly, The modeling of F0 by the HMM method is complicated because F0 is discontinuous in the voiced and unvoiced areas.

- Thirdly, HMM cannot predict the duration information very accurately, which is very important for high-quality TTS. If the inappropriate phoneme duration is used, the naturalness and expressiveness of synthetic speech will be reduced.

Aiming at the problem that the prosodic feature parameters are too smooth and the synthesized speech lacks prosody in the HMM-based speech synthesis system, much researches on improving the prosody of synthesized speech and generating expressive speech have emerged. In 2008, Yamagishi et al. [40] explored an advanced Japanese expressive speech synthesis system based on HMM. They use a maximum likelihood linear regression model to achieve control of spectral features and prosodic features, and use speech style interpolation and adaptive technology. In 2009, Tang et al. [41] proposed to use the difference method to predict the prosody, and predict the prosody change parameters (F0, duration and intensity) for each phoneme. Inanoglu et al. [42] proposed a method of emotional transformation of segment selection, which directly searches the F0 segment in training corpus by using the tandem frame. These studies enable the HMM model to model prosodic features more accurately, and the synthesized speech is more natural and vivid.

Aiming at the discontinuity problem of F0 in the acoustic and silent regions, multi spatial distribution HMM (MSDHMM) was developed by using the combination of discrete and continuous distribution [38], which became the default modeling method of the advanced HMM synthesis system at that time. On the other hand, for the duration model in the HMM speech synthesis system, researchers have also conducted a lot of research [42, 43].

In addition to the above studies, there are still a large number of studies on the HMM expression system to improve the prosody of synthetic speech in the TTS system. In 2010, Yu et al. [44] used two new decision tree models to extract word-level prosodic patterns from natural English speech and then embedded prosodic models into an HMM-based speech synthesis framework. In the same year, Badino et al. [45] automatically detected contrast word pairs with text features and used enhanced context-sensitive tags to synthesize prosody. They pointed out that this method can effectively convey contrast information. Moreover, Turk et al. [46] explores speech conversion and modification techniques to reduce data system collection and processing while maintaining acceptable quality and naturalness.

These studies make the HMM-based speech synthesis system achieve advanced performance. However, only a few works focus on the prosodic synthesis of Mandarin, and cannot automatically generate expressive speech with prosodic information from the original text. Mandarin is standard Chinese, a language which is tonal type. Every syllable which has the same phoneme sequence has four tone types, and meanings of every tone differs. The earlier kernel model has been proved to apply to Mandarin tone recognition [47] and Mandarin speech synthesis [48].

The research on the integrated expressive speech synthesis system of Mandarin did not appear until 2010. Wen et al. [49] proposed a prosody conversion method for Mandarin speech based on the phonetic core model. This method no longer converts the F0 contour of the entire syllable, but models the prosody features of each syllable core, thereby avoiding the problem of data sparseness. At the same time, the mapping function is constructed by carefully selected tonal model parameters, which is to better capture the tone information of Mandarin and achieve higher perception accuracy. The Institute of automation, the Chinese Academy of Sciences [50] proposed a speech synthesis system based on HMM to support Mandarin stress synthesis. The maximum entropy model is proposed for the first time, which uses only the text features to generate the Mandarin stress in the prosodic words. At the same time, a linear adaptive model is proposed, which can obtain the corresponding adjustment parameters, and modify it according to different voice features by analyzing the stress tags in the corpus. Although the proposed maximum entropy model makes it possible to design a data-driven prosodic model, the proposed linear adaptive model is essentially generated from a manually marked corpus, which will cost a lot of manpower and material resources. A similar method [51], which uses a training database with manual prosody markers to estimate the context-sensitive information commonly available in HMM, is based on parametric speech synthesis. Wang et al. [39] proposed an F0 generation model, which can improve the prosody feature generation quality of the HMM model by re-estimating the F0 value in the pitch tracking error area and the unvoiced area. Every Mandarin phoneme is required a priori knowledge of Vu (voiced/unvoiced) and applies it to Vu decision-making. The grammar features extracted from the output of the Stanford parser are designed to predict the duration of Mandarin phonemes. Through this improvement, a clear relationship can be obtained between the generated prosodic features and their background language information. Thus, the prosodic features can be flexibly controlled in the TTS based on HMM. However, the model still needs a lot of manual intervention to mark, which leads to heavy modeling workload and low model scalability.

According to the above research, these expressive speech synthesis models in the early stage are all rule-based methods. The basic idea is to make rules manually, which can generate prosodic structures from the grammar of a sentence. We have also found that the rule-based method will consume a lot of manpower and material resources, because it needs to extract and update a huge number of rules. At the same time, the rule-based model is not scalable for different languages. Since then, annotated speech corpus has been developed, and many data-driven methods have emerged, some of which are classic methods such as decision trees [52] and maximum entropy [53].

The data-driven method first extracts the prosodic features of the text (including vocabulary and syntax), then trains the statistical model according to the feature parameters, and finally predicts the prosodic features of the unlabeled text. Mandarin prosody model based on data-driven method has also been widely investigated. In 2010, Hsia et al. [54] proposed a method for modeling and generating pitch in Mandarin speech synthesis based on the Hidden Markov model using prosodic hierarchy and dynamic pitch features. Supervised classification and regression tree (S-CART) is used by the model to predict prosodic structure, and the pitch prediction model can be estimated from the training corpus. However, the model still relies on a large corpus of manually marked word body structure for high-level tone modeling which increases the complexity of the model. In 2013, Yu [55] proposed to use syntactic information to predict prosodic parameters directly. The model can use rich syntactic tags and relationships to improve the modeling of prosodic parameters and does not need a large manual annotated prosody corpus but there is still a lack of high-level prosody modeling and syntactic analysis, which leads to the lack of long-term feature modeling of F0. Therefore, a hierarchical F0 structure should be introduced to analyze more syntactic context information. For the problem that F0 long-term prosodic representation modeling of the traditional HMM model is insufficient, a double-layer F0 modeling method is proposed in [56]. In the prosodic modeling of statistical parametric speech synthesis, the advantages of the QTA (quantitative target approximation) model are fully utilized, and the F0 prediction method of Mandarin speech synthesis based on HMM is improved by filtering after extracting the F0 features of syllable level. Although these hierarchical structures play a certain role in the long-term modeling of context information, the extracted features are still not enough to fully represent the complex and higher dimensional features of human speech, which is difficult to break through the bottleneck of HMM parameter modeling. In the prediction of speech synthesis acoustic characteristic parameters, the introduction of a deeper structural model has become the focus of research.

The parameter prediction model based on Deep Neural Network (DNN) gradually showed its advantages. DNN can train the mapping of complex language features to acoustic feature parameters. The most important thing is that DNN-based methods can model the correlation between speech frames based on long and short-term context information, thereby greatly improving the synthesis of speech Naturalness.

Speech Synthesis Model Based on Deep Neural Network. Speech synthesis based on HMM maps linguistic features to the probability density of voice parameters with different decision trees. Not like the approach basing on HMM, the deep learning approach straightly use deep neural networks to map linguistics features to acoustic features, of which the efficiency has proved to be very high when learning the inherent characteristics of data. In the research of deep learning based speech synthesis, many models have been put forward, and we will briefly introduce these models.

- **Restricted Boltzmann Machine (RBM)** [57], a randomly generated neural network that can learn the probability distribution through input data sets. It is commonly used as a density model to generate the spectral envelope of acoustic parameters in the acoustic field. RBM can alleviate the over-smoothig problem in HMM-based speech synthesis. Because it can more effectively describe the distribution of a high-dimensional spectral envelope. Although the RBM predicted spectral envelope is very close to the original spectral envelope, the quality of the model is easily affected by training data issues. At present, this model has been widely used in speech signal modeling, such as speech recognition and spectrogram coding.
- **Multi-distributed Deep Belief Network (DBN)** [58], through the use of layer-by-layer training, solves the optimization problem of deep neural networks, so that the network can reach the optimal solution as long as the network is fine-tuned. In the field of speech synthesis, DBN allows all syllables to be trained in the same network, thereby eliminating the problem of training data fragmentation. It is worth

mentioning that this model does not model speech frames, but directly models syllables, effectively alleviating the excessive smoothness of synthesized speech caused by frame averaging.

- **Deep Mixed Density Network (MDN)** [59, 60], by using the duration prediction model, effectively solves the single model problem and the inability to predict the variance of the traditional DNN model in modeling acoustic feature parameters and significantly improves the voice Synthetic naturalness. However, this model still has two problems: Because it can only model a fixed period, only limited context information can be used; The model can only be mapped frame by frame.

- **Recurrent Neural Network (RNN)** [61] is used to solve the problem that the previous model is difficult to model context information. However, the traditional RNN can easily cause gradient attenuation and gradient explosion, and cannot learn long-term context-dependence. To solve these problems of traditional RNN, the author [62] proposed a long short-term memory (LSTM) model, which can make full use of context information and effectively solve the problem that traditional models in speech synthesis cannot establish long-term dependencies for processing.

With the research and development of the neural network model, the speech synthesis model based on deep learning is becoming more and more mature. Compared with the HMM model, it can synthesize more natural and expressive speech, and its excellent performance has been proved. However, there are still many problems in the model for Chinese speech synthesis. For example, the regional diversity of Chinese speech, the polysemy of Chinese words, and the diversity of syntactic prosody bring huge challenges to Chinese speech synthesis based on deep learning [63]. Given the special problems in Chinese speech synthesis, researchers have carried out a lot of research work, we will briefly introduce it.

In 2016, Zheng et al. [64] discussed the new application of continuous lexical embedding and Bidirectional Long- and Short-Term Memory Cyclic Neural Network (BLSTM) model in stress prediction of Chinese speech synthesis. The model adopts an unsupervised learning method, which can effectively capture semantic and syntactic attributes, and achieves good Mandarin stress prediction performance. In 2018, Zheng et al. [65] discussed the deep neural network acoustic model that can produce Chinese exclamation and interrogative speech, the bidirectional long and short-term memory cyclic neural network (BLSTM) model and the forward neural network (FNN). In the proposed model, the shared layer of multi-style BLSTM can take advantage of the commonness among different speaking styles, thus converting the learned knowledge into new speech styles. This is very friendly to text to speech synthesizer for speech styles (such as Mandarin) with few training resources or limited resources. In 2019, Zhu's work [66] discussed the tonal and phonetic knowledge in the Chinese TTS model and emphasized the importance of designing linguistic information stimulus to train and evaluate the TTS model. Liu et al. [67] studied a cross-language multilingual TTS method, which can generate natural and understandable native speech for invisible speakers. The author uses WaveNet to train Cantonese pronunciation and can be used to generate Mandarin. Li [68] proposed an acoustic model of synthetic speech emotion. The proposed model uses the regression network based on CBHG (1-D Convolution Bank + Highway Network + Bidirectional GRU) module to model the dependence between language features and acoustic functions, making acoustic parameters more suitable for regression tasks and waveform reconstruction. In real-time speech synthesis, the model can generate expressive interrogative and exclamatory speech with high audio quality. However, there are still some deficiencies in the model, which need to be improved in many aspects, such as adaptive training for speakers and more complex emotional language generation (such as happiness, anger, and sadness).

The SPSS speech synthesis system based on DNN has made significant progress in the field of speech synthesis and achieved very good performance. However, these TTS systems are usually composed of individually trained components (including text analysis front-ends, parameter prediction models, and speech synthesizers), so the errors of each component may be compounded. Moreover, the construction of these models depends on professional knowledge in the field of linguistics, so it is very laborious for the researchers of deep learning. With the proposal of the end-to-end speech synthesis model, synthesized speech under a unified framework has gradually become the mainstream of research in the field. Compared with the model trained by multiple components separately, the end-to-end system shows significant advantages:

- Training can be performed based on a large number of <text, speech> pairs, and uses as few manual annotations as possible.
- Phoneme-level alignment is not required.
- Unified single model, no error compound.

We will briefly introduce the end-to-end speech synthesis including its development and model structure afterward.

3 End-to-End Speech Synthesis

3.1 The Proposal of the Seq2Seq Model

In 2014, the Google Brain team and Yoshua Bengio team proposed the Seq2Seq model [69, 70] for machine translation-related problems. This model uses RNN and LSTM to map a sequence as input to another output sequence. The accuracy of machine translation has been significantly improved due to the proposed model. Moreover, the model has been widely used in automatic coding, classifier training, syntactic analysis, automatic text summarization, intelligent speech system, speech synthesis, and recognition, etc.

In the Seq2Seq model, the encoder will compile the input sequence and compress all its information into feature vectors of corresponding dimensions. However, as the sequence continues to grow, the Seq2Seq model will have two problems when processing longer data:

- No matter how long the input is, it is encoded into a vector with a fixed length. Therefore, coding will lose more information when the model is processing long sentences. This is also not conducive to the subsequent decoding work.

- In the decoding process, different output uses the same context information, which will also bring difficulties to decoding. To solve these problems, it is necessary to introduce an attention mechanism so that the model can accurately get more critical information to the current task goal selected from the input sequence and output sequence.

3.2   Introduction and Development of Attention Mechanism

In 2014, Bahdanau et al. [71] first introduced the Soft Attention Model (Soft AM) to machine translation (see Fig. 1). The author proposes a machine translation model with an attention mechanism. This model mainly includes an encoder constructed using a bidirectional RNN (BiRNN) and a decoder that introduces a soft-aligned attention mechanism. Among them, the BiRNN in the encoder is used to generate an annotation sequence of context information. In the annotation sequence, each h_i can calculate the corresponding weight value a_i for different target words, and finally calculate the context vector of the aim word s_i. The decoder uses annotation sequence information and weight information given by the encoder to select the corresponding target so that it can learn to automatically align during translation, which is the so-called attention mechanism.

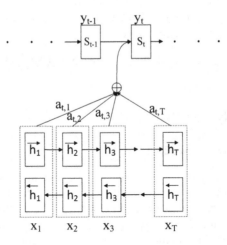

Fig. 1. (Decoder) Given the source sentence (x1, x2,..., xT), try to generate a graphical description of the model of the t-th target word yt.

The research group of Huawei teacher Li Hang proposed [72] to apply the Encoder-Decoder framework with attention model (AM) to the dialogue robot application (Fig. 1). The input to the Encoder-Decoder is a dialogue, and the output of the Encoder-Decoder is the response of the dialogue robot, and its training data uses the dialogue data in the Weibo comment. This research proves that AM-Encoder-Decoder is effective in the dialogue system (Fig. 2).

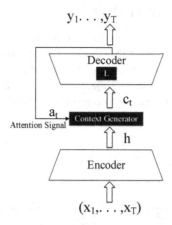

Fig. 2. Attention mechanism applied in dialogue system.

Google's paper [73] uses the Encoder-Decoder framework with the AM model for syntactic analysis, as well as the Soft AM model. The paper [74] applies the Encoder-Decoder with AM to the generative text summary, which is essentially a Soft AM model and proves that the model is effective.

The Manning research group of Stanford University proposed two AM models [75]: Global Attention Model and Local Attention Model. The Global Attention Model is essentially Soft AM. The Local Attention Model is a windowed Soft AM. It first estimates an alignment position Pt, and then takes a probability distribution similar to Soft AM in the window range of D around P_t.

Google's paper [76] proposes to use the AM model to solve the problem of the question answering system. This paper proposes two AM models: 'Attentive Reader' and 'Impatient Reader', where Impatient Reader is Soft AM, also known as dynamic AM, and Attentive Reader is static AM. Dynamic AM requires calculating the word alignment probability of each word in the input sentence corresponding to each word in the output sentence. Static AM proposes that for the entire output sentence, it is sufficient to obtain an attention distribution probability distribution for the input sentence as a whole, and does not require each word to be calculated independently. Because in the Q&A scenario, for a question, its focus is the answer in the article, so the whole question sentence has a probability of attention distribution.

The paper [77] uses the Encoder-Decoder framework with AM to do speech recognition and proposes the idea of forced forward AM. When Soft AM gradually generates the target sentence words, it is gradually generated from front to back. The forced forward AM adds constraints: when generating the target sentence words, if an input sentence word is already aligned with the output word, then it is basically not considered to use it later, because the input and output are gradually going. Moving forward, so it looks similar to mandatory alignment rules moving forward.

3.3   Speech Synthesis Based on ARST

In 2016, Wang et al. [78] were the first to use the seq2seq method with an attention mechanism to try an end-to-end TTS system. They proposed an original end-to-end parametric TTS model, which uses an attention-based cyclic sequence sensor (ARST) to map text strings directly to acoustic trajectories. 'End to end' means that text analysis and acoustic modeling are integrated into a unified model (Fig. 1 and Fig. 3).

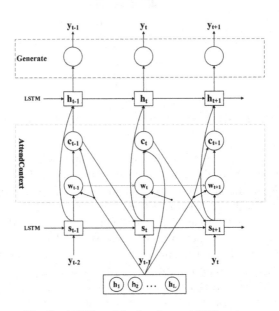

Fig. 3. ARST model of end-to-end TTS system.

This model uses a dual LSTM architecture and introduces a content-based attention mechanism, because compared with the content distance between frames, the semantic distance between words in high-dimensional space is relatively large, which makes the attention mechanism more distinctive. At the same time, to solve the problem that the information in the experiment is invalid due to the too large text size when ARST extracts the sentence level context information of the whole input text sequence, a window opening technique is introduced to help aligns text and acoustic tracks, which reduces computational complexity.

Although this model integrates text analysis and acoustic modeling framework to a certain extent, it does not achieve true end-to-end speech synthesis. The reasons are as follows:

First, its seq2seq model needs to learn alignment with the help of a pre-trained HMM aligner. So, it is hard to say how much alignment power seq2seq itself has learned. Secondly, in order to train the model, several techniques (such as windowing, input quantization, and sampling) are used, and the author points out that these techniques are harmful to synthetic prosody. Thirdly, it predicts the vocoder parameters as intermediate feature expression, so it needs a vocoder receiving parameter to synthesize speech. Fourthly, the training input of the model is phoneme data rather than characters, and due to the problem of error accumulation, only phrases with less than 8 Chinese characters can be synthesized. In addition, the convergence speed and stability of content-based attention mechanisms need to be improved. Zhang et al. [79] proposed a new forward attention method. Compared with the content-based attention mechanism, it can converge faster and obtain better acoustic feature representation.

Obviously, the performance of the end-to-end speech synthesis system based on ARST still can't compete with the baseline system, but this attempt shows that the research on a complete end-to-end TTS synthesizer is an exciting research field.

3.4   Speech Synthesis Based on WaveNet

WaveNet [80] is a power generation model of the original audio waveform (Fig. 1). Its ideas are borrowed from PixelRNN [81] or PixelCNN [82] model in the field of image generation. It is a complete probabilistic autoregressive model proposed by Deepmind in 2016. It can use all previously generated samples to predict the probability distribution of the current audio samples, and can directly model the waveform using the DNN model trained by real voice recording to generate a relatively strong voice (Fig. 4).

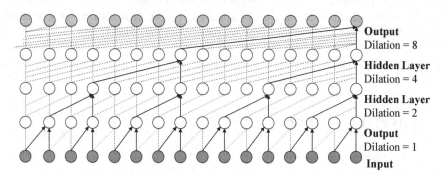

Fig. 4. Wave Net.

As an important part of WaveNet, extended causal convolution can ensure that WaveNet can only use 0 to $t-1$ sampling points when producing the t-th, and make the receptive field increase exponentially with the depth of the model, so that the model can learn large-span context information and establish dependence. In addition, in the actual observation, the model not only extracts the speech features from the audio but also extracts other features, such as the sound quality, the speaker's breath, and mouth movements.

The joint probability formula of the generated waveform X = {x1, x2,..., xT} is:

$$p(x) = \prod_{i=0}^{T-1} p(x_{i+1}|x_1, x_2, \ldots, x_i) \tag{1}$$

WaveNet based model consists of the training section and generation section. The training section records the real waveform from the human speaker as the input sequence. The generation section samples the network to generate synthetic speech.

When generating speech with a specified speaker or text type, it is often to introduce local and global conditions to control the synthesized content.

Although WaveNet can directly generate speech comparable to real human voice, it still has some shortcomings:

- The model is autoregressive and serial, so the value of each sampling point depends on all previous sampling points, resulting in limited speech synthesis speed.
- It is required to adjust the acoustic characteristics generated by the existing TTS front-end, so it is only used as a vocoder to synthesize speech, not an end-to-end model.
- The quality of WaveNet synthesized speech is limited by the performance of the front-end text analysis model.
- To solve these problems, DeepMind proposed an improved version of WaveNet based on the probability density distillation method, Parallel WaveNet [83].

Probability density distillation enables the student model to effectively learn the probability distribution of the teacher model. The algorithm uses the joint probability density of any two data points in the feature space to model the probability distribution of the distance between the two data points. Then by minimizing the difference in the joint density probability estimates between the teacher model and the student model, the probability distribution learning is achieved. The student network is a relatively small CNN, similar in structure to the original WaveNet (Fig. 1). But there is a key difference between the two: In the student network, each sample is generated independently, which means that from the first word to the last word, as well as the entire sentence in between, can be generated at the same time (Fig. 5).

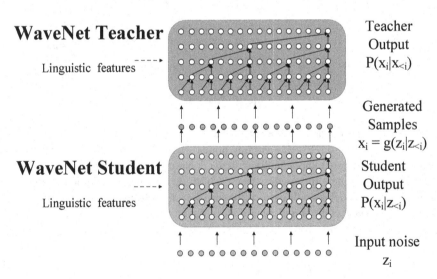

Fig. 5. Parallel WaveNet.

Therefore, parallel WaveNet can generate speech samples 20 times faster than the original WaveNet. However, there is still a problem. Whenever the model needs to be retrained, WaveNet teachers should be trained first, and then WaveNet students should be trained. In addition, the performance of students' WaveNet largely depends on the training of WaveNet teachers.

3.5 Speech Synthesis Based on CHAR2WAV

In 2017, Sotelo et al. proposed Char2Wav [84], This is an end-to-end TTS model that can be trained directly based on character data (Fig. 1). Char2Wav has two components: the reader at the front end and the neural vocoder at the back end. The reader consists of an encoder and a decoder. The encoder accepts phoneme or text as input, which is a BiRNN structure. The decoder is an RNN structure with an attention mechanism, used to generate acoustic features as the input of the vocoder. Neural vocoder refers to an extension of SampleRNN [85], which generates original waveform samples from the middle representation. As you can see, unlike the previous voice model, Char2Wav can generate voice directly from the text (Fig. 6).

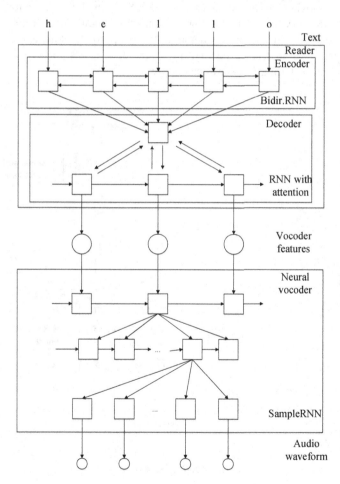

Fig. 6. Char2Wav model.

Char2Wav integrates front-end and back-end and learns the whole process end-to-end. This process eliminates the need for linguistic expertise, thus eliminating a major bottleneck in creating synthesizers for new languages. In theory, only relying on the model itself to learn from the data, the model can be applied to any language synthesis without knowing the corresponding linguistic knowledge.

But despite this, the model is still not fully end-to-end, mainly for two reasons. First, the output of Char2Wav is essentially the vocoder parameter, which is used as the input of SampleRNN [85] and outputs the synthesized speech, so the model itself is not end-to-end. Second, seq2seq and SampleRNN need to be pre-trained separately, instead of training from scratch under a unified framework, so they are not a complete unified model. But it is undeniable that the model laid a solid foundation for the later end-to-end model and became the starting point for further development.

3.6   Speech Synthesis Based on TACOTRON

In 2017, the Google team proposed Tacotron [86, 87], which is a recognized complete end-to-end speech synthesis model. For a given <text, audio> pair, it directly trains a TTS model which can reduce the demand for manpower feature engineering. Furthermore, since Tacotron is a model basing on character levels, theoretically nearly all types of speech including Mandarin can apply it.

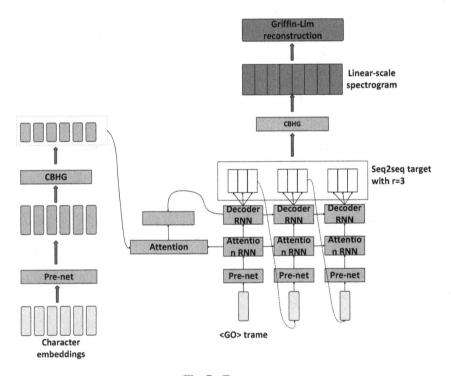

Fig. 7. Tacotron

Compared to previous research on end-to-end speech synthesis models, Tacotron's contribution is remarkable. It does not require a lot of manual engineering to extract language features or use complicated components like HMM aligners, it can directly predict the original spectrogram from the text and estimate the phase in the score map through iteration information to reconstruct the audio (Fig. 7) by using the Griffin-Lim algorithm [88]. You can train the entire model from scratch by simply performing a simple standardization process on the training text.

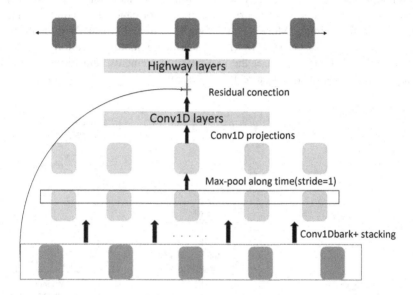

Fig. 8. CBUG Module.

In terms of model details, the core module of Tacotron is a CBHG module for extracting sequence feature expression (Fig. 8). This module uses non-causal convolution, batch normalization, residual connection, and maximum pooling with a step size of 1. The generalization ability of the model has been significantly improved. At the same time, CBHG is also used in the post-processing network of the model to learn how to predict the spectral amplitude, and finally synthesize audio through Griffin-Lim.

Tacotron is a complete end-to-end model, which has attracted a large number of researchers to conduct extensive research on it. Some studies implemented the open cloning of Tacotron to reproduce high-quality speech as clear as the original work. Kingma et al. [89] introduced a Variant Autoencoder (VAE) on the basis of Tacotron, so that the model can extract the potential features of the speaker's speech style to control the speech style of speech synthesis.

Since the Griffin-Lim waveform synthesizer used by Tacotron is already a very early model, the output voice sounds to contain traces of artificial synthesis. Therefore, some works began to combine Tacotron and WaveNet to improve the model. For example, Deepvoice2 [90] uses Tacotron as a front end to convert the input text into a linear spectrogram, and then uses the vocoder WaveNet to directly synthesize speech from the linear spectrogram. Besides, the author proposed the Tacotron 2 system in [91] (Fig. 9).

This method uses the Mel spectrogram generated by Tacotron as the input of the modified WaveNet to generate synthetic speech with naturalness close to human voice. It is worth mentioning that this model is more concise than Tacotron. It no longer uses the CBHG module and GRU cycle layer, but instead uses the ordinary LSTM and convolutional layer, which greatly simplifies the structure of the front-end model. At the same time, the WaveNet model is modified in Tacotron 2, which uses a smaller receptive field and a shallower network, and can still generate high-quality speech.

Although Tacotron 2 has achieved extraordinary results in end-to-end synthesized speech, the system requires very strict machine performance and requires numerous effective data for training. Moreover, the WaveNet model is usually difficult to synthesize audio at speeds over 16 kHz without sacrificing quality. Therefore, it is difficult for the synthesized audio to meet the real-time requirements, and further research is needed to deploy the system in a real-time system.

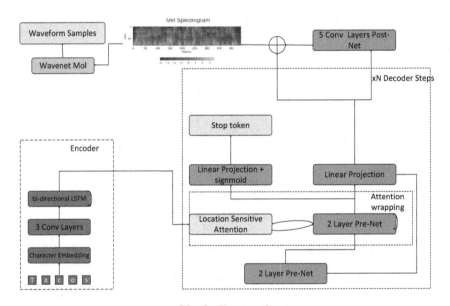

Fig. 9. Tacotron 2.

3.7 Speech Synthesis Based on Convolutional Neural Network (CNN)

End-to-end system based on Tacotron has realized gratifying performance, but it still has shortcomings. Large repetitive units in the Tacotron model cause the high cost of model training, and makes it highly dependent on high-performance machines. At the same time, these end-to-end systems are based on RNN, whose autoregressive characteristics leads to very slow training speed. Researchers have done a lot of work to solve these issues.

In 2018, Tachibana et al. [92] proposed a deep convolution (CNN) network with a guided attention mechanism, whose training speed is much faster than the most advanced neural system based on RNN. In the previous speech synthesis models, most models are based on RNN, only WaveNet is a full convolution structure. However, [92] is different from WaveNet. WaveNet uses full convolution structure as a vocoder or back-end, while [92] uses full convolution structure as front-end (and most back-end processing) of the synthetic spectrum while using a simple vocoder as back-end can obtain voice with equivalent quality. Since then, DeepVoice 3 [93] proposed a novel, fully convoluted character to spectrum graph architecture for speech synthesis (Fig. 10). The architecture can be fully parallel computing (but note that the model itself is not parallel), which lets the process of training much faster than the model based on RNN. The data set used by DeepVoice 3 is also very large, and there are also considerable requirements for traffic processing on the hardware. If the system is to be deployed in production and replace the existing TTS system at the same cost, further optimization is still needed.

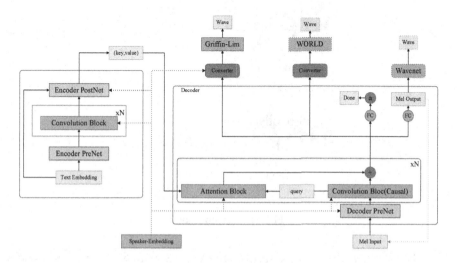

Fig. 10. DeepVoice 3 based on convolutional neural network.

Although the speech synthesis speed of DeepVoice 3 is much faster than that of RNN based model, the slow reasoning speed is still an urgent problem due to the autoregressive characteristics of WaveNet model. A lot of researches are improved by using parallel WaveNet, but the model must use the complex Monte Carlo method, which leads to the instability of actual training.

In 2019, Ping et al. [94] proposed the ClariNet model, which is a full convolution TTS model based on DeepVoice 3. It first proposed a neural architecture that synthesizes waveforms directly from text rather than a spectrum, which can quickly conduct end-to-end training from scratch. It is worth mentioning that all components in Clarinet directly feed their hidden representation to other components (Fig. 11). WaveNet no longer takes spectral features as input, but directly receives hidden representations learned from attention mechanism through intermediate processing, which is the key to successfully train from scratch. In addition, WaveNet is simplified in [94], and parallel computing to a certain extent is achieved without sacrificing sound quality.

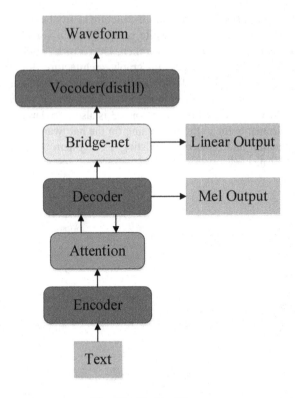

Fig. 11. Text-to-Wave.

Although CNN based models (such as DeepVoice 3, WaveNet) can be processed in parallel during training, they still need to be run in sequence when they are synthesized, because the input element at the next time step must be generated in advance. Ping et al. [95] then proposed the ParaNet model. The first fully parallel neural TTS system was realized by applying the parallel vocoder based on IAF and proposing a non-autoregressive text to spectrum model. Although the coder architecture of ParaNet is the same as the autoregressive model's, the decoder predicts the entire spectral sequence in a feedforward manner, which is based on the hidden representation. Therefore, the training and synthesis of the model can be carried out in parallel. At the same time, the author points out that the non-autoregressive ParaNet, whose synthesis speed is 46.7 times higher than that of DeepVoice 3, has fewer attention errors and the speech quality does not cause too much loss.

With the rapid development of the end-to-end TTS system, compared with the traditional TTS system, it has made great advantages. How to further optimize the front end to bridge the gap between text and voice, improve training efficiency, reduce training costs, and perform expressive speech synthesis in multi-scene and cross-language will become the focus of the next research.

3.8   Flow-Based Generative Network for Speech Synthesis

At present, most speech synthesis models based on the neural network are autoregressive, which means that the forecast of every sample point always relies on the previous prediction sample points, so the training is serial in nature. Therefore, parallel processors such as GPU or TPUs cannot be fully utilized. These models are usually difficult to synthesize audio at a speed of more than 16 kHz while ensuring the quality.

Due to the bottleneck in the synthesis speed of autoregressive models, many types of research on non-autoregressive models have been carried out. For example, Parallel WaveNet [83], Clarinet [94] and MCNN are used for spectrum inversion [96]. More than 500 kHz audio on GPU can be synthesized by these techniques, but autoregressive models are often easier to train and implement than these models. In addition, Parallel WaveNet and Clarinet need two networks, one for students and one for teachers. The basic student network of Parallel WaveNet and Clarinet uses Inverse Autoregressive Flow (IAF) [97]. Although the IAF network can be run in parallel when reasoning, the automatic recursion of the flow itself makes the IAF's calculation efficiency low. Teacher networks are used to train the student network to approach real possibilities by the works in order to get over that problem. These methods are difficult to reproduce and deploy because it is difficult to train these models greatly to convergence.

In 2019, a team of NVIDIA researchers developed a flow-based network called WaveGlow [98] because it combines ideas from Glow and WaveNet (Fig. 12). The network can generate high-quality speech from the Mel spectrum, and only uses a single network and possibility loss function for training. Although the model is simple, on NVIDIA V100 GPU, more than 500 kHz speech is synthesized: more than 25 times

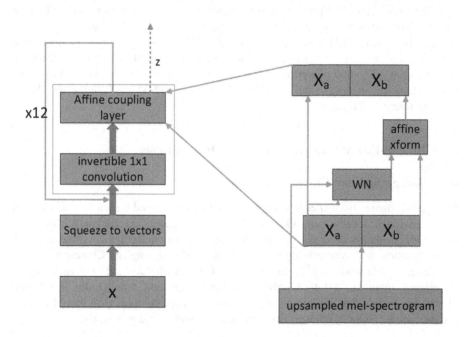

Fig. 12. WaveGlow.

higher than real-time. The average opinion score shows that trained on the same dataset, the audio quality it provides is as great as the best publicly available WaveNet implementation. It can be said that the research makes the process of speech synthesis deployed on a real-time system a great step forward.

However, compared with autoregressive and IAF models, flow-based models need deeper layers and more parameters. The parameters of WaveGlow are about 200M, while those of WaveNet and clarinet are only 1.7M, which makes the latter more popular in production deployment.

In 2020, Baidu Research Institute proposed WaveFlow [99]. It is a flow-based generative model like WaveGlow, which defines an invertible mapping between audio x and latent z and enables closed-form computation of the likelihood through the change of variable formula.

WaveFlow-based small-footprint model (5.91M parameters, this is 15 times smaller than the classic WaveGlow speech synthesis model) can achieve 40 times faster than real-time synthesis of high-fidelity speech on NVIDIA V100 GPU (MOS: 4.32). A unified view of likelihood-models for raw audio also provided by WaveFlow, which permits us to trade inference parallelism for model capacity explicitly and includes both WaveNet and WaveGlow as special cases. However, it should be noted that WaveFlow is a vocoder and cannot directly convert text to speech, so the effect of speech synthesis is still restricted to the front-end model.

Miao et al. [100] proposed a flow-based end-to-end natural TTS model, Flow-TTS, which is also the first TTS model which makes use of flow in spectrogram generation network. The experiment pointed out that the quality of synthesized speech is also better than Tacotron 2 and the non-autoregressive model FastSpeech, and the inference speed of Flow-TTS is 23 times that of the autoregressive model Tacotron 2, showing the power of the flow-base model in processing the original audio data ability.

Related research [101] also proposed Glow-TTS, these Flow-base models show extremely fast speech synthesis speed (Glow-TTS can generate one minute of speech end-to-end in 1.5 s) and powerful speech Generating ability. The application of Flow-base technology in fields such as Voice Conversion and Voice Cloning will be an exciting research direction.

4   Chinese-Based End-to-End Speech Synthesis

4.1   Background and Current Situation

Since 2017, the study of speech synthesis based on end-to-end has entered a period of ultra-high-speed development. Google, Baidu, Nvidia, and other research institutions have been constantly bringing forth the new, striving for perfection in synthesis speed, style migration, and synthesis naturalness. Compared with English, Chinese has many difficulties in text analysis [19]. For example, Chinese characters do not express pronunciation; there are a lot of polysyllabic characters and tone sandhi in Chinese characters. The rhythm of Chinese pronunciation is more complex than that of English pronunciation. There is no clear division between words and words, etc.

At present, the back-end models of the neural vocoder, such as WaveNet [80], WaveRNN [102], and WaveGlow [98], can hardly be distinguished from the real human voice. However, compared with the back-end vocoder model, the front-end text processing module has made little progress. The TTS front-end is designed to extract various language and phonetic features from the original text to enchant the synthesized speech's clarity and naturalness. How to deal with the alignment between text and speech and how to extract complete and accurate acoustic features are the main work of the front-end model, which directly influences the performance of the end-to-end TTS system. For the English based TTS system, the advanced front-end model has been able to extract the accurate acoustic representation from the original text with high efficiency and low complexity. However, for the TTS system of Mandarin, most of the front-end models are unable to extract the acoustic features covering the diversity of Mandarin texts from the limited training data set.

The front end of the Chinese TTS system contains a series of Natural Language Processing (NLP) blocks, including text normalization (TN) [103], Chinese word segmentation (CWS) [104], part of speech tagging(POS) [105], polyphonic disambiguation (PPD) [106], and prosodic structure (PS) prediction [107]. We will give a brief introduction to these main modules:

- **CWS and POS tagging.** Mandarin is a character-based language which is different from English, and there are no spaces between words. So, you need to use Chinese Word Segmentation to extract word boundaries from the original text. The key to construction is accurate word boundaries. Part Of Speech tagging plays an significant role in disambiguating polyphonic speech, especially for Mandarin with many polyphonic characters.

- **Text Normalization.** TN is the process which is changing non-standard characters into clearly pronounced spoken characters. Usually, a rule-based method (using regular expression matching) is used to perform this conversion.

- **Polyphonic Disambiguation.** The G2P conversion of Chinese characters mainly focuses on the ambiguity of polyphonic characters. About a thousand characters in Chinese text are polyphonic, so polyphonic disambiguation is very important for Mandarin TTS, because different pronunciation always leads to different meanings of sentences. Multi-tone disambiguation is usually classified as a classification problem. Therefore, it is necessary to learn a classifier for each character to predict the correct pronunciation in a given context.

- **Prosodic Structure Prediction.** The typical prosodic structure of the Mandarin TTS system is usually divided into three levels, including Prosodic Words (PW), Prosodic Phrases (PP), and Intonation Phrases (IP). These three prosody levels reflect three different pause times in natural speech signals. The task of prosody structure prediction is usually formulated as a problem of sequence labeling [108]. In the input text sequence, for each word or character, the prosodic boundary label sequence of Break (B) or Not Break (NB) should be predicted (Fig. 13).

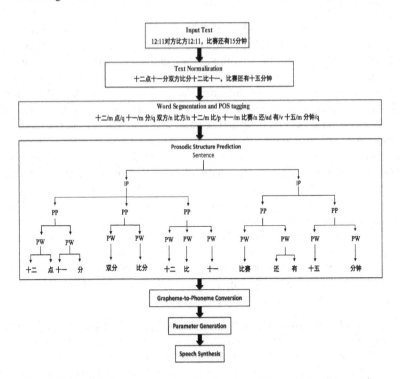

Fig. 13. A typical text processing pipeline from Mandarin text to speech.

At present, RNN-based seq2seq models have been greatly applied to speech synthesis and NLP tasks, but these models usually a huge-scale number of training data is required to realize good performance. Especially for input with complex acoustic features such as Mandarin characters, the problem of label sparseness is serious, and it is difficult to extract accurate and complete acoustic features from a front-end model based entirely on neural networks. Most of the existing models require manual annotation and training based on rules [109]. With the increasing development of neural network models today, let the front-end model learn more linguistic knowledge by itself, reduce human intervention, and be able to train a complete end-to-end speech synthesis model from scratch, which is an inevitable challenge. Given the complexity and particularity of Mandarin texts, researchers have conducted many studies on building a Mandarin end-to-end TTS system, which we will introduce in detail in the next section.

4.2 Related Research

Preliminary Work. ARST [78] is the first Mandarin TTS system to work end-to-end, and it is also the first to use the seq2seq method with an attention mechanism. The model integrates text analysis and acoustic modeling framework to a certain extent, bypassing the limitation of linguistic knowledge, and let the model automatically learn the alignment.

However, this model has many limitations and is not a true model of end-to-end. In actual training, a pre-trained HMM aligner is needed by the model to help the seq2seq model learn how to align, and it is difficult to determine how much alignment the seq2seq itself has learned [86]. At the same time, the model has the problem of error accumulation, and can only synthesize phrases with less than 8 Mandarin characters, and the final synthesized speech is also a certain gap with the baseline system. But [78] is the first exploration of end-to-end Mandarin TTS, which has important reference value for future research. Besides, Zhang et al. [79] proposed a new forward attention method to obtain a content-based attention mechanism. This method is suitable for the Mandarin TTS system and can achieve faster convergence speed and faster convergence than the content-based attention model in ARST. Better acoustic characteristics and naturalness of synthesized speech.

In 2019, the study [66] assessed the cognition of tone-3 sandhi and tonal republic in Mandarin acquired by advanced TTS models. Tone sandhi is a forced classification change of tone type which adjacent tone causes. The tone-3 sandhi is the most common example which is the change from tone-3 to tone-2 when a tone-3 character is followed by another tone-3 character. The current advanced TTS system Tacotron 2 + Wave-Glow was used to train standard Mandarin and test and score synthesized speech. Although the Tacotron 2 model can generate highly natural speech, it still cannot effectively deal with the tonality classification in Mandarin, which was shown by the experimental results. Especially in long sentences, the model changes the tone at incorrect syntactic boundaries, resulting in tone errors.

It can be seen from the above studies that the advanced TTS model cannot completely acquire the basic language rules in the present methods based on data-driven, and the rules learned by the neural network cannot be as complete and clear as those summarized in linguistics. Especially for languages with complex linguistic knowledge such as Chinese-Mandarin, the most powerful neural network cannot fully obtain all linguistic rules. Based on this situation, how to simultaneously use the advantages of data-driven and rule-based methods in the Mandarin TTS system to build a unified Mandarin end-to-end TTS system has become an important research direction. Next, the article will present the unified Mandarin TTS system.

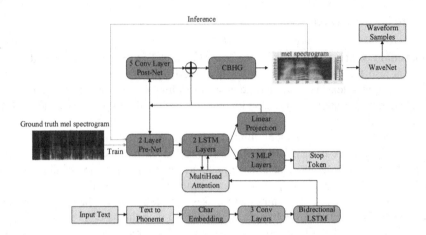

Fig. 14. Mandarin end-to-end TTS solution

Unified Model. Wang et al. [109] proposed a Chinese speech synthesis model based on Tacotron framework (Fig. 14). In this model, multi attention is used to perform attention operation through parameter matrix mapping, and then multiple sub attention results are spliced together, which is similar to the process of convolution check-in CNN to extract features from an image, which can effectively obtain the information in the sequence so that the cohesion between words and the prosodic change of the whole sentence is closer to the human voice when the decoder predicts the audio.

This project aims at the situation that English can only be synthesized end-to-end in the industry, and has achieved gratifying results. However, this scheme does not solve the problem of Chinese polyphone recognition completely, and synthetic speech cannot completely avoid the noise, and there are unreasonable pauses in the speech. The CBHG module and Grifin-Lim vocoder used in the model are no longer suitable for the advanced TTS system, and the model still needs further improvement.

Similar studies include [110], DOP-Tacotron, which is an end-to-end Mandarin TTS system Tacotron framework based that can be quickly trained. The system replaces the original CBUG module with the DOP module, reducing the parameters to 35.5% of the original model, greatly reducing the training time. However, the voice quality generated by this model (MOS is 3.683) is still far behind the real human voice. The fully data-driven model cannot obtain all the characteristic information of the Chinese voice well. How to build advanced encoders and decoders to better handle the complex information of Chinese speech is an important research direction.

A knowledge-based language coder (Fig. 15) is proposed in [111] and applied to a character-based end-to-end Mandarin TTS system. The model is based on the architecture of Tacotron 2 but provides more information than the encoder in Tacotron 2. The model is developed with a multi-task learning structure, which can provide powerful language coding functions and learn rich language knowledge from original Chinese characters. According to the particularity of Mandarin, the model designs several sub-tasks:

- It takes character to phoneme (G2P) as the first subtask of training knowledge language coder, which is used to alleviate syllable pronunciation errors in synthetic speech.
- Use word tokenization as a second subtask to reduce word tokenization errors. It predicts the BMES (start, middle, end, single element) on each character tag.
- To improve the performance of the first two subtasks and enrich the semantic knowledge in language coding, POS tags and word embedding are also part of the multi-task learning framework. The POS tag subtask predicts POS tags for input characters that are copied from the corresponding POS tags. The word embedding subtask predicts the word vectors of input characters, which are also copied from the corresponding word vectors.

The knowledge-based language coder takes Chinese character sequence as input to generate language code, and the multi-task decoder uses language code as input to predict subtasks. Compared with the most advanced TTS method, the system can greatly alleviate syllable pronunciation errors and word marking errors, and improve the naturalness and clarity of synthesized speech, which was shown by the experimental results. It is easy to see that the system combines the rule-based and data-driven methods well, and achieves strong language coding performance and gratifying achievements. However, there are still many problems in the framework, which are worth investigating. The proposed knowledge-based language coder contains many early design components that are mature for improvement. TTS will be the next step in the development of TTS.

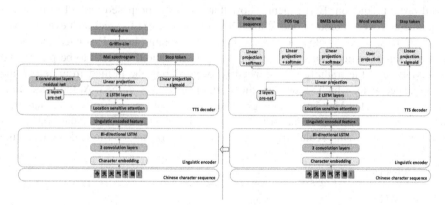

Fig. 15. (Left picture) The architecture of an end-to-end TTS system based on Chinese characters, (right picture) the architecture of training a knowledge-based language encoder. After training, the knowledge-based language encoder will be transferred to the end-to-end TTS system based on Chinese characters.

Due to the complexity of Mandarin language knowledge, there is a huge demand for the front-end of the TTS system. At present, advanced systems adopt multi-task learning to solve the problem of feature extraction and coding of Mandarin text. Data baker studies the Mandarin boundary prediction based on multi-task learning [112] and proposes to use the multi-task learning framework (MTL) to optimize the three independent tasks of Mandarin boundary prediction. The author found that after the introduction of the multi-task learning framework, the model size of the Mandarin boundary prediction model was reduced by nearly half, and the overall prediction performance was improved by 0.8%. This shows that the MTL model has great advantages in engineering applications (memory consumption, CPU resource consumption, etc.).

Zou et al. [113] proposes that since the multi-task learning method cannot completely solve the pronunciation problem, a pre-trained dictionary network (Fig. 16) was introduced by the proposed model to improve pronunciation through joint training. When the confidence of Pinyin is not high enough, Pinyin embedding will be replaced by dictionary embedding. The introduction of dictionary network corrects the pronunciation of multi tone characters and uncommon characters in Chinese to a certain extent, which provides a new idea for the research of the Chinese TTS system. However, due to the introduction of the dictionary network, there is a significant vector space mismatch between TTS encoder output and dictionary encoder output in this model. How to deal with the matching problem of joint training and build a unified front-end model will be a great challenge.

A unified front-end model of the Mandarin TTS system is proposed in [114] to significantly simplify the workflow of Mandarin TTS system. In the framework of encoder and decoder, the proposed model directly generates three linguistic features, which are voice, tone, and order from the input of original text, as the input of back-end vocoder, and extracts the potential representation of CWS and POS through the auxiliary module (Fig. 17) simultaneously. Compared with the front-end pipeline, this front-end model achieves excellent performance in multi-tone disambiguation and word order prediction. Experiments show that when the proposed unified front end is implemented with Tacotron and WaveRNN, the synthesized speech achieves a MOS score of 4.38, which is close to the real human recording (4.49). However, the model still has some shortcomings, such as the auxiliary module that needs to be pre-trained separately, and the training data is needed to pre debug the unified front-end in the actual experiment, which shows that the model is not really unified. At the same time, for the complicated Mandarin language features, the model only extracts three features, which are tone, tone color, and order, as the back-end input. Whether the system has good robustness and scalability is questionable. For an end-to-end system, the

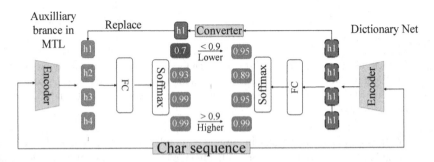

Fig. 16. Dictionary guidance and error correction mechanism. The auxiliary branches in multi task learning is shown on the left. On the right is a pre trained dictionary network that maps character sequences to phonetic sequences. Owing to the confidence level of 0.7 which is below the threshold, the 'blue' hidden representation is replaced by the 'purple' hidden representation.

intermediate process should be transparent to the operator. That is to say, the acoustic features extracted from the text by the front-end model should be unrestricted, and all the acoustic features can be learned and aligned by the model itself. Finally, the hidden form learned by the front-end model is passed to the back-end synthetic speech. Therefore, it is against the end-to-end principle to extract three linguistic features from the front-end.

From the above research findings, for the TTS system of Mandarin, the accuracy of previous text standardization is closely related to the quality and accuracy of the acoustic features extracted from the text by the front-end model. The quality of text normalization directly affects the alignment and convergence speed of front-end model training. Especially for Mandarin, which has almost no acoustic information, the early standardization work is particularly important. Given the particularity of Mandarin text, research [115] proposes a hybrid text normalization system (Fig. 18). The system has the advantages of text preprocessing based on rule model and neural network model at the same time and has realized remarkable results in the standardization of Mandarin text. Compared with the system based on rule, the proposed model improves the

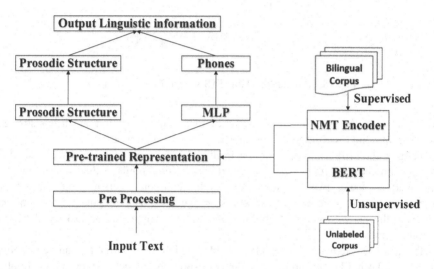

Fig. 17. Architecture of the front-end using pre training text representation.

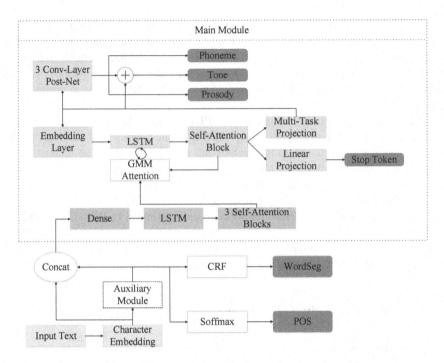

Fig. 18. Unified Mandarin TTS system front - end model.

performance of the system and the accuracy of text normalization and it has stronger expansibility and great improvement potential.at the same time.

Yang et al. [116] proposed a similar front-end input preprocessing model (Fig. 19). The performance and robustness of the text processing module of the front-end will be improved by using two encoders with multi attention mechanism to extract the potential semantic representation of words or characters as the input of TTS front-end task, and the performance of ambiguity and word order prediction tasks will be significantly improved.

There are also relevant studies [16, 17, 117] which improve the text analysis ability of the Mandarin TTS system through the corresponding model algorithm and simplify the text analysis front end of the Mandarin TTS system. It can be seen that most of the current research is focused on the construction of the front-end model of the Mandarin TTS system. How to obtain accurate acoustic information from Mandarin characters with almost no acoustic information is challenging research work. After exploration, the hybrid system based on rules and the neural network has gradually become an important method to deal with TTS tasks in Mandarin.

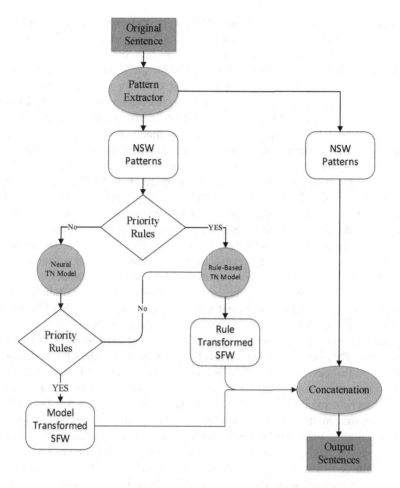

Fig. 19. Flow chart of mixed text normalization system.

5   Discussion

5.1   Summary

The earliest Mandarin speech synthesis system was based on parameters. However, due to the poor text analysis ability of the synthesizer at that time, the generated speech was very mechanical and could not generate the appropriate prosodic structure. After entering the 20th century, the serial speech synthesis system based on waveform or corpus has become the most advanced Mandarin speech synthesis system because of its high naturalness. With the extensive application of synthetic speech technology in production and life, the construction of an expressive speech synthesis system full of rhythm and emotion has become another goal of speech synthesis. For a corpus-based speech synthesis system, the quality and expressiveness of it is completely restricted by corpus. At this time, the statistical parametric speech synthesis (SPSS) is favored by researchers, since it can easily modify the prosodic parameters of the synthesized speech to overcome the shortcomings of the traditional model which is difficult to change the way of the speaker, and can synthesize high-quality speech.

The early SPSS system is mainly based on Hidden Markov Model (HMM), but the HMM based model is insufficient in modeling the long-term relevance of speech context, and the synthesized speech is usually too smooth and lacks rhythm. Especially for Mandarin, which has complex text information and highly depends on context information, the HMM-based speech synthesis model cannot achieve satisfactory performance, so an advanced Mandarin speech synthesis system is constructed. Accompanied by the deep learning developed rapidly in the field of speech synthesis, a Mandarin speech synthesis system of deep learning has been developed by researchers. The speech synthesized by these models has very high speech quality and can synthesize expressive speech with complex emotions. However, the construction of these models often depends on a lot of professional knowledge in the field of linguistics, which is not friendly to the researchers of deep learning. Moreover, the grammatical rules and semantic features of Mandarin are very complicated, and a large number of independent components need to be trained independently to extract complex text features. Not only a great deal of manpower and material resources will be cost by that but also the errors of each component will be compounded, which will reduce the robustness of the model and affect the synthesized speech's quality.

Based on the end-to-end speech synthesis method, a unified speech synthesis model is proposed. The model can learn speech synthesis from character text from the beginning. In that case, researchers do not need to master a lot of linguistic knowledge and hand over the complex semantic coding to the machine. With the application of attention mechanism in speech synthesis and the models based on RNN and CNN have been widely studied, the end-to-end model has been able to produce speech comparable to the real human voice in the English synthesis system, and has become the most advanced speech synthesis system. But for Mandarin, the end-to-end model is far from perfect. Chinese is a hieroglyphic character. Compared with phonetic characters like English, it is difficult to achieve text to speech alignment in an end-to-end system. Most of the front-end models cannot extract the acoustic features covering the diversity of Chinese text from limited data sets. In last several years, most of the research is based on the construction of the advanced front-end model of the Mandarin speech synthesis system. How to effectively standardize the Mandarin text, significantly encode a large number of semantic information and extract complete high-quality acoustic features is an important research direction. At the same time, the hybrid system based on rule and neural network provides a new important clue to solving this problem.

5.2   Research Direction

Although the end-to-end model has achieved extraordinary results, it is far from perfect. The front-end model based on deep learning has strong learning and expression ability, but there are still some problems. For example, the prediction of the prosody structure is unstable and requires a huge data set; the model debugging is troublesome, because it completely relies on the self-learning ability of the neural network, so errors are difficult to locate. Next, we will discuss some research directions about end-to-end systems and Mandarin speech synthesis:

- **Better front-end text analysis and processing.** Since researchers proposed the end-to-end TTS model, the back-end vocoder model has developed rapidly and has reached the most advanced performance [83, 98]. However, the front-end text feature analysis model progresses relatively slowly. At present, the fully convolutional front-end model based on CNN has achieved gratifying results in the TTS field, especially the efficiency of the parallel architecture is much higher than that of the traditional RNN structure. However, the CNN model's ability to capture long-distance features of the text is quite lacking compared with the traditional RNN model [118]. The Google team proposed the Transformer front-end feature extraction model in machine translation research [119], which has powerful parallel capabilities and excellent long-distance feature capture capabilities, and the extraction capabilities of semantic features also exceed the RNN model and CNN model [118]. At present, the three front-end models of RNN/CNN/Transformer have become a hot topic in speech synthesis research [120, 121]. The research how to further integrate the advantages of various models, improve model performance and training efficiency, reduce training costs, and integrate with industrial production will be major in this field.

- **Application of Generative Adversative Nets.** Recently, Generative Adversative Nets has achieved great success in image generation, audio generation, and other fields [122, 123]. It will also be good research to apply the idea of Generative Adversative Nets to an end-to-end TTS synthesis system in future.

- **Improve training efficiency and reduce training costs.** The current advanced CNN-based end-to-end speech synthesis models show wonderful results, but a huge number of high-quality <text, speech> data setting for training, which are high-cost and time-consuming to train, is required by them usually. Although the advanced end-to-end model has obtained excellent parallel processing capabilities, it has strict requirements on machine performance and is very unfriendly to researchers who do not have high-performance machines and high-quality data sets. At the same time, if it is to be deployed in production and life in real-time, the model needs to continue to be optimized to reduce costs. The hybrid system that combines artificial design rules and neural network self-learning provides useful clues to reduce data sets and reduce training costs. What kind of rules can be combined with neural networks to build efficient and low-cost models will be a new research idea.

- **More applications for voice-related scenarios.** In addition to text synthesis speech synthesis systems, applications in other speech scenarios such as machine translation, cross-language synthesis, and multi-speaker speech synthesis [18] are also good research directions.

- **The combination of software and hardware realizes deep parallelization.** The end-to-end deep neural network model requires a lot of data operations, and parallelization is an indispensable part of improving network efficiency. At present, the advanced end-to-end model has been parallelized at the software level. The design and production of targeted high-performance hardware that meets the needs of deep neural networks is also an important topic for future research.

- **Mandarin optimization.** For Mandarin, it is difficult to achieve excellent synthesized speech quality based on data-driven learning. Because of the lack of phonetics of characters, the neural model cannot learn accurate and effective character-to-speech alignment. Therefore, for the synthesis of Mandarin, based on certain rules is necessary at present, but how to effectively combine the rules in the neural model is also a challenging task.
- **More advanced neural network model to obtain more powerful learning ability.** For modern Chinese, there is a certain relationship between pronunciation and the characters themselves. Just as native Chinese speakers, the pronunciation of the corresponding characters is based on the underlying acoustic characteristics of the characters to a certain extent. Accompanied by the deep neural networks developed rapidly, models with more powerful learning capabilities may solve the current system performance bottlenecks. Complete data-based end-to-end Mandarin synthesis based on attention will also be an important research direction.

6   Conclusions

This article systematically reviews the development of Chinese-Mandarin speech synthesis research, compares the advantages and disadvantages of different methods, focuses on the research of end-to-end technology, and explored future research directions to contribute to the development of speech synthesis. It provides systematic research ideas and a relatively complete research context for the research of Chinese-Mandarin speech synthesis and related speech synthesis fields, and provides a better foundation for further research.

References

1. Parlikar, A., Black, A.W.: Data-driven phrasing for speech synthesis in low-resource languages. In: Proceedings of 2012 IEEE International Conference on Acoustics, Speech and Signal Processing (ICASSP), pp. 4013–4016. IEEE (2012)
2. Takamichi, S., Toda, T., Shiga, Y., Sakti, S., Neubig, G., Nakamura, S.: Improvements to HMM-based speech synthesis based on parameter generation with rich context models. In: Proceedings of the INTERSPEECH, pp. 364–368 (2013)
3. Chen, L., Gales, M.J.F., Braunschweiler, N., Akamine, M., Knill, K.: Integrated automatic expression prediction and speech synthesis from text. In: Proceedings of 2013 IEEE International Conference on Acoustics, Speech and Signal Processing (ICASSP), pp. 7977–7981. IEEE (2013)
4. Bigorgne, D., et al.: Multilingual PSOLA text-to-speech system. In: Proceedings of 1993 IEEE International Conference on Acoustics, Speech, and Signal Processing (ICASSP), pp. 187–190. IEEE (1993)
5. Portele, T., Steffan, B., Preuß, R., Sendlmeier, W.F., Hess, W.: HADIFIX-a speech synthesis system for German. In: Proceedings of the Second International Conference on Spoken Language Processing (ICSLP'92), pp. 1227–1230 (1992)

6. Hunt, A.J., Black, A.W.: Unit selection in a concatenative speech synthesis system using a large speech database. In: Proceedings of 1996 IEEE International Conference on Acoustics, Speech, and Signal Processing Conference Proceedings (ICASSP), pp. 373–376. IEEE (1996)
7. Sagisaka, Y., Kaiki, N., Iwahashi, N., Mimura, K.: ATR μ-talk speech synthesis system. In: Proceedings of the Second International Conference on Spoken Language Processing (ICSLP'92), pp. 483–486 (1992)
8. Tao, J., Zhao, S., Cai, L.: Research on Chinese speech synthesis system based on statistical prosody model. J. Chin. Inf. Process. **16**(1), 1–6 (2002). https://doi.org/10.3969/j.issn.1003-0077.2002.01.001
9. Zhang, D., Chen, Z., Huang, H.: Design and implementation of mapping address algorithm in Chinese text-to-speech system. J. Softw. **13**(1), 105–110 (2002)
10. Zhang, W., Wu, X., Zhao, Z., Wang, R.: A method of cutting voice database based on virtual variable length. J. Softw. **17**(05), 983–990 (2006)
11. Dong, M., Lua, K.T.: Using prosody database in Chinese speech synthesis. In: Proceedings of the Interspeech, pp. 243–246 (2000)
12. Chou, F., Tseng, C., Lee, L.: A set of corpus-based text-to-speech synthesis technologies for Mandarin Chinese. IEEE Trans. Speech Audio Process. **10**(7), 481–494 (2002). https://doi.org/10.1109/TSA.2002.803437
13. Li, Y., Tao, J., Zhang, M., Pan, S., Xu, X.: Text-based unstressed syllable prediction in Mandarin. In: Proceedings of the Interspeech, pp. 1752–1755 (2010)
14. Li, Y., Tao, J., Xu, X.: Hierarchical stress modeling in Mandarin text-to-speech. In: Proceedings of the Interspeech, pp. 2013–2016 (2011)
15. Yang, C., Ling, Z., Dai, L.: Unsupervised prosodic phrase boundary labeling of Mandarin speech synthesis database using context-dependent HMM. In: Proceedings of the ICASSP 2013, pp. 6875–6879. IEEE (2013)
16. Yang, F., Yang, S., Zhu, P., Yan, P., Xie, L.: Improving Mandarin end-to-end speech synthesis by self-attention and learnable Gaussian bias. In: Proceedings of 2019 IEEE Automatic Speech Recognition and Understanding Workshop (ASRU), pp. 208–213. IEEE (2019)
17. Zhang, C., Zhang, S., Zhong, H.: A prosodic Mandarin text-to-speech system based on Tacotron. In: Proceedings of 2019 Asia-Pacific Signal and Information Processing Association Annual Summit and Conference (APSIPA ASC), pp. 165–169. IEEE (2019)
18. Xiao, Y., He, L., Ming, H., Soong, F.K.: Improving prosody with linguistic and bert derived features in multi-speaker based Mandarin Chinese neural TTS. In: Proceedings of the ICASSP 2020 - 2020 IEEE International Conference on Acoustics, Speech and Signal Processing (ICASSP), IEEE, pp. 6704–6708 (2020)
19. Lu, Y., Dong, M., Chen, Y.: Implementing prosodic phrasing in chinese end-to-end speech synthesis. In: Proceedings of the ICASSP 2019 - 2019 IEEE International Conference on Acoustics, Speech and Signal Processing, pp. 7050–7054. IEEE (2019)
20. Lei, S., Lee, L.: Digital synthesis of mandarin speech using its special characteristics. J. Chin. Inst. Eng. **6**(2), 107–115 (1983). https://doi.org/10.1080/02533839.1983.9676732
21. Huang, T., Wang, C., Pao, Y.: A Chinese text-to-speech synthesis system based on an initial-final model. Comput. Process. Chin. Orient. Lang. **1**(1), 59–70 (1983)
22. Zhou, K., Cole, T.: A chip designed for Chinese text-to-speech synthesis. J. Electr. Electron. Eng. Aust. **4**(4), 314–318 (1984)
23. Zhou, K.: A Chinese text-to-speech synthesis system using the logarithmic magnitude filter. J. Electr. Electron. Eng. Aust. **6**(4), 270–274 (1986)

24. Qin, D., Hu, N.C.: A new method of synthetic Chinese speech on a unlimited vocabulary. In: Cybernetics and Systems'88, Proceedings of the Ninth European Meeting on Cybernetics and Sytems Research, pp. 1223–1230 (1988)
25. Shi, B., Lu, S.: A Chinese speech synthesis-by-rule system. In: Speech, Hearing and Language: Work in Progress, U.C.L. Number 3, pp. 219–236. University College London (1989)
26. Cai, L., Liu, H., Zhou, Q.: Design and achievement of a Chinese text-to-speech system under windows. Microcomputer **3** (1995)
27. Chu, M., Lu, S.: High intelligibility and naturalness Chinese TTS system and prosodic rules. In: Proceedings of the XIII International Congress of Phonetic Sciences, Stockholm, pp. 334–337 (1995)
28. Hwang, S., Chen, S., Wang, Y.: A Mandarin text-to-speech system. In: Proceedings of the ICSLP 96, pp. 1421–1424. IEEE (1996)
29. Suen, C.: Computer synthesis of Mandarin. In: Proceedings of the IEEE International Conference on Acoustics, Speech, and Signal Processing Conference Proceedings (ICASSP), pp. 698–700. IEEE (1976)
30. Shih, C., Sproat, R.: Issues in text-to-speech conversion for Mandarin. Int. J. Comput. Linguist. Chin. Lang. Process. **1**, 37–86 (1996)
31. Chou, F., Tseng, C.: Corpus-based Mandarin speech synthesis with contextual syllabic units based on phonetic properties. In: Proceedings of the IEEE International Conference on Acoustics, Speech and Signal Processing (ICASSP), pp. 893–896. IEEE (1998)
32. Tseng, S.: Spontaneous Mandarin production: results of a corpus-based study. In: Proceedings of the International Symposium on Chinese Spoken Language Processing, pp. 29–32. IEEE (2004)
33. Gu, H., Wang, K.: An acoustic and articulatory knowledge integrated method for improving synthetic Mandarin speech's fluency. In: Proceedings of the International Symposium on Chinese Spoken Language Processing, pp. 205–208. IEEE (2004)
34. Xu, J., Fu, G., Li, H.: Grapheme-to-phoneme conversion for Chinese text-to-speech. In: Proceedings of the International Conference on Spoken Language Processing (2004)
35. Zhang, J.T.F.L., Jia, H.: Design of speech corpus for mandarin text to speech. In: Proceedings of the Blizzard Challenge 2008 Workshop (2008)
36. Cai, L., Cui, D., Cai, R.: TH-CoSS, a Mandarin speech corpus for TTS. J. Chin. Inf. Process. **21**(2), 94–99 (2007)
37. Tokuda, K., Yoshimura, T., Masuko, T., Kobayashi, T., Kitamura, T.: Speech parameter generation algorithms for HMM-based speech synthesis. In: Proceedings of 2000 IEEE International Conference on Acoustics, Speech, and Signal Processing. Proceedings (Cat. No. 00CH37100), pp. 1315–1318. IEEE (2000)
38. Tokuda, K., Masuko, T., Miyazaki, N., Kobayashi, T.: Multi-space probability distribution HMM. IEICE Trans. Inf. Syst. **85**(3), 455–464 (2002)
39. Wang, M., Wen, M., Saito, D., Hirose, K., Minematsu, N.: Improved generation of prosodic features in HMM-based Mandarin speech synthesis. In: Proceedings of the Seventh ISCA Tutorial and Research Workshop on Speech Synthesis (SSW7-2010) (2010)
40. Yamagishi, J., Masuko, T., Kobayashi, T.: HMM-based expressive speech synthesis-towards TTS with arbitrary speaking styles and emotions. In: Proceedings of the Special Workshop in Maui (SWIM) (2004)
41. Tang, H., Zhou, X., Odisio, M., Hasegawa-Johnson, M., Huang, T.S.: Two-stage prosody prediction for emotional text-to-speech synthesis. In: Proceedings of the Interspeech, pp. 2138–2141 (2008)
42. Inanoglu, Z., Young, S.: Data-driven emotion conversion in spoken English. Speech Commun. **51**(3), 268–283 (2009)

43. Wu, Y., Kawai, H., Ni, J., Wang, R.: Discriminative training and explicit duration modeling for HMM-based automatic segmentation. Speech Commun. **47**(4), 397–410 (2005). https://doi.org/10.1016/j.specom.2005.03.016

44. Yu, K., Mairesse, F., Young, S.: Word-level emphasis modelling in HMM-based speech synthesis. In: Proceedings of the ICASSP, pp. 4238–4241. IEEE (2010)

45. Badino, L., Andersson, J.S., Yamagishi, J., Clark, R.A.: Identification of contrast and its emphatic realization in HMM-based speech synthesis. In: Proceedings of the INTER-SPEECH, pp. 520–523 (2009)

46. Turk, O., Schroder, M.: Evaluation of expressive speech synthesis with voice conversion and copy resynthesis techniques. IEEE Trans. Audio Speech Lang. Process. **18**(5), 965–973 (2010). https://doi.org/10.1109/TASL.2010.2041113

47. Zhang, J., Hirose, K.: Tone nucleus modeling for Chinese lexical tone recognition. Speech Commun. **42**(3–4), 447–466 (2004)

48. Sun, Q., Hirose, K., Gu, W., Minematsu, N.: Generation of fundamental frequency contours for Mandarin speech synthesis based on tone nucleus model. In: Proceedings of the Eurospeech, pp. 3265–3268 (2005)

49. Wen, M., Wang, M., Hirose, K., Minematsu, N.: Prosody conversion for emotional Mandarin speech synthesis using the tone nucleus model. In: Proceedings of the Twelfth Annual Conference of the International Speech Communication Association (2011)

50. Li, Y., Pan, S., Tao, J.: HMM-based speech synthesis with a flexible Mandarin stress adaptation model. In: IEEE 10th International Conference on Signal Processing Proceedings, pp. 625–628. IEEE (2010)

51. Yang, C., Ling, Z., Lu, H., Guo, W., Dai, L.: Automatic phrase boundary labeling for Mandarin TTS corpus using context-dependent HMM. In: Proceedings of 2010 7th International Symposium on Chinese Spoken Language Processing, pp. 374–377. IEEE (2010)

52. Shao, Y.Q., Sui, Z.F., Han, J.Q., Wu, Y.F.: A study on Chinese prosodic hierarchy prediction based on dependency grammar analysis. J. Chin. Inf. Process. **22**(2), 116–123 (2008)

53. Li, J., Hu, G., Wang, R.: Chinese prosody phrase break prediction based on maximum entropy model. In: Proceedings of the INTERSPEECH, pp. 729–732 (2004)

54. Hsia, C., Wu, C., Wu, J.: Exploiting prosody hierarchy and dynamic features for pitch modeling and generation in HMM-based speech synthesis. IEEE Trans. Audio Speech Lang. Process. **18**(8), 1994–2003 (2010). https://doi.org/10.1109/TASL.2010.2040791

55. Yu, Y., Li, D., Wu, X.: Prosodic modeling with rich syntactic context in HMM-based Mandarin speech synthesis. In: Proceedings of 2013 IEEE China Summit and International Conference on Signal and Information Processing, pp. 132–136. IEEE (2013)

56. Gao, L., Ling, Z., Chen, L., Dai, L.: Improving F0 prediction using bidirectional associative memories and syllable-level F0 features for HMM-based Mandarin speech synthesis. In: Proceedings of the 9th International Symposium on Chinese Spoken Language Processing, pp. 275–279. IEEE (2014)

57. Ling, Z., Deng, L., Yu, D.: Modeling spectral envelopes using restricted Boltzmann machines for statistical parametric speech synthesis. In: Proceedings of the 38th IEEE International Conference on Acoustics, Speech and Signal Processing, pp. 7825–7829. IEEE (2013)

58. Gehring, J., Miao, Y., Metze, F., Waibel, A.: Extracting deep bottleneck features using stacked auto-encoders. In: Proceedings of the IEEE International Conference on Acoustics, Speech and Signal Processing, pp. 3377–3381. IEEE (2013)

59. Zen, H., Senior, A.: Deep mixture density networks for acoustic modeling in statistical parametric speech synthesis. In: Proceedings of the 39th IEEE International Conference on Acoustics, Speech and Signal Processing, pp. 3844–3848. IEEE (2014)
60. Bishop, C.M.: Mixture density networks (1994)
61. Graves, A., Schmidhuber, J.: Framewise phoneme classification with bidirectional LSTM networks. In: Proceedings of the IEEE International Joint Conference on Neural Networks, pp. 2047–2052. IEEE (2005)
62. Graves, A., Fernández, S., Gomez, F., Schmidhuber, J.: Connectionist temporal classification: labelling unsegmented sequence data with recurrent neural networks. In: Proceedings of the 23rd International Conference on Machine Learning, pp. 369–376 (2006)
63. Xie, L., Lee, T., Mak, M.-W.: Guest Editorial: Advances in deep learning for speech processing. J. Signal Process. Syst. **90**(7), 959–961 (2018). https://doi.org/10.1007/s11265-018-1333-3
64. Zheng, Y., Li, Y., Wen, Z., Liu, B., Tao, J.: Text-based sentential stress prediction using continuous lexical embedding for Mandarin speech synthesis. In: Proceedings of 10th International Symposium on Chinese Spoken Language Processing (ISCSLP), pp. 1–5. IEEE (2016)
65. Zheng, Y., Li, Y., Wen, Z., Liu, B., Tao, J.: Investigating deep neural network adaptation for generating exclamatory and interrogative speech in mandarin. J. Signal Process. Syst. **90**(7), 1039–1052 (2018)
66. Zhu, J.: Probing the phonetic and phonological knowledge of tones in Mandarin TTS models. In: Proceedings of 10th International Conference on Speech Prosody 2020, pp. 930–934 (2020)
67. Liu, Z., Mak, B.: Cross-lingual multi-speaker text-to-speech synthesis for voice cloning without using parallel corpus for unseen speakers. arXiv preprint arXiv:1911.11601 (2019)
68. Li, H., Kang, Y., Wang, Z.: EMPHASIS: an emotional phoneme-based acoustic model for speech synthesis system. arXiv preprint arXiv:1806.09276 (2018)
69. Cho, K., et al.: Learning phrase representations using RNN encoder-decoder for statistical machine translation. arXiv preprint arXiv:1406.1078 (2014)
70. Sutskever, I., Vinyals, O., Le, Q.V.: Sequence to sequence learning with neural networks. In: Proceedings of the Advances in Neural Information Processing Systems, pp. 3104–3112 (2014)
71. Bahdanau, D., Cho, K., Bengio, Y.: Neural machine translation by jointly learning to align and translate. arXiv preprint arXiv:1409.0473 (2014)
72. Shang, L., Lu, Z., Li, H.: Neural responding machine for short-text conversation. arXiv preprint arXiv:1503.02364 (2015)
73. Vinyals, O., Kaiser, Ł., Koo, T., Petrov, S., Sutskever, I., Hinton, G.: Grammar as a foreign language. In: Proceedings of the Advances in Neural Information Processing Systems, pp. 2773–2781 (2015)
74. Rush, A.M., Harvard, S., Chopra, S., Weston, J.: A neural attention model for sentence summarization. In: Proceedings of the ACLWeb. Proceedings of the 2015 Conference on Empirical Methods in Natural Language Processing (2017)
75. Luong, M., Pham, H., Manning, C.D.: Effective approaches to attention-based neural machine translation. arXiv preprint arXiv:1508.04025 (2015)
76. Hermann, K.M., et al.: Teaching machines to read and comprehend. In: Proceedings of the Advances in Neural Information Processing Systems, pp. 1693–1701 (2015)
77. Chorowski, J., Bahdanau, D., Cho, K., Bengio, Y.: End-to-end continuous speech recognition using attention-based recurrent NN: first results. arXiv preprint arXiv:1412.1602 (2014)

78. Wang, W., Xu, S., Xu, B.: First step towards end-to-end parametric TTS synthesis: generating spectral parameters with neural attention (2016)
79. Zhang, J., Ling, Z., Dai, L.: Forward attention in sequence-to-sequence acoustic modeling for speech synthesis. In: Proceedings of 2018 IEEE International Conference on Acoustics, Speech and Signal Processing (ICASSP), pp. 4789–4793. IEEE (2018)
80. Oord, A.V.D., et al.: WaveNet: a generative model for raw audio. arXiv preprint arXiv: 1609.03499 (2016)
81. Oord, A.V.D., Kalchbrenner, N., Kavukcuoglu, K.: Pixel recurrent neural networks. arXiv preprint arXiv:1601.06759 (2016)
82. Van den Oord, A., Kalchbrenner, N., Espeholt, L., Vinyals, O., Graves, A.: Conditional image generation with PixelCNN decoders. In: Proceedings of the Annual Conference on Neural Information Processing Systems, pp. 4790–4798 (2016)
83. Oord, A., et al.: Parallel WaveNet: fast high-fidelity speech synthesis. In: Proceedings of the International Conference on Machine Learning, PMLR, pp. 3918–3926 (2018)
84. Sotelo, J., et al.: Char2Wav: end-to-end speech synthesis (2017)
85. Mehri, S., et al.: SampleRNN: an unconditional end-to-end neural audio generation model. arXiv preprint arXiv:1612.07837 (2016)
86. Wang, Y., et al.: Tacotron: towards end-to-end speech synthesis. arXiv preprint arXiv: 1703.10135 (2017)
87. Wang, Y., et al.: Tacotron: a fully end-to-end text-to-speech synthesis model, vol. 164. arXiv preprint arXiv:1703.10135 (2017)
88. Griffin, D., Lim, J.: Signal estimation from modified short-time Fourier transform. IEEE Trans. Acoust. Speech Signal Process. **32**(2), 236–243 (1984)
89. Kingma, D.P., Welling, M.: Auto-encoding variational Bayes. arXiv preprint arXiv:1312. 6114 (2013)
90. Gibiansky, A., et al., Deep Voice 2: multi-speaker neural text-to-speech. In: Proceedings of the Advances in Neural Information Processing Systems, pp. 2962–2970 (2017)
91. Shen, J., et al.: Natural TTS synthesis by conditioning WaveNet on Mel spectrogram predictions. In: Proceedings of 2018 IEEE International Conference on Acoustics, Speech and Signal Processing (ICASSP), pp. 4779–4783. IEEE (2018)
92. Tachibana, H., Uenoyama, K., Aihara, S.: Efficiently trainable text-to-speech system based on deep convolutional networks with guided attention. In: Proceedings of 2018 IEEE International Conference on Acoustics, Speech and Signal Processing (ICASSP), pp. 4784–4788. IEEE (2018)
93. Ping, W., et al.: Deep Voice 3: scaling text-to-speech with convolutional sequence learning. In: Proceedings of the Sixth International Conference on Learning Representations, pp. 1–16 (2018)
94. Ping, W., Peng, K., Chen, J.: ClariNet: parallel wave generation in end-to-end text-to-speech. arXiv preprint arXiv:1807.07281 (2018)
95. Peng, K., Ping, W., Song, Z., Zhao, K.: Parallel neural text-to-speech. arXiv preprint arXiv: 1905.08459 (2019)
96. Arık, S.Ö., Jun, H., Diamos, G.: Fast spectrogram inversion using multi-head convolutional neural networks. IEEE Signal Process. Lett. **26**(1), 94–98 (2018)
97. Kingma, D.P., Salimans, T., Jozefowicz, R., Chen, X., Sutskever, I., Welling, M.: Improved variational inference with inverse autoregressive flow. In: Proceedings of the Advances in Neural Information Processing Systems, pp. 4743–4751 (2016)
98. Prenger, R., Valle, R., Catanzaro, B.: WaveGlow: a flow-based generative network for speech synthesis. In: Proceedings of the ICASSP 2019–2019 IEEE International Conference on Acoustics, Speech and Signal Processing (ICASSP), pp. 3617–3621. IEEE (2019)

99. Ping, W., Peng, K., Zhao, K., Song, Z.: WaveFlow: a compact flow-based model for raw audio. In: Proceedings of the ICML (2020)
100. Miao, C., Liang, S., Chen, M., Ma, J., Wang, S., Xiao, J.: Flow-TTS: a non-autoregressive network for text to speech based on flow. In: Proceedings of the ICASSP 2020 - 2020 IEEE International Conference on Acoustics, Speech and Signal Processing (ICASSP), pp. 7209–7213. IEEE (2020)
101. Kim, J., Kim, S., Kong, J., Yoon, S.: Glow-TTS: a generative flow for text-to-speech via monotonic alignment search. arXiv preprint arXiv:2005.11129 (2020)
102. Kalchbrenner, N., et al.: Efficient neural audio synthesis. arXiv preprint arXiv:1802.08435 (2018)
103. Ebden, P., Sproat, R.: The Kestrel TTS text normalization system. Nat. Lang. Eng. **21**(3), 333 (2015)
104. Sproat, R., Emerson, T.: The first international Chinese word segmentation Bakeoff. In: Proceedings of the Second SIGHAN Workshop on Chinese Language Processing, pp. 133–143 (2003)
105. Màrquez, L., Rodríguez, H.: Part-of-speech tagging using decision trees. In: Nédellec, C., Rouveirol, C. (eds.) ECML 1998. LNCS, vol. 1398, pp. 25–36. Springer, Heidelberg (1998). https://doi.org/10.1007/BFb0026668
106. Zhang, H., Yu, J., Zhan, W., Yu, S.: Disambiguation of Chinese polyphonic characters. In: Proceedings of the First International Workshop on MultiMedia Annotation (MMA2001), pp. 30–31. Citeseer (2001)
107. Shi, Q., Ma, X., Zhu, W., Zhang, W., Shen, L.: Statistic prosody structure prediction. In: Proceedings of 2002 IEEE Workshop on Speech Synthesis, pp. 155–158. IEEE (2002)
108. Huang, Z., Xu, W., Yu, K.: Bidirectional LSTM-CRF models for sequence tagging. arXiv preprint arXiv:1508.01991 (2015)
109. Guo-liang, W., Meng-nan, C., Lei, C.: An end-to-end Chinese speech synthesis scheme based on Tacotron 2. J. East China Norm. Univ. Nat. Sci. **2019**(4), 111 (2019)
110. He, T., Zhao, W., Xu, L.: DOP-Tacotron: a fast Chinese TTS system with local-based attention. In: Proceedings of 2020 Chinese Control and Decision Conference (CCDC), pp. 4345–4350. IEEE (2020)
111. Li, J., Wu, Z., Li, R., Zhi, P., Yang, S., Meng, H.: Knowledge-based linguistic encoding for end-to-end Mandarin text-to-speech synthesis. In: Proceedings of the INTERSPEECH, pp. 4494–4498 (2019)
112. Pan, H., Li, X., Huang, Z.: A Mandarin prosodic boundary prediction model based on multi-task learning. In: Proceedings of the INTERSPEECH, pp. 4485–4488 (2019)
113. Zou, Y., Dong, L., Xu, B.: Boosting character-based Chinese speech synthesis via multi-task learning and dictionary tutoring (2019)
114. Pan, J., et al.: A unified sequence-to-sequence front-end model for Mandarin text-to-speech synthesis. In: Proceedings of the ICASSP 2020–2020 IEEE International Conference on Acoustics, Speech and Signal Processing (ICASSP), pp. 6689–6693. IEEE (2020)
115. Zhang, J., et al.: A hybrid text normalization system using multi-head self-attention for mandarin. In: Proceedings of the ICASSP 2020–2020 IEEE International Conference on Acoustics, Speech and Signal Processing (ICASSP), pp. 6694–6698. IEEE (2020)
116. Yang, B., Zhong, J., Liu, S.: Pre-trained text representations for improving front-end text processing in Mandarin text-to-speech synthesis. In: Proceedings of the INTERSPEECH, pp. 4480–4484 (2019)
117. Yan, Y., Jiang, J., Yang, H.: Mandarin prosody boundary prediction based on sequence-to-sequence model. In: Proceedings of 2020 IEEE 4th Information Technology, Networking, Electronic and Automation Control Conference (ITNEC), pp. 1013–1017. IEEE (2020)

118. Tang, G., Müller, M., Rios, A., Sennrich, R.: Why self-attention? A targeted evaluation of neural machine translation architectures. arXiv preprint arXiv:1808.08946 (2018)
119. Vaswani, A., et al.: Attention is all you need. In: Proceedings of the Advances in Neural Information Processing Systems, pp. 5998–6008 (2017)
120. Karita, S., et al.: A comparative study on transformer vs RNN in speech applications. In: Proceedings of 2019 IEEE Automatic Speech Recognition and Understanding Workshop (ASRU), pp. 449–456. IEEE (2019)
121. Zheng, Y., Li, X., Xie, F., Lu, L.: Improving end-to-end speech synthesis with local recurrent neural network enhanced transformer. In: Proceedings of the ICASSP 2020–2020 IEEE International Conference on Acoustics, Speech and Signal Processing (ICASSP), pp. 6734–6738. IEEE (2020)
122. Engel, J., Agrawal, K.K., Chen, S., Gulrajani, I., Donahue, C., Roberts, A.: GANSynth: adversarial neural audio synthesis. arXiv preprint arXiv:1902.08710 (2019)
123. Donahue, C., McAuley, J., Puckette, M.: Adversarial audio synthesis. arXiv preprint arXiv: 1802.04208 (2018)

Author Index

Printed in the United States
by Baker & Taylor Publisher Services